The Petrol Navy

By the same author

The Harwich Striking Force:
The Royal Navy's Front Line in the North Sea, 1914–1918

British Naval Trawlers and Drifters in Two World Wars

The Power and the Glory:
The Story of Royal Navy Fleet Reviews from Earliest Times to 2005

Battle in the Baltic:
The Royal Navy and the Fight to Save Estonia and Latvia, 1918–1920

Southern Thunder:
The Royal Navy and the Scandinavian Trade in World War One

Bayly's War:
The Battle for the Western Approaches in World War One

Securing the Narrow Sea:
The Dover Patrol 1914–1918

Blockade:
Cruiser Warfare and the Starvation of Germany

Formidable:
A true story of disaster and courage

The Coward? The Rise and Fall of the Silver King

The Scapegoat:
The Life and Tragedy of a Fighting Admiral and Churchill's Role in his Death

www.steverdunn.com

The Petrol Navy

British, American and Other Naval Motor Boats at War 1914–1920

STEVE R DUNN

Copyright © Steve R Dunn 2023

First published in Great Britain in 2023 by
Seaforth Publishing,
A division of Pen & Sword Books Ltd,
47 Church Street,
Barnsley S70 2AS
www.seaforthpublishing.com

British Library Cataloguing in Publication Data
A catalogue record for this book is available from the British Library

ISBN (HARDBACK) 978 1 3990 6285 5
ISBN (EPUB) 978 1 3990 6287 9
ISBN (KINDLE) 978 1 3990 6288 6

All rights reserved. No part of this publication may be reproduced or transmitted in any form or by any means, electronic or mechanical, including photocopying, recording, or any information storage and retrieval system, without prior permission in writing of both the copyright owner and the above publisher.

The right of Steve R Dunn to be identified as the author of this work has been asserted by him in accordance with the Copyright, Designs and Patents Act 1988.

Pen & Sword Books Limited incorporates the imprints of Atlas, Archaeology, Aviation, Discovery, Family History, Fiction, History, Maritime, Military, Military Classics, Politics, Select, Transport, True Crime, Air World, Frontline Publishing, Leo Cooper, Remember When, Seaforth Publishing, The Praetorian Press, Wharncliffe Local History, Wharncliffe Transport, Wharncliffe True Crime and White Owl

Typeset and designed by Ian Hughes, www.mousematdesign.com

Printed and bound in Great Britain by CPI Group (UK) Ltd, Croydon, CR0 4YY

For Vivienne, with love

Contents

List of Plans   9
List of Abbreviations   10

Introduction   13
1   Yachting and the Development of the Motor Boat   17
2   A Strategic Gap and a Motor Boat Solution   30
3   To War in Boats   39
4   The Birth of the Motor Launch   49
5   Motor Launches versus U-boats and Mines   70
6   In Distant Waters   91
7   Operation ZO – The Raids on Zeebrugge and Ostend   106
8   The Corinthians of ZO   124
9   Motor Launch Losses   132
10   The Sea Skimmers   140
11   The American Submarine Chasers   155
12   The Splinter Ships Go to War   175
13   Motor Boats in the Italian, French and German Navies   194
14   Armistice, Occupation and a Revolution   214
15   In Russia and the North Sea   234
16   Last Rites   252
17   Conclusions   267

Appendices

1	Motor Boats Lost 1914–1918	276
2	British and World Merchant Shipping Losses, 1917 and January – April 1918	277
3	Tonnage of Allied and Neutral Merchant Shipping Lost, 1914–1918	278
4	The Motor Launch VC Citations	279
5	Motor Launch Losses, 1914–1918	281
6	Number of USN Submarine Chasers Based in Europe by Port, 1918	282
7	Armistice Military Occupation Clauses	283
8	Menu, Dinner 23 April 1919	284
9	Dobson and Steele VC Citations	285
10	Motor Launch Losses Post-war, 1918–1920	286

The Plans	287
Author's Notes	300
Notes and Sources	301
Bibliography	307
Index	310

List of Plans

Plan of a Thornycroft river launch	287
A plan by her builder of the 53ft motor boat *Hippocampus*	287
The side, deck and sheer plan of a motor launch	288
Plan of a USN sub chaser	289
The inboard plans of a 110ft USN sub chaser	290
The outboard plans of a 110ft USN sub chaser	290
Technical drawing, lines of a Thornycroft 40ft CMB	292
General arrangement of a Thornycroft 55ft CMB	294
72ft coastal motor boat for minelaying	296
72ft coastal motor boat designed for minelaying	298

List of Abbreviations

A/S	Anti-Submarine
ASC	Army Service Corps
BMBC	British Motor Boat Club
C	French submarine chasers acquired from the USA
CMB	Coastal Motor Boat
CNVM	Corpo Nazionale Volontari Motornauti, the Italian Naval Reserve
DCB	Distant Control Boat
ECB	(German) Electrically Controlled Motor Boat
EEF	Egyptian Expeditionary Force
Elco	The Electric Launch Company
GRT	Gross Register Tons
M	Monitor
MAS	either *Motoscafo Armato Silurante* or *Motoscafi AntiSommergibili*, Italian motor boats
ML	Motor Launch
MMA	Marine Motoring Association
MMR	Mercantile Marine Reserve
PDH	Portable Directional Hydrophone
PSG	Portable General Service Hydrophone
RFA	Royal Fleet Auxiliary
RN	Royal Navy
RNR	Royal Naval Reserve
RNR(T)	Royal Naval Reserve Trawler Section
RNCV	Royal Naval Coast Volunteers
RNAV	Royal Naval Artillery Volunteers
RNMBR	Royal Naval Motor Boat Reserve
RNVR	Royal Naval Volunteer Reserve
RNAS	Royal Naval Air Service
SC	Submarine Chaser
SNO	Senior Naval Officer
SVAN	Societa Veneziana Automobili Navali, an Italian shipyard
USN	US Navy
USNRF	US Naval Reserve Force
V	French *Vedettes*, largely US-built MLs

Very bold, very gallant was he
Who first built a ship
And set sail down wind
Seeking a country he didn't see
And a shore he didn't know
    Wace, *Roman de Brut* (1155)

One who never turned his back but marched breast forward,
Never doubted clouds would break,
Never dreamed, though right were worsted, wrong would triumph,
Held we fall to rise, are baffled to fight better,
Sleep to wake.
    Robert Browning, *Epilogue to Asolando* (1889)

'Believe me, my young friend, there is nothing – absolutely nothing – half so much worth doing as simply messing about in boats'.
    Kenneth Grahame, *The Wind in the Willows* (1908)

Sing me a song of a frail ML
May the Lord have mercy upon us,
Rolling about in an oily swell
May the Lord have mercy upon us,
Out on a high explosive spree,
Petrol, Lyddite and TNT,
Looking for U-boat 303,
May the Lord have mercy upon us.
    Anon, *The Song of the Sea Slugs*
    (quoted in Nutting, *Cinderellas of the Fleet*, p54)

HMS *Lightning* (1876), the first seagoing vessel to be armed with an explosive cylinder driven by a compressed air engine. The illustration is from *Scientific American*, Supplement 7 July 1877. *(Author's collection)*

Introduction

Britain's navy played a key role in the eventual defeat of Germany in the First World War. Much has been written about the battles of Heligoland Bight, Dogger Bank and Jutland, of the Zeebrugge and Ostend raids, and of the destroyers of the Dover Patrol.

But these famous actions did not decide the outcome of the war. It was the battle of attrition, fought in the North Sea and elsewhere, to starve Germany of supplies through naval blockade which ruined German morale and eventually brought that country to its knees. And it was the hard-fought battle against the U-boats in the North Sea and the Western Approaches which ensured that food, men and armaments reached Britain and her Allies. It was the Royal Navy's eventual success in this campaign which ensured that the British population was fed and watered throughout the conflict and that Allied arms and manufacturing prevailed in the end.

Key to these two successes was the role of the auxiliary naval forces. Rich men's private yachts, cross-channel ferries and sundry other commercial craft were taken up by the Admiralty and commissioned as temporary warships. Steam trawlers and drifters were hastily removed from their peacetime activities and converted to minesweepers or anti-submarine patrol vessels. Over three thousand fishing vessels were used by the Royal Navy in this fashion, in the main manned by their fishermen crews. They are remembered in fishing ports all round Britain's coast to this day.

But there was another category of vessel that was to play a key part in these auxiliary forces, and in the regular navy; and that was the small, durable, motor boat, armed with torpedoes or anti-submarine weapons. The concept of a small manoeuvrable craft, capable of carrying an offensive explosive charge dates back to 1864, when a retired Italian army officer, Capitano Giovanni Luppis, developed a 'mobile spar torpedo', an explosive charge that was guided by two wires. A British engineer, Robert Whitehead, furthered Luppis' work and came up with 'an automobile torpedo' that could be detonated below a ship's waterline. In April 1871 the Admiralty purchased the rights to the Whitehead device for £15,000 and it was further refined at Woolwich. Then British boatbuilder John Isaac Thornycroft adapted the weapon to his fast steam launches. The first boat of such design was accepted by the Royal Navy as HMS *Lightning* (1876). *Lightning* was in effect a steam launch, relatively fast for the time. She had two drop collars to launch torpedoes; these were replaced in 1879 by a single torpedo tube in the bow. She also carried two reload torpedoes amidships.

But fitting a steam engine into such craft was a difficult piece of naval architecture. Coal, stokers, boilers: all had to be found a place in a small space. The inception of the internal combustion engine gave naval planners a new opportunity to consider the concept – a petrol-powered vessel. The development of the marine internal combustion engine in the early years of the century led to the rise of motor-powered small craft, motor boats and motor-powered yachts. And an obvious extension of this new technology was its use in naval vessels.

The parts that these boats took are not well known today; and less renowned too is the role in the auxiliary forces played by the amateur yachtsmen and motor boat enthusiasts of the country. In the years immediately before the First World War, sport featured the gentleman amateur as never before. Relatively wealthy and with copious free time, these so-called 'Corinthians', with their carefully nurtured, seemingly effortless success, dominated the sporting world and nowhere more so than competitive yachting and motor boat racing.

In 1912 a group of these sporting motor boat owners had suggested to the Admiralty that their vessels too could assist in the defence of Britain. This led to the creation of the Royal Naval Motor Boat Reserve (RNMBR). At the beginning of the war, these marine sportsmen and owners of motor pleasure launches responded to the clarion call of *noblesse oblige* and brought forward their vessels and themselves for naval service in the auxiliary forces. Owners came with their boats and in exchange were given a commission in the RNMBR, a minimum of training, a rifle or machine gun, and set to all types of work in harbours and along the littoral. During the war, a total of 194 motor boats were so employed as naval auxiliaries. The boats' owners, now RNMBR officers, came from the landed gentry, the peerage and the monied middle class; they were gentlemen amateur sailors turned warriors.

But by mid 1915 it was clear that the demands of naval duty had proved too much for the motor pleasure boats and that they were structurally unfitted for the task. A fortunate meeting in the USA led to their replacement by Elco motor launches (MLs), of which 550 were eventually purchased from the Elco company of America. Constructed according to the methods of mass production pioneered by Henry Ford, these craft were built in record time and began to be commissioned into the Royal Navy from October 1915. Around the same time, the RMBR was disestablished and its men absorbed into the Royal Naval Volunteer Reserve (RNVR). The officers transferred to command the MLs, while their original craft were decommissioned back to civilian life.

The Elco launches gave great service for the rest of the war, almost entirely officered by RNVR personnel, in duties that included hunting U-boats, minesweeping, convoy escort and smoke-laying. And three Victoria Crosses were won in these craft at the Zeebrugge/Ostend raids of 1918.

This book tells the story of how the RNMBR and the MLs came into being, describes the men who brought them into existence, and how they were manned. The narrative also details the design and technical development of the Elco boats, from a chance meeting in New York to their production in Canada at the rate of one a day. The actions and day-to-day duties involving ML boats are examined, as is the character of the amateur sailors who commanded and crewed them.

But this was not the only example of motor-powered small war craft in the Royal Navy. In 1915 some serving naval officers developed another concept, the hydroplaning coastal motor boat or CMB, many of which served with great distinction in the later part of the war, especially at Zeebrugge and Ostend and with the Harwich Force. These craft were the province of regular Royal Navy sailors, as well as volunteers, and were not considered 'auxiliary'. At least 116 of these remarkable boats were produced and the story of their development and use is considered.

Post-war, both MLs and CMBs saw valuable service, inter alia, in the Occupation of the Rhineland, policing and defending the Rhine waterways, and in the Baltic Campaign of 1918–1920 where three VCs were won in them. The book examines their usage and success in these little-known deployments.

Britain was not alone in using diminutive motor-powered boats for war. In Italy, the MAS torpedo-carrying motor craft achieved some success, including sinking a battleship. And in France, motor launches (*vedettes*), supplied by the Royal Navy and acquired direct from Elco, played their part.

Germany too made use of small motor vessels, building twenty-one torpedo-armed *Luftschiffmotorboote* together with some *Fernlenkboot* remotely controlled designs. And when America entered the war, she built a considerable fleet of so-called 'sub chasers' (also known as 'splinter ships'), wooden-built and specifically designed to counter the threat from U-boats. They were deployed in British and European waters just before the war's end and post-war continued to serve with their British sisters in Europe and Russia.

And it was American manufacturing drive and know-how that allowed the petrol navies of Britain, France and the USA to come to fruition. US shipyards and designers were the source for many of the vessels deployed.

The stories of these small, versatile motor craft, largely utilised in coastal waters, have rarely been told. They were 'The Petrol Navy', a new type of war machine which owed its existence to the recent development of the marine internal combustion engine and opened new tactical opportunities for maritime powers.

In both Britain and the USA, such vessels were almost entirely crewed and commanded by volunteers. The contribution to the Allied war effort that these little craft and their officers and crews made is largely overlooked. In this book, the author hopes to both rectify these omissions and provide a tribute to the work of these men and boats, both in the Royal Navy, the USN and in the navies of both friend and foe. Although primarily from a British perspective, the intent is a celebration and commemoration of the motor boat at war.

Please note: the twenty-four-hour clock is employed throughout. Where ante-meridian/post-meridian was used in the original it has been converted. Naval ranks and other titles given to individuals are the ones they held at the time of the incident narrated. A date in brackets after the name of a vessel is its year of launch. Names of towns are the ones used at the time of the war. The book does not follow a strict chronology but rather a thematic one, which examines a topic through time before moving on to others. And finally, weights: a warship's size was generally reckoned as 'displacement tonnage', cargo vessels as 'gross register tons' or grt (a measure of internal volume).

1
Yachting and the Development of the Motor Boat

There has probably never been a better time in British history to be alive than the twenty or so years preceding the First World War – as long as you were rich, or at least substantially well off. Advances in health care meant that a man of means had an increased possibility of living his three score and ten, and a growing consumerist society presented the opportunity for wealth creation as well as wealth retention.

Immediately before this period, it had not been all beer and skittles for the landed rich. Britain fell into a severe agricultural depression in the 1880s which lasted until Edward VII's ascension to the throne.* Rental income from land holdings fell sharply, and the aristocracy had to sell land, houses and other treasures to stave off their decrease in ready money. Fortunately, American millionaires simultaneously filled their homes with the treasures of the Old World, bought into the troubled estates and married their daughters into these suddenly less wealthy aristocratic families, desperate for English status and titles for themselves and their offspring. They also provided staggeringly large dowries.†

Additionally, by the time of the extended Edwardian era, the period between 1900 and 1914, society was no longer a small, exclusive circle confined to those of aristocratic birth, but had expanded to include those who had made their wealth through trade or banking. Travel was cheap and easy, since one needed no passport or visa before the Russian or Ottoman borders. Tax on income or capital had been trivial, and technological advances were exciting and opened up new horizons for pleasure and commerce. Innovative technical designs came to the market one after the other, including, inter alia, telephones, typewriters, sewing machines, motorcars, aeroplanes and wireless radio.

The influence of the Prince of Wales (later King Edward VII) dominated the latter part of the nineteenth century. His mannerisms of dress, speech,

---
* Corn imports from Australia and the USA, combined with more efficient bacon production in Denmark and new refrigerated ships bringing beef from South America, caused agricultural rents to drop by an average 22.6 per cent between 1878 and 1893. The price of wheat fell from 46 shillings per quarter in 1870 to 22 shillings in 1894 (Offer, *An Agrarian Interpretation*, p93).
† The 9th Duke of Marlborough was one of the pioneers in 1895, marrying Consuelo Vanderbilt and receiving a dowry of \$2.5 million, perhaps \$70 million today. He told his unfortunate bride that he only married her to save Blenheim Palace.

leisure, amusements, and those whom he chose to befriend, were imitated by the aspirants who wished to be accepted in society. Edward opened the doors of society to those previously excluded from it by birth, occupation or religion – people such as the Rothschilds, Sassoons and Cassells – American millionaires, and the nouveau riche from the British Empire. As long as they had money and/or were amusing, they were in. Thus Edward's sporting interests influenced the leisure choices of society. There were at least two 'sports of kings', not just horse racing. For though he loved the turf, Edward delighted in sailing too, especially Cowes Week, as did his younger son, later George V, who served in the Royal Navy until 1892.

And with increased leisure time, at least among the middle and upper classes, other sports grew too. Cricket, football, rugby and rowing all boomed during this period, as did tennis, croquet and golf. To a greater or lesser extent, royalty, the aristocracy and the monied bourgeoisie participated in all of these interests. But they were careful with whom they played or competed and on what basis.

The cult of the amateur

It was a trope of the age that one should not be seen to try too hard at anything. To work in trade was of a lesser status than to live off rental or capital. The future Admiral Sir Percy Scott remembered his father: 'it was a principle with him never to make a fuss about anything, and he impressed upon me that every occurrence, whatever it might be, should be taken with imperturbable quiet. He would quote that passage from "Pelham",* who declares that among the properly educated a calm pervaded all their habits and actions, whereas the vulgar could take neither a spoon nor an affront without making an amazing noise about it'.[1]

To work hard at school or university was considered poor form; better one should make friends, play sports, roister and be seen as a 'jolly good egg'. Professionalism in sport was seen as infra dig, as it suggested effort. Successful sportsmen should be amateurs (with certain exceptions such as jockeys, who were paid substantial sums to ensure that their lordly horse-owning patrons won) and losing should be taken in good part; better to participate fairly and lose, than win by taking an advantage or through poor sportsmanship.

Such behaviours and beliefs applied in Britain's senior service as well. In the Royal Navy, 'advertising' – pushing oneself forward or striving overmuch to be successful – was a social crime. Indeed, it could be positively deleterious

---

* *Pelham, or, the Adventures of a Gentleman*, was a novel by Edward George Bulwer-Lytton, written in 1827.

to one's reputation to perform too well in a scholastic manner. It was not necessary, or even desirable, to be academically gifted in order to progress in the Edwardian and Victorian navy. Cleverness was looked at somewhat askance and the furtherance of academic study was not encouraged. A 'three-oner' – a man who obtained first-class passes at his Seamanship Board, Royal Naval College and the HMS *Excellent* Gunnery School – was suspect and 'three-oners' were held in contempt by many in the navy as being 'too clever by half', as were officers who pursued outside interests. Fitting in socially and coming from the 'right' background was deemed more important.

The army was the same. Horace Smith-Dorrien was one of the better British generals in the 1914–1918 war. As a captain, he attended the army staff college in 1887. He found his two years there very pleasant: 'I enjoyed every minute,' he wrote later. 'I do not think we were taught as much as we might have been, but there was plenty of sport and not too much work.'[2] He never managed to find the library but still passed out.

Even in battue shooting, so beloved of Edward VII and George V, it was a crime to be seen to try too hard. At the end of the nineteenth century, the best shot in Britain was Lord de Grey (later the Marquess of Ripon). He liked to pretend that his mass killing of birds was effortless and 'was annoyed to be discovered in the library of a country house before breakfast, practising changing guns with his loader'.[3]

Corinthians

The right sort of amateur sportsman was called a Corinthian. There was even a football club named Corinthian FC. It was founded in 1882, entirely amateur, and grounded in the concept of fair play. The club produced sixteen English national team captains, including Reginald Erskine 'Tip' Foster, still the only man to have captained an English international team at both cricket and football. Another who played football for Corinthian and cricket for England was C B Fry. He appeared seventy-four times for the club, competed for England at football once and won twenty-six Test cricket caps. He also held the British long jump record and was offered the throne of Albania. In 1908 he became Captain Superintendent of the Training Ship *Mercury*, a nautical school primarily designed to prepare boys for service in the Royal Navy.*

In cricket, amateurs changed in separate dressing rooms from the professionals. One of the most prestigious matches was that between the public schools of Eton and Harrow at Lord's each year. Another high-ranked

---

* When war came, Fry was made an honorary captain in the RNR. According to *The Globe* newspaper, 'he would stride about in his uniform looking every inch like six admirals' (Sandford, *The Final Over*, p66).

cricket fixture was that held annually between the Gentlemen (amateurs) and the Players (professional).* A cricketer such as the Indian prince and England Test batsman K S Ranjitsinhji, ruler of the princely state of Nawanagar, who won fifteen international caps between 1896 and 1902, was admired for his effortless artistry and apparent lack of effort at the crease.

And the term 'Corinthian' came to have a considerable resonance in the world of yachting. In the *Shorter Oxford English Dictionary,* the word 'Corinthian' is defined as 'a wealthy amateur of sport'.[4] But *Brewer's Dictionary of Phrase and Fable* goes further, giving as its meaning 'a gentleman sportsman who rides his own horses on the turf or sails his own yacht'.[5] As with cricket, yacht races had once been the vehicle for betting, and rich men used to race yachts in much the same manner as they raced horses – for large prizes and with the use of highly professional methods. Yachts such as these were crewed entirely by paid hands with professional skippers. There was little scope for amateurs in such a set-up. But by the second half of the nineteenth century, such racing became unfashionable. By 1892, the yachtsman Frank Cooper, writing in his book *Sailing Tours,* was able to state that 'a Corinthian sailor … is one capable of managing a craft either single-handed (if she is small enough) or with the assistance of other amateurs'.† And sailing really did become the sport of kings (and queens).

The rise of the yacht club

It was Charles II who popularised the yacht. Whilst in exile in Holland, the King had become enamoured of the Dutch vessel known as a *jacht*. Charles's early experience of Dutch *jachts* led him to desire similar vessels for himself. His return to the English throne was celebrated by the city of Amsterdam, which presented him with a luxurious 60ft yacht, including a crew of twenty, named the *Mary*. The first English-built yacht was the *Katherine*, of length at the keel 49ft and beam 19ft. By 1685 there were twenty yachts in the royal squadron (there would be twenty-five over the two reigns of Charles and his brother James), including one specially built and launched in 1670 for Queen Henrietta, named *Saudadoes* ('greetings to you' in Portuguese), although only seven were truly royal and assigned to the immediate service of the King and royal family.

Soon the first organised regatta took place, a forty-mile race on the Thames in 1661 between *Katherine* and *Anne,* James, Duke of York's new yacht. The King himself was at the helm of *Katherine* – and unsurprisingly won. A new sport was born.

---

* This tradition did not end until 1962.
† And the term persists. Even in the 2020s, there exists the Royal Corinthian Sailing Club (est 1894) and the Cowes Corinthian Yacht Club (est 1852).

The ex-America's cup challenger *Thistle*, later Kaiser Wilhelm II's *Meteor*.
(Author's collection)

With the rise of sailing, came the yacht club. By the 1800s, yachting had grown to include the world's wealthiest men. Yacht clubs began to form in the eighteenth century to accommodate the new interest shown and codify and establish races and rules. The first yacht club in the world, called the Cork Water Club, later the Royal Cork,* was established in Ireland in 1720, followed by the Lough Ree Yacht Club in 1770 (again in Ireland), and the Starcross Yacht Club in 1772 in England.

Probably the most famous of all the English yacht clubs, the Royal Yacht Squadron, was founded on 1 June 1815 at the Thatched House Tavern in St James's, London, as 'The Yacht Club' by forty-two gentlemen interested in yachting. It welcomed the Prince Regent as a member in 1817. Three years later, when the Regent became George IV, it was entitled the Royal Yacht Club. The club organised yacht racing as part of its annual regatta, which eventually became known as Cowes Week. And in 1833 William IV renamed the club the Royal Yacht Squadron. The Squadron hosted royal visitors of many nations over the years and maintained strong links with the British

---

* With a clubhouse built in 1854 to the designs of Anthony Salvin, the go-to architect for the minor aristocracy.

Lord Crawford's auxiliary steam yacht *Valhalla* (1892), depicted in 1901 by Antonio de Simone. *(Author's collection)*

monarchy and Royal Navy. Members' yachts were given the suffix RYS to their names and permitted to fly the White Ensign of the Royal Navy.

The German emperor brought his *Meteor*, the 1887 ex-America's Cup challenger *Thistle*, to Cowes in 1892. This encouraged Edward, Prince of Wales to build *Britannia*, one of the most successful racing yachts in the calendar. Lord Crawford's* beautiful ship-rigged yacht *Valhalla* cruised far afield and was a noted visitor in Cowes Week; she was also a competitor in the 1905 Transatlantic Race for the German Emperor's Cup. Cowes became one of the social events of the season.

Yacht clubs sprang up all over Britain and attracted noble and wealthy members and patrons. The Royal Harwich Yacht Club boasted Queen Victoria as its patron from 1847 to 1901, followed by King George V between 1911 and 1936. The Harwich regattas had become the opening event for each season's 'Big Yacht Class' and attracted most of the famous racing yachts of the time, including *Britannia*.

Or consider the Royal Western Yacht Club: founded as the Port of Plymouth Royal Clarence Regatta Club in 1827, it became the Royal Western in 1833. Its original aims were to hold an annual regatta, to organise an active social programme and to stimulate improvements in naval architecture through yacht racing. In its early years its principal strength was in long-

---

* James Lindsay, 26th Earl of Crawford.

distance cruising and its members' yachts, wearing the Blue Ensign* – a privilege given to them in a warrant granted by Queen Victoria – were to be seen in many far-flung places.

And as a final example, the Royal Temple Yacht Club was founded in 1857 by a group of yachtsmen sailing from the Temple Steps, on the River Thames in the centre of London. Club racing started on the Thames, but increasing commercial traffic on the river made racing ever more difficult. Races began to be moved further and further down the river, until eventually it was decided that a more suitable base for racing should be found. This proved to be at Ramsgate, where a new clubhouse was opened in 1896. At the turn of the century two thousand members dined annually at the Hotel Cecil.† The Commodore at that time was Baron Nathaniel Mayer de Rothschild, who was often accompanied by his close friend, Edward, Prince of Wales. A Royal Charter was granted in 1897 and the Admiralty Warrant to wear the Blue Ensign was given in 1898.

And the growth of yacht clubs and racing brought the need for a unified code of conduct. In 1875 the Yacht Racing Association agreed a set of rules which would govern what were then called 'sailing matches' – rules which are broadly the same today.

Running a large racing or pleasure yacht was expensive. Paid crews were necessary, servants and cooks if touring; berths and mooring when at sea cost money. Thus money, aristocracy and yachting went hand in hand. No surprise then, that yacht clubs were seen as exclusive and snobbish. But as the twentieth century dawned, technological advancement provided the opportunity for a different type of sailing, and a different sort of club.

The advent of the motor launch and motor boat

Several inventors developed their own versions of practical automobiles with petrol-powered internal combustion engines during the last two decades of the nineteenth century. Perhaps the best known of these was Karl Benz, who built his first automobile in 1885 in Mannheim. Benz was granted a patent

---

* Prior to the reorganisation of the Royal Navy in 1864, the plain blue ensign had been the ensign of one of three squadrons of the Royal Navy, the Blue Squadron. This changed in 1864, when an Order in Council provided that the Red Ensign was to be allocated to merchantmen, the Blue Ensign to be the flag of ships in public service or commanded by an officer in the Royal Naval Reserve, and the White Ensign was allocated to the navy. Thus, after 1864, the plain blue ensign was permitted to be worn, instead of the Red Ensign, by three categories of civilian vessel. First, British merchant vessels whose officers and crew included a certain number of retired Royal Navy personnel or Royal Naval Reservists, or commanded by an officer of the Royal Naval Reserve in possession of a government warrant. Secondly, Royal Research Ships by warrant, whether manned by former Royal Navy personnel or Merchant Navy personnel. And thirdly, British-registered yachts belonging to members of a defined list of yacht clubs, thirty-four in number, including eleven in the Antipodes.
† A grand hotel built 1890–96 between the Thames Embankment and the Strand in London. Shell-Mex House now stands on the site.

for his creation on 29 January 1886 and began to manufacture them two years later.

Around the same time, people began to experiment with putting an internal combustion engine into a boat. Probably the progenitor was Priestman Brothers, with a working launch built in 1888. James Dennis Roots of London fitted a launch with a petrol engine, which he used to run on the Thames between Richmond and Wandsworth in 1891 and 1892; and in 1897 the Daimler company in Coventry offered powered boats for sale*.

But the advent of the new century sparked a sudden rush of development, as it was at about this time that the British and continental motor car manufacturers began to turn their attention to motor boat construction.

Many of the engines so deployed were unsuitable for marine use but companies such as Thornycroft and Napier and Sons specialised in boat work, and development was further enhanced when a cup was offered by Lord Northcliffe, then Alfred Harmsworth and owner of the *Daily Mail*, for international competition. The contest was to be confined to boats of a maximum overall length of 40ft, built and engined in the country which they represented, with no other restrictions imposed. Queenstown, near Cork, was the venue for the first such race, held in 1903, and a number of innovative vessels were demonstrated.

It was won by the famous racing driver Selwyn Francis Edge† in a 40ft, steel-hulled, 75hp Napier-engined craft named *Napier I*. With an eye for publicity (he was the representative for Napier cars), Edge had trained a

Dorothy Levitt piloting the 1903 cup winning motor boat *Napier I*.
(Author's collection)

---

* The Daimler Motor Company (Coventry) was registered as the first British car manufacturer in January 1896.
† Winner of, inter alia, the 1902 Gordon Bennett motor car race.

The petrol launch built for King Edward VII by Tom Tagg and Sons in 1903.
It was kept in the royal boathouse at Datchet. *(Author's collection)*

female co-pilot, the tall and very beautiful Dorothy Levitt, who worked for him as a secretary (and was probably his mistress), to be the first woman to compete in a motor boat race, but it was his name as owner and entrant that went on the trophy. Miss Levitt had achieved reported speeds of 19.3mph (16.8 knots)*.

The contest was repeated at Seaview, Isle of Wight, in 1905, with the Thornycroft company entering five boats; one of the entrants was Commander Mansfield Smith-Cumming, later to be in charge of Britain's Secret Intelligence Service as the original 'M'. A Napier-built boat eventually won the competition. And by 1909, the Thornycroft boat *Gyrinus II* carried off the *Prix de la Méditerranée*, apparently exceeding 22 knots.

Meanwhile, petrol-driven motor craft had acquired the royal imprimatur in 1903 when King Edward VII purchased one. He took his first trip in it on Whit Monday afternoon, sailing on the Thames near Windsor, wearing a soft grey hat and a navy-blue suit, and accompanied by Prince Louis of Battenberg (at that time the Director of Naval Intelligence at the Admiralty,

---

* On 8 August 1903 Levitt drove the Napier motor boat at Cowes and again won the race. She was then commanded to the royal yacht by King Edward VII, where he congratulated her on her courage and skill, and discussed the performance of the boat and its potential for British government despatch work.

with the rank of captain), Lord Esher (Reginald Brett, 2nd Viscount Esher) and the Honourable John Ward (second son of William Ward, 1st Earl of Dudley). This was the first petrol launch to be built for the monarchy and was designed and constructed by Messrs Tom Tagg and Sons of Molesey.

And the use of the internal combustion engine soon reached Africa too, when the Crown Agents for the Colonies commissioned two light draught vessels from Thornycroft's for use on the West African rivers. Delivered in early 1906, they were built of galvanised steel and were powered by four-cylinder Thornycroft engines which ran on petrol or paraffin. One, *Spider*, used screw propulsion and 'attained a mean speed of 8 knots with a load of four tons and a draught of twelve inches'.[6] In the other, the engine drove a stern paddle wheel.

The advent of powered boats and racing led naturally to the formation of motor boat clubs. According to *The Times*, the British Motor Boat Club (BMBC) was founded in November 1904 by a group of between 'fifty and sixty gentlemen well known in the automobile world … having for its objects the development of the motor boat and the encouragement of racing and cruising events for boats with internal combustion engines'.[7] Perhaps unsurprisingly, one of the founder members was John Walter Brooke, chairman of Messrs J W Brooke and Co of Lowestoft who were 'among the early workers on the application of the internal-combustion engine to marine propulsion'.[8]

The BMBC had been preceded by the creation of the Marine Motoring Association (MMA) in 1903, which was intended to be the official body governing motor boat racing. It was stated at the outset that the prevailing idea of the BMBC 'was not one of hostility to the Automobile Club or the MMA, but rather that this proposed club should carry out a programme of encouragement under the rules already laid down by the existing bodies'.[9] The use of the word 'motoring' in the club's title perhaps reflects one of reasons for motor boat popularity. The Locomotives on Highways Act of 1896 restricted powered road vehicles to 14mph. The Motor Car Act of 1904 raised this to 20mph. But many motor cars could cruise at twice that speed, and so those with a need for fast and/or reckless driving turned to motor boats, for which there were no limits.

The first gathering of the BMBC was in May 1905 and it attracted twenty-five craft and a large crowd at Kingston upon Thames, where the event took place. The club admiral was a retired Royal Navy officer, Admiral Sir William Robert Kennedy KCB, Commander-in-Chief at The Nore between 1900 and 1901, and the vice admiral was Archibald Kennedy, 3rd Marquess of Ailsa, founder of the Ailsa Shipbuilding Company.

Meanwhile, the MMA inaugurated annual reliability trials in 1904,

Admiral Sir William Robert Kennedy, one of the founding members (and club admiral) of the British Motor Boat Club. A prolific author, he had written about sport in the navy and an autobiography of his naval days. *(Author's collection)*

administered from the following year by the Motor Yacht Club at Poole. And another annual event was created in 1906, a rally from London to Cowes.

Other organisations soon sprang into existence. The Royal Sussex Yacht Club (whose successive patrons were Queen Victoria, King Edward VII and George V) was already a major force in the yacht-racing movement and held an annual regatta each August. In 1905 the officers of the club decided to run a race for motor boats as part of this event, and other yacht clubs were not far behind.

A Sussex Motor Yacht Club was founded in Brighton in 1907. Francis, Viscount Curzon (later the 5th Lord Howe), accepted the position of commodore. He had joined the Royal Naval Volunteer Reserve (RNVR) on leaving school and was appointed commanding officer of the Sussex

Division, based in Hove, and with the rank of commander RNVR that same year. The vice commodore was Sir Theodore Vivian Samuel Angier, a wealthy shipping-line owner and prominent Liberal Unionist. Millionaire Alfred Gwynne Vanderbilt* presented the Venture International Challenge Cup to the SMYC. This was a large Edwardian silver trophy decorated with an enamelled SMYC burgee and engraved 'Sussex Motor Yacht Club, The Venture, International Challenge Cup'.

In Scotland, from the year 1906 there were three clubs for motor boaters, the Scottish Marine Motor Club, Clyde Motor Boat Club and Clyde Motor Yacht Club. A leading light in these associations was James Cleland Burns, 3rd Lord Inverclyde, from the family of Cunard fame.

And by 1913, the *Spectator* magazine was reporting that 'In brief, ... in spite of admittedly good arguments on the other side, the general use of the auxiliary motor in sailing yachts will act on the whole in the right direction by making yachtsmen undertake adventures which they would formerly have shunned'.[10] Motor boating was here to stay.

The spirit of the age

The men who formed the membership of these yacht and motor boat clubs all largely subscribed to a particular view of the demeanour necessary to be considered a 'good sort', a pillar of their societies and a well-regarded member of their club. The concept of gentlemanly behaviour was closely entwined with the dominant moral codes of the late Victorians and Edwardians. These were derived from their reverence for the chivalric, the lost Eden of Arthurian legend, Camelot, the Round Table and from their obsession with imperial England as a new Rome. The educational system was founded on the Latin and Greek classics for that very reason.

As a result, public schools and colleges tended to produce a breed of men who were devoid of guile and conditioned to believe in romantic notions of honour, glory and sacrifice. These educational establishments raised boys to believe in the high-minded values of chivalry that were all the more potent because they had not been tested in the real world. And as one historian has written, 'every public schoolboy was familiar with the *Iliad* and the *Odyssey* and the poetry – with its emphasis on honour, discipline, athleticism and courage in the face of death – spoke across the ages about what it meant to be a gentleman and a scholar at the height of empire'.[11]

Launcelot and Galahad were admired for their honour and virtue as

---

* Alfred Vanderbilt was an extremely wealthy sportsman and a member of the famous Vanderbilt family. He died in 1915 when the luxury liner RMS *Lusitania* was torpedoed and sunk by *U-20*. *Alfred* gave up his life vest to a child-carrying female passenger.

much as for their fighting ability in the Camelot tales. In the *Iliad*, Sarpedon, one of the Trojan allies, urges his fellows to take their place in the front line of the attack on the Greeks so that no one may later call them cowards. And the Greek heroes always feared what other people would say about them if their behaviour did not come up to what was expected; they felt *aidos* (shame) if they slipped from their high standards.

As historian Margaret MacMillan put it, in relation to the First World War, 'the young British officers who went to the front had been raised on the classics and hoped … to fight like the Greek and Roman heroes'.[12] These golden lads 'represented the old chivalry of England … moulded in the gentleman image … they were confident in their role as standard bearers of a code entitling them to be called, in Marc Anthony's words, "all honourable men"'.[13] And 'honour could not be drunk by babies from their mother's breast and then kept for ever. It could only be earned in conflict or when faced with shame … honour was not heritable. Each generation had to earn it anew.'[14]

And patriotism and pride in Britain was an important belief too, set deep in the national psyche. Ulric Nisbet left Marlborough School in July 1914; on the outbreak of war he felt 'it wasn't a matter of "our country right or wrong". Our country was 100% right and Germany 100% wrong … the British Empire was the greatest the world had ever known and its greatness was due to the superior qualities of the British. Foreigners weren't cast in the same mould'.[15]

Another hallmark of the gentleman was speech. 'In the later years of the reign of Queen Victoria and into the twentieth century, almost all "gentlemen" and "ladies" spoke with what can only be described as a marked nasal drawl. Words such as "off", "gone", "often" and so on were pronounced "orff", "gorn", "orfen". This way of speaking was instantly recognisable as that of an acceptable member of the class – and hence of the amateur spirit which, it was generally agreed, the class represented'.[16]

Belief drives behaviour and behaviour produces culture; and hence the idealised gentleman was brave, loyal, and chivalrous towards females, put public duty before his own interests, and took part in activities for love rather than financial gain. These values were applied to a wide range of activities during the nineteenth century. Science, sport, politics and the arts were all defined by this *beau idéal* of the 'gentleman amateur'. These were the men who would volunteer in their thousands to Kitchener's New Armies when war came or, if a sailing or motor boat club member, seek an opportunity to serve in Britain's naval forces.

2

A Strategic Gap and a Motor Boat Solution

While the Edwardian age ran to its close, a fundamental change in the world order was taking place. Germany's defeat of France in the Franco-Prussian War of 1870, and the subsequent unification of Germany under a Hohenzollern Prussian king, caused France to seek new friends and Britain to worry about the rapidly industrialising state, with growing naval and expansionist ambitions, that lay across the waters of the North Sea.

With assistance from King Edward VII, an Entente Cordiale was agreed between Britain and France that buried past differences, and which was signed on 8 April 1904. The two most powerful nations in Europe had

Admiral Sir John 'Jacky' Fisher, First Sea Lord 1904–1910 and 1914–1915, the man who more than anyone recognised the need for a new strategy in the North Sea and created the First World War Royal Navy, in a painting by Hubert von Herkomer. *(Author's collection)*

reached a concord, but it posed a challenge to Germany's influence in Europe and the world, and caused a paranoid Kaiser Wilhelm II to imagine that Germany was being encircled by its rivals.

At the same time, the Royal Navy gained a new executive head. First Sea Lord Admiral Sir John (Jacky) Fisher, a dynamo in human form and a man possessed of both a reforming zeal and the energy to implement his plans, took office in October. Fisher recognised that the most likely enemy that Britain would have to face was not France but Germany. Admiral von Tirpitz, with the enthusiastic backing of Kaiser Wilhelm II, was creating an Imperial German Navy designed to raise his country to first-class naval status. With other factors, including an anti-British stance during the Boer War and the German government's refusal to consider an alliance with Britain, except on terms that guaranteed Germany a free hand and hegemony in Europe, Fisher was convinced that Germany was now the most probable foe. His political master, First Lord of the Admiralty Lord Selborne, certainly agreed with him. In a memo to the Cabinet, Selborne noted that 'the great new German navy is being built up from the point of view of war with us'.[1]

To ensure that Britain had the necessary concentration of forces, Fisher instigated a reorganisation of the fleets. He recalled ships from far-flung postings, concentrated the navy where he expected it to have to fight (the Channel and the North Sea) and scrapped 150 ships, deeming them 'too weak to fight and too slow to run away'. Five battleships were withdrawn from the China station in 1904. The standing South American, North American[*] and Pacific squadrons were abolished. As Andrew Lambert has written 'by early 1906 the centre of naval effort was shifting from the Mediterranean to the North Sea; Germany was not only the most likely but also the only realistic enemy. Russia was no longer a naval power and the French navy had collapsed'.[2]

Fisher created a new entity – the Home Fleet – to be based on Sheerness, where easy access to the North Sea and the German coastline could be obtained and which was announced by the Admiralty on 24 October 1906. He stripped the Mediterranean, Atlantic and Channel Fleets of battleships and cruisers to make up this new force and backed it up with ships from the reserve.

Under international law, close blockade of an enemy's ports was legal, but the closing-off of large areas of the seas to them was not.[†] This close blockade had been the Royal Navy's traditional strategy. But Jacky Fisher

---

[*] The North America and West Indies station was reinstated in 1913.
[†] The Treaty of Paris (1856, and subsequently re-ratified at the Hague Conventions of 1899 and 1907) gave legal basis to the concept of blockade. The agreement, among other things, permitted 'close' but not 'distant' blockades. A belligerent was allowed to station ships near the three-mile limit to stop or inspect traffic with an enemy's ports; it was not allowed simply to declare areas of the high seas comprising the approaches to the enemy's coast to be off-limits.

foresaw that the submarine, the torpedo, and light inexpensive craft which could deliver them, made the shallow and confined North Sea unsuitable for the battleships and other large vessels of the navy's battlefleet. Nor, in any case, could warships stay close to the continental coastline, as in the days of the Nelsonian frigates of old. They were too vulnerable to underwater attack and too dependent on regular refuelling. Instead, he strongly advocated a distant blockade, in which the North Sea was sealed off at either end and patrolled only by light craft.

Two years after Fisher had retired, on 16 December 1912 Admiral George Callaghan, CinC Home Fleet, was instructed that in time of war he should base himself at the Firth of Forth and sweep the North Sea, without going more than halfway across. When in 1913 First Lord of the Admiralty Winston Churchill pressed a madcap scheme for the close blockade of the Heligoland Bight and the capture of the island of Borkum, Callaghan was dismissive, stating that close blockade was no longer a viable strategy. And Chief of the Admiralty Staff Admiral Sir Henry Jackson noted on 16 October 1913 that 'our war plans lay down definitely that one of our objects of war is to bring economic pressure on Germany by stopping her oversea trade',[3] thereby creating great social unrest.

Accordingly, as the likelihood of conflict with Germany grew, Scapa Flow was designated the main battlefleet base. The Firth of Forth was developed for naval purposes at Granton, Invergordon and Rosyth. The Nore command, which included Chatham and Sheerness Royal Dockyards, gained in importance. It might be noted that in adopting this strategy, Britain ignored international treaties in determining that its approach to countering Germany would henceforth be based on a distant blockade.

Distant blockade and a problem

The strategy of distant blockade left the North Sea, and with it Britain's eastern seaboard, bereft of large British warships. Nor were there sufficient small ships, destroyers, minesweepers, etc, to police and protect the coast. In 1910 the Admiralty decided that it would co-opt fishing boats, trawlers and drifters to close this gap and act as auxiliary minesweepers and patrol vessels. These little ships would be hired or purchased from their civilian owners in time of war. To man them a new naval reserve would be created as a sub-section of the Royal Naval Reserve (RNR).

The RNR had been created by the Naval Reserve Act of 1859, itself a product of the invasion scare of the same year. For one month a year, merchant sailors and fishermen were given gunnery training on drill ships stationed around the coast. When war was declared they were liable to be drafted to the fleet or reserve ships. As first created, the RNR consisted of up to thirty thousand merchant seamen and fisherman whom the navy could call on in times of crisis. By 1914, membership was drawn from professional officers and ratings of the mercantile marine, the fishing fleet and ex-naval ratings. For the former, it was voluntary, but many major steamer companies encouraged their employees to join. After basic training, further periodic training with the fleet was undertaken.

It was decided to expand the naval reserve through the creation of a special reserve for fishermen, the Royal Naval Reserve – Trawler Section. The first skipper to join the RNR(T) signed on in Aberdeen on 3 February 1911 and approval was given to recruit 1,278 men to crew 142 trawlers.[4] By April 1912, only forty-two were ready, but Commander Reginald Plunkett noted at the time that 'in war we shall have 140 trawlers available [for minesweeping].'[5] *

But there was another group of sailors who had a close and intimate knowledge of the coastline of Britain, and also had vessels capable of sailing around it: the yachtsmen and motor boat owners of the nation.

The foundation of the motor boat reserve

By 1912, war clouds were gathering around Europe, dimming the glow of post-Edwardian radiance. First there was the Agadir incident: this was a crisis triggered by the deployment of a large force of French troops to the interior of Morocco in April 1911. Germany did not necessarily object to France's expansion of its African influence, but wanted territorial compensation for herself. Berlin threatened war, sent the gunboat *Panther* to the port, followed by the cruiser *Berlin*, and roused German nationalists to bellicosity. Negotiations between Germany and France resolved the issue, but the British government, in the person of Chancellor of the Exchequer Lloyd George, made it clear that Britain would not stand idly by if Germany threatened French or British interests. 'If Britain is treated badly … as if she is of no account in the cabinet of nations, then I say emphatically that peace at that price would be a humiliation intolerable for a great country like ours to endure,' Lloyd George thundered in a speech at the Mansion House in London. The speech was interpreted by Germany as a warning that she could not impose an unreasonable settlement on France.

Then there were two Balkan Wars in 1912 and 1913, which threatened to pull the major powers into conflict. First, four Balkan states (Bulgaria, Serbia, Greece and Montenegro) ganged up on, and defeated, the Ottoman Empire. But then the victors fell out, and Bulgaria fought against the original combatants of the first war while facing a surprise attack from Romania from

---

* This proved to be a wild underestimate of the need. Over three thousand trawlers and drifters were taken up during the course of the war.

the north. The conflicts ended with the Ottoman Empire losing the bulk of its territory in Europe. Austria–Hungary, although not a combatant, became relatively weaker because of the emergence of a strengthened and much-enlarged Serbia. And this new ascendancy led the Serbians to press for a union of the South Slavic peoples, which directly threatened Austro-Hungarian interests. Russia, Germany and Austria were at loggerheads over Slav rights; France was aching for revanche after her losses in 1870; Germany felt hemmed in and deprived of the colonies and status which she felt she deserved. And Britain thought that her pre-eminence in trade and maritime supremacy was challenged by Germany. Europe seemed to be on the edge of conflict.

This threat caused some boating enthusiasts to consider how they might be of use to their country if war came. Edward Keble Chatterton, author and a yachtsman member of the Royal Thames Yacht Club (founded in 1775 by Prince Henry, Duke of Cumberland and Strathearn), wrote that 'it arose from the desire of yachtsmen to become of use to the navy in time of war. But actually, this enthusiasm took shape owing to the action of the chief motor boat clubs'.[6] Representing three thousand members, the BMBC approached the Admiralty in 1912 and an Admiralty committee was formed under the chairmanship of Vice Admiral Sir Frederick Samuel Inglefield, at the time Admiral Commanding Coastguards and Reserves, to study the potential role of the motor pleasure craft. According to Chatterton, 'this officer reported in November 1912 that motor boats would be able to patrol and carry out examination service in estuaries and harbours, detect hostile submarines … act as despatch boats and so on'.[7] In these duties, small vessels were preferable and the petrol-powered motor boats were conceptually appropriate, for a steam engine was not well suited for such light craft.

As a result of this favourable conclusion, the Admiralty proposed that a motor boat reserve be created, affiliated to the Royal Naval Volunteer Reserve in the same manner as the RNR(T) was to the RNR. The RNVR had been set up in 1903 and was open to civilians with no prior sea experience. Keen sailors or mere landlubbers, all were welcome. There were originally five divisions, stationed in Bristol, London, Tyne, Mersey and Clyde, where civilian volunteers were trained in shore-based drill halls and aboard warships no longer required by the Royal Navy. The RNVR uniform was distinguished from that of the regular navy by its buttons stamped with RNV, and the wavy gold braid of its sleeve insignia which led them to become known colloquially as the 'Wavy Navy'.

The RNVR was not the first volunteer 'amateur navy'. The Sea Fencibles had been formed from longshoremen, bargees, fishermen, etc, for coastal defence during the French revolutionary wars. This was disbanded at the end of the conflicts, but in 1852 a Manning Committee recommended the formation of a new organisation, the Royal Naval Coast Volunteers (RNCV), which in time was replaced in 1874 by the Royal Naval Artillery Volunteers (RNAV). 'Only those at least moderately well-to-do could really afford to serve their country in the RNAV', and as a result membership was targeted on the 'rowing and yachting gentlemen of good social standing'.[8] This organisation bore many of the hallmarks and *tenue* of a yachting or gentleman's club and was disliked by the regular naval officers and the Admiralty, which starved it of support. There was some rejoicing when the Admiralty succeeded in getting the RNAV suppressed in 1891.

But the beast would not lie down, and had some powerful supporters. One such was Hugh Oakeley Arnold-Forster*, who shared a barge-yacht with W L Wylie, the well-known marine painter. In 1900 he became Parliamentary Secretary to the Admiralty under Lord Selborne, the new First Lord, in which position he was able to agitate from within. He gained agreement to the formation of a committee to study the issue of a volunteer organisation. With the support of individuals such as the Marquess of Graham (James Graham, later 6th Duke of Montrose), who held a master mariner's certificate, and C E H Chadwyck-Healey QC, who had been a lieutenant in the RNAV and had an honorary commission in the RNR, pressure was brought to bear, which the Admiralty fought hard against.

There were at least three reasons for the Admiralty's historical opposition to the volunteers. First, they clung to the view that it took years to make a sailor and that there was an arcane knowledge and skill set which could only be learned with years before the mast. But the demise of sailing ships made this argument specious. Secondly, there was a special cachet to being a Royal Navy man in the late nineteenth century; the volunteers were seen as trying to 'cash in' on this public adulation without putting in the 'hard yards', and this was resented. And thirdly, all of the volunteer bodies to date had not been governed by the Naval Discipline Act – the regular navy had no power to control and punish such men. When the volunteers' representatives on the investigating committee offered that the new organisation would willingly be subject to the Act, there was no longer a viable ground for Admiralty resistance. The Naval Forces Act of 1903 amended the 1859 Royal Naval Reserves Act and the Admiralty was authorised to 'raise and maintain a force to be called the Royal Naval Volunteer Reserve'. The RNVR was born.

In a very class-conscious regular naval world, the RNR was looked on with disdain by the regular navy, as being 'trade', but the RNVR was now tolerated, mostly because they were 'gentlemen'. There was a popular saying in the pre-1914 navy: 'Royal Navy – gentlemen and seamen; Royal Naval

---
* Later, Secretary of State for War between 1903 and 1905.

Reserve – seamen but not gentlemen; Royal Naval Volunteer Reserve – gentlemen trying to be seamen.'

The motor boat scheme had progressed to the point where Rear Admiral John de Robeck, Admiral of Patrols 1912–1914, had drawn up a training scheme for the motor boat crews and his successor, Commodore George Ballard, was given a small committee of naval officers and motor yacht club luminaries to help set up a detailed plan. The Royal Naval Motor Boat Reserve (RNMBR) had come into being; it was ten years since Dorothy Levitt had won the inaugural motor boat race. The internal combustion engine had joined the navy.

Who were the motor boat men?

Three civilians seem to have been most influential in the development of the RNMBR: Lord Inverclyde, Morton Smart and Sir Francis Armstrong. James Cleland Burns, the 3rd Lord Inverclyde, came from a family distinguished in the church, in medicine and as general merchants. But the family is best remembered in the field of shipping, for his grandfather and uncle, James and George (1st Baronet of Wemyss Bay), were the developers

James Burns, 3rd Baron Inverclyde, one of the founding 'motor boat men'.
(US Library of Congress, LC-DIG-ggbain-29288)

of the Cunard Steamship Company Limited, while he himself was chairman of the Burns Steamship Company.

George's son John (1829–1901) succeeded his father as baronet and became head of Cunard, which by that time was among the world leaders in passenger shipping. John was created the 1st Baron Inverclyde in 1897. He was a keen yachtsman and was among those responsible for setting up the Clyde Industrial Training Ship Association, which brought the sailing vessel HMS *Cumberland*, a veteran of the Crimean War, for use as a boys' training ship in the Gareloch. Lord Inverclyde's eldest son George succeeded his father as 2nd Lord Inverclyde, and as chairman of Cunard, but died childless and so his younger brother James (born 1864) assumed the title of 3rd Lord Inverclyde.

Like his father, he was an enthusiastic yachtsman. Lord Inverclyde was Commodore of the Royal Clyde Yacht Club, Vice Commodore of the Royal Northern Yacht Club and the Royal Highland Yacht Club and a member of the Royal Yacht Squadron. He was also an all-round sportsman, served as president of the Scottish Hockey Association, distinguished himself as a cricketer and lawn tennis player, and was president of the Lorne Curling Club. It has already been noted that Lord Inverclyde was a leading light in the Scottish motor boat movement, and he no doubt brought his contacts, standing and enthusiasm to the Admiralty.

Morton Warrack Smart was a famous surgeon, specialising in the treatment of muscular and joint injuries, using a method which he described as 'graduated muscular contractions'. Born in 1878, the son of the well-known Scottish artist John Smart RSA RSW, Morton was educated at Watson's College, Edinburgh, and went on to become a medical student at the university. There his studies were interrupted by the outbreak of the South African War, in which he served as a private in the Highland Brigade. Returning to Edinburgh at the end of the war, he graduated MB and ChB, and shortly afterwards moved to London.

Here, as well as establishing himself as a prominent medical man, he became greatly interested in yachting and motor boat racing and by 1914 was vice president of the International Motor Yacht Union, Commodore of the British Motor Boat Club and chairman of the Marine Motor Association. Smart had seen the possibilities of high-speed motor boats in war, and he served on the initial Admiralty committee under de Robeck and Ballard. He too brought his knowledge and connections to the Royal Navy's cause.

The third civilian member of the team was Sir Frances Philip Armstrong, 3rd Baronet of Ashburn Place. His father had been the owner of *The Globe* newspaper and received a baronetcy as a result of his services to the Unionist party. He had a long-standing interest in motorised transport of all types.

The two Royal Navy leading lights on the motor boat committee were Admiral Inglefield and Rear Admiral Cresswell John Eyres. Inglefield had been superseded as Admiral in Charge of Coastguard and Reserves at the end of 1912, but continued to chair the motor boat forum. Eyres, latterly captain of HMS *Temeraire* (1907), had been advanced to flag rank in June 1913 and, although clearly a clever man with four firsts as a lieutenant (in gunnery, torpedo, seamanship and from the Royal Naval College), had the recommendation of being available when the committee was formed.

They were assisted by Paymaster Martin Gilbert Bennett RN*, who acted as secretary to the group, and for technical advice they were 'loaned' the services of Engineer Lieutenant Commander Frank Rheuben Goodwin RN†.

A new command

The post of Admiral of Patrols was established on 1 May 1912 as a command designed to patrol the eastern coast of Britain. Rear Admiral John de Robeck hoisted his flag in the old cruiser *St George* (1892) at Harwich and thus took command of the 5th, 6th, 7th and 8th Destroyer Flotillas. It was publicly announced on 16 April that the office of the Admiral of Patrols would be at the Admiralty.[9] It did not seem to be an overly demanding position, at least initially. Captain (later Admiral) Walter Cowan, de Robeck's chief of staff, was an enthusiastic huntsman, as was de Robeck. The latter kept two horses near Banbury and Cowan had one nearby at Kineton. Their work caused them to travel all over the country and to the Admiralty; however, according to Cowan, 'the hunting took some arranging', but 'the two of them found time in some miraculous way to fit in their country pursuits'.[10]

By early 1914, the role of the flotillas was redefined as being responsible for coastal defence, where they would be supplemented by units of the newly envisaged Auxiliary Patrol, composed of trawlers, drifters, yachts and motor boats. De Robeck was succeeded by Commodore George Ballard on 1 May 1914 and it was he who ultimately commanded the Auxiliary Patrol vessels at the outbreak of war. But in October 1915 Ballard's position was abolished and command of the local patrol forces passed to the Home Command CinCs, the admirals for Dover, Nore, Portsmouth, Plymouth, Rosyth, Orkney and Shetland, and the Coast of Ireland. By then, the civilian leisure motor boats and their volunteer crewmen had been at war for fourteen months.

---

* Bennett served as Deputy Judge Advocate of the Fleet from 1930 to 1933 and retired as a paymaster rear admiral. His son was the naval officer and historian Captain Geoffrey Bennett.
† The son of Engineer Vice Admiral Sir George Goodwin KCB MIME HON LLD, Frank Goodwin's attachment to the RNMBR did his career no harm, for he won the DSO ('for exceptional work under very trying conditions in bringing HMS Dartmouth to port after she was torpedoed', *London Gazette* 30258, 28 August 1917) during the coming war and ended his career as an engineer rear admiral himself.

3

To War in Boats

War with Germany was declared on 4 August 1914. *The Times* averred that 'the position in Europe is one of breathless anticipation of the beginning of hostilities on a large scale'.[1] At Old Trafford, where Lancashire were playing Yorkshire at cricket, the amateur Mr A H Hornby (Harrow, Trinity College Cambridge, Lancashire club captain and son of the great A N 'Monkey' Hornby, one of only two men to have captained England at rugby union and cricket) had to leave the ground at 1330 in response to a call from the War Office – which resulted in him reappearing with the rank of captain in the Remount Department.

And all across the country, men rushed to volunteer or were called up for service. Take, for example, the scenes at Fraserburgh in Scotland. In the 4 August edition of the *Fraserburgh Times*, the newspaper noted that:

> the calling out of the Royal Naval Reserve* created great excitement in Fraserburgh, where hundreds of Highland hired men, engaged meantime on the herring fishing boats, are members of the Reserve. During Sunday forenoon, 257 men presented themselves at the Custom House, and received their warrants. In the afternoon at 1530 a special train, carrying 233 reservists, left Fraserburgh for Portsmouth. Unparalleled scenes were witnessed at the railway station, where several thousand assembled to give the men a hearty send-off. They marched from the Custom House to the station, headed by the Fraserburgh pipe band, under the charge of Leading Seamen Alexander Sim and Noah Killoh, both of Fraserburgh. For fully half a mile along the railway thousands of spectators lined the embankments on both sides, and tumultuous cheers were raised.

At the other end of Britain, at Brixham nearly every family was affected by mobilisation and the town's annual regatta was abandoned. Men were commanded to report to the Customs House on the quay and depart for the naval barracks at Devonport. The cottage hospital nurses turned out to cheer

---

* The RNR was activated at 0125 on 2 August 1914 after a meeting of the Army Council, chaired by Prime Minister Asquith.

them off and the chairman of the urban district council presided over the singing of the National Anthem at the railway station. In Looe, Cornwall, the men mustered on the quay and were marched to the railway station. In Falmouth the call-up was announced by the town crier. And the King's Proclamation summoned the RNVR to active service for the first time; the force was only eleven years old.

The great and the good toured their estates encouraging men to volunteer. In Leicestershire, at Redmile on his estates, the Duke of Rutland lectured an audience in the school hall, championing the chivalric ideals of honour, valour and sacrifice. 'If we had attempted to keep out of this war, we should have violated every honourable principle ... we should have been guilty of one of the most cowardly actions that a country ... has ever been guilty of,' he thundered.[2] His people came forwards in droves.

Meanwhile, the Admiralty started to requisition, hire or purchase the civilian vessels, both commercial and domestic, that it needed to fight a war.

The Auxiliary Patrol

The trawlers, drifters, yachts, motor boats, paddle steamers and all other assorted civilian craft taken up by the Royal Navy were known as auxiliaries, and initially either joined what became known as the Auxiliary Patrol or the Minesweeping Service.

Those vessels intended for minesweeping duties 'belonged' to the Minesweeping Division, headed from 4 September 1914 by Rear Admiral Edward Francis Benedict (Ned) Charlton*, as Admiral of Minesweepers, with his flag in the 279grt armed yacht *Zarefah* (ex-*Maretanza V*), armed with two 3pdr guns. She had been built in 1905 by George Brown of Greenock for Sir John Denison-Pender†, was hired by the Admiralty in 1914, purchased by them in 1916 and was sunk by a mine in May 1917. As the war progressed and mining became heavy, and a considerable menace in areas such as the North Sea, yachts were sometimes deployed as minesweepers, but this activity was largely the preserve of trawlers and paddle steamers.

However, most yachts and motor boats joined the Auxiliary Patrol. At the outbreak of war, the defence of the coastline of Britain was divided into twenty-seven patrol areas, each under a senior naval officer, often a 'dug out' (a retired senior officer recalled to duty) with a shore base. All were ultimately under the aegis of the Admiral of Patrols. There were also eleven patrol areas in the Mediterranean, variously subject to British, French or

---

* Charlton was succeeded at the end of 1915 by Rear Admiral the Hon Edward Stafford Fitzherbert (later 13th Baron Stafford).
† Chairman and managing director of the Eastern Telegraph Company (later Cable & Wireless).

Italian (after 1915) control. Patrol groups were set up to try to keep the seaway clear of enemy minelayers, U-boats, coastal raiders, invasion, etc. These were 'composed at first of armed yachts, trawlers and motor boats with officers drawn from the RNVR. The standard unit consisted of a yacht, four trawlers and four motor boats [and these] were sent to Scapa, Rosyth and other places where they were most needed'.[3]

Motor boats were scattered around the country. Five operated at Stornoway and another nine in the Shetland Islands zone. Eight were at Orkney and Cromarty had ten. Tyne had fifteen, Humber five, Great Yarmouth nine, Dover eight and Portsmouth twenty-five.

The motor boats and the motor men

From the onset, the RNMBR had sprung into action. Inglefield's committee now became the executive body for running the motor boat reserve. Inverclyde, Armstrong and Smart all received commissions as commanders RNVR and the group was joined by two other yachtsmen, commissioned as RNVR officers, to assist in the work on the ground – section officers Lieutenant Commander Francis Joseph Richardson for England and Lieutenant Robert Gibson for Scotland.

The call went out for boats and men came from far and wide, bringing their motor craft with them. Vessels of between 3 to 65 tons were taken. Their owners were given a commission in the RNMBR, the boats were painted grey with a white identifying numeral on the bow, equipped with a white ensign, and a rifle or other small arm, and sent off to harbour duties or local patrol functions. The Admiralty paid a charter fee and owners enrolled their own crews, who were supplied with a service certificate. These crewmen were known as 'motor boatmen',[4] and their service number had the suffix 'MB'.

The duties of the RNMBR were officially defined as 'for services during the war, for patrol and despatch work, etc, or such duties as the Admiralty may from time to time direct'.[5] Typically, apart from

A Royal Navy Motor Boat Reserve sweetheart brooch, made of silver on tortoiseshell. It depicts a crowned laurel wreath, the centre bearing 'RNMBR' above a fouled anchor, with a solid silver back. Sweetheart brooches were extremely popular in the First World War and were given by servicemen to their wives, girlfriends, mothers, etc, who would wear them as a charm and memento. *(Author's collection)*

working with the patrol groups, motor boat duties might include 'patrolling in the roadsteads, estuaries, off harbours, examining shipping, controlling traffic, taking out orders to trawlers and checking they were on station, putting pilots aboard and so on'.[6] By October, their tasks had been formalised as being 'for the purpose of examining the coast, harbours and inlets and denying the use of these places to the enemy'.[7]

Sub Lieutenant Gordon Maxwell in motor boat number 35, *Minou*, offered a more light-hearted view of the tasks of the RNMBR:

> The boats we had to work on then were of all shapes and sizes, and our duties were varied; duty boats, patrol, emergency (which usually meant hanging about doing nothing), and pilot boats. The last-named work was by far the best, from our point of view, and everyone, I think, looks back with pleasure on the days when they were attached to the pilot cutter *Jessica* and the merry parties aboard that trim, comfortable little craft. The pilots were good fellows and made us welcome. I was always sorry when that twenty-four-hour duty was over.

A number of Scottish motor fishing drifters were also enrolled in the RNMBR and commanded by yachtsmen, and by November 1914 'there were 120 craft in the RNMBR'.[9] This swelled to 180 by the end of December, together with eleven RNMBR gentlemen shown on the Navy List with no boats.[10] The volunteers were given an RNVR rank of sub lieutenant, lieutenant or, in one instance, lieutenant commander. This latter distinction went to Francis Richardson (see above) who had brought his boat *Dragonfly* (motor boat no 21) with him.

Who were these latter-day knight errants who arrived with their maritime steeds? They were varied in terms of personality, but not in status. Here were the upper classes going to war, the British aristocracy and the gentry in arms. Forty-five-year-old Gilbert Sackville, 8th Earl de la Warr, loved cricket and in 1894 and 1896 got together sides which played the South Africans and Australians respectively at Bexhill. He himself took part in both matches, scoring 0 and 8 not out in the first game and 1 in the second. But it got him into *Wisden*. Now he brought his boat *Osprey* to the war. He would die of pneumonia on active service in December the following year.

The Honourable Charles Watson Sholto Douglas was the second son of Sholto George Watson Douglas, 19th Earl of Morton. He volunteered, but brought no craft with him. By contrast, the Hon Thomas John Wynn, who on 19 July 1916 became 5th Baron Newborough, of Bodvean, County Caernarvon, brought *Nord Est*.

Thirty-one-year-old Algernon Arthur St Lawrence Lee Guinness, who would succeed to the Ardilaun peerage in 1915, came with *Perlona*. Guinness was an avid and successful racing driver, who – on entering his inheritance in 1906 – covered the Ostend speed trials at a top speed of 117mph. The same year he bought a massive 18-litre V8 Darracq that in September 1907 took him to 115 mph at Brooklands racing track. That same year he was third in the Isle of Man Tourist Trophy and placed second and third in two circuits of the Ardennes. He came second in the 1908 Isle of Man Tourist Trophy, but in the 1913 French Grand Prix at Picardy Guinness failed to make a turn at 80mph and crashed through a barrier, killing a spectator and ending up, unhurt, in a river. He also had a sideline in motor boat racing.

Ninian Ballantyne Stewart, whose father owned the yacht *Maria*, registered at 786 tons, and was a founding partner of the department store chain House of Fraser, arrived with the motor boat *Catriona*. The *What Next* belonged to thirty-eight-year-old Sir George Charles Keppel Johnstone, 9th Baronet Westerhall, who lived at 'Rothsay', West Cowes, and whose family motto was *Nunquam non paratus*, 'never not ready'; he was certainly ready enough to join the RNMBR.

A little further down the social scale, Edward Keble Chatterton, author and yachtsman, brought *Burrastow*; solicitor Arthur Hildebrand Ramsden Tagore commanded *Pursuit*. Engineer and inventor John Godfrey Yule Delmar-Morgan, who lived in prestigious Tite Street, Chelsea, had his boat *Mansura*. Recently divorced John Henry Atkinson Bell* appeared in *Jean* (his ex-wife was called Stella Ethel – perhaps there's a story there). Forty-year-old Louis Charles Bernacchi, an Australian physicist and astronomer best known for his role in several Antarctic expeditions, arrived with *Frances*. He had been on Captain Robert Falcon Scott's 1901 to 1904 polar expedition and Scott was best man at Bernacchi's wedding in 1906. Lawrence Maxwell Waterhouse, BMBC member and managing director of electrical engineers Simplex Conduits of Birmingham, brought his motor yacht *Amice*, which the navy counted as a motor boat (number 36). And Morton Smart, who by 1914 had been medically qualified for twelve years, was appointed as a naval surgeon. But within a day or two he was transferred by the Admiralty to a fighting job, presumably in the light of his role on the motor boat committee and general experience of the type.

Not all of the motor boats which came the Admiralty's way were the result of pure altruism, however. John Walter Edward Douglas-Scott-

---

* The fact that Bell was divorced confirms his wealthy status. Before 1914 divorce was rare; it was considered a scandal, confined by expense to the rich, and by legal restrictions requiring proof of adultery or violence to the truly desperate. In the first decade of the twentieth century, there was just one divorce for every 450 marriages.

Montagu, 2nd Baron Montagu of Beaulieu, was a passionate motorist, who had taught himself to be an engineer after attending Eton and Oxford. On 17 March 1915 his secretary wrote to Edward Marsh, aide to First Lord of the Admiralty Winston Churchill, explaining the financial difficulties of his employer and asking if the Admiralty would be interested in buying his motor boat.[11]

The hurried and improvised nature of the recruitment can be seen in the personnel records kept by the Admiralty. The service records for regular officers (and ratings) were on pre-printed forms, ruled and formatted into various heading and completed in a (more or less) copperplate hand. In contrast, the paperwork for the officers of the RNMBR were scrawled on a plain, unruled, untitled piece of white paper, looking for all the world like a discarded shopping list.* Nonetheless, by July 1915, there were 278 officers in the RNMBR, three commanders, two lieutenant commanders, 131 lieutenants and 142 sub lieutenants.[12]

Travels abroad

And the RNMBR was not confined to Britain. As historian Christopher Phillips has noted:

> the canal and river systems of northern France and Belgium in 1914 were, from a transportation point of view, undoubtedly among the finest in the world. Across the two nations ran almost ten thousand miles of navigable waterways that – unlike in Britain, where the spread of the railways had severely curtailed the use of canals for the bulk carriage of goods – remained an integral component of the local and regional freight traffic infrastructure. In 1905 the total quantity of freight carried by water in Belgium amounted to 53,345,000 tons, approximately half of the nation's entire goods and merchandise traffic. The outbreak of war in August 1914 brought this traffic almost entirely to a standstill. However, the 'permanent way' of the canal and river network remained relatively undamaged by the opening campaigns and – in many areas – within the hands of the Allies.[13]

And where there was water, there should be the Royal Navy. Rear Admiral Eyres was sent to France with Morton Smart as his chief of staff. With them went three 60ft Thornycroft-built motor boats – *Penelope, Mary Rose* and *Dorothea* – originally intended for the Turkish government, together with four small motor boats and the motor yacht *California* (which the navy

---

* As were those for all RNVR officers.

categorised as a motor boat). Each was armed with at least one 3pdr and a Maxim.

This small force was placed under the First Army's HQ in March 1915, but was never put to aggressive use. So, at the end of May the Royal Navy asked for their boats back and eventually despatched them to Gallipoli. They were shipped aboard transports to Mudros, where they arrived in midsummer and were joined by another motor boat, *Anzac*, sent from the Suez Canal, and *Oomala*, again carried by freighter and attached to the consular service in the eastern Mediterranean for intelligence work.

By contrast, *California* travelled through the French riverine and canal systems to reach Marseilles, from whence she motored via Genoa and Malta to reach Mudros. Here these six pleasure boats were designated the Motor Gunboat Flotilla and placed under the command of Morton Smart, now rated with the rank of commander. They were despatched to patrol the harbour mouth at Aivali, a Turkish port from which U-boats were said to be operating. *Mary Rose* and *Penelope* both came under fire during this duty and the flotilla was moved to the Gulf of Smyrna in September.

Similarly, in July 1915 motor boats from the RNMBR were sent to Egypt to replace *Anzac* and help protect and patrol the Suez Canal. At this point in the war the canal, 101 miles long from Port Said in the north to Suez in the south, was viewed as a defensive barrier in itself and the British held the west bank, leaving the east and Sinai desert to the Turks (the line of defence was moved to the east bank at the end of 1915).

The motor boats deployed were *Nina d'Asty*, *Puffin II*, *My Lady Molly*, *Minnehaha*, *Eothen* and *Memphis* (motor boats 120, 108, 36, 11, 144 and 147). The latter had already seen service in France, operating around Armentières, and was fitted with steel protection plates and a Maxim machine gun in the bows. She was commanded by a London-born avid yachtsman, thirty-three-year-old Sub Lieutenant Christopher Noel Luker RNVR, who later wrote that patrolling the canal was not a dull affair:

> Spies were caught almost nightly, swimming the canal, and they were not alone or unarmed. One or two of their number would remain on the Turkish side of the Canal and open fire should the one crossing the canal be discovered. The advantage was entirely with them, as they chose a spot where the banks are high and afford plenty of cover. However, the spy trouble was eventually overcome.[14]

The RNMBR men and their craft were based at the village of Osmailia on Lake Timsah, which was also home to the canal pilots.

Within two months, *Memphis* and her commander were sent to the Great

Bitter Lake at the north end of the canal and here conducted night patrols on the eastern side of the lake, searching for Turkish reconnaissance units. 'The usual procedure was to drift, as the current sets along the shore', wrote Luker 'and in the early hours of the morning we would "fetch up" somewhere near Kabret, the station at the entrance to the canal on the southern side. Some mines were laid in the Great Bitter Lake and a Holt steamer was damaged but able to proceed to Suez'.[15] *Memphis* sustained this role for six months. Eventually, around April 1916, the motor boats were relieved of their patrolling duties and replaced, being distributed to various points on the canal until their commanding officers were recalled to England to retrain.

And the RNMBR was represented in the Salonika campaign as well. British naval motor boat units patrolled Lake Langaza and Lake Beshik from 1915. Not the least of their problems was getting the motor boats to the lakes: 'there seemed only one way; hoist them to the quay and load them onto pontoon wagons'.[16] Given the lack of roads, it took the resultant wagon train a whole day to transport its cargo just three miles. One of the men involved was Thomas Lawrence Burls Eve, who had joined the motor boat reserve in December 1914, but in March 1916 he was 'demobilised to take up an appointment' under War Office control in the Salonika campaign, where he worked with the Army Service Corps (ASC) motor boats. He remained a naval officer, but was paid for by the army. By June he was back on the Admiralty's books, for 'duty with the motor boats in Salonika'.[17] In this post he was mentioned in despatches on 29 March 1917 by the CinC British Salonika Force (Lieutenant General George Milne) for 'distinguished services during the past six months'.[18] In December his services seemed to be no longer required and he transferred to the books of the old cruiser and depot ship *St George*.

The development of anti-submarine nets

The arrival of the amateur sailing enthusiasts meant that the Royal Navy found itself with men joining the service who brought with them knowledge and skills not necessarily associated with naval officers. For instance, it was a member of the RNMBR who came up with one of the main anti-submarine devices of the early war. Lieutenant Francis Richard Sam Bircham was an engineer and motor boat owner, whose craft *Mayfair* was one of the first to be put into service with the RNMBR and designated motor boat number 1. Independently wealthy, he lived at 76 Jermyn Street and was a member of the Wyndham Club in St James's Square, whose stated objective was 'to secure a convenient and agreeable place of meeting for a society of gentlemen, all connected with each other by a common bond of literary or personal acquaintance'. It cost twenty-five guineas* to join!

On the outbreak of war, *Mayfair* and Bircham were sent to patrol in the Forth area, where the Battlecruiser Fleet was anchored above the Forth Bridge. Here his engineer's brain fell to thinking about a sort of anti-U-boat boom to protect the moored warships. By the end of 1914, he had been put on the books of HMS *President* and was working on his ideas under the Director of Naval Operations. For Bircham had invented the indicator net.

This was a light, steel-wire net, sections of which were stopped by a jackstay buoyed with bottle-glass floats and shot and laid by armed drifters. The net could be up to 100ft long and made into longer lengths by clipping them together. Some were kept extended by the drifter proceeding at low speed, others permanently moored. The nets were fitted with buoys which were released by the violent motion of the submarine manoeuvring against it or by a hydrostatic trigger when the buoy was dragged under. When fouled, the buoy released a calcium carbide flare which allowed the drifter and/or other vessels to track the victim's progress. The work on the Forth indicator-net barrier was complete by February 1915 and the admiral commanding the coast of Scotland (Sir Robert Swinburne Lowry) expressed his 'appreciation of [the] rapidity with which the work was done, reflecting great credit on all concerned'.[19]

By April 1915, these had developed into EC mine nets. These were fitted with small mines, which were powered from batteries carried on the drifters or, in the case of the EC II net mine, armed hydrostatically and fired when one of its eight contacts were pressed, exploding against a U-boat's flanks. Initially they were intended to be towed, but this proved more dangerous to the drifter than any U-boat, and they were thereafter always moored, though tended by a fleet of drifters to maintain them in good repair.

Indicator nets were widely utilised around the coast of Britain and Ireland to deny ports to U-boats, and also used to make barriers to submarines, such as the cross-channel Dover Barrage. And the idea sprang from the head of a motor boat sailor. In 1915 Their Lordships gave the Admiralty Board's thanks to Bircham for 'the thought and time given to the use of indicator nets'.[20]

* * * * *

Fishermen, yachtsmen, motor boat enthusiasts, people for whom the sea was a living, and others for whom it was a pleasure, all came together for

---
* Equivalent to over £3,000 at the time of writing.

the defence of Britain. As Julian Corbett put it in the navy's *Official History* after the war:

> the whole seafaring population, in so far as it was not needed for other work vital to the national life, gathered to the struggle before it was six months old … so by the end of 1914, and without any previous preparation, our nation was in arms upon the sea. Such a reawakening of the old maritime spirit which had lain dormant for so many ages must always remain as one of the most absorbing features of the war, and the strangeness of the revival is the more impressive when we remember that it was mainly the mine and the submarine, the very last words of the naval art, that threw us back to the methods of the Middle Ages.[21]

4

The Birth of the Motor Launch

The motor boats and crews of the RNMBR were long on enthusiasm and courage, but short on practicality. During the first winter of the war, it became clear that 'many of the motor boats could not keep the sea in bad weather'.[1] The larger ones, of 20 to 30 tons, could at least patrol bays and exposed areas such as the mouth of the Humber. But the smaller craft proved useless except for picket work, patrolling harbours, pilotage or carrying despatches. In any case, it is difficult to know what they would do if they found an enemy submarine or surface vessel. Only one in ten of the motor boats were (lightly) armed, and only two or three had radio. Various methods of attacking submarines were essayed; divers were sometimes carried, who were meant to go over the side and interfere with a U-boat's periscope or diving planes. Another scheme was for a black hood and large hammer to be carried. The hood was to be placed over the lens of the periscope and the hammer used to smash it. For all the well-meaning volunteerism of the gentlemen amateurs, the Corinthian spirit was not enough and no successes from the use of these methods was reported.

Nonetheless, the Admiralty did allot a motor boat one success against a U-boat. The motor boat *Salmon* (number 192) was built in 1915 and was just 40ft long. She had no cabin, but her Sterling engine* could push her up to 20 knots. *Salmon* was one of six fast motor boats presented to the Royal Navy by a wealthy American and New York Yacht Club member, Alexander Smith Cochran. He had been the owner of the racing schooner *Westward*, which had won a famous race against two German yachts, *Germania* and *Meteor* on 1 August 1910.

Just before midnight on 5 July 1916 *Salmon* and her commander, Sub Lieutenant Francis Edward Temple-West RNVR, were on patrol off Lowestoft. Temple-West had only joined the RNVR on 14 February; now he was using a hydrophone set to search for German minelaying UC-type submarines operating out of the Flanders ports. Temple-West homed in on a buzzing hydrophone signal, which indicated there was a submarine around, until he seemed to be right over the contact, then went to full speed ahead and dropped a depth charge. This exploded, followed by a much more violent

---

* Manufactured by the Sterling Gas Engine Company of Buffalo, New York.

detonation which threw a column of water 50ft in the air. It seemed clear that his charge had found a target, and as pieces of white-painted wood, gratings, and bubbles came to the surface, and the hydrophone contact had ceased, he was certain he had sunk a U-boat. Their Lordships told him that 'he showed skill and intelligence in the way he carried out an attack on an enemy submarine on the night of 5 July'. But they noted that 'destruction was not thought conclusive'.[2]

But in 1919 the Admiralty credited *Salmon* with sinking *UC-10* (although on 21 August 1916).[3] However, when a prize payment on behalf of this success was made to the prize fund, *UC-10* was allotted to the submarine *E-54* and *Salmon* shown to have sunk *UC-7*.[4] No doubt the crew were proud of their achievement, and Temple-West was awarded the DSC in 1919 for 'Services in Action with Enemy Submarines'.[5] The medal was inscribed 'July 5th 1916 Sinking U-boat'. But later scholarship showed that *UC-7* had been mined on 5 July 1916, north of Zeebrugge.* No U-boat was in fact destroyed by a motor boat.

Seven of these RNMBR pleasure boats were lost in war service, three of them to fire and three in the sinking of the ship bearing them to Cardiff (see Appendix 1). And by early 1915, it was clear that their limited capabilities were of little use in the war against the growing menace of the submarine. U-boats sank 749,000 tons of British merchant shipping (total British losses 855,721) in the whole of 1915.[6] The country needed small, capable, anti-submarine vessels, faster and better armed than the Auxiliary Patrol's trawlers, more durable than the motor boats. And it needed lots of them. An 'accidental' meeting would provide the answer. But first we must examine a small American boatbuilder.

The Elco Boat Company

In 1879 one William Woodnut Griscom of Philadelphia patented an electric motor that could be used for marine purposes, and the following year he started a company to sell his invention, the Electric Dynamic Company. In 1892 the business went bankrupt and was purchased by the owner of the Electric Storage Battery Company (branded as Exide), Isaac Leopold Rice.

Meanwhile, the Electric Launch and Navigation Company, later known as the Electric Launch Company (Elco), was assembling small electric boats and sourcing its batteries and engines from what was now Rice's two businesses, while subcontracting out the construction of the hulls. Elco became famous overnight at the Columbian Exposition of 1893 in Chicago, where fifty-five of its launches, each 36ft long and driven by battery-powered

---

* Such investigations also demonstrated that *E-54* had sunk *UC-10*, however, on 21 August 1916.

The Columbian Exhibition of 1893 made Elco boats famous. Here is a view of the centrepiece of the Beaux-Arts design, seen looking west from the peristyle and showing the Court of Honour and Grand Basin. One of Elco's launches can be seen bottom left and others centre right and left. *(Author's collection)*

electric motors, carried over a million passengers on the waterways of the Exposition between 15 April and 31 October. Seeing an opportunity for further vertical integration, Rice purchased Elco in 1899 and began construction of an Elco boatbuilding facility at Bayonne, New Jersey*.

On the back of its success in Chicago, Elco-built boats became a desirable commodity. Industry and world leaders bought into the brand: John Jacob Astor possessed four, Grand Duke Alexander of Russia and his cousin, Tsar Nicholas II, owned Elco launches. Henry Ford and Thomas Edison each purchased an Elco boat and moored their vessels at their adjoining Florida estates.

---

* A city set on a peninsula located between Newark Bay to the west, the Kill Van Kull to the south, and New York Bay to the east,

The company's managing director for the pleasure boat division was Henry Randolph Sutphen, who had joined the firm in 1892. As his chief designer, in 1906 he employed a young naval architect, Irwin Chase. They adopted building techniques based on those pioneered by Henry Ford, breaking the process down into small, repetitive steps. Then came the war.

A meeting

In February 1915 Henry Sutphen was in a hotel in New York when he met up with 'a well-known English shipbuilder … presumably on secret business of the Admiralty'.[7] They fell to talking about the menace posed by the U-boats. By his own account, Sutphen ventured to suggest the use 'of a small number of motor launches for attacking and destroying submarines. My idea was to have a mosquito fleet big enough to patrol the waters of Great Britain'.[8] They would be about 80ft long and be capable of 19 knots. His interlocutor asked how many he could build of that type; Sutphen, making it up as he went along, suggested fifty.

The 'well known shipbuilder' was in fact Sir Trevor Dawson*, managing director of the defence contractor Vickers. He had been sent to America by First Lord of the Admiralty Winston Churchill at the head of an arms-buying delegation. The meeting was unlikely to have been accidental, as Vickers had brought submarine licences from Rice and at one time had held shares in Elco. Indeed, given that Dawson was on friendly terms with First Sea Lord Jacky Fisher, it is entirely possible that Dawson and his team already had Admiralty approval in principle to procure such vessels before they left Britain.

A few days later, they met formally; Sutphen was informed that the Admiralty would give him a contract for fifty vessels. This was great, except that he had no idea how to build them. But a contract was signed on 9 April 1915.

American derring-do came to the rescue and by 1 May Elco had the frames of the first boat erected. That was the same day as the *Lusitania* set out on her fateful voyage; a week later she was sunk by a U-boat with staggering loss of life, including 128 Americans. This disaster prompted the Admiralty to up the order – to an additional five hundred vessels. Elco were contracted to provide 550 motor launches for delivery by 16 November 1916 for a total of $22 million or about £8,400 per boat (perhaps £890,000 in today's money).

---

* Dawson was himself a former naval officer, having joined *Britannia* as a cadet in 1881 and served until leaving the RN in the rank of lieutenant in 1896. His commission on the Emergency List was restored in 1902.

The contract specification called for a minimum speed when fully loaded of 19 knots, combined with a cruising radius which required a fuel capacity of 2,000 gallons. The boat should be able to maintain station in any weather and have the facility to carry a deadweight of 20,000lbs (which was equivalent to the weight of the guns, ammunition, water and supplies of a patrol). Simplicity and standardisation were the key to producing the boats quickly and so the design details were kept simple; for example, there was no double planking of the hull for strength. And in order to transport the vessels to Britain, the agreement specified that the boats had to be of a size to fit four at a time on the deck of a steamer for transit across the Atlantic.

But there was a problem. The USA was officially neutral in the war. In fact, large parts of American commerce were doing very nicely, thank you, selling goods to all sides, including food and other supplies to Germany. But US President Woodrow Wilson had set out American policy very clearly in 1914:

> The United States must be neutral in fact as well as in name during these days that are to try men's souls. We must be impartial in thought as well as in action, must put a curb upon our sentiments as well as upon every transaction that might be construed as a preference of one party to the struggle before another.[9]

Therefore, in order to avoid any embarrassment or conflict with the US government for such an overt supply of war craft to Britain, while the first fifty boats were built at Bayonne, Sutphen and the Admiralty urgently sought a base in Canada in which to construct the remaining vessels. The first New Jersey-built batch of fifty was painted white (and camouflaged as yachts so as not to appear to be warships) and sailed on their own bottoms to Halifax for onward delivery to the UK. Subsequently, parts were made in Bayonne but assembled in two Canadian shipyards, Canadian Vickers of Montreal (*ML-51–260*) and Davie Shipbuilding, Lauzon, Quebec (*ML-262–550*), facilities leased by Elco. Such was the pressure on schedules that Elco's usual suppliers of bronze components (rudders, quadrants, etc) could not meet demand, and the famous glassmaking and sculpture-producing company of Tiffany's in New York was called upon and contracted to provide them. Motive power came from a pair of Standard 220hp engines.

That summary of the process is what the official documents tell us. The reality was a little different. The anonymous author ('M-P-S') of the pamphlet *Hounding the Hun* was the son of a British shipyard owner doing 'work experience' in the draughtsmen's office of the Elco works when war broke out. He noted that when American banks were asked to finance the deal, they were disbelieving: 'How can a plant which has built perhaps a dozen yachts a year produce a submarine chaser a day?'[10] they asked. Sutphen was obdurate: 'Our standardisation will do it … if you won't help, we'll have to do it alone'.[11]

M-P-S was sent to report on the Quebec yard which was eventually contracted to assemble nearly three hundred craft. It was, he reported, 'a rock pile … very good for cows', with 'workmen [who were] rough Canadian backwoodsmen, most of whom had never seen a motor boat'.[12] Few of them spoke English.

M-P-S took charge of the assembly process and used the methods of Ford et al, with small groups assigned to one definite operation. Every single keel, frame, knee, deck, fitting and piece of machinery was made in New Jersey. Each item needed to be perfectly cut to size, and not only for the assembly, for the pieces were moved by train direct to the shipyards and they had to meet railway clearances in both countries. Whole freight trains carried entire flotillas of kit craft 380 and 580 miles to Montreal and Quebec respectively, where the boats were assembled and launched.

The boat parts arrived labelled and were put together like working out a jigsaw puzzle, and the completed vessels then shipped off to Halifax for acceptance testing and afterwards to England. When winter closed the river with ice, they shipped the finished motor launches (known as MLs) to Halifax by rail, sending the 80ft boats on 60ft lumber rail wagons. Eighty-four boats were sent in this manner until the waterways opened up again in February 1916. Every day for a year and a half a completed boat rolled off the production line; 550 were built in 488 days. The last one was delivered on 3 November 1916; it was a stunning achievement by Sutphen and his Elco team.* It took 130 separate voyages from Halifax to England to convey all 550 boats over to Britain (usually four to a ship). Once in Britain the boats were armed and commissioned at Portsmouth.

Nor did Elco's service end there. A further thirty were ordered in July 1917, the final one of which arrived in February 1918.

The Elco motor launch

Built of wood, primarily yellow and Oregon pine and white oak, the two batches of MLs had slightly different dimensions. MLs *1–50* measured 75ft in length, 12ft in beam and had a draught of 3ft 8in. MLs *51–500* were

---

* Elco eventually built 720 MLs (Nutting, *Cinderellas of the Fleet*, p20), with at least two being deployed by the US Navy and many finding their way into civilian hands after the war.

slightly larger, being between 80ft and 88ft long*, 12ft 2in across and drew 3ft 10in. The change in length came about as it had been found that it was easier to maintain the specified speed with a longer hull. The first fifty vessels weighed in at 34 tons, the second at 37 tons.

All were powered by Standard Motor Construction Company engines. Based in Jersey City, NJ, the company had started life in 1900 as a manufacturer of marine engines. Each ML was fitted with two of their six-cylinder petrol engines, which could together produce around 450hp and drive the craft at about 19 knots. Range at a cruising speed of 15 knots was 1,000 miles, which doubled at 11 knots. A feature of the technology was that there was no reverse gear – the motors were connected directly to the propeller shaft. To start the engines required a blast of compressed air, carried in bottles on board. The motors could be initiated either ahead or astern, but to transition between the two meant stopping the engines, operating a small hand-lever to change the direction of the air blast, and then starting them again. This could be tricky to do when the crew was under pressure.

The initial impression created by the launches amongst regular RN officers when they first arrived in Britain was less than favourable. It was believed that 'no craft under 130ft would be capable of standing up'[13] to the rough waters of the North Sea. The Inspector of Lifeboats went out on one and 'his report on their seaworthiness was depressing'.[14] And it cost an additional £3,000 to fit them out.[15] But longer acquaintance proved that 'uncomfortable, wet and inadequate for certain work they might have been but they lived through much bad weather and made some outstanding voyages'.[16]

Arming the motor launches

Armament was fitted in Britain prior to commissioning. There is confusion in the published literature as to how the motor launches were armed. Some sources state 13pdr guns, others 3pdr, or even 3in. In fact, initially it was intended that the boats carry a modified army 13pdr gun†. Vice Admiral Reginald Bacon (who commanded the Dover Patrol from 1915 to the end of 1917) described these as 'Old Horse Artillery 13pdrs in a ship mounting on their foredeck'.[17] Sub Lieutenant Gordon Maxwell remembered training on these at Whale Island before being assigned to his vessel.[18] But these guns were earmarked in late 1916 for the new concept of Defensively Armed

---
* To give a frame of reference, at an average 80ft the length was 1.2 times the length of a cricket pitch, wicket to wicket, or 1.3 times the distance between a baseball pitcher and the batter.
† Developed by Vickers from the Royal Horse Artillery Mk II. It was of 3in calibre and fired a 16lb 4oz shell.

A motor launch 3pdr gun and proud skipper. *(Author's collection)*

Merchant Ships, cargo vessels armed for defence against U-boats and with navy gunners on board, and most that had been fitted to MLs had been removed by the end of the year. The motor launches were instead equipped with a 3pdr (although fifty MLs retained the 13pdr to the end of the war).

The 3pdrs were mainly old Vickers Mark I, first used in 1904 on battleships and armoured cruisers as an anti-torpedo boat weapon, and removed later as the longer ranges at which actions were expected to be fought rendered them useless. They fired a shell of just over 3lbs to a maximum range of around 8,000yds, dependent on elevation. Lewis machine guns and a few rifles or pistols completed the gunnery fit-out.

For anti-submarine purpose they carried lance bombs, and from late 1916 depth charges, together with primitive hydrophone listening equipment. MLs could also carry smoke discharging equipment, anti-aircraft weapons and their versatility meant that all sorts of inshore operations came their way.

Comparisons

Given that the MLs were intended as anti-submarine (A/S) boats, it is interesting to compare the relative size and armament of the hunter and the hunted.

MLs were 75–88ft in length, could manage 19 knots on a good day and cruise at 15 knots. They were armed with a 3pdr gun. An ocean-going *U-27*-class U-boat of 1912–1914 build was 212ft long, could attain 16.4 knots surfaced and was equipped with a 10.5cm (4.1in) gun and six torpedoes.

The smaller coastal submarines were perhaps an opponent more likely to be encountered around the coast of Britain. The *UB-II* type of 1915–1916, usually based on the Belgian ports, could manage 9.5 knots on the surface, was 119ft long and carried an 8.8cm (approximately 3.5in) gun and six torpedoes. The minelaying *UC-II*-class of 1915–1917 ran at 11.6 knots, was 160ft in length and carried an 8.8cm weapon and seven torpedoes.

It can be readily seen that the MLs were considerably smaller than their foes and far from achieving parity in gun armament.

Crewing the motor launches

MLs *1–3* were commissioned at Portsmouth by 14 October 1915. But while the building of MLs was being feverishly pursued across the Atlantic, changes were taking place in the RNMBR as well.

At the end of October 1915 the position of Admiral of Patrols was eliminated. George Ballard, the incumbent, had incurred the distrust of Chief of the Naval Staff Vice Admiral Sir Henry Oliver and, as Oliver put it, 'I could not get him shifted … so I took bits of his command away at the north and south ends till there was none left'.[19] Responsibility for the Auxiliary Patrol now fell to the admiral in whose jurisdiction they operated.

At the same time, the RNMBR was abolished as a separate body, perhaps a recognition that the motor pleasure boats had simply not been up to the tasks required. Administration was folded into the general Auxiliary Patrol organisation and the men of the RNMBR were instead assigned to the RNVR, with their vessels progressively decommissioned and reduced in number until mid 1916, leaving but a few to serve in the later phases of the war.

Inglefield had, in any case, been assigned by the Admiralty in June to the formal investigation in the loss of the *Lusitania*, under Lord Mersey. The government was keen to blame *Lusitania*'s master, Captain William Turner for the loss, and 'Admiral Inglefield clearly believed it was his duty to ensure that the inquiry took government views on board and that its findings were not contrary to government expectations'.[20] In this mission Inglefield failed, for 'in the end Lord Mersey chose not to blame Captain Turner explicitly, despite obtaining confirmation through Admiral Inglefield that the government would be happy for him to do so'.[21] Inglefield faded from the scene and was placed on the retired list at his own request on 9 June 1916.

Undoubtedly, one of the challenges the Royal Navy faced in acquiring so many motor launches so quickly was providing crew. Two officers were required for each boat; fortunately, the MLs had something in common with a motor boat – petrol engines, motor propulsion, limited accommodation – and the officers of the quondam RNMBR were swiftly transferred to command the new launches.

For example, Ninian Stewart, now skipper of the motor boat *Colonsay*, was assigned to command the second launch to be commissioned, *ML-2* on 12 October 1915 and captained five MLs in the course of the war.[22] Arthur Tagore took over *ML-23* on 15 December 1915, and would have another three boats before the end of the conflict.[23] And Sir Arthur Lee Guinness took command of *ML-59*. Douglas Gordon Prynne had brought his own boat, *Platypus* (motor boat number 4) in 1914. Subsequently he commanded *ML-31*, and served at Port Said in her. Later he trained as an instructor for

ML-22, which served at Dover. *(Author's collection)*

ML-59, commanded by racing driver and motor boat racer Sir A Arthur St L Lee Guinness. (Author's collection)

hydrophone operations, in which post 'he carried out his duties with ability and proved a competent instructor'.²⁴

However, some didn't make the cut. John Kinghorn joined the RNMBR in November 1914 and moved to the staff of the Senior Naval Officer, Belfast in March 1915. But he resigned in January 1916 and refused a request to rejoin.²⁵ And John Henry Atkinson Bell commanded his motor boat *Jean*. He was advanced to lieutenant in June 1915, but on 31 May the following year was admitted to Haslar Naval Hospital. Discharged as physically unfit, he was reassigned to the Transport Department at Cowes.²⁶

A rich source of ML officers was the yachting community. Author and yachtsman Edward Keble Chatterton transferred from his motor boat *Burrastow* to *ML-181* and was placed in command of the motor launch flotilla stationed at Queenstown (Cobh). Portly and short, his less than svelte appearance provoked a rash of gently mocking cartoons from his underlings. Edwin S Turner was a small boat sailor, who owned two sailing craft named *Bab* and *Rani IV* and wrote many articles for *Yachting Monthly* magazine. He had joined the RNVR at the start of the war and served in MLs in the North Sea and then in the West Indies (where in 1917 he got married in Trinidad, aged thirty-eight. He died two years later). And mining engineer and yachtsman Eugene Lang joined the RNMBR in 1914 and then was sent on a course of instruction at HMS *Fisgard*, the engineer and artificer training school. Surviving this, Lang took command of *ML-7* on 1 March 1916.

Yachting artists featured prominently. Geoffrey Allfree commanded

ML-307 pictured in 1917. She remained in the navy until at least May 1924 and was disposed of by 1927. *(Author's collection)*

ML-247. Kent-born, after leaving school he served for several years in the merchant marine and in 1910 was awarded his master's mate certificate. A talented painter, he left the sea for art and was made an official war artist in January 1918. Arthur Briscoe was another ML captain and artist. Pre-war he owned a 3-ton cutter, *Doris*, and held his first one-man show in 1906 at the Modern Gallery in Bond Street, entitled *Round the North Sea and Zuyder Zee*, which included thirty-five watercolours. He also wrote and illustrated *A Handbook on Sailing* and executed pictures for the *Illustrated London News*.

Donald Maxwell was a keen yachtsman who went as far as to live in one. He trained in London at the Clapham School of Art, the Slade School of Fine Art, and the Royal College of Art. He wrote and painted extensively for *Yachting Monthly* and other magazines, and in 1909 he became a regular correspondent for the *Daily Graphic* and the illustrated weekly *The Graphic*. Donald was in the motor boats, in Prynne's *Platypus*, and then MLs *59* and *154* prior to taking command of *ML-139*, after which he was appointed a war artist in Mesopotamia. His brother Gordon, another talented yachtie, author and artist, had joined the RNMBR and commanded the motor boat *Minou*. In 1916 he took responsibility for *ML-314*. Or consider Frank Henry

Algernon Mason. He was a young cadet at HMS *Conway* at Birkenhead before he trained as a marine engineer with Parsons & Co. But it was art that was his first love and he transitioned to being a professional artist in 1898, exhibiting at the Royal Academy from 1902. Thirty-nine years old when war broke out, he was commissioned into the RNVR in December 1914 and assigned to the RNMBR. A year later he commanded *ML-33*, *ML-154* and *ML-194* in the North Sea and in Egypt; additionally, he was appointed an official war artist to the Admiralty.*

One of the more interesting recruits to the MLs was Limerick-born Edward Conor Marshall O'Brien. He was a boatbuilder and naval architect whose designs included *Saoirse* (in which he single-handedly circumnavigated the globe between 1923 and 1925). A committed Irish republican, another of his boats, *Kelpie*, was used for gun-running in 1914. On 26 July nine hundred guns were brought by *Kelpie* and more by the yacht *Agard* (owned and skippered by Erskine Childers of *Riddle of the Sands* fame) to Howth harbour for the use of the Irish Volunteers (of which O'Brien was a member).

When war came, amazingly, Conor O'Brien eventually joined the RNVR. It was not necessarily a happy time for either him or the service. As a sub lieutenant in April 1916, his service record indicates that his conduct was reported twice – but for what we will never know as a large ink blot obscures the missing words.[27] In September he was on the books of the depot ship *Hermione* (see below) for a course of instruction, after which he took command of *ML-425* in November, *ML-102* in December and then *ML-551* before eventually becoming captain of the armed yacht *Sayonara* in March 1917.

Another remarkable sailor who joined the MLs was Edward Isaac Sycamore, widely regarded as the leading British yacht skipper of his generation. His yachting victories included six Royal Cups and two Albert Cups. At the outbreak of war, Sycamore was skipper of the yacht *Isabella Alexandra* (owned by Edmund Luttrop) which, together with the Kaiser's yacht *Meteor*, were being towed to Cowes for the annual August Cowes Week by a German navy torpedo boat. When war was declared they were taken back to Cuxhaven, where the crew of *Isabella Alexandra* was interned. They were released after about a week and returned to the UK via Denmark. In May 1917, aged nearly sixty-two, Sycamore joined the RNVR and took command of *ML-350* at Newlyn seaplane base. Later he commanded *ML-5* at Calshot and then Dundee.

---

* The Imperial War Museum has fifty-six of his paintings.

ML-524 depicted in 1918. She appears to have a non-standard canvas roof to the wheelhouse. (Author's collection)

Canada and New Zealand were fertile ground for ML officers and, indeed, the Admiralty sent a mission to Canada in May 1916 specifically to enlist men for the Petrol Navy. Its publicity handbill proclaimed that:

> Representatives of the British Admiralty have arrived in Canada for the purpose of entering officers and men for service in the motor craft employed in the Auxiliary Patrol … the British Admiralty calls for two classes of recruiting; 1) commissioned officers for deck duties in patrol motor boats and 2) mechanics to run the engines. [For officers] a good knowledge of practical seamanship … [and] elementary navigation is desirable.[28]

Lieutenant John D Hunter was typical of the Canadians who joined the RNVR. Toronto-born, he was a salesman on the staff of the Harris Abattoir Company, but came to England in 1916 and joined the volunteers. His only qualification for naval life was that he was a good athlete and an avid canoeist, a member of a canoe club in his home city. On 8 June 1917 Hunter became commander of *ML-211*, aged just twenty-three years old, and was employed in patrol duties in the English Channel. Another was Collamer Chipman Calvin, scion of an affluent and well-known family from Garden Island near Kingston, Ontario. After training, he joined *ML-558*.

And the Torpedo Bay Navy Museum in Auckland, New Zealand, notes that 'the motor launches acquired by the Royal Navy in 1916 had a large proportion of New Zealanders as officers and motor mechanics'. It is estimated that some two hundred Kiwis served in the motor boats.[29]

What about the remaining eight or so crew for the MLs? The personnel needed included motor mechanics, deckhands, signalmen, cooks, etc. They came from the RNVR (chief motor mechanics, for instance), while others were RNR or MMR. Given the relative novelty of petrol engines within the RN, the mechanical positions were the most challenging roles to fill and the navy felt it necessary to advertise for such men. In early 1916 *The Motor Ship and Motor Boat Magazine* carried this advertisement:

> In addition to the demand for skilled mechanics and good motor-boat drivers with knowledge of engines (particularly hot-bulb engines), there is at the moment a special need for a number of men who have been accustomed to marine motors, preferably of large size and of the paraffin type, for service in a special branch of the Forces. These men must have had mechanical experience, and good pay will be given.[30]

By the end of the war, 2,500 mechanics were employed in the motor launch section.[31]

The physical make-up of a typical ML crew can be seen from that of *ML-403*, blown up on 22 August 1918 while salvaging a German torpedo on the Yorkshire coast. It comprised a lieutenant and sub lieutenant, both RNVR, a coxswain, leading deckhand RNR, able seaman RN, three deckhands RNR, chief motor mechanic RNVR and a motor mechanic.

The officers were often leisure boaters or yachtsmen and the like, with temporary commissions in the RNVR; and the crews, like the officers, were amateurs too, from every walk of life. They called themselves the 'Emmelites'. The wide variety of backgrounds that made up these sailors was attested to by Signalman Edwin F King RNVR: 'Take our boat; skipper – dentist; second in command – bank clerk; two petty officers – motor mechanics; coxswain – a butcher; myself – a cinema projectionist; cook – a clerk; first seaman – an overlooker in a Lancashire mill; second seaman – an inshore fisherman'.[32]

HMS *Helicon* (1865), which as *Resource II* was intended to be the depot ship for the motor launch men. She is shown here in a painting by George Pechell Mends, who himself came from a naval family. (© *National Maritime Museum, Greenwich, London, NMM PAF6174*)

The ML officers had first to be trained. Assigned onto the books of HM Ships *President* and *Victory* for administrative purposes only, they went through eight weeks of courses, with an exam at the end of each one. Navigation and signalling were taught at an old institute in Southampton; courses at HMS *Vernon* covered mine, torpedo and depth charges. HMS *Fisgard* gave instruction on engineering topics; and HMS *Excellent* for gunnery. On passing out they were appointed to their boats.

HMS *Hermione*, which became the second and little appreciated depot ship for the ML men at Portsmouth, photographed around 1904.
(US Navy History and Heritage Command, NH 60448)

Hermione at a later date. She was equipped with two 6in and eight 4.7in guns, plus a variety of smaller weapons and had a design speed of 19 knots. *(Author's collection)*

For accommodation, the navy provided the old yacht HMS *Resource II* (1865). She was hired for the purpose in October 1915. Originally the 'Fast Paddle Despatch' steam paddler *Helicon*, she was renamed *Enchantress* when used as the Admiralty yacht. Sold off in 1905 to the Royal Motor Yacht Club (RMYC), she became their floating clubhouse until the navy hired her back. Such luxury as she offered did not last long, for she burnt out six weeks later.

The now homeless ML men awaited her replacement with expectations which were disappointed when HMS *Hermione* finally appeared. She was an *Astraea*-class protected cruiser launched at Devonport in 1893.* To the men who would live on her she had another name. According to Sub Lieutenant Gordon Maxwell:

> she was a good old ship, but had been out of commission for some time, I believe, or used as a prison ship, or something of that sort, and the men dubbed her the 'vermy one', and not without living reason, till she was fumigated and burnished up, for when she arrived, she was certainly not quite as immaculate as she might have been.

Nonetheless there was considerable demand for her doubtful luxuries:

---

* In 1896 *Hermione* had formed part of a Special Service Squadron, created as a result of the infamous 'Kruger Telegram' which Kaiser Wilhelm II had sent to President Kruger on the occasion of the Jameson Raid. She then joined the China station and played a part in the Boxer Rebellion of 1900. Periods in reserve, the Home Fleet and as a potential airship tender followed and at the outbreak of war, she became guard ship at Southampton.

the disposal of the officers' cabins during the first few days of muddle, before things got straightened out a bit, was of the nature of a game of general post. Only those on boat duty were supposed to sleep on board, which meant about ten spare cabins to about twenty men. If you found a vacant one you commandeered it at once and asked no questions.³³

Sailing the motor launches

Despite their versatility, life at sea in a motor launch was unpleasant in all but the calmest weather. According to M-P-S, who returned to England in 1916 to serve on the MLs as an RNVR officer, 'the name we like best ourselves [for the boats] is the "Movies". There is something about the name Movie which seems to fit; for an ML is nothing if not movement'.³⁴ The MLs were lively in any sort of sea. Gordon Maxwell described a typical day:

there is a certain liveliness in the North Sea on this morning, quite a high sea is running, and soon the boat is feeling this, no boat sooner than an ML, and before long she is 'shipping it green.' Patrol may be a bit monotonous at times, but it can never be called dry work, anyhow in the winter. There are days when, however much you may wrap yourself up in oilskins, you will still get soaked, and your sea boots act as involuntary foot baths of ice-cold water. But this is a thing you have to grin (or curse) and bear on an ML on a rough day. Nor is the general wetness confined to the deck, as clothes, and boots

ML-399 at sea. (Author's collection)

testify if not worn for a few days, and a calm day is as bad as a rough one for this form of dampness.

Towards midday the wind abates a little, but not so the cold, and oilskins give place to duffel coats – thick wool, yellowy-brown coats with hoods, and which, if worn with these up and baggy trousers of the same material, give the appearance of a ship manned by giant teddy bears.[35]

Eating was next to impossible:

meals on an ML are 'movable feasts,' where the right hand never knows what the left hand may be doing, for while the latter is conveying food to the mouth the former is probably chasing the plate across the table or picking up a chop from the seat. No meal on patrol is ever dull.[36]

The lack of comfort extended in other ways too. Officers' quarters were right aft, a sleeping cabin and a wardroom – a small room about the 'size of a fair-sized dining table',[37] also described as 'where two can turn round and three becomes a crush'.[38] Moving towards the bow, next came the galley and amidships, the engine room, with the chart house just forward of it. The magazine was next ahead and adjoined the forecastle, 'where the crew sleep and have their being – rather a crowded being'.[39] On deck, the engine room ventilators discharged right around the commander and helmsman. And 'originally they had the noisiest of exhausts, enough to frighten a submarine miles off'.[40]

Initially, the MLs were fuelled by petrol, a significant fire hazard, and problems with the engines overheating and catching alight resulted in a decision in mid 1916 to use a mixture of one part petrol to two parts kerosene. The fire hazard worried some, if not all, skippers. According to Signalman King, in MLs at Scapa Flow, his first skipper was an Australian who announced to the bridge party, after due thought, that:

this is a small ship made of wood. We carry 5,000 gallons of petrol, plenty of paraffin, a magazine crammed with explosives. Depth charges full of TNT. A cigarette end or an absent-minded cook could easily start a fire and what would be left of us? And who would know. So I have decided that we must train ourselves to perfection in the most necessary thing to do – I mean abandoning ship.[41]

A sailor hands down into a ML two G-type depth charges. These were small, portable, hand-dropped bombs containing 35lbs of TNT or Amatol. They were intended for use by smaller vessels which could not carry D or D*-types, or as a backup to those where only a limited number of the larger weapons could be carried. *(Author's collection)*

One day they practised a full abandonment, but their dinghy was sucked out to sea and their motor launch seemed in danger of becoming a new *Marie Celeste*. The engineer, a man of faith, muttered, 'Man proposes, God disposes.' 'You go to hell,' roared the Aussie skipper. 'We're on the way,' murmured the coxswain.[42] Fortunately, the current took them to a whirlpool which turned them around and they rowed furiously back to their boat.

Pre-war, Commander Francis Fitzpatrick Tower RNVR was a gentleman of leisure and keen yachtsman who lived in London and on the Isle of Wight, where he sailed regularly. Aged fifty-five when war broke out, Tower immediately joined the RNVR, commanded an armed yacht, served on a Q-ship and by 1917 was in charge of flotilla of fourteen MLs based at Kingston*, northeast Ireland. There he found the motor launches hard-worked but occasionally temperamental. '[They] were always an anxiety,' he wrote, 'but everyone connected with them was keen and did their duty resulting in a good deal of useful work; only the constant repairs were trying, though unavoidable'.[43]

And even the navy's own Training Department, writing in 1933, thought that 'motor launches, of which there were 550, were not suitable for patrol work in winter'.[44]

So, the Elco motor launches were not perfect. But as a replacement for the motor pleasure boats, and as a platform for a multiplicity of tasks, they were heaven sent. As Vice Admiral Bacon of the Dover Patrol (which boasted thirty-one MLs at the end of 1917) wrote, '[they] were useful for most purposes for which they were not originally intended. What a gallant little flotilla they were'.[45] Motor launches were a worthy addition to the Royal Navy's wartime list, although strangely neglected in subsequent histories.

---

* Now Dún Laoghaire.

5

Motor Launches versus U-boats and Mines

The Elco motor launch was primarily conceived as an anti-submarine platform. But its small draught meant that it was soon also pressed into work as both a minelayer and a minesweeper in shallow waters where larger vessels could not proceed. In their 'exhaust exploding wooden craft',[1] the amateur sailors patrolled home waters winter and summer, searching for U-boats and mines.

Anti-submarine work

Pre-war, many in the navy had considered the submarine an underhand weapon, 'Fisher's toys' as Admiral Sir Charles Beresford disparagingly called them, only suitable for weaker naval powers or coastal defence. However, successive naval manoeuvres confirmed the potency that submarines could possess. In the 1904 summer trials, the umpires 'considered that the subs fully achieved their various functions'. In 1908 the navy deployed twenty-five undersea boats for defensive work off the Firth of Forth; and in 1909 they were 'used very successfully for coast defence'. In the 1913 anti-invasion manoeuvres, the submarine commanders 'considered … that an enemy's transports could be so damaged so as to render a military landing on any part of our coasts ineffectual'.[2] According to Commander Reginald A R Plunkett, 'the big ship officer now realises what a serious menace threatens him'.[3]

Nonetheless, no one was really prepared for the losses of merchant ships which Germany's U-boats brought about from early 1915. That year, a total of 1,307,900 gross register tons (grt) of Allied and neutral shipping was sunk, most of it by U-boats. And in 1916, this rose to 2,327,300grt.* Hence the pressing need to bring anti-submarine vessels into service and the rush to get the motor launches built and shipped.

But when the MLs first came into service, Britain lacked a credible anti-submarine (A/S) weapon, barring catching one on the surface and shelling it. For specific A/S purposes, the MLs were originally equipped with lance bombs, to be hurled at an enemy U-boat. This was a hand-thrown weapon, comprising a 7lb charge of Amatol attached to a wooden handle some

---

* And would reach a massive 6,235,900grt in 1917.

The crew of *ML-574*, one of the last built, with their 'catch' for dinner, the fish probably killed by a depth-charge explosion. *(Author's collection)*

4ft 6in long. The lance bomb was a contact weapon, designed to explode when it hit a hard surface, such as a U-boat's hull, and was to be swung around the head of a strong seaman and then flung at the enemy; an effective range of 75ft was claimed. The device was introduced in April 1915 and supplied to the small craft of the auxiliary patrol.

Anyone making such a throw, which would from necessity have to be close in, would be lucky to survive the subsequent explosion unscathed, always assuming that an ML could actually sneak up to a surfaced submarine. And if the enemy was submerged, then the weapon was useless. Lance bombs were not withdrawn from use until early 1917; in that time twenty thousand units had been produced, but no U-boat had ever been sunk by the method. Perhaps as a result, some MLs were fitted with a steel 'shoe' on the lower bow to facilitate ramming U-boats; *ML-229*, which will be met again in Chapter 14, was one so equipped.

To attack an underwater U-boat, a submersible explosive device was necessary – the depth charge. Primitive depth charges had existed for some time before the war, made from aircraft bombs attached to lanyards which would trigger their charges. A similar idea was a 16lb guncotton charge in a lanyard-rigged can, known as the 'depth charge Type A'. It was fired by a float and wire system, but problems with the lanyards tangling and failing to function led to the development of a chemical pellet trigger, known as the Type B. These could be set to explode at a depth of 40ft but they were far from adequate.

In December 1914 Admiral John Jellicoe, CinC Grand Fleet, had asked HMS *Vernon* to develop a more powerful device. The resultant weapon was based on a standard Mark II mine, which was fitted with a hydrostatic pistol (ie, actuated by water pressure) preset to fire at 45ft and launched from a stern platform. Weighing 1,150lbs this so called 'cruiser mine' was, in fact, a potential hazard to both the dropping ship and the putative enemy. But further improvement was swift. By January 1916, the first really effective depth charge, the Type D, became available. These were barrel-like casings containing a high explosive, TNT or Amatol. There were initially two sizes, Type D, with a 300lb charge for fast ships, and Type D-star with a 120lb charge for those ships too slow to clear the danger area of the more powerful charge. A hydrostatic pistol set to a preselected depth detonated the charge and they were supplied with two depth settings of 40 or 80ft.

From mid 1916 some MLs were fitted with a depth-charge rack at the stern. But supply and space constraints meant that generally only two D-star type were carried with four smaller G-type (just 35lbs of TNT) in addition from later in the year. By 1917, a new water-pressure-activated pistol could fire the depth charges at 100–200ft, allowing use of Type D on most ships. But manufacturing was still constrained and, in any case, the room available restricted the number that a motor launch could carry.

Another issue preventing the killing of U-boats was locating them if they were underwater. Some of Britain's greatest scientists were recruited to bring their powers to bear on this challenge and much development work was done at the Royal Navy's station at HMS *Tarlair*, at Aberdour in Scotland, and later at Harwich too, where the Admiralty Experimental Research Establishment, a mixture of naval and civilian staff, worked on the problem. After a number of false starts, they were able to create the Portable General Service (PSG) model of hydrophone listening equipment. This was a non-directional tool also known as a 'drifter' for its mode of operation. The operator dangled it over the side of a stationary ship and sat on deck listening. The device was lowered to a depth of 20–30ft and the operator tried to 'centre' any sound he heard in his two headphones by turning a small

An officer aboard a British motor launch using a hydrophone. The precarious nature of the job is clearly visible. *(© Imperial War Museum, IWM, Q20837)*

control wheel. When centred, the plot gave him a bearing which, unfortunately, could be 180 degrees out, as the device could not detect which direction along the bearing the submarine lay.

This was followed by the Portable Directional Hydrophones (PDH), which entered service in 1917. PDHs were directional and comprised two diaphragms carried in a larger, ring-shaped body; they responded to sound approaching each plate broadside on. PDH sets could be used at low speed and eradicated the possibility of a 180-degree error. But they were subject to interference from water noise.

From mid 1916 MLs began to be equipped with the PSG sets. These required the engines and the boat to stop, so that the flow noise of water and resonance produced by the reverberation of the propeller/engine did not block out the sound of a U-boat. Some enterprising commanding officers of the MLs 'fitted their craft with square sails so they could move in silence'[4] and change their position without alerting their prey. Lieutenant Gordon Maxwell described the process. 'Sometimes the engines are stopped,

An early British hydrophone PSG set. *(US Navy History and Heritage Command, 109948)*

and we drift for an hour with the hydrophone out. This is an undersea telephone, and a man waits in the chart-house with the receivers to his ears for a submarine to "ring up".[5]

In 1917 the MLs were generally organised in A/S hunting flotillas of six boats each. Some eighty-two such groups were formed over the later course of the war. As but one example, MLs *181*, *187*, *320*, *325*, *410*, *487*, *132* and *167* at Queenstown were equipped as a U-boat hunting flotilla in April 1918 and sent over to be based at Holyhead, patrolling in the Irish Sea. Two of them (*325* and *187*) were fitted out with W/T sets, which added weight and an extra crewman, but allowed the leader, Lieutenant Commander Charles Vernon Lowcay Norcock, a 'dug-out' officer who had retired from the navy on medical grounds in 1910, to control operations from *ML-325*.

Admiral Jellicoe noted that:

> these vessels were equipped with the directional hydrophone as soon as its utility was established and were supplied with depth charges. In the summer of 1917 four such hunting flotillas were busy in the Channel … they certainly contributed to making the Channel an uneasy place for submarine operations.[6]

A favourite tactic was to lay-to off the many anti-submarine nets along the coast to attack any submarine that became entangled in the snare.

But the hydrophone was an imperfect tool. For instance, on 20 July 1917 four motor launches based at Newhaven had tracked a submarine by their hydrophones for about six miles. They had never actually located her and had to abandon the chase because the sea got up slightly and the hydrophones ceased to pick up the U-boat signal from the wave noise. And another example of some of the disadvantages faced by the hydrophone ML flotillas could be seen on 29 July near the Arklow Bank light vessel. At 1400 the MLs detected a submarine, which they tracked for over two hours on minimal indications in the receivers. But the noise of passing commercial traffic drowned out the signal and contact was lost.

The process of hydrophone tracking and the stop–start requirement in order to dip the microphone is well illustrated by the log entries for *ML-325* on 16 July 1918. Operating from Holyhead, *325* started hydrophone watch at 0730. At 1250 she thought she had a contact; *ML-407* and the armed trawler *Greta* came up to help. At 1835 they dipped again and dropped depth charges on a patch of oil. At 1945 they stopped again and at 2030, *325* released her two depth bombs. At 2230 she stopped to listen, went ahead at 2100 and at 2350 went back on stationary hydrophone watch.[7] It was a long, tiring day and no U-boat was sunk, or even seen.

The MLs would be on duty in the Channel or lower North Sea both day and night. The different patrol areas provided different experiences. Three of them – the West Roads, Hills Bank and Zuydcoote Pass – were centred on Dunkirk, and MLs were based at the harbour there, as an outstation of the Dover Patrol. The West Roads patrol was essentially a straight line about a mile off the harbour entrance; Hills Bank was similar, but further to sea and more uncomfortable because it was outside the shelter of the sandbanks. And Zuydcoote was considered quite dangerous and comprised two MLs every night, keeping watch for enemy vessels leaving Ostend or Zeebrugge. Night patrol was particularly hazardous:

> Vigilance is always necessary, but this must be doubled during the hours of darkness. A look-out man must be stationed forward to warn the bridge of any object ahead, which may be a mine, a wreck, or a buoy, and recognition lights must be kept in readiness to be turned on in case of a challenge by another patrol boat. So, with engines running dead slow and every nerve alert, on through the blackness the ML prowls, with all lights extinguished save a couple or so in the engine-room, invisible from without, and the searchlight ready for instant use.[8]

MLs served in the Western Approaches too, as part of the Coast of Ireland Command under the irascible Admiral Sir Lewis Bayly at Queenstown. The first MLs to join Bayly's forces departed Falmouth on 4 September 1916, arriving two days later having ridden out a storm. They were attached to the Queenstown depot ship HMS *Colleen**. MLs were soon serving at all of the principal Irish patrol zones, especially XVI (Kingstown), XVII (Lough Larne), XX (Galway Bay, Berehaven), and XXI (Queenstown).[9] By January 1917, fifty-four MLs were stationed in Irish waters, rising by two a year later.

At the main base of Queenstown, there were twenty-four on 1 January 1917 and sixteen the following year,[10] of which six were equipped as a hydrophone flotilla. The motor launches would patrol along the Irish littoral, looking for U-boats or Sinn Fein gun-running activity. The MLs would be out for two days, returning to base to replenish stores and fuel. The weather was often unpleasant, with strong westerly winds and heavy seas, but they came to know where they could take shelter, such as the small town of Kilrush, a seaport on the estuary of the River Shannon. *ML-374* was a frequent visitor there; the local bank manager even invited the crew of the ML for Christmas dinner.

Neither he nor his wife was at home when the crew arrived for their repast, but a splendid dinner was laid out, including whiskey and stout. Having enjoyed themselves immensely, they left a note of thanks, a large bag

---

* HMS *Colleen* was a *Satellite*-class barque-rigged composite screw sloop of 1,420 tons and originally named *Royalist*. Built in 1883, she was hulked as a depot ship in 1900 and renamed *Colleen* in 1913.

of brown sugar (a luxury at the time) and a tin of tobacco. It transpired that the bank manager was a member of the local Sinn Fein and thought it best not to be at home when the navy called. But he held no antipathy towards the men, just the British government.

MLs in action

Despite this constant patrolling, MLs and U-boats seldom physically encountered each other, although the mere presence of a pod of MLs may, of course, have kept the U-boat down or caused it to avoid the area. But when a submarine was found, the men of the motor launches did not flinch from conflict.

Perhaps the most unusual of these encounters came on 17 September 1916. MLs *206*, *234*, *240* and *248* were secured to the deck of the converted collier SS *Belleview*, being transported with their crews from Portsmouth to Port Said. After leaving Malta, bereft of escort even though one had been expected, at 1000 a U-boat was sighted on the starboard beam. *Belleview* was equipped with a gun, but nonetheless the ML commanders called their gun crews to their action stations. The U-boat submerged, but at 1210 was seen on the surface, coming up rapidly on the starboard quarter. *Belleview* opened fire and the U-boat replied, whereupon something went wrong with *Belleview*'s weapon and the MLs commenced firing while fully fixed to the decks of their carrier.

This exchange of fire between MLs and U-boat continued for two hours and, while the engagement was taking place, captains and crews hastily prepared the MLs for sea in the event of having to abandon ship. The U-boat fired shrapnel and HE and one shell hit *ML-234*, smashing through the cabin and the deck into the hold; fortunately, the fuse broke off as it passed through the flimsy wooden launch and it did not explode. Eventually, the submarine tired of the game and submerged, not to be seen again, and *Belleview* continued the rest of her voyage unmolested. There cannot have been many naval duels in history between ships on a ship and an enemy assailant. The captain of the collier, James Ernest Churchill RNR, a retired RN lieutenant, was awarded the DSC for his (limited) role in the action,[11] but the MLs received no recognition at all!

ML-211, commanded by Lieutenant John Hunter RNVR, a Canadian met in Chapter 4, became involved with a U-boat on 23 July 1917. For the previous two days, there had been indications that a submarine was lurking in Lyme Bay, and Admiral Sir Alexander Bethell, Commander-in Chief, Devonport, ordered a strong force to try to find and sink it. The destroyer *Sunfish* (1895), from the local defence flotilla, the Devonport armed drifters and the hydrophone motor launches from Dartmouth were positioned to the east of Berry Head. An armed trawler patrol was spread along a line which ran from the centre of Lyme Bay to the south of Start Point. Lines of mined nets were laid out near Dartmouth and the Eddystone light. And to complete the dispositions, a seaplane was ordered to patrol the western end of Lyme Bay.

Throughout the night, the hydrophone-equipped MLs drifted with their engines stopped, using the northeasterly flood tide to carry them towards the centre of Lyme Bay, where the submarine was thought to be lying on the bottom. It was a fine, still night, and in the early morning the hydrophone set in *ML-211* heard the sound of a U-boat starting its engine. The ML went to full speed and minutes later a U-boat loomed out of the gloaming. Hunter opened fire and the submarine dived to escape, but now it was precisely located – surely it would be sunk. Over-eagerness let it slip away. On hearing the sound of gunfire, the motor launches started up and sped to support their sister; and the noise of their engines swamped all other sounds in the hydrophones. Contact was lost.

Lieutenant John Francis Buller Kitson RNVR, another Canadian from British Columbia, joined the RNVR in July 1916 – having made his own way to England – and was assigned to *Hermione* for the motor launches. Described as 'good mannered and very zealous',[12] he had taken command of *ML-357* in December 1916. On 12 December 1917 Kitson's boat was part of the escort of a coastal convoy off the Cornish coast. It was very much a British Empire affair, for in addition to a Canadian commanding officer, *ML-357*'s second in command was a New Zealander, J W Laurie Stubbs from Auckland.

It was a misty winter's day and suddenly Kitson spotted a U-boat on the surface, just 70yds away. He called for full speed and collision stations, and rammed his craft into the enemy submarine. The U-boat dived, wounded but not crippled – which could not be said of Kitson's boat, for the impact had stoved the bows in. In sinking condition, the ML crew could not have been happy to see the U-boat surface again. Stubbs manned the 3pdr himself and got six shots off at the enemy before it once more submerged.

Kitson and his crew endured a very tricky time until they managed to beach the craft near Penzance. And the Admiralty certainly appreciated the attack, which drove the U-boat away from the convoy to seek easier pickings. Their Lordships commented that 'great credit is due to him for his behaviour and action on this occasion',[13] and Kitson received the DSC for his efforts.[14] Stubbs, Chief Motor Mechanic John Marland, Chief Motor Mechanic George E Crabb, Leading Deckhand J H Willacy, Deckhand J H Hooley, Deckhand CH Proctor, and Deckhand Norman Wright were all mentioned in despatches and the Admiralty awarded a bounty of £1,000 to be shared amongst the crew.

Twenty-seven-year-old Lieutenant Ferrand Paget had been one of the motor boat men. He had returned to England from Bangkok, where he worked as a trader, joining in October 1915 and serving in number 52, *Eun Mara*. After a course at HMS *Fisgard* at the beginning of 1916, he served in several MLs before assuming command of *ML-168* in August 1917.

On the night of 18/19 April 1918 Paget was on patrol in the Otranto Strait when he spotted a U-boat on the surface, no more than 100yds away from his ship. He immediately opened fire, scoring a hit on the conning tower and causing the submarine to dive. Steering over the spot where she disappeared, he dropped his depth charges and was rewarded with a brief glimpse of a black, conning tower-like object breaking the surface, which then vanished. Paget was mentioned in despatches 'in recognition of his prompt action in attacking an enemy submarine'.[15] Later scholarship showed that no U-boat was lost that night.

The only verified example of a motor launch being solely responsible for sinking a U-boat came in the spring of 1918 in the Mediterranean. In the early morning of 21 April *ML-413* was on hydrophone watch, stopped and silent, four and a half miles from Almina Point, Ceuta. Her commander was Scots-born Lieutenant Joseph Stephen Bell, who had joined the RNMBR in January 1915 and initially served in the motor boat *Armida* (number 68). He had taken command of one of the first MLs to arrive in Britain, *ML-4*, on 23 September 1915, 'for trials', so had clearly been highly regarded. At 0400 Bell heard the sound of a vessel's engine approaching quickly. He immediately called for full speed and turned on his forward lights to find a surfaced U-boat passing across his bows, no more than ten yards away. The submarine dived but Bell dropped his two depth charges over the spot and then went silent again to dip his hydrophone.

No underwater noise was detected, but as dawn broke, Joseph Bell was able to see debris and large quantities of oil across the surface of the water. He and his men had sunk *UB-71* with all thirty-two of its crew. The Admiralty recognised his achievement, noting 'Their Lordships appreciation [was] expressed of [sic] the prompt and able service in which the attack was carried out'.[16] And Bell was awarded the DSC for his efforts, 'for services in action with enemy submarines'.[17]

MLs played their part in the sinking of another U-boat later in the year. *ML-135* was one of a division of MLs all fitted with the PDH hydrophone and operating off Dartmouth under the direction of the destroyer *Opossum* (1895), part of the Devonport Local Defence Flotilla. On 8 August the German minelaying submarine *UC-49* was laying a field off Start Point when she fouled one of her own mines, which detonated. The explosion was observed from *Opossum* and the MLs began a search with their hydrophones, dipping and drifting, such that when *UC-49*, which had been lying on the seabed, restarted her motors at 1520, her approximate position could be plotted and the destroyer and launches dropped depth charges over the spot.

More depth charges were dropped just before 1800 and then *Opossum* noisily withdrew, hoping to convince the U-boat commander that her persecutors had left the scene. Nearly twenty minute later, the U-boat surfaced, but only 200yds from the lurking *ML-135*. Lieutenant George Livingstone Cassidy, another Canadian ML commander, fired three rounds from *135*'s 3pdr at close range and *Opossum* opened fire with her 12pdr and 6pdr guns.

Admiral Sir John Jellicoe, CinC Grand Fleet and First Sea Lord 1916–1917, who admired the work of the MLs. *(Author's collection)*

Immediately, the submarine descended under the water again, but this time with her bows at an angle of fifty degrees. Several more depth charges were dropped by *Opossum*, bringing up oil and bubbles. And the next day, having located the wreck by sweeps, more depth bombs were dropped, to break it up and confirm that the submarine had been sunk. Debris came to the surface, including a light bulb manufactured in Vienna, proof enough. *UC-49* was lost with all hands.

Lieutenant Cassidy received the DSC for 'services in motor launches';[18] and he had the signal distinction of receiving it from the hand of Admiral Sir John Jellicoe. As Jellicoe later wrote of the action, 'this engagement held peculiar interest for me, since during my visit to Canada in the winter of 1919 the honour fell to me of presenting to a Canadian – Lt G L Cassidy RNVR – at Vancouver the DSC awarded by his majesty for his work in ML number 135'.[19]

The final encounter between a motor launch and a U-boat took place two days before the Armistice, once more off Alina Point. On 9 November 1918 *ML-155* was on night patrol, when at around midnight she saw a U-boat on the surface and gave chase. A Very light was fired by an accompanying launch, *ML-373*, and *155* saw the submarine submerge and dropped her two depth charges. This brought the U-boat back to the surface and the flare attracted the Q-ship *Privet* to join the action, firing her 4in and 12pdrs and making hits on the conning tower, and then dropping more charges as the enemy submerged once more. According to Edward Keble Chatterton, the U-boat *U-34* was the victim and 'by half past twelve the submarine was destroyed'.[20] But whatever or whomever it was that was attacked that night, it probably wasn't *U-34*, which had sailed on 18 October and was never heard of again. She was in all likelihood lost before this date.

Only one U-boat kill can definitively be assigned to a ML. But their very presence on patrol, hunting for submarines and criss-crossing coastal waters, saved many lives by keeping U-boats submerged, using up their precious battery power, and forcing them to leave convoys and other tempting targets alone. Gordon Maxwell encapsulated this point when he wrote:

> a submarine will not attack a patrol boat if it can help it, and it is often more useful to keep one of the former under the water, locating its position with the hydrophone if it moves, than to drive it away or engage it; for fresh boats can be brought up by a scout, and, as a submarine can only stay a certain time under and must come up to charge its batteries, its chance is small in these circumstances. This is known as 'sitting on a submarine.' Naturally they get away sometimes, for the sea is a wide place, but they are at least rendered harmless while in the vicinity of a war channel.[21]

MLs and mines

The Royal Navy had not embraced the use of mines and mining before the war with very much enthusiasm. There was a strong body of opinion at the Admiralty that the widespread deployment of mines was poor strategy: 'Mines were regarded as sneaky weapons, resented because they seemed to favour weaker powers by denying Britain the fruits of her overwhelming maritime superiority'.[22] Such denigration was also because the Admiralty saw mines as a defensive weapon and the navy prided itself on being an offensive force, seeking the next Trafalgar, which would destroy the German High Seas Fleet in a climactic sea battle. Mining near enemy coasts would deter the foe from coming out into open seas for that much-wished-for conclusion.

As a result, although considerable technical innovation had taken place at HMS *Vernon*, the navy's torpedo and mine school, the Royal Navy had not especially focused on the development of the mine as a serious weapon of war. As naval historian Nick Lambert noted, 'since 1894 Admiralty policy had been to suppress the system and suspend further experimentation … in the hope that rival powers perhaps would not realise its full potential'[23] and adopt them too.

After the Russo-Japanese war, a Mining Committee had been established at the Admiralty, and in November 1908 it reported some far-reaching conclusions. The committee plumped for the fixed-wire sweep; converted torpedo gunboats were to be used as fleet minesweepers and specifications for replacement vessels specifically designed for minesweeping were drawn up. Nothing more was done to further this latter recommendation.

Thus Britain entered the First World War with a small fleet of minesweepers, which were actually old torpedo boats, dating from the nineteenth century, and which had been converted to fit the minesweeping needs as then perceived. They were only ten in number and were fitted out as minesweepers at the end of 1908 and during 1909. But surely, ten mine-clearance vessels would hardly be enough in time of war?

And so it proved. The trawlers of the RNR(T) and other auxiliary patrol vessels were converted for minesweeping and bore the brunt of the burden in the early years of the conflict. Both sides began to mine defensively and offensively, to deny the use of the sea to their enemy. The North Sea in particular became infested with mines, to the point where British and German fields extended some 150 miles out into the North Sea from the Heligoland Bight and a wall of mines, with swept breaks in it for access, extended all the way up Britain's east coast.

The advent of German 'UC'-class minelaying submarines from mid 1915 worsened the situation. Now small localised fields could be laid right up to the coast in deep or shallow waters, and in secret. Commander Taprell Dorling at Harwich noted that 'one felt compelled to give the enemy full marks for his submarine minelaying. The *UC* boats from Zeebrugge used to plant their detestable eggs in the very approaches to Harwich harbour with uncanny prescience'.[24] He thought that mines had become a particular bugbear by 1916: 'the whole area between Orford Ness and the North Foreland soon became an ocean graveyard. Our chart became spotted with the little red ink symbols denoting sunken ships'.[25] And submariner William Guy Carr felt that the mines 'were thicker than peas in pea soup'.[26]

The problem was that trawlers and other sorts of minesweepers could not operate in shallow waters, or when the tide had ebbed to produce shallows. Trawlers drew some 13ft; the new purpose-built minesweepers coming into service drew between 7 and 8ft. But the MLs drew just 3ft 8in.

And so a new role came about. The versatility of the ML showed in its use as both a minelayer and a minesweeper. The dangerous task of minesweeping was allocated to MLs where a field had been laid in waters too shallow for the general run of mine-removal vessel. Frequently they swept in flotillas of four in quarter-line formation, using a kite to hold the sweeping cable extended. MLs also worked in pairs, towing between them the navy's traditional A-sweep, in which a single steel wire was towed between two parallel vessels and used to sever the mooring cables of mines. At other times a paravane sweep was used, consisting of:

> a pair of paravanes towed off the quarters … thereby offering no protection to the boat from which they were towed. Extending out at an angle of approximately forty-five degrees, the towing cable of the paravane encountered the mooring wire of the mine, deflecting it out to the paravane where it was cut by the steel knives in the head of the latter. After being cut adrift the mine was exploded by gunfire.[27]

Lieutenant Guy Carr observed that 'motor launches (MLs) were used in such shallow waters when the weather was calm'. The MLs were 'admirably suited for exploring suspected minefields and the sinking of mines both above and below water'.[28] And Edward Keble Chatterton noted that by late 1916, 'MLs were now actually being used for this purpose, their light draught and the use of serrated wire* being most suitable'.[29] Not everyone was enamoured of the MLs as minesweepers, however. Vice Admiral Reginald Bacon of the Dover Patrol thought 'motor launches were fine-weather boats

---

* Serrated wire, which gave a better cutting 'edge', had been introduced in 1916.

The American Keystone View Company created this image of the newly invented paravane sweeping device. The body copy tells that 'The latest invention gotten out to aid the Allies in cleaning up European waters of German mines, is the Paravane. Shaped somewhat on the style of a torpedo, it is dragged through the waters by a minesweeper. The sharp knife seen on top is used for cutting the chains that hold the mine in place. The mine, then floating to the top of the water, is exploded by rifle fire'. *(US National Archives, 45511976)*

only; to rely on these to sweep for mines was like leaning on a rotten reed, since a very moderate sea put them *hors de combat*.[31]

At least mines were more visible than a submarine's periscope:

> A periscope is a very difficult thing to see. Even when you know it is there it is none too easy; but not so a floating mine. Its size renders this fairly simple to locate, except, of course, at night, when you may be on it before the look-out man can give the alarm. Sinking mines by rifle fire is interesting and exciting work; a specially heavy rifle or a Lewis-gun are used, and the mines make splendid targets. If a mine is more than usually obstinate the gun is employed as well. It is not only floating mines that have to be accounted for, but also those washed ashore, which have to be towed off the beach into deep water before they are sunk. These are not all German, some being our own which have broken away from the numerous minefields owing to bad weather.[31]

Dealing with mines was a difficult and dangerous task, but all in a day's work for a motor launch.

And not only were motor launches used for sweeping mines, they were pressed into service to lay them too, a job nobody had envisaged when they were designed. Their draught often allowed them to access waters other minelayers could not.

Minelaying MLs were fitted with tracks on either side carrying two mines nested in their sinkers. To lay their 'eggs', three or four divisions of four motor launches would go out to sea in line ahead. A buoy usually marked where the mines were to be laid and further bearings would be taken on arrival to confirm the position. An eight-point turn was then signalled, bringing them to line abreast at intervals of about 75ft. The senior officer then fired a rocket as the signal to commence laying and the starboard forward mine would be dropped. Thirty seconds later, the port forward one followed, then after the same interval the aft starboard and finally the remaining portside one. Behind the layers, the last ML carried danbuoys which were dropped to indicate the field's location and its dimensions.

Releasing a mine from a Royal Navy minelaying ML, photographed in 1918. *(US Naval History and Heritage Command, NH 61107)*

A highly stylised etching of an ML (*ML-105* or *106*) bringing fuel to a seaplane, drawn for the *Illustrated London News* of 12 January 1918 by Charles Pears. In reality, the seaplane would be unable to take off in the sea state depicted! *(Author's collection)*

Convoy

Convoying of merchant ships as an anti-U-boat system was introduced by the Admiralty during the first half of 1917 as a response to rocketing losses of cargo vessels in the face of the German unrestricted U-boat campaign, which commenced at the beginning of February. Sinkings immediately plummeted. But in London during October 1917, Fleet Paymaster Ernest Thring noticed that, whilst convoy as constituted had worked, substantial losses were being suffered after the convoy split up and ships sailed for their final and separate destinations or when heading to the convoy assembly point (a process that in the next war would come to be known as 'unbuttoning' and 'buttoning').

Consequently, smaller groups of ships came to be escorted through coastal waters, and this job too fell to the auxiliary patrol, the trawlers and the MLs. It was on such a duty that *ML-357* had encountered her U-boat (see above).

Maids of all work

Apart from martial use, the MLs filled many other roles. Lieutenant Maurice Patrick Shea RNVR, a Canadian from Montreal, commanded one of the MLs working with the Grand Fleet at Scapa and then Rosyth. He had been the first man in Canada to enlist in the RNVR and now his work entailed

ML-463 alongside, probably at Aberdeen in late 1916 or 1917, with seemingly disinterested civilians. *(Author's collection)*

patrolling and convoying, but also any sort of role which seemed beneath the dignity of larger RN ships. For instance, his boat was once tied up to a pier for several days to provide power to an air station. And on one occasion he was required to furnish electric current for a film show to entertain the otherwise bored matelots.

Another task for the MLs was that of air rescue launch. Motor launches were attached to most of the RNAS coastal air stations to cruise offshore when aircraft or seaplanes were taking off. The career of Edward Sycamore in this capacity at Newlyn, Calshot and Dundee air bases was noted in Chapter 4.

If a pilot fell into the drink, the MLs were there to pull him out. So impressed were the ladies living near the Newlyn air base that they presented a memorial to the motor launch men at the war's end to thank them for their efforts.

This rescue role was also filled when warships were flying off their aeroplanes. When the battlecruiser *Indomitable* launched her Sopwith Pup from the top of the midships 12in gun turret, a ML was always standing by.

ML-215 and some of her sisters tied up somewhere in Patrol Area V, with a small admiring crowd. (Author's collection)

On one occasion it failed to show up, but Lieutenant 'Dickie' Bird RNAS took off anyway. His aeroplane failed to fly and he went straight into the sea. *Indomitable* launched a rescue boat and the rather damp aviator was annoyed to find the crew more interested in salvaging his engine than himself.

And the adaptability of these little craft even led to pecuniary gain. Warships and auxiliaries received salvage money for saving ships, cargoes and ship's boats. On three occasions, the *London Gazette* records MLs as benefiting. On 21 November 1916 *ML-295* played a role in the salving of SS *Zwaluw*. The following year, SS *Bethlehem* gave *ML-23* (together with the gunboat *Halcyon* and *P-22*) some cause for celebration in April and May. And on 8 September 1917, the ketch *Annie* was salvaged by *ML-299*.

* * * * *

The vital part played by MLs in defending Britain's seaways and keeping the seas for her trade and supply is often overlooked. But, as this chapter has demonstrated, the motor launches and their volunteer crews were a valuable component in maintaining Britain's command of the seas.

ML-313 in dry dock in late 1916 or 1917. Note the twin propeller shafts.
(Author's collection)

6

In Distant Waters

The Elco motor launches served in many different theatres of war outside of British waters, and particularly in the Mediterranean. Here their versatility and utility found many uses, especially around the Italian coast and in the eastern Mediterranean.

In the Adriatic Sea

In 1915 the threat to Allied shipping in the Mediterranean from Austrian and German U-boats stationed at the Austro-Hungarian naval bases of Pola (now Pula) and Cattaro (now Kotor) led the Royal Navy to create a net barrier across the entrance to the Adriatic, between Brindisi in Italy and southeast to Corfu off the Albanian coast. It was known as the Otranto Barrage.

To maintain the sixty-mile barrier, lay and tow the nets, and intercept U-boat excursions, a force of over 120 hired drifters was deployed, towing steel indicator nets (see Chapter 3). Historian John Winton believed that

Steam yacht *Catania*, used as a depot ship for the MLs at Taranto. *(Author's collection)*

ML-516, patrolling the Otranto Barrier. Many of the MLs used in the Mediterranean were camouflaged with broad white stripes painted over a dark blue-grey in order that they were not mistaken for U-boats. Her depth charges are clearly visible.
(© Imperial War Museum, IWM Q63063)

'there was an Alice in Wonderland element about the concept of the submarine net barrage. Because salmon could be caught in nets stretched across river estuaries so … bigger fish such as U-boats could be caught in bigger nets … this belief persisted for years in the face of conspicuous failure'.[1] And demonstrable success in sinking U-boats in the Otranto nets was elusive too. So in mid 1916 it was decided that further anti-submarine resources were necessary and that the motor launches would provide them.

First to arrive was the armed yacht *Catania*, which reached Taranto at the end of July. Built in 1895, she was a steel screw steamer of 589 tons owned by twenty-eight-year-old George Sutherland-Leveson-Gower, 5th Duke of Sutherland* and a leading light in the Royal Yacht Squadron. She was taken into service by the Admiralty on 7 September 1914 with her owner in command and served with the yacht patrol at Cromarty. In 1915 the duke was sent to serve with the British Military Mission to the Belgian Army but

---

* Later, Under Secretary of State for Air from 1922 to 1924, Paymaster General from 1925 to 1928, and Under Secretary of State for War from 1928 to 1929.

the following year he returned to command his yacht and sail her to Italy. Now fitted as a workshop, she was to serve as parent ship for the Adriatic-based MLs.

Four MLs arrived on the deck of a collier in August and another four were offloaded and proceeded to Mudros under their own power. More came on 3 September, and by 1 January 1917, the ML flotilla boasted thirty-six boats, growing to forty-two the following year.

Some journeys to reach the Adriatic were more difficult than others. MLs *206*, *234*, *240* and *248* had to fight their way through from the deck of a collier, as narrated in Chapter 5. And three were lost in a similar battle on 14 September 1916, with another two perishing the same way on 8 June 1917 (see Chapter 9). In July 1917 a flotilla of eight MLs was assembled at Portsmouth awaiting transport to the Mediterranean. This was intended to be by merchant ship, as was usual for such voyages, but the exigences of war meant that no transport was available. It was decided that they would sail under their own power instead. They were under the command of the redoubtable Morton Smart, now a commander RNVR, and he determined that the flotilla would use the French river and canal system to gain entry to the Mediterranean. On 11 July MLs *432*, *438*, *440*, *505*, *516*, *530*, *535* and *539* departed Pompey for Le Havre and then Rouen. The canal and riverine systems of France, much used for transport in the war and also much neglected, caused delays and other problems, but eventually the MLs reached Marseilles on 31 July. They had incurred some damage from propellers grounding, striking lock sides and running into hidden tree branches, and this necessitated repairs before they could progress.

ML-505 and *535* left France on 8 August for Gibraltar and arrived three days later. This was a run of seven hundred miles with no friendly port on

A motor launch wearing the Otranto paint scheme of grey and white, painted by Donald Maxwell RNVR, an ML officer and official war artist. (*Author's collection*)

hand in case of difficulty, although they did have an escort in the form of the *Arabis*-class sloop *Marguerite*. The remaining six MLs departed Marseilles on the 19th and proceeded via Villefranche, Genoa, Spezzia, Leghorn, Naples and Messina, where *428* and *432* split away for Malta. The other four reached Taranto on 3 September. The little wooden craft and their amateur officers and men had sailed 2,246 miles over twenty-six days of actual motoring – a remarkable achievement.

The MLs patrolling the Otranto barrier were largely based at Gallipoli, a small port forty-five miles southeast of Taranto, with an outstation at Tricase, a very primitive port, but located directly on the Adriatic coast at the very heel of Italy. 'The little harbour at Tricase,' wrote Lieutenant Gordon Maxwell:

> will always live in the memory of motor launch adventures in the Adriatic, for it was used exclusively by MLs, no others of His Majesty's ships being able to adapt themselves to its Lilliputian proportions. Those boats at work on the Otranto anti-submarine barrage were wont to run in there for shelter and as many as six have been known to berth there at once. Airmen reported that on these occasions a more splendid imitation of a newly opened sardine tin could not be imagined when viewed from a height.[2]

Tactically, the MLs patrolled five miles north of the drifter-maintained net barrage, with the objective of forcing the U-boats to submerge before reaching the nets, thus increasing the chance of ensnaring them through

Sunrise, a motor launch off Gallipoli (Italy), by Donald Maxwell. Note the dark and light grey stripes of the camouflage scheme. *(Author's collection)*

reduced visibility and speed, and compelling them to use their batteries for propulsion.

As elsewhere, the use of motor launches could be limited by bad weather. And their grey paint and small size made them difficult to see, which presented the danger that they might be mistaken for U-boats. As a result, they eventually had white diagonal lines painted on their hulls to avoid incidents. Unfortunately, this also had the effect of making them more visible to the enemy, so it was somewhat of a cleft stick.

Enemy contact was uncommon, although *ML-168* was given a 'probable' success for attacking a U-boat on 18 April 1918 (see Chapter 5). But for all the effort and patrolling put into the maintenance of the net barrier, it proved fairly permeable. Only one submarine, the Austrian *U-6* (1909)*, was verifiably caught by the indicator nets in the barrage's first two years.

The motor launches were not confined to the heel of Italy. By the end of 1916, in addition to Taranto, Gallipoli and Tricase, they were also stationed at Genoa, Marseilles, Brindisi, Venice, Corfu, Oran, Crete, Salonika, Mudros, Alexandria and Malta. By September 1918, there were forty-one patrolling the Otranto barrier.

The eastern Mediterranean

The MLs played a crucial role in the eastern Mediterranean campaign. Those based at Port Said engaged in patrol work and escorted ships passing into or out of the harbour. Lieutenant Luker, last met in Chapter 3, had returned to the east after an eight-week-long conversion course to motor launches in Portsmouth. He thought that of their various tasks:

> the most pleasant was escorting. We assisted in escorting outward-bound convoys from fifty to a hundred miles, weather permitting, and meeting incoming convoys about forty miles out. Convoys usually consisted of about twenty ships and looked most impressive surrounded by destroyers, sloops, and other craft darting about in all directions.[3]

In 1916 the nearest Turkish base to Port Said was at El Arish, about seventy miles along the coast and occupied by the Turks since the end of 1914, where there was a large force of infantry, artillery and aircraft under German command. The Royal Flying Corps (RFC) made regular raids against this position from their base at Kantara (now El Qantara) and the MLs had an important part to play in their safety.

---
* On 13 May 1916.

On the eve of a raid, a signal would be sent to the ML base and one or two would slip at around 2200 and head towards El Arish, where they would lie off the coast in wait, sometimes in the company of armed trawlers. At dawn, the RFC attack would go in, and if a British aeroplane was hit, the pilot would try to land in the water near to the attendant MLs. Because of the likelihood of retaliation from the air, the MLs did not stop to launch a dinghy, but tried to pick the downed crew directly from the water, no easy task.

On occasion, the German aircraft arrived in time to bomb the rescue launches. In June 1916 *ML-38*, under the command of Lieutenant John Melville Shillington* RNVR, was chased out to sea for many miles, while fifteen bombs rained down on the vessel. And when these had been exhausted, the Germans attacked with machine guns, only to be repelled by rifle fire from the launch.

The returning MLs were sometimes greeted by trawlers carrying oil bags, for calming the waters, for the sea was shallow and nasty breaking waves could develop quickly. Lieutenant Luker thought that 'the flying men were not always good sailors and some said that the worst part of the whole thing was the trip back in the ML'.[4]

All this time the Egyptian Expeditionary Force (EEF)[†], under General Sir Archibald James Murray, had been reinforcing its position and supply lines following the Battle of Romani in August 1916, when a combined Ottoman and German empire army had been forced to retreat to Bir-el-Abd after a British victory. Through the following three months, this defeated force continued to retire further eastwards to El Arish, while the captured territory stretching from the Suez Canal was consolidated and garrisoned by the EEF. This included the continuing construction of the railway and water pipeline, and the denial of passage across the Sinai desert to the Ottoman forces by destroying water cisterns and wells.

By December 1916, construction of the infrastructure and supply lines had sufficiently progressed to enable the British advance to recommence during the evening of 20 December. By the following morning a mounted force had reached El Arish to find it abandoned. But replenishment of supplies across the burning desert of the Sinai Peninsula from Kantara was a real issue for the troops, and instead El Arish was to be used as a port of supply. The MLs were critical in enabling this to happen, for the harbour had to be rid of mines to allow the lighters to enter and discharge both stores

---

* Shillington's career demonstrates the potential pitfalls of overseas naval service. In May 1916 he had been admitted to an Australian-run hospital in Ismailia with influenza. Discharged on 8 June, he went straight into the action described above. When in command of *ML-151* in the West Indies he was invalided to hospital with enteric fever, and was discharged as medically unfit as a result in September 1918 (ADM 337/117/794, TNA).
† Formed in March 1916 when two Egyptian commands were merged into one.

and the labour corps. As Anthony Bruce has written, 'El Arish marked the end of the Sinai Desert and offered British forces direct access to the Mediterranean. No time was wasted in making use of this facility and the first supplies were landed there two days later'.[5] Despite the trying tides and shallow waters, the motor launches acted as minesweepers and cleared the way for the cargoes to land. The anchorage gave no shelter to them and some remained until Christmas 1916, but the supply route to Murray's troops via El Arish was kept clear.

The remainder of the MLs returned to Port Said, but in March and April 1917 the deep-sea trawlers which patrolled out in the Mediterranean off Port Said were removed to participate in the (unsuccessful) two battles for Gaza. Instead, the MLs were pressed into service, patrolling forty to sixty miles off the coast at the 100-fathom line. This was difficult work, for which the little boats were unsuited, and it 'was a most anxious and wearing time for COs and crews',[6] as it put the MLs right in the track of shipping. They patrolled in pairs but, concerned that at a distance MLs resembled a submarine, they tried to keep well away from potential accidents. Noel Luker wrote that:

> on dark nights and with no lights this was not always easy. On two occasions we were nearly rammed, once by a sloop and once by a liner. Other boats had similar experiences. The trawlers eventually returned and resumed their old job, for which we were thankful.[7]

The failure to take Gaza led, unsurprisingly, to a change of command. General Murray was relieved and replaced on 27 June 1917 by General Edmund Allenby, large and irascible, known as 'The Bull'. His mission, as directly given to him by Prime Minister Lloyd George, was to take 'Jerusalem by Christmas'.[8] He devised a plan for the taking of Gaza, which began with a preliminary bombardment by artillery and gunfire from French and Royal Navy warships from the sea. These included a cruiser and four monitors, the latter heavily gunned but of limited draught, suitable for shallow coastal waters. The infantry attack began on 1 November, and Gaza was captured on the 7th.

The MLs from Port Said took part in this third attack on the town, being used as protection against U-boats and to patrol round the larger ships that were bombarding the city. They were not directly targeted by enemy gunfire, but had some narrow escapes from shots aimed at the larger ships. Although Gaza was seized without naval loss, a destroyer and a monitor* were

---

* HMS *Staunch* (1910), an 'H'-class destroyer, and *M-15*, a 9.2in monitor, both sunk on 11 November by *UC-38*.

General Allenby, 'the deliverer of Jerusalem', and the man whose army the MLs supplied as he advanced up the Syrian coast. *(Library of Congress, LC-DIG-pga-13058)*

torpedoed shortly after the town had fallen, both victims of a submarine, despite the attendance of the motor launches.

The navy was immediately at work landing supplies at Gaza, with the MLs as escort. Lieutenant Luker recalled that:

> we were in company with *ML-9* and *ML-248*, escorting a store ship to Gaza. We arrived at dawn to see only the masts of the [sunken destroyer and monitor] vessels showing above the water. The weather was bad and the glass falling. *ML-248* hung on to the stern of an anchored trawler and we chose a spot to leeward of the sunken monitor from which quantities of oil were rising, affording us unbroken water if a heavy swell.[9]

But no sooner had they hunkered down than a signal ordered them back to Port Said, owing to a report of bad weather approaching. 'We had some difficulty in getting our anchor, the ML putting her bows under several times,' wrote Luker:

> All kinds of things were floating past us from the sunken monitor, signal pads, clothing, cabin furniture, and dead bodies. *ML-39* was

compelled to 'slip', and our passage back was a stormy one, the worst I have ever experienced in an ML. Some seas broke over the bridge, carrying away the forward ventilators and all sorts of deck gear. However, we got back safely, and without serious mishap.[10]

With the road to Jerusalem now open before him, Allenby began a carefully planned drive north. On 9 December the Turks evacuated, while the civic authorities hurried to find someone to surrender the keys of the city to; they first tried some cooks of the London Regiment and eventually settled for a lieutenant colonel of the Royal Field Artillery. On the 11th Allenby entered the Holy City, sacred to the three monotheistic religions, on foot as a gesture of humility.

Bull run

Initially, Allenby was pressed by the Cabinet to push on, but he first wanted to ensured that his right flank was secure. Nonetheless, in February 1918 Lloyd George secured an agreement at a meeting of the Supreme War Council in Versailles that there would be a renewal of the campaign in Palestine. But then came the great German offensive on the Western Front, which began on 21 March 1918. Allenby was ordered to strip his command of British army divisions and send them to France, replacing them with Indian army formations. It was not until September 1918 that he was able to resume the offensive.

On 19 September the Battle of Sharon commenced, south of Haifa. Here, the British artillery was supported by fire from two destroyers off the coast. Nazareth was captured and then, on the 23rd, Haifa. This brought the MLs to the fore again and they were the first craft to enter the Bay of Haifa on the Palestine coast. The waters were extensively mined and the motor launches swept a passage in for the trawlers and supply vessels.

Haifa became the base for the MLs, although not a pleasant one. Bad weather had the MLs continually crossing six miles from one side of the bay to the other in search of shelter. During one such passage of severe weather, Sub Lieutenant Hunt of *ML-206*, rowing a boat from one launch to another, was caught in an easterly squall and carried out to sea. He wasn't missed for some time and when eventually three MLs put out to find him, there was no trace. It was over twenty-four hours later that he was eventually picked up south of Cape Carmel, suffering from dehydration and exposure. Hunt survived, a very lucky man.

Meanwhile, the Ottoman army had been broken at the Battle of Megiddo and withdrew towards Damascus. Allenby was encouraged from London to drive on for Aleppo and took Damascus on 1 October. The MLs were now

Motor launches off Sidon, by Donald Maxwell. *(Author's collection)*

tasked with helping to maintain his supply lines as the British forces advanced up the coast. The ports of Tyre and Sidon became important supply dumps for the army, as the overland supply chain now stretched back over 150 miles.

Tyre was captured on 4 October, but the first British vessel to enter its

ML-248 entering Tyre, by Donald Maxwell. She was the first boat into the harbour after the town fell. *(Author's collection)*

harbour was *ML-248*, under the command of Lieutenant Arthur Harvey Wells. Wells had joined the RNVR in January 1916 and had been assigned to one of the few remaining motor boats, *Anacapa* (number 112) in March. In July he had taken command of *ML-34* at Port Said, and in December transferred to *248*. Now he nosed towards Tyre harbour, his searchlight breaking the gloom. MLs were the only ships that could enter the port:

> The other craft – trawlers, drifters, food hulks, etc – were forced to anchor outside the harbour. The army had pushed on from Haifa, and was marching up the coast towards Tyre and Sidon, and was dependent to a large extent for supplies from the sea. The flotilla arrived off Tyre at dawn; two minesweeping trawlers swept a channel and the ML went right into the ancient harbour, feeling her way along by the lead. It is not an easy entrance even for an ML and in some places was only a matter of clearing by inches.[11]

On her starboard side was a pile of stones that looked like a ruined tower, on her port hand a low line of debris and fallen pillars ending in a tower-like mass of masonry; ahead, on every accessible outcrop or viewpoint, hundreds of ragged figures, gesticulating and shouting.

ML-248 was followed in by *206* and the work of clearing the harbour

ML-206 entering Tyre, by Donald Maxwell. *(Author's collection)*

began. Apart from mines, all sorts of snags and obstructions blocked the channel. Her commander told Gordon Maxwell that:

> Tyre is a miserable place, as seen from the north side, where there is an apology for a harbour. It is really the ancient site, and broken traces of the old mole abound. Jagged fragments of masonry stick out from the water and jumbled masses of columns, which make it a tortuous channel. A few small fishing-boats constitute its shipping. A more desolate scene it would be impossible to imagine, her walls shattered and her towers broken down.[12]

But the MLs cleared a passage and soon surf boats began the work of unloading the supply lighters, plying to and fro to the beach. Food and ammunition began to flow to the army.

Sidon was taken on 6 October and cleared in a similar manner. And Lieutenant Wells's part in this success was not overlooked. On 8 April 1919 he was gazetted with the DSC, 'for excellent service in connection with the landing of stores on the coast during the advance, doing much to expedite and assist this important work upon which so much depended'.[13]

By the 8th, Beirut had been evacuated by the Turks and occupied by the advancing armies. Again, a motor launch, *ML-240*, was the first to enter the harbour, accompanied by a Royal Navy armed yacht and followed (at a distance) by two French destroyers. No mines were found and an enthusiastic welcome was given by the waiting crowd of inhabitants. As Allenby's forces pressed on, taking Homs on 16 October and Aleppo nine days later, two MLs, *234* and *206*, were left at Beirut and operated between there and Tripoli.

HMS *Agamemnon* (1906), four 12in, eight 9.2in guns. The Turkish Armistice was signed on board on 30 October 1918. *(Author's collection)*

During October Turkey sued for an armistice and the date for its signing was agreed to be the 30th. After three days of negotiation, at noon on that day the peace was signed by the Ottoman Minister of Marine Affairs, Rauf Bey, and Rear Admiral Somerset Arthur Gough-Calthorpe RN, CinC Mediterranean, on board the pre-dreadnought *Agamemnon* anchored in Mudros harbour, at the Greek island of Lemnos.

Lieutenant Luker heard of it:

> on our wireless about twenty miles from Beirut, when making a passage to Haifa. The armistice with Austria we celebrated in Tripoli, and we arrived in Beirut on the eve of the German armistice. However, celebrations in these parts of the world were of a modest nature, for there was too much poverty and distress surrounding the victors to allow of any open demonstration. Apart from the firing of a few Very lights, everything went on as usual.[14]

Admiral Somerset Arthur Gough-Calthorpe who signed the Armistice of Mudros.
(Author's collection)

The amateur sailors had been vital in keeping the army fed and watered as they drove the Turks out of Palestine and Syria.

And in the Aegean

On 10 October 1918 Temporary Sub Lieutenant Fred Cooper RNVR departed from his home town of Southampton for Cherbourg on the London and South Western Railway ferry SS *Lydia* (1890). From there he took a train to St Germain, boarded another one and eventually, many trains later, arrived in Taranto on the 19th. There he took another ship to Istea, then more trains until he finally arrived in Salonika on 25 October and joined *ML-228* the following day. She was one of a number of MLs supporting General Franchet d'Espèrey, in overall command of the Allied Army of the Orient, in actions against the Bulgarian and Austro-Hungarian enemy, although by the time Cooper got to join his motor launch, the Bulgarians had already signed an armistice (on 29 September) and left the field.

He had been on the books of *Hermione* from 13 July, learning to sail in the MLs. Now he transferred to the muster of the Aegean flagship *Europa* (1897), a *Diadem*-class protected cruiser armed with sixteen 6in guns. His *ML-228* was one of twenty-one MLs in Mediterranean Auxiliary Patrol Area VIII, a much-reduced number from the previous year, when there had been forty-two. The depot ship for the MLs was *Osiris* (1898), a passenger liner converted to an armed merchant cruiser before being repurposed as a depot ship in April 1915.

Cooper was soon at work, with his ML escorting a freighter to Mudros on 27 October, although bad weather made them put in for shelter at Kondia, and making the return journey two days later. But he was then struck down by some sort of eye infection and sent to first the 50th general hospital and then to the 52nd. By the time he rejoined his vessel, the war was over.

Bravery in Trinidad

The motor launches were even found in the West Indies. Trinidad was rich in oil and provided the Admiralty with millions of gallons during the war. Additionally, at the outbreak of war the largest and most powerful wireless station in the West Indies was located in Port of Spain. As a result, the perceived threat to Trinidad and Tobago was very high. And once German submarines began operating off the coast of the Americas*, there was much concern that the shipment of oil would be targeted and interrupted. As a result, a flotilla of twelve MLs was sent in late 1916 to patrol the Caribbean

---

* Starting with *U-53* in October 1916.

ML-285. (Author's collection)

waters and remained there until the end of the war. The Royal Garrison Artillery followed with supplies of modern guns for harbour defence.

One of the motor launches was *ML-289*, based at Port of Spain. On 29 December some cotton waste stored in a wooden cupboard in the magazine of *289* caught fire. When the hatch was opened a sudden smell of burning and the issue of smoke alerted twenty-seven-year-old, Northumberland-born, Deckhand John George Stanners RNR that a magazine explosion was likely. Without hesitation, Stanners plunged into the magazine flat and emerged carrying a mass of burning material, which he threw over the side. Moored alongside *289* was *ML-285*, where Deckhand Rupert Walter Bugg RNR noticed Stanners' actions and jumped over from his own vessel, entered the magazine area and extinguished the remainder of the fire. It is certain that the speed of action and the courage shown by these men in the face of considerable danger averted a serious fire and saved two MLs and the lives of their crews. The powers-that-be agreed: both men were awarded the Albert Medal for Saving Lives at Sea[15] in recognition of their efforts.*

* * * * *

Motor launches served with great versatility across a wide range of naval theatres. Apart from the activities noted above, by the beginning of 1918 there were also MLs at Gibraltar (nineteen), Malta (eighteen), Egypt (seventeen) and 'On Special Service'. Nearly all were commanded by the men of the RNVR.

---

* Rupert Bugg died in the Spanish flu epidemic on 22 March 1919, while John Stanners chose not to exchange his Albert Medal for a George Cross following the change in the Royal Warrant of 1971. He died three years later.

7

Operation ZO – The Raids on Zeebrugge and Ostend

The apotheosis of the motor launches was surely during Operation ZO, the raids on Zeebrugge and Ostend in 1918.

The raids were an attempt to close the egress for German U-boats from their highly protected base at Bruges. Once Belgium had fallen to Germany, the Kaiserliche Marine quickly established a U-boat base at Bruges, from which they could exit via canals reaching the sea at Zeebrugge and Ostend. From here, the U-boats wreaked havoc on British shipping in the North Sea and the Western Approaches.

Various attempts were made to limit the U-boats' freedom. During 1916 and 1917, bombardments designed to damage the canal lock gates were undertaken without success. And the most visible deterrent was the Dover Barrage, a cross-channel mine and net barrier, which went through no less than four iterations during the war, and the real or apparent failure of which was responsible for two of the three admirals commanding at Dover losing their commands.

This lack of success was also the cause for a rapid increase in British and neutral shipping losses to mines and U-boats once Germany declared unrestricted submarine warfare from the beginning of February 1917. The situation seemed so dire that on 27 April First Sea Lord Sir John Jellicoe was moved to tell the War Cabinet, via the First Lord, that:

> the real fact of the matter is this. We are carrying on the war at the present time as if we had the absolute command of the sea, whereas we have not such command or anything approaching it. It is quite true that we are masters of the situation so far as surface ships are concerned, but it must be realised – and realised at once – that this will be quite useless if the enemy's submarines paralyse, as they do now, our lines of communication.
>
> Without some such relief as I have indicated [inter alia 'the import of everything that is not essential to the life of the country is ruthlessly and immediately stopped'] – and that given immediately – the navy will fail in its responsibilities to the country and the country itself will suffer starvation.[1]

Convoy was the ultimate answer to this problem and with its introduction, losses became somewhat more manageable. But many still wanted to deal with the nest of vipers that lurked on the Belgian coast. One who did was Vice Admiral Roger Keyes who, after conniving in the firing of his predecessor at the end of 1917, took command of the Dover Patrol, and he wanted to attack the German base.

This was not a new idea. Back in the early days of the war, Captain Herbert Richmond, serving in the Admiralty as Assistant Director of the Operation Division, had minuted on 13 October 1914 a recommendation that the ports of Zeebrugge and Ostend be blocked before the Germans took them (which they did two days later). Then in 1916 Vice Admiral Lewis Bayly, commanding the Western Approaches from his base at Queenstown and thus in the thick of the anti-submarine effort, produced a detailed plan for landing troops in occupied Belgium to seize Ostend and Zeebrugge. Ambitious in scope and objective, it called for men and equipment that were both in short supply and was quietly shelved.

Vice Admiral Roger Keyes, who presided over Operation ZO. *(Author's collection)*

Shortly afterwards, the offensively minded Commodore Reginald Tyrwhitt at Harwich also produced a proposal. This called for the destruction of the lock gates by an explosive-packed blockship protected by smoke and poison gas. The possibility that the poison gas would impact on the local populace was something he had overlooked, but the Admiralty didn't and rejected the idea. Undismayed, Tyrwhitt recast his thinking and now proposed an attack on Zeebrugge harbour Mole and the capture of the town itself to effect operations against the German flank. Admiral Bacon, commanding at Dover, was asked for his views on the concept and deprecated it.

When Roger Keyes arrived at the Admiralty in October 1917 to take over as Director of Plans, it coincided with the failure of the Third Battle of Ypres, which was unsuccessful in an attempt to throw back the Germans and allow for the taking of the Belgian ports. German U-boats were destroying more than 500,000 tons of shipping each month, but were losing no more than two submarines per month in return. Keyes reasoned that the immediate tasks were to stop the transit of submarines through the Strait of Dover and, importantly, to nullify the problem at source by denying the Germans the use of the Belgian ports.

Keyes forwarded his thoughts to First Sea Lord Jellicoe and Jellicoe passed them on to Bacon, asking for a response. In reply, Bacon suggested that the long, curved harbour Mole could be stormed by men landed by means of a forward mounted ramp from a monitor and that they could then storm the lock gates and destroy them. To distract the Germans, he proposed a bombardment of the German heavy gun battery at Knokke to convince them that the landing was intended for that location, not the harbour. In these ideas was the genesis of the plan that became the Zeebrugge and Ostend raids.

Bacon presented his strategy at the Admiralty on 18 December 1917. The concept of landing troops on the Mole (a long barrier protecting the harbour from the sea and at the time the longest in the world) appealed to Keyes' aggressive temperament and he persuaded the Admiralty Board that the operation should proceed. Bacon was unofficially told that he was to command the attempt, to take place in February; but then he was fired. Keyes would run what now became Operation ZO.

St George's Day Eve, 1918

A small armada of ships set sail towards the Belgian coast at 1700. There were nine monitors, eight light cruisers, seven flotilla leaders, forty-four destroyers and torpedo boats, twenty-four CMBs (coastal motor boats) – and sixty-one motor launches, the largest assembly of them in one place ever made. Additionally, there were minesweepers, submarines, two ex-River Mersey ferries, *Iris* and *Daffodil*; and six very old cruisers, *Vindictive, Thetis, Intrepid, Iphigenia, Brilliant* and *Sirius*. The latter five vessels were packed with concrete; the former was heavily protected and carried all sorts of close-range firepower, including howitzers and a flame-thrower. There were also two old submarines, each crammed with explosives. Two hundred Royal Marines and a naval landing party were loaded on board the ferries and *Vindictive*. In all, 166 craft were present. Keyes, with his flag in the destroyer *Warwick*, led the flotilla out with the MLs formed up in three divisions in line ahead.

Originally intended to take place in early April, the plan for the operation was straightforward in outline, but complex in execution. Under cover of smoke and bombardment, *Vindictive* and the ferries *Iris* and *Daffodil* were to land the marines on Zeebrugge harbour Mole, from whence they would destroy German gun positions and prevent the enemy from interfering with the remainder of the operation. Explosive-packed submarines would position themselves under the viaduct which joined the Mole to the mainland and blow themselves up, destroying the bridge and hence the enemy's pathway for resupply of men and equipment to the Mole. *Thetis*, *Intrepid* and *Iphigenia* would sail into the harbour and sink themselves in the Bruges canal entrance, thus blocking entry and exit for the foreseeable future. Meanwhile, *Sirius* and *Brilliant* would head for Ostend with their escort and under the command of Commodore Hubert Lynes (a noted ornithologist in peacetime) would sink themselves to obstruct that canal link too.

It looked simple, but there were many 'moving parts' and inter-dependences. The harbour and its environs were heavily protected with guns of large and small calibre alike. The tides were difficult and there was only one dredged channel into Zeebrugge harbour proper. There were constantly shifting sandbanks in the immediate approaches and there were bound to be hidden German minefields. To take advantage of the high tides they would have to go in at around midnight. Navigation would be by dead-reckoning and a light onshore wind was essential to ensure the success of the smokescreen. It was a tough ask and one which Keyes (and previously Bacon's) intelligence officer, Captain Herbert Grant, had argued strongly against, to no avail.

The operation had originally been planned for 10/11 April and the armada had actually sailed before strong winds meant that it had to be abandoned when they were actually lying off Zeebrugge. The recall signal was a single letter flashed in Morse on a lamp. Not all ships received the message; on *ML-558*:

a signal cancelling the operation had been made but we didn't get it. Suddenly we were a perfect whirlpool of confusion. Big ships and little ships seemed to be coming and going in all directions … imagine a hundred or more ships , in close company, all without lights, making a sixteen-point turn.²

What is more, the Germans knew they were coming. During the confusion of the first, abortive, sailing, coastal motor boat *CMB-33* had managed to get itself grounded and captured by the Germans off Ostend. Against all instructions, the commander was carrying his secret orders and navigation charts on board; it did not take the Germans very long to work out that an assault on Zeebrugge was in the offing. Added precautions were taken, with more men and guns moved into the immediate area.

The raid was to be an all-Royal Navy affair, to restore that body's prestige in the public eye after the disappointments of Jutland and the much-lamented lack of a climactic sea battle and victory. After the 11 April failure, the Board of Admiralty instructed Keyes to stand the men down. Losses to submarines were thought to be abating under the effect of convoy (see Appendix 3); and Room 40, Admiralty Intelligence, had word that submarine commanders had been instructed not to risk the Dover Strait and the Barrier. But Keyes persuaded First Sea Lord Rosslyn Wemyss (who had replaced Jellicoe on Christmas Eve 1917 when the latter was dismissed from his post) to intercede for him, and promised early action.

Volunteers

The operation involved eighty-two officers and 1,698 men, and every man in the blockships was a volunteer. The call had gone out for officers and men to take part in a 'secret and dangerous mission'. Officers were sought who were unmarried or lacked dependants. In the MLs nearly all the officers, and most of the men, were RNVR. Many had originally served in the RNMBR. Now these latter-day Galahads, the code of Corinthian chivalry still burning bright, were headed towards the Belgian coast, with *pro patria* their intent but quite possibly *mori* in their minds. Thirty-one-year-old rating Percy Pointer in *ML-512* described how they felt. 'Our blood tingled and we laughed and jumped like schoolboys at a football match'.³

Coastal motor boats and MLs rushed ahead of the force and laid smoke around Zeebrugge harbour. Destroyers formed a screen on the seaward side of the advancing landing vessels and blockships. Despite the smoke, the defences were hitting home on *Vindictive*, the old cruiser deployed to land the attacking force on the Mole. Then, at 2356, the wind changed direction and *Vindictive* was exposed to view. She became a charnel house, as every German gun that could bore on her. Half the men of the landing parties were killed or badly wounded. The commanding officers and their deputies of both the marine and naval landing parties were killed. Her captain, Alfred Carpenter, increased speed and ran for the protection of the seaward side of the Mole. At 0001 on St George's Day he bumped into it, over 400yds from the intended landing place.

Vindictive had been fitted with narrow landing brows (gangplanks) for the men to run up to access the Mole. Many had been smashed away by shellfire and others destroyed by the vessel's sudden banging against the concrete wall. Carpenter could not get his ship to lie still against the wall. Massive grappling hooks, which were meant to secure the ship, proved incapable of being deployed in the teeth of machine-gun fire. Finally *Daffodil*, arriving three minutes after *Vindictive*, and commanded by a half-blinded Lieutenant Harold Campbell, took matters in hand by using her bow to push the old cruiser tight against the Mole. After fifteen minutes under heavy gunfire, men began to inch up the gangplanks onto dry land – and into a hail of machine-gun fire. They could only arrive in penny packets due to the narrowness of the brows and their limited number. This was precisely what Bacon had warned against when he had recommended a broad ramp and front exit, allowing for a rush of men to overwhelm an enemy. Worse, the men on *Daffodil* could only get off her via her bow and a transit of *Vindictive*'s shell-swept decks. It was wholesale slaughter.

Because of the delay from 11 April, the altered timings meant high tide was 4ft lower than planned and men on *Iris*, intended to disembark onto the Mole alongside *Vindictive*, could not get off her and were quickly improvising ladders and ropes. *Iris* could not get her grapnels to seize on the harbour wall. When finally deployed, marines and naval ratings fought with bayonets, cutlasses, rifles and their fists.

On water, Lieutenant Richard Douglas Sandford managed to drive his explosive-laden submarine into the harbour and up against the viaduct connecting the Mole and land. The explosion achieved its objective and the viaduct was downed but as the crew attempted escape in a skiff, most were wounded. Eventually they were rescued by a picket boat commanded by Sandford's elder brother and transferred to a destroyer.

Now three more old cruisers entered the harbour. *Thetis* was meant to ram the lock gates, but staggered under the weight of enemy fire and finally reached a timber breakwater just short of the objective, where Commander Ralph Sneyd blew his charges and sank her. Half the ship's small crew were dead or wounded, but the living were rescued from the boats they had taken to by *ML-526* under Lieutenant Hugh Alexander Littleton RNVR (nicknamed 'the Doctor'), who braved a torrent of enemy fire to lift the men off. As he was about to leave the area, there was a shout from behind that there was another boatload coming up; without hesitation, Littleton turned around back into the inferno of fire and collected them too. As *Yachting Monthly* had it, he was asked, 'Do you mind waiting a moment, I think there are some more men coming'. Littleton's answer surprised his interlocutor: 'You priceless old thing, of course I can't wait for them … I'll go back for them.'[4] Once more under way, he again stopped to pick up a man from the water and now with sixty-odd survivors aboard *ML-526* found her way outside the Mole and ran for Dover. On arrival, Littleton was amazed to find that the boat's only damage was a machine-gun bullet through the after hatch and a piece of shrapnel which had pierced the roof of the bridge house.

Meanwhile, *Intrepid*, commanded by Lieutenant Stuart Bonham-Carter, should logically have attempted the task which *Thetis* had failed to complete, but her commander followed his orders to the letter and instead sank his ship across the canal channel.

The motor launches

The MLs had been told off for a number of tasks – smoke-laying, rescue of men from the blockships, distracting the defenders, suppression of U-boats, etc. *ML-448* and *ML-538* had been detailed to lay smoke to cover an opening bombardment from the monitors. They were using a new technology specifically invented for the occasion by Wing Commander Frank Arthur Brock RNAS, scion of the famous fireworks family*. Brock's new and improved smokescreen, or 'artificial fog' as he preferred to call it, was ingenious. A chemical mixture, mainly chlorosulphonic acid, was injected directly under pressure into the hot exhausts of the motor launches and other small craft, or the hot interior surface of the funnels of destroyers. With water vapour present, a thick cloud was formed. The smoke was as dangerous to the user as it was hindrance to the enemy. Signalman William Wood, serving on HMS *Warwick*, described it as 'hardly smoke, more like fog. The acid made it nip the eyes and sting the face so that it was necessary to smear one's exposed parts with Vaseline. The other ingredients of the gas choked when one tried to breathe, hence the use of respirators.'[5]

The MLs came under heavy fire from coastal batteries as they laid down the screen, but they were successful, and at 2320 the monitors opened a

---

* Amongst Brock's contribution to the war effort thus far were the Dover Flare, used in the illumination of the Dover Barrage, the Brock Colour Filter and the Brock Bullet (or Brock Incendiary Bullet or Brock Anti-Zeppelin Bullet). The first German airship to be shot down was destroyed by this projectile.

covering fire on Zeebrugge and Ostend, trying to suppress the defences. There were nine of them with guns from 15in to 7.5in in calibre. They were joined by the Royal Marine and Royal Navy siege artillery that had been placed in the dunes in France.

The MLs were everywhere. *ML-382* was based at Dunkirk and had been detailed to lay smoke to protect the twin 12in-gunned monitor *Lord Clive* (1915). The launch's commanding officer, thirty-three-year-old Lieutenant Gerald Ashburner Mooring Aldridge RNVR, left harbour on 22 April with other MLs to join with the bombardment force in the Dunkirk Roads. 'There were a large number of ships,' he recorded in his diary, 'waiting to proceed into action, anchored off Malo-les-Bains … we hung onto the monitor and in due course moved off towards Ostend'.[6] *Lord Clive* and her escort took up position two to three miles off Nieuwpoort. At 2250 *ML-382* and *ML-287* started up their smoke generators and *Lord Clive* opened fire at 2210. Shellfire from the shore bracketed Aldridge's boat just 50yds away, although he hid in his own smoke and was unhit, while shrapnel burst overhead but again spared the little craft.

Laying the smoke was not without its problems. 'The gas operator, 1st Air Mechanic Drake, suffered from cold feet and was of little use,' wrote Aldridge, and the ship's engineers had to take over. 'The smoke at times was very bad in the engine room as the acid was leaking through a joint. The gas masks came in very useful'.[7]

ML-424 was putting down smoke off the coast when she was disabled by heavy gunfire and her captain, twenty-nine-year-old Lieutenant Oswald Robinson* killed, together with two deckhands. Lieutenant John Robinson RNVR, second in command, took charge, decided to abandon the boat and managed to get the wounded away in the dinghy, then destroyed the vessel by setting fire to the engine room. Another launch, *ML-128*, had been detailed with *ML-110* to place calcium lights at the entrance to the harbour, but an engine breakdown put an end to her mission, and she was sunk with the loss of five men. *ML-110* was commanded by forty-one-year-old Lieutenant Commander James Dawbarn Young RNR, who had volunteered to light the entrance. He had preceded the blockships towards the harbour entrance where his vessel came under sustained enemy fire and he was hit three times, mortally wounding him. Despite his injuries, Young gave orders to abandon and sink his crippled ship, and Lieutenant George Bowen RNVR smashed a hole in the ML's bottom with an axe, before emptying a magazine from her Lewis gun into the craft to ensure that it sank. Young was rescued,

---

* 'A wonderfully clever mimic and actor' (Maxwell, *Motor Launch Patrol*, p118), he left a young wife. His body was never found, having been blown off his bridge by an explosion.

but died on the way back to Dover. Meanwhile, *ML-128* got going again and her commander, Lieutenant Raphael Saunders RNVR, now went into the maelstrom of the harbour to rescue *ML-424*'s remaining crewmen.

ML-558, Lieutenant Commander Lionel Sheard Chappell RNVR, had been laying smoke to protect *Vindictive*. She also carried on board the flag captain, Captain Ralph Collins RN, who had charge of the whole motor-launch flotilla. When the blockships arrived, Collins passed on a rough bearing for them to follow and then laid smoke to screen first *Vindictive* and then *Iris*:

> Every now and then when they came to the end of their short patrol the smoke blew away from them, exposing the ML to the full glare of the searchlights from the Mole, and the only thing to do was to turn sixteen points into their own smoke and make their way back again and renew the manoeuvre. This the ML kept up during the time that the storming party from *Vindictive* landed on the Mole, and undoubtedly saved them from much of the fire from the western shore batteries.[8]

Chappell's craft was hit by a large shell, which landed on top of the magazine hatch and would have blown them to kingdom come, but it ricocheted on to a box of ammunition and blew that up instead. Chappell's

'*ML-282* rescuing men during the Zeebrugge Raid, 23 April 1918', by W L Wylie (© National Maritime Museum, Greenwich, London, PAD 9929)

number one, Canadian-born Lieutenant Collamer Calvin, managed to extinguish the flames.

ML-512, another launch on smoke-laying duty, was attacked by a remotely controlled motor boat, directed from a Gotha bomber circling above. By dint of hiding in her own smoke, she managed to escape.

Lieutenant Percy Dean RNVR, in *ML-282*, had followed *Intrepid* and *Iphigenia* into the canal itself and loitered there under heavy fire to pick up the blockship crews. He met with *Iphigenia*'s overloaded cutter and, with small arms and machine-gun fire directed at his ML from only yards away, stopped to rescue the men from the cutter, towing the empty vessel astern as well. On his opposite bow, a skiff from *Intrepid* bumped alongside and those men too were taken onto his by now heavily overcrowded boat. When his launch could take no more on board and was low in the water, men were directed to the cutter. Dean now attempted to leave, stern first, but in doing so she grounded and damaged the propellers, but he pressed on. Having picked up all the men he could see, Dean spotted a single Carley float with one person on it, to the stern of *Intrepid*. Again, he went to the ship and plucked the man, who turned out to be her captain, Lieutenant Bonham-Carter, from the raft. Eventually *ML-282* had 109 men on board, so overloaded that she was almost underwater and would not answer her helm for there were too many feet standing on the rudder cables. Dean had to steer using the engines. Going out of harbour she was badly hit by enemy gunfire, killing her coxswain and wounding her second in command, Lieutenant James Courtenay Wright RNVR. All the while, the motor launch was towing *Iphigenia*'s cutter; when Dean finally got clear of the Mole, he cut it adrift to save the men he already had on board. 'His ship was a shambles, with dead and dying … in the forecastle and after-cabin, men were already in their final agonies'.[9] Three helmsmen had been hit at the wheel, two of them receiving fatal injuries. Riddled like a sieve, eventually *ML-282* reached *Warwick* and transferred her huddled masses. Dean then headed first for Deal to land some hospital cases and then finally to Dover.

> That an ML, whose full complement is ten all told, should have been able to get out of harbour with over a hundred men on board would have been wonderful under peacetime conditions; but when we consider that the feat was performed amidst a tornado of gunfire, some idea of the achievement can perhaps be imagined.[10]

With the raid in tatters, somehow *Vindictive* got men back on board and slipped the harbour. Carpenter was injured, but he conned the ship to the protection of the waiting destroyers and nursed her back to Dover. *Iris* and

Daffodil too managed to get back to port, the former guided by her dying navigating officer, Lieutenant George Spencer RNR, gasping out the courses to steer. She had been badly damaged as she pulled away from the Mole and then hit amidships by a shell which killed or injured many Royal Marines on board, who probably thought they were sailing to safety. During her painful return, Keyes called out to *Iris* from his flagship *Warwick*. 'Do you want anything?' he shouted across. A tense voice, quivering with emotion, replied, 'For God's sake send us doctors and dressings, we are a boatload of wounded.' 'How many killed?' responded Keyes. 'Seventy killed and wounded,' came the answer.[11]

Motor launches were still trying to get home. *ML-420* suffered a collision in the smokescreen, which severely damaged her bows. Her CO, Lieutenant Herbert Tracey, first thought he would have to abandon, but *ML-252* picked up his distress calls and came up to stand by him. The engines worked, but only a slow crawl was possible with the condition of the bows. When daylight came, the two boats took the canvas identification signal from the top of the bridge house and rigged it as a temporary patch for the holes in her bow; they finally entered Dover at 1430.

That evening, Collamer Calvin was at dinner with some other officers who had gone on the raid at a 'little hotel over St Margaret's Bay'. They were amused when 'some of the guests asked us if we had heard heavy firing the night before'.[12]

The raid on Ostend

The intended and simultaneous raid on Ostend was a complete failure. By the simple expedient of moving the Stroombank navigation buoy one and a half miles to the east, and removing the Bell buoy altogether, the Germans ensured that Commander Alfred Edmund Godsal in *Brilliant* could not find the harbour entrance in the dark. Groping along the coast, he ran hard into a sandbank, and *Sirius*, following close behind, ran into him. That was the end of that. They blew their charges and the crews abandoned ship.

Eighteen MLs under the command of Captain Ion Hamilton Benn RNVR had left Dunkirk for Stroombank Buoy to create the smokescreen for the blockships. This they did successfully, despite heavy gunfire from the shore.

ML-283, Lieutenant Keith Robin Hoare RNVR, went alongside *Sirius* and took off her crew, as well as some of *Brilliant*'s, who had left their ship in a whaler. With his crew plus seventy-five rescued men on board, his craft was now very top-heavy and rolled badly; nonetheless, Hoare managed to struggle to Dunkirk safely.

Lieutenant Rowland Bourke RNVR in *ML-276* had followed the blockships

A postcard depicting *ML-557* and *ML-532* at Zeebrugge at the end of the war. Both boats took part in Operation ZO, *532* being Ion Hamilton Benn's command. *(Author's collection)*

in, having laid part of the western smokescreen. He went first alongside *Sirius*, but could get no response from her, and then *Brilliant*, the latter despite her engines still running astern; on four occasions he went up against her, taking survivors off each time and repeatedly pelted with gunfire from the shore batteries. In all, he rescued thirty-eight officers and men, including Commander Godsal.

But Bourke's day was not yet over. After departing the wrecked cruiser for the last time, he received an SOS signal from Hamilton Benn in *ML-532* asking Bourke to stand by him, as he had damaged his launch by running into the side of *Brilliant* in the dense smoke whilst attempting to take men aboard. Under heavy gunfire, Bourke took Benn's vessel in tow and, despite the rope parting three times, both craft made it back to port.

For others, the day had ended more peaceably. At 0210 on the 23rd *Lord Clive* had ceased firing and by 0645, the monitor and Lieutenant Aldridge's *ML-382* were back at Dunkirk. In response to many inquiries, the senior naval officer at Dunkirk issued a signal to all his commanding officers: 'with regard to the ZO operations, all the commodore can say at present is that parts of it are excellent and that the conduct of all engaged in the Ostend operations was admirable throughout'.[13]

But the U-boats' exit at Ostend remained undamaged.

Ostend (again)

Dissatisfied with the outcome at Ostend, but claiming a famous victory at Zeebrugge, Keyes now proposed a second raid on Ostend to finish the job. Commodore Lynes again volunteered to lead it, and the old cruisers *Sappho* and the much knocked-about *Vindictive* were pressed into service as blockships. Opinion at the Admiralty was against the operation, but Keyes once more persuaded Wemyss to let him proceed. Captain Grant was disgusted, and argued so strongly against the plan that Keyes' chief of staff requested that he be transferred, as did Grant himself. Grant wrote that Keyes 'believed his own heroics', and requested Keyes not to mention him in his despatches.[14]

Once again, it was a failure. The force, which included sixteen motor launches, sailed on 9 May, but *Sappho* broke down at the outset and so *Vindictive* had to go it alone. Commander Alfred Godsal (now commanding *Vindictive*) and Lynes had carefully consulted charts of Ostend following the previous operation's failure due to the repositioning of navigation buoys. Their efforts were rendered worthless by a sudden fog which obliterated all sight of the shore. Steaming back and forth across the harbour entrance in the fog as the covering monitors and German shore batteries engaged in a long-range artillery duel over their heads, Godsal tried to find the piers marking the entrance to the canal. During this period, the accompanying MLs lost track of the cruiser and it was only on the third pass that *Vindictive* found the entrance, accompanied by just one of the launches. Heading straight into the mouth of the canal, guided by a flare dropped by the motor launch, *Vindictive* became an instant target of the German batteries and was badly hit, the shellfire seriously damaging her propellers.

Commander Godsal intended to swing *Vindictive* broadside on into the channel mouth, but as he ordered the turn, the right screw broke down completely, preventing the cruiser from fully turning. At that moment the problem became academic, for a heavy shell from on shore hit Godsal directly and blew up the bridge and most of the people on it, including First Lieutenant Victor Crutchley RN. Crutchley, a giant of a man, staggered to the wheel and attempted to force the ship to make the full turn into the channel. It was to no avail, as she was stuck fast on a sandbank.

Crutchley ordered the charges blown and the ship abandoned, making a check of the ship himself by torchlight before leaping over the side into the only launch which had kept up with the ship, *ML-254*, commanded by Lieutenant Geoffrey H Drummond RNVR. His vessel had suffered grievously at the hands of the onshore gunners and was on fire, Drummond himself was wounded in three places, and his second in command, Lieutenant

Gordon Ross RNVR*, and a deckhand were dead and the coxswain wounded. But Crutchley was 'a tower of strength. He reduced the fire [on board], bound up the wounded and put a tourniquet round my leg,' remembered Drummond.[15]

Together they took *ML-254* out of the harbour mouth, proceeding astern, while carrying thirty-eight survivors from *Vindictive*'s fifty-five crewmen huddled on deck, where they remained exposed to machine-gun fire from the shore. As Drummond turned his boat seawards and proceeded back to the offshore squadron, one of the missing launches passed him. It was *ML-276*, once more under the command of Lieutenant Rowland Bourke. He and his crew had worked night and day to get his battered boat fit for sea again and they were now again in the thick of the action. As his coxswain, Bourke now had a schoolteacher from Lowestoft, Leading Deckhand Joseph Hamshaw, who had volunteered in order to get leave to visit his wife and family!

Drummond called to Bourke that he believed there were still men in the water and Bourke immediately headed to the harbour to search for them. Drummond meanwhile set course to rendezvous with *Warwick*, but was near collapse, so Crutchley temporarily took over, using his massive frame to bail whilst standing up to his waist in water.

Hearing shouts for help, Bourke entered the harbour, but could not find anyone. Despite heavy machine-gun and artillery fire, he returned to the old cruiser four times before they discovered a sailor and *Vindictive*'s badly wounded navigator, Lieutenant Alleyne, in the bottom of a boat. Bourke heaved them on board, to be joined by two more ratings who appeared from nowhere and jumped aboard, but as he did, two heavy shells struck his launch, smashing the lifeboat and destroying the compressed air tanks. This stalled the engines and caused a wave of corrosive acid to wash over the deck, severely damaging the launch's hull, and almost suffocating the unconscious Alleyne, whom Bourke had installed in his own cot below deck. The acid began to eat its way through the deck and, on contact with the water in the bilges, began to smoke. Bourke had to rush to pull Alleyne out of the bed before he was gassed.

The shells also killed Coxswain Hamshaw; Bourke's second in command was Sub Lieutenant James Petrie RNVR, who had volunteered for the rescue work. Petrie had been number one in *ML-559*, but as that vessel was not tasked to take part in the raid, he asked to transfer for service on *276*. With Hamshaw dead, he leapt to the wheel and tried to steer the launch out of Ostend harbour, while machine guns from the piers targeted his vessel.

---
* In 1915 Ross was the first Canadian to join the RNAS; he later transferred to the RNVR.

Undeterred, Petrie next manned the Lewis gun and returned fire at both pier heads. Then he sighted three wounded men in the water and personally assisted them into the launch, being exposed all the time to heavy fire. Under heavy attack, the boat staggered out of the harbour and was taken in tow by a monitor, which also took off the worst of the wounded. After the operation, Bourke's launch was discovered to have fifty-five bullet and shrapnel holes, with two crew killed.

Lieutenant Sir John Meynell Alleyne, 4th Baronet Alleyne of Four Hills, Barbados, was a twenty-nine-year-old regular officer who had volunteered for *Vindictive*, as he had three years' experience as a navigating officer off the Belgium coast. As he remembered it, he had been wounded in the back when descending from the monkey island to the conning tower, and it 'bowled me over and put one leg out of action'.[16] Alleyne was slumped on the floor when 'Abandon Ship' was sounded, and was unceremoniously hoisted onto the back of a chief quartermaster, carried out, and dropped into the water. Seeing a rope trailing from a ML, he grabbed it, but couldn't get on board, and then the boat took off at speed and he 'went down like a paravane'.[17] When he was able to surface, he saw another ML closing in on him and likely to use him as a fender, so he let go and the two boats disappeared into the darkness. Alleyne swam back to *Vindictive*, where he found a ship's boat with one end in the water and one on the davit head, and a seaman in it. The rating pulled him in and Alleyne told him to climb up the rope and cut the boat free of the davit. Suddenly there was an intense outbreak of firing and an ML raced into view at full speed. As she came abreast of the shattered cruiser, a voice called out, 'Is anybody there?' and 'We holloa'd our best and she ran up alongside,'[18] and he was able to clamber aboard.

But Sir John's ordeal was not yet over:

> We lay on the upper deck while she steamed full speed out of the harbour. I was a bit amazed at the time by a rather heavy rating who insisted on lying on top of me as I was pretty sore, and it was not until sometime afterwards that I realised that the gallant fellow was making a splinter screen of himself.[19]

When finally ashore, Alleyne discovered that he had been hit by a machine-gun bullet, which had gone through a button of his monkey jacket and come out the back.*

---

* Alleyne survived the war. In May 1919 his mother, Lady Alleyne (née Suzanne Meynell), presented Bourke with an inscribed silver coffee pot and Petrie a silver inkwell in gratitude for saving her son.

Meanwhile, Drummond's vessel was severely damaged; her forecastle was flooded and despite sending all possible men to the stern, the water was slowly gaining on the efforts of both the pumps and bucket-wielding sailors. Moreover, Drummond's injuries included a bullet through the shoulder and the near loss of his left leg. Both he and Crutchley made constant SOS signals to seaward by lamp, which were eventually picked up by *Warwick* at 0315. Keyes ordered destroyers to surround her, but she was too badly damaged to be towed. Eventually, *ML-254* transferred her survivors to *Warwick*, whose first officer, Lieutenant Frederick Trumble*, had left the bridge to supervise the discharge of the wounded to his ship. As he lent over the side, his head was blown apart by a round from the launch's forward Lewis gun; although the magazine was off, one round had been left in the breech and was triggered by the violent motion of the vessel.[29] Keyes ordered the launch to be sunk.

Meanwhile, other motor launches had been putting themselves in the way of danger. For example, Hamilton Benn, once more leading the MLs, this time from *ML-105*, Commander William Wordie Watson's boat, managed to place a Holmes light† in a charted position on the Stroombank as a navigation mark. Another ML placing marker buoys was *ML-556*, under Lieutenant Rawsthorne Proctor RNVR. This boat was one of the third batch ordered, and must only just have arrived in England. It was brand new and with a scratch crew. As Lieutenant Maxwell put it:

> owing to a slight eleventh-hour alteration in the plans of the MLs, it became necessary to find someone almost at the last moment to take on the none too enviable task of marking the Bell buoy, which is well inshore from the Stroom Bank and not far from the harbour mouth. Lieutenant R Proctor undertook to do this in *ML-556*, in spite of the fact that his boat was so newly commissioned as to be incomplete in many important details, and possessed a crew who were as new to ML life as the boat itself. However, by very strenuous hustling, Lieutenant Proctor managed to get some semblance of order out of chaos, and to instruct his crew (first having to learn it himself) in the art of dropping smoke-floats.[21]

Having achieved his aim, Proctor busied his crew with making smoke to protect the monitors, popping in and out of his own smokescreen to avoid the fire from onshore. So successful was he in this that the launch received

---

* Trumble, a good cricketer, had represented the navy against the Army at Lords in the 1914 fixture.
† A canister, attached to a float, containing calcium carbonate and calcium phosphide, which ignite spontaneously on contact with the water to emit copious fire and smoke.

not a single hit. This was all the more laudable, as Proctor was in charge of a ML section, screening the monitors.

Another section leader was Lieutenant Commander Jean S Miéville RNVR in *ML-280* who 'led his unit with skill and judgment in a very exposed position, and it was largely due to him that the screen was so extremely successful in his section'.[22]

Lieutenant Commander Saunders in *ML-128* was once again in the thick of it. As his launch approached Ostend piers, he ran into a smokescreen, lost his way, and ended up almost on the beach 200yds from his objective, where the launch came under sustained fire from the shore batteries. Saunders called for full speed, but his boat was riddled by machine-gun fire, one man killed and sixty-six bullet scars later counted on the vessel.

Finally, *Warwick*, with Keyes on board and now carrying a deck-load of wounded men, hit a mine and began to sink. The destroyer *Velox* was lashed alongside and survivors from *Warwick*, *Vindictive* and *ML-254* transferred across to her. Thus entwined, this sad combination reached Dover early the following morning. Sixteen British sailors died. And the canal was not blocked. It was another failure. And a final attempt at a further raid was quietly dropped.

Although Keyes claimed Zeebrugge was a success, the blockships were in the wrong position when sunk and only managed to obstruct the canal for a few days. The Germans removed two piers in the western bank of the canal near the blockships and dredged a channel through the silt near the sterns of the blocking vessels, and were then able to move submarines along the channel past them at high water. Captain Edward 'Teddy' Evans was emphatic that the canal was not blocked. He could, he noted, 'easily take the *Broke* [his destroyer] past the blockships at high tide'.[23] The official historian recorded later that before the raid two submarines entered or left the Flanders bases each day, and continued at that rate during the week after the raid[24] and the German official history recorded that the conduct of the war suffered 'only minor and temporary restrictions'.[25] What is more, at Zeebrugge the lives of 227 brave men had been lost and another 356 men badly wounded.

Two MLs were destroyed at Zeebrugge and another at Second Ostend. Six motor launch officers and crew perished in the first raid and four more on 9/10 May. Another would die of wounds four months later*. And the

---

* This man was CPO Roy Leslie Alexander, one of the two hundred or so New Zealanders who served in the RNVR's motor boats. He had been amongst the first Kiwis to volunteer for the MLs and served as a chief motor mechanic in a motor launch during Operation ZO, for which he was awarded the DSM (*London Gazette* 30807, 19 July 1918). Wounded in the raid, he died of his injuries on 21 August.

bravery of the motor launch men was recognised with the unprecedented award to the motor launches of three Victoria Crosses, to Lieutenants Dean, Drummond and Bourke; all of them were RNVR (see also Appendix 4). As Gordon Maxwell later wrote, 'it requires courage of no mean order to stand on the unprotected deck of a frail wooden craft and go steadily into an enemy port under a murderous fire, and go alongside a ship that is being hammered by half a dozen shore batteries'.[26] But they did it anyway.

8

The Corinthians of ZO

Who were the ML officers who so distinguished themselves at Zeebrugge and Ostend?

We might start with someone who represents the *beau idéal* of the yachtsmen warriors, Ion Hamilton Benn. A founder member of Charlton Athletic AFC, a pre-war honorary colonel of the 20th (Woolwich & Blackheath) Battalion of the London Regiment, quondam mayor of Greenwich, Conservative MP for Greenwich 1910–1922, a director of the Port of London Authority since its inception, and a partner in the timber merchants Price and Peirce. Benn had joined up in October 1914, aged fifty-one, displaying the full *noblesse oblige* of an English gentleman.

Hamilton Benn was a most enthusiastic yachtsman, and a member of the Yacht Racing Association, the Royal Thames, Royal Corinthian (naturally), Royal Norfolk and Suffolk Yacht Clubs, as well as the Junior Carlton. He sailed a 92-ton yawl named *Betty*, designed by Arthur Payne and built by Hansen of Cowes. *Betty* was a very successful racing boat. In 1905 she won a Royal Yacht Squadron prize, and first and second prizes at the Ostend Regatta, second prize at Torquay Regatta, and first prize at the Royal Dart Yacht Club Regatta. In 1906 she won the German Emperor's Cup in the Dover–Heligoland race. Despite his age, Benn served with distinction.

ML-55, flying Hamilton Benn's command pennant when part of the Dover patrol. *(Author's collection)*

He commanded the MLs of the Dover patrol, was awarded the DSO in 1916 for his actions in the bombardment of Zeebrugge and Ostend[1] and received the CB for his part in Operation ZO.[2]

Some of the ML men in the raid had been in the RNMBR from the inception of the war. Lionel Sheard Chappell joined in the motor boat *Kia Ora* on 16 September 1914, transferring to *ML-5* in September the following year. He had won a DSC for 'his coolness and courage in the presence of the enemy',[3] awarded on 26 June 1917, and would gain a DSO in 1919 'for distinguished services during the war'.[4]

Keith Robin Hoare was another from the RNMBR, having joined in November 1914 and transferring to *ML-21* twelve months later. In his childhood he learned to sail at the Isle of Wight and was the stepson of C B Fry (see Chapter 1)*, and a regular visitor to the Frys' naval training ship *Mercury* during his childhood. Immediately prior to the raid, on 12 April 1918 Hoare and another ML officer, Lieutenant Arthur Bagot, had been awarded the Albert Medal for saving life at sea, gazetted on 20 August 1918 (see Chapter 13). Hoare had already won the DSO and the DSC for previous acts of bravery, and would gain a bar to his DSO for his actions in Operation ZO. The Corinthian figure of C B Fry clearly cast a long shadow over him. After the war, he stayed with the sea, managing a fleet of fishing trawlers.

A DSO was also presented to Lieutenant Raphael Saunders RNVR, who additionally gained accelerated advancement to lieutenant commander. Saunders had started the war in the motor boat section on the very last day of 1915 as a temporary sub lieutenant, despite it being largely moribund by this time, having been a leading seaman in the RNVR until that point. In August 1916 he transferred to *Hermione* and the motor launches, and took command of *ML-128* in June 1917.[5] In his despatch after the raids, Keyes noted of Saunders that:

> this officer volunteered for rescue work at Ostend in command of *ML-128*. In company with *ML-283* he went in after *Vindictive* to look for survivors. When near the shore he came under heavy fire – his signalman was killed and Lieutenant Brayfield and one of the crew wounded. This officer showed great coolness, setting a fine example to his men throughout, and was of the greatest assistance in organising the smoke screen.[6]

Hugh Littleton was another motor boat man, who started the war with his motor boat *Trident* on service at Queenstown in the Coast of Ireland

---

* And the natural son of Charles Arthur Richard Hoare, senior partner of C Hoare & Co, bankers.

Command. He was awarded the DSO for his work during the raids. The citation noted that he 'handled his motor launch in a magnificent manner. Embarked over sixty officers and men from *Thetis* under heavy machine gun fire at close range. It was solely due to his courage and daring that his boat succeeded in making good her escape with the survivors'.[7]

Herbert Tracey served initially on *Stately*, one of the motor fishing vessels co-opted into the RNMBR. He was mentioned in despatches, as he had 'showed skill and judgement which assisted in the success of the smoke screen in his section', during the raid.[8]

And forty-year-old Commander James Dawbarn Young RNVR, killed at Zeebrugge, was in peacetime a surveyor turned barrister, whose father had been president of the Royal Institution of Chartered Surveyors. Outside of the law, his passion was yachting and he joined the RNVR immediately war commenced. Young had taken command of *ML-12* in October 1915 and been appointed a lieutenant commander in charge of a division of MLs at Dover in July 1917.

Another volunteer from the legal profession was Lieutenant Gerald Ashburner Mooring Aldridge, in peacetime a solicitor in Dorset, a profession he returned to post-war. His daughter Margaret had been born just one month after the start of the war.

Percy Dean's second in command, Lieutenant James Courtenay Keith 'Shiner' Wright, twenty-six years old at the time of the action, was an amateur of a different cut. He had joined the Royal Naval Volunteer Reserve's London Division in June 1904. Thereafter, until the start of the war, he served on active duty for a month each year, gaining advancement to chief petty officer in January 1911. His great love was training field-gun crews for competing with the teams of the Royal Navy – which led to his team winning a final at Olympia against HMS *Excellent*.

During the action he had been wounded in the stomach. Taken to the hospital ship *Liberty*, the doctors pronounced that he would not live. In an action which demonstrated the better side of Roger Keyes' nature, Keyes phoned First Sea Lord 'Rosy' Wemyss and asked him to request of the King an immediate grant of a DSC to Wright, so that he could be decorated before his death. This was done, but in fact, Wright recovered and eventually went back to sea in command of the armed yacht *Mairi* in December 1918. His final command was *ML-53*, prior to being demobilised in December 1919. He married in 1921 and died thirty years later.

And Sub Lieutenant James Petrie, who received the DSC for his actions in *ML-276*, was the son of a prominent jute merchant and bag manufacturer from Greenock, also named James. James junior took over the firm after the war and sold it in 1925 to Thomas Boag, another bag manufacturer, leaving

Britain for Hong Kong, where he became managing director of Davie, Boag and Co. In 1933 Petrie founded the Hong Kong Naval Volunteer Force and was appointed its commanding officer in 1936, maintaining that role when it was officially reconstituted as the Hong Kong RNVR. When war came again, James served as a commander in the RNVR, and was involved in the demolition and scorched-earth policy carried out in Singapore and Malaysia prior to the arrival of the Japanese.

Percy Dean

What of the three motor launch VC recipients? Percy Thompson Dean was 'an experienced yachtsman'.[9] Aged forty at the time of Operation ZO, Dean was the scion of a well-known and wealthy Blackburn, Lancashire, family whose wealth came from cotton spinning and slate manufacture. The Deans were a prominent middle-class family with strong economic and political associations in the neighbourhood; both his paternal grandfather and his maternal uncle were former mayors of Blackburn. Percy was sent away to be educated at Bromsgrove School, where he did not distinguish himself, except on the fives court. This did not unduly concern him, for he entered the family slate business and, in fact, proved a successful businessman, reviving the concern, John Dean Ltd, which had fallen into decline since the death of his father, and was regarded as a good and fair employer. In the immediate pre-war years, Dean lived the life of the prosperous upper middle class. He contracted the first of his three marriages in 1906*, and entered politics, becoming a councillor and chair of the local Conservative and Unionist party in 1913. For recreation, he sailed; Dean was a skilled yachtsman and a popular member of the West Lancashire Yacht Club (founded 1894). A friend recalled how 'all his spare time from Easter to September ... was spent racing or cruising in small boats ... with a cruise to the Irish and Scottish coasts for his summer holiday ... no paid hand was carried in those days and the little ship always made its port in seamanlike style'.[10]

When war broke out, Dean tried to join the army, but was rejected owing to tendon damage in his leg, sustained when washing his feet in a hand basin. Instead, he parlayed his sailing ability into a commission in the RNVR as a sub lieutenant, joining *ML-101* in October 1916 and was made a lieutenant in April 1917. For his actions in the raids, Dean was advanced to lieutenant

---

* Dean married Mabel Ratcliffe in 1906 and had a son. Following his wife's sudden death in 1907, he married Jeanne Marie Klein in 1908, by whom he sired a daughter. They divorced in 1921 and in 1927 he married Marian Rebecca, the widow of Lieutenant Colonel James Ogden Hardicker (a solicitor and Manchester Regiment volunteer, who died in 1919 of consumption contracted at Gallipoli).

commander, backdated to 23 April 1918, and was presented with his Victoria Cross at Buckingham Palace on 31 July. Before then, he had been hailed in Blackburn as a local hero, and on 3 July had accepted the nomination to stand as Blackburn's Conservative candidate at the first post-war election. Five months later, the VC was a Member of Parliament, having beaten the eminent Labour politician, wartime pacifist and incumbent, Philip (later Viscount) Snowden*. Percy Dean was demobilised on 8 January 1919 and his portrait was painted by Edgar Bundy ARA. It is now in the collection of Blackburn Museum and Art Gallery. Bravery, a sportsman, political community service, a benign employer – Dean exemplified the Corinthian spirit.

Geoffrey Drummond

Geoffrey Heneage Drummond also came from privilege. Born on 25 January 1886, he was the third of seven sons of Algernon Heneage Drummond† and his wife Margaret Elizabeth, née Benson. The Drummonds were part of a banking dynasty and divided their time between Cornwall Gardens, London, and Maltman's Green‡, a house in Gerrards Cross. The latter was the setting for many summer gatherings, when the guests would often include their cousins, the Bowes-Lyons, including Elizabeth, the future wife of George VI. He attended Evelyn's preparatory school, Eton, but at the age of nine had a bad fall down stairs and dislocated his neck. From then on, Drummond suffered from severe headaches and spent only a few more terms there; likewise, after he had entered Christ Church College, Oxford, he soon left and eventually finished his education at Wye Agricultural College. His injury did not prevent him working as a land agent in Staffordshire and in the Australian Outback. He also began to practise what became his favourite recreation, yachting, and in the years before the Great War did a great deal of sailing around the south coast and on the continental littoral.

When war came, Drummond was so anxious to serve that he endured a course of manipulation on his neck at the hands of a Swedish specialist, and gained sufficient improvement to be accepted by the RNVR on 2 January 1916. He served initially at Poole in a drifter, then as second in command of an ML, before heading to Scapa Flow, where the dull routine of patrol was ended by a bad attack of sciatica. 'After being lifted out of my bed by my crew and literally hauled on deck for about a week', he wrote, 'I had to give up and go to hospital'.[11] After sick leave, he ended up in MLs running out of Dunkirk, from whence he volunteered for Operation ZO.

---
* Dean's parliamentary career was not extensive for he stood down at the 1922 election.
† Algernon initially served in the Rifle Brigade in India and is possibly best known as the originator of the tune to the Eton Boating Song.
‡ Which became a preparatory school in 1918.

Geoffrey Drummond VC. *(Author's collection)*

Regrettably, the award of a VCs does not guarantee a good life. Demobilised in 1919, he teamed up with a friend, Hugh Littleton (see above) driving and repairing a small fleet of lorries from a base at Waterloo Station. Initially, business was good, but it didn't last, and the strain told on Drummond. By the late 1920s, he was living off his pension and touring the country in search of work. Eventually, a family friend gave him a clerical job at ICI.

However, if England was not good to him, Drummond's patriotism was demonstrated once more when the second war came. Despite fragile health, he tried to re-enlist in the RNVR. Rejected as too old and unfit, he joined the River Emergency Service on the Thames and subsequently transferred to the Royal Naval Patrol Service as a second hand in July 1940. His old friends Roger Keyes and Ion Hamilton Benn lobbied for him to get a commission in the RNVR, but before any pressure could tell, fate intervened. In spring 1941, while carrying a heavy sack of coal, Drummond's left leg, weakened by the effects of his injuries twenty-three years earlier, gave way and he fell, hitting his head on the deck housing. He suffered bad concussion and died in St Olave's Hospital, Rotherhithe, on 21 April. Geoffrey Drummond, yachtsman, broken in body but not in soul, died for his country.

Rowland Bourke

The third motor launch VC was the exception to the yachtsman rule. He was not a pleasure sailor, lived in Canada, and was the youngest of the three, being twenty-six years old at the time of the raids.

Rowland Richard Louis Bourke was born in Redcliffe Square, London, the son of Isidore McWilliam Bourke, a retired surgeon major of the 72nd (Seaforth) Highlanders, from Curraleigh, County Mayo, and his Italian second wife, Marianna (née Carozzi). Around 1898, at the time of the gold rush in the Klondike, Isidore Bourke joined a flood of emigrants seeking their fortune out west. He went to Dawson, in the Yukon territory of northwest Canada, where he established the city's first hospital. Rowley, as he was generally known, and who had remained in England to be educated by a number of Roman Catholic orders, followed his father to Canada aged eleven, in 1902.

They settled in Dawson, where Isidore established the town's first hospital. But disaster soon struck; one of Rowley's adopted cousins, Cecil, was accidently killed in 1907 by an explosion while clearing tree stumps at their ranch at Crescent Bay, Nelson, British Columbia. Nearly blinded by the blast, Rowley was severely injured and left with permanently damaged eyesight. Such was the impact on the family, they immediately emigrated to New Zealand. Rowley, however, returned and was farming a property at Nine Mile (British Columbia) when war broke out. He tried to enlist in Canada's armed forces but was rejected on account of his eyesight and thick glasses.

To contribute to the war effort, he instead donated a waterfront lot from his land to be raffled off, with proceeds going to a local patriotic fund supporting the families of serving soldiers. But this did not assuage his desire for action. He left Canada for England, paying his own way, and finally convinced the RNVR to sign him up as a sub lieutenant on 7 January 1916.

After courses at Greenwich and Southampton, he was posted to Larne, in the Coast of Ireland Command, where he took command of *ML-341*. But the next year was filled with dull routine, patrols and little excitement. He

Rowland Bourke VC in later life, depicted in 1941. *(Author's collection)*

requested a transfer and in November 1917 joined the Dover Patrol, just before Keyes took command. Due for leave in Canada, he postponed it when Benn told him that 'he was short of officers', and 'very important operations were expected very soon'.[12] When Bourke heard that a secret call for volunteers was in the air, he applied, was rejected on account of his eyesight, and relentlessly badgered his commanding officer until it was agreed that he would command *ML-276* as a stand-by rescue launch in the first Ostend raid, where he won a DSO for the part he played in it.

Following the operations, apart from winning the VC and DSO, he was appointed a Knight of the Legion of Honour by the French government[13], was mentioned in despatches and promoted to lieutenant commander, with seniority dated back to 23 April 1918.

Bourke was another who would come to the colours again in the Second World War. He was instrumental in organising a Fishermen's Reserve to patrol the west coast of Canada. He served as a recruiting officer, and in 1941 returned to the sea, with the Royal Canadian Navy Volunteer Reserve as commander of the armed trawler HMCS *Givenchy*, minesweeper HMCS *Esquimalt*, and the stone frigate, HMCS *Burrard*. Bourke ended his naval career in 1950 in the rank of commander RCN.

Basically shy, Rowley Bourke was a man who would not be deterred by his handicap, 'a modest man [who] disliked too much attention and positively detested having his photograph taken',[14] and another 'gentleman amateur' who made a difference.

* * * **

The amateur sailors had made a big impression. Captain (later Admiral) Alfred F B Carpenter RN VC, who was awarded the Victoria Cross for his actions in command of *Vindictive* in the Zeebrugge raid, noted of the ML sailors:

> the more one considered the dependence upon seamanship, the practical use of technical knowledge, the mental and physical strain, the value of perfect discipline and the initiative called for ... the greater is one's admiration for those fine fellows of whom the majority had seen comparatively little of sea life and had lacked the severity of training which is inseparable from the naval profession.[15]

9

Motor Launch Losses

Twenty-four motor launches were lost during the war (for a summary, see Appendix 5).

Fire

The most common reason for loss was fire, accounting for nine of them. This is perhaps unsurprising, given that they were petrol-engined; later this was changed to a mixture of petrol and kerosene, but it was nonetheless still highly inflammable. In the crowded engine compartments, the slightest spill of fuel on a hot engine, or a spark in an atmosphere rich in petrol vapour, might trigger an explosion. And wooden ships burn well.

Indeed, 1916 saw three such loses. *ML-19* was destroyed by fire while lying at Shotley, across the water from Harwich, on 31 January. *ML-40* suffered the same fate at Suez on 18 May. And *ML-49*, newly arrived at Taranto, having been shipped strapped to the deck of a collier, was destined for the Dardanelles. But on 10 September, when she went alongside the Commercial Railway Jetty to take on fuel, there was a large explosion which destroyed the launch completely.

Taranto was the scene of another burned out motor launch in 1917. *ML-534* had arrived at the port on 31 March, as part of a deck cargo of four launches on the transport *Belleview*. She was intended to operate in the Aegean, but whilst fitting out on 13 April there was an explosion and fierce fire which not only destroyed the little vessel, but also took the life of her commander, Lieutenant Samuel George Hill RNVR, and injured two more officers and four ratings. Hill, from Blessington, County Wicklow, had originally joined the RNMBR in October 1915, just as it was winding up.

And a week later in Poole harbour there was another engine-room explosion, this time *ML-431*, while lying alongside the jetty on 22 April. Sub Lieutenant Charles Nash RNVR was trapped below in the wreckage and would surely have died had not two men from another ML, Chief Motor Mechanic Ernest Pooley and Deckhand Herbert Powley, boarded the burning craft, found Nash and carried him away, just before *431*'s aft petrol tanks detonated. An account in the *London Gazette* described the scene:

the flames were every instant drawing nearer to the spot where Sub Lieutenant Nash lay buried, and it was clear that there was imminent danger of the after petrol tanks exploding at any moment. Regardless of the fact that this would mean certain death to them, Powley and Pooley jumped on board the vessel and succeeded in extricating Sub Lieutenant Nash from beneath the wreckage and carrying him to the jetty. As they were leaving the boat the whole of the after part burst into flames, and, in all probability, had they been delayed for another thirty seconds all three would have perished. Deckhand Powley, who led the way on board the burning motor launch, had subsequently to be sent to hospital suffering from the effects of fumes.[1]

Both Pooley, a New Zealander,* and Powley were awarded the Albert Medal for Saving Life at Sea for their troubles.

ML-52 was attached to the submarine depot at Fort Blockhouse as tender to submarines on exercise. She caught fire while moored in Sandown Bay on 29 November and was completely destroyed. And even when under refit, MLs were vulnerable to fire. *ML-55* burnt out on 28 January 1918 whilst being refitted in the Sittingbourne yard of Messrs Wills and Packham.†

ML-356 was part of the ML contingent assembled for Operation ZO. On 12 April 1918 the engine room of the launch exploded at Dover, after a collision with another vessel, and the forward petrol tanks burst into flames. Several of the ML's crew were blown overboard by the explosion, including her commander, Lieutenant Frederick Martin RNVR‡, and the remainder were driven aft by the fire. From there they were taken off in a skiff. Flames began to issue from the cabin and burning petrol spread on the surface of the harbour; it was clear that the petrol tanks and the depth charges on board *356* could explode at any moment, and destroy the surrounding vessels.

Lieutenant Keith Robin Hoare, already met in Chapter 7, along with Sub Lieutenant Arthur Bagot§, realising the threat, jumped into a dinghy and rowed out towards the crippled vessel. When they gained the blazing boat, the pair

---

* Pooley had been born in Auckland in 1883 and was one of eight children. After the war he married and lived in the USA and Canada before his death at the early age of forty-seven.
† Wills and Packham were brick makers, based at Crown Quay, Sittingbourne, who owned a fleet of barges, some of which they built themselves. During the First World War they also built torpedo boats and hulls for flying boats.
‡ Martin, from Southend-on-Sea, had joined the RNVR in the motor drifter Benaigen, but had applied for a shore posting – which was refused – in August 1916. Instead, he was sent to *Hermione* for a course in motor launches. After the incident of 12 April, he went before a medical board and was not passed fit until the war was over, whereupon he was demobilised on 23 December 1918 (ADM 337/121/355, TNA).
§ Bagot, Australian-born but living in Canada, joined the RNVR in 1916. He was a great-grandson of Admiral Edward Hawker and a first cousin of Lanoe Hawker, flying ace and posthumous Victoria Cross recipient.

removed the depth charges in spite of the flames. They prevented an explosion and damage to the other craft in the vicinity together with potential loss of life.

Both men were advanced in rank for their bravery, and Hoare and Bagot were awarded the Albert Medal. Gazetted on 20 August 1918, the citation noted that 'the King has been graciously pleased to approve of the award of the Albert Medal for Gallantry in Saving Life at Sea to Lieutenant Commander Keith Robin Hoare, DSO, DSC, RNVR, and Lieutenant Arthur Gerald Bagot, DSC, RNVR'.

Another motor launch lost to fire was *ML-64*. And it resulted in a further award of an Albert Medal too. On 10 June *64* was lying in Granton harbour, part of Commodore James Startin's command, when she exploded and caught fire. A retired admiral, Startin was a 'character', and in his earlier days had been noted as a fearless horseman, gymnast and athlete. As a vice admiral he had been placed on the Retired List on 14 September 1914, aged sixty, but was reactivated into the RNR four days later. Jellicoe described him as 'the life and soul of the patrols and minesweepers working from Granton, frequently at sea with the decoy ships fitted out there'.[2]

ML-64 was immediately enveloped in flame, and Startin himself set out in *ML-324* to direct the firefighting operation. Arriving at the stricken vessel, Startin saw that the engine room was burning fiercely and was informed that the engineer was trapped below. The sixty-four-year-old warrior didn't hesitate for a moment. He jumped down the launch's hatch and succeeded in recovering the trapped man unaided, despite the fact that the bulkhead between the engine room and the forward tanks had been blown down by the force of the explosion, and that the fire was blazing at the sides and on top of the forward tanks, which were thus liable to burst at any moment. 'The action of Commodore Startin in entering the engine-room before the fire was subdued showed the utmost possible gallantry and disregard of personal safety'.[3] Despite Commodore Startin's bravery, the crewman, twenty-five-year-old Chief Motor Mechanic Herbert Mann RNVR, died of his injuries. On 20 August the King awarded Startin the Albert Medal for Gallantry in Saving Life at Sea in recognition of his efforts. James Startin's son, Robert, had already been awarded the same decoration in 1916, making them the only father and son duo to have been so recognised.

Wrecks

MLs were somewhat flimsy craft, and very skittish in even the lightest of seas. In bad weather they could be a real handful, so it is a little surprising that only three motor launches were wrecked during the war.

ML-197 was part of the Coast of Ireland Command based at Queenstown. She was commanded by Canterbury-born, thirty-seven-year-old Lieutenant Alan Leonard Dorney Skinner, who had originally joined the RNMBR and served in the motor boat *Morandy* (number 146). He had been appointed to *197*, initially as a relief, and confirmed in the position at the end of September 1916. On 31 January 1917 Skinner was on anti-submarine patrol between Carnsore Point and Helwick Head when a strong gale sprang up from the southeast. The launch could make no seaway and was driven ashore near to the Ballincourty Lighthouse on the shores of County Waterford. The crew was able to get off safely, but the ML was a total wreck. Engines, guns and stores were eventually salvaged and the hull left to rot where it had run aground. Skinner was 'cautioned to exercise greater care in future'.[4] He redeemed himself in 1918 when Their Lordships gave their 'appreciation of his gallant behaviour in *ML-304* when on fire on 29 April',[5] and Skinner was mentioned in despatches for 'Services in the Auxiliary Patrol and Minesweeping between the 1st January and 30th June, 1918'.[6]

Gale-force winds accounted for *ML-278* as well. She was driven against Dunkirk Pier while serving in the Dover Patrol on 15 January 1918 and became a total loss. Her commander, Lieutenant Anthony Charles Mackie RNVR, was – like Skinner – able to make amends, winning the DSC in *ML-279* for his actions on 9/10 May off Ostend in Operation ZO, where he was 'of great assistance carrying out smoke screen work under heavy fire for one and a half hours'.[7] In his official despatch, Keyes noted that 'he pluckily carried on his smoke screen work under fire for one and a half hours after breaking the starboard shaft, retiring with the rest of the flotilla, when operations were completed, under one engine'.[8]

The final wrecked motor launch was also the most tragic. On 29 September 1918 four motor launches were caught in a bad storm near St Ives Bay, to which they retreated for shelter. However, the wind continued to increase, shifting to the northeast at 1930 and reaching hurricane force. The MLs found themselves being driven towards the shore and decided to head for the better shelter of Mounts Bay. Two boats managed to get going into deeper water; two had engine problems. The local lifeboat put out to help them, but one launch managed to right its issues. The other, *ML-247*, had suffered engine failure and could not restart them. Her commander was an experienced yachtsman, twenty-nine-year-old Lieutenant Geoffrey Stephen Allfree RNVR, painter and official war artist, already noted in Chapter 4. Battered by the winds and unable to get any steerage way on, Allfree and his vessel were driven towards the rocks at Clodgy Point, crashed onto the 'Oar Rock'* and blew up – either from the detonation of the depth charges or from accumulated petrol vapour.

---

* The author has been unable to find a feature in the St Ives area with that name. Possibly, the official record has transliterated Hor Point, west of Clodgy Point.

Lifting an ML: an ML being hoisted into the water, painted by Lieutenant Geoffrey Stephen Allfree RNVR. Initially he had trained as a mariner, but became a professional artist. When war broke out, he volunteered and was commissioned as a sub lieutenant in the RNVR in October 1914. Allfree died in September 1918 when his command, *ML-247*, grounded in a gale and blew up. *(Author's collection)*

Despite the lifeboat launch, there was no salvation for *247*. Geoffrey Allfree and seven of his eight crew died; the lone survivor (a seaman named Patrick Young) was washed ashore and resuscitated by people watching from the beach. Allfree left his wife Mary pregnant with their second child. She never remarried. A brass plaque in the church of St Nicholas, in the village of St Nicholas-at-Wade, records Mary's loss: 'In loving memory of/ Geoffrey Stephen Allfree/ Lieutenant RNVR/ drowned on active service/ September 29th 1918 aged 29/ RIP'.

Misadventure

A month earlier, *ML-403* had also blown up, but in different circumstances. In August 1918 a torpedo was discovered floating in Runswick Bay, five miles

A Motor Launch on a Dock Wall, also by Allfree, shows it sitting mounted on a cradle which is supported by struts on the dockside. *(Author's collection)*

north of Whitby. It was surmised that it was German, and Lieutenant Commander Victor Bowden-Smith RN of the submarine depot ship *Lucia* was sent to investigate. He had been briefly attached to HMS *Vernon*, the RN's mine and torpedo school, before service in the Dardanelles in *Euryalus*. Bowden-Smith took a dinghy out to view the find and decided it could be salvaged intact. In the afternoon of the 22nd *ML-403* was despatched to assist.

Watched by crowds on the beach, and under Bowden-Smith's orders, she manoeuvred to pick up the torpedo and it was lifted out of the water with slings. Bowden-Smith now resolved that he would remove the firing pistol, and in so doing detonated the weapon. This was followed by the sympathetic explosion of four depth charges on deck, destroying the ML and killing ten men, including Bowden-Smith and the launch's commander, Lieutenant Arthur Whiting RNVR, pre-war an engineer in London and a keen yachtsman and motorist; Whiting's second in command, Belfast-born Sub Lieutenant Norman Giles Paton RNVR, another peacetime enthusiast for yachting, also perished, as did twenty-one-year-old Chief Motor Mechanic Archibald Allen RNVR, from Edinburgh. There was only one survivor.* The explosion smashed windows of houses in Runswick and some roofs were damaged, while the stern of the vessel was blown about 110yds onto the beach.

Bowden-Smith, the son of a Hampshire clergyman, is remembered at St Nicholas Church, Brockenhurst, his father's living, where a plaque on the east wall of the north aisle reads:

> In Piam Memoriam/ Lieut Commander/ Victor James Bowden-Smith RN/ HMS *Lucia* 10 Submarine Flotilla/ who was killed in the great war by an accidental/ explosion, whilst engaged in the act of recovering/ a German torpedo, which was adrift in the/ North Sea near Runswick, August 22nd 1918/ aged 31/ Mors Janua Vitae.†

Mines were inherently dangerous to all types of vessels, but especially the lightly built motor launches. Despite this, and the fact that they were sometimes used for minesweeping, only one ML was sunk by a mine. On 20 October 1918 the monitor *M-21*, in company with *M-27*, was ordered to Ostend. In the evening, as she approached West Pier, there was a sudden explosion which wrecked the fore part of the ship. She had hit a mine and sank some four hours later. The following day, a flotilla of motor launches was sent to search for the minefield. The method chosen, inherently dangerous in itself, was to form a line abreast and slowly sail towards the shore with a rifleman in the bows to shoot at and sink any mine spotted. *ML-561* saw a floating mine, and her commander, Lieutenant John Eiston Purvis RNVR, took upon himself the responsibility of potting it, sending all the crew to the stern of his vessel and taking the rifle up to the bows. As he did so, there was a loud explosion, which blew the front off the launch and killed Purvis; *ML-561* had hit another, unobserved, mine. Other launches came to her assistance and tried to tow the vessel to the large monitor *Terror*, but the ML foundered and sank.

Thirty-year-old Purvis, born in Alnwick, had previously commanded *ML-54*, spent six months on 'special service' (which often meant Q-ships), and had taken command of *ML-562* on 30 January 1918.[9] His selflessness

---

* The coxswain survived. He had been feeling unwell for several days and was laid down in the forecastle at the time of the explosion. Rescued, he was taken to Middlesbrough hospital where he was detained for several weeks.
† Mors Janua Vitae translates as 'Death, the Gate to Life'.

and sense of honour and responsibility had cost him his life, with less than a month of the war remaining.

As for the remainder, MLs *254*, *110* and *424* were sunk during Operation ZO and have been noted in Chapter 7. *ML-474* ran aground near Chios, was abandoned and then destroyed by Turkish shore-based shellfire. And five MLs were lost in two separate sinkings of the cargo vessel carrying them. On 14 September 1916 ss *Inverbervie* was torpedoed by the Austrian *U-4* off Cape Rizzuto, on passage for Taranto with *230*, *253* and *255* aboard. Six men were killed in the attack and a fourth ML was floated free as the cargo ship went down. And on 8 June 1917 ss *Hunstrick* was sunk by a torpedo from *U-39* off Cape Spartel, Algiers, with the loss of fifteen men, and *540* and *541*. They had been bound for Salonika.

For such fragile vessels, built in such quantity, the losses seem less than one might expect. Perhaps this is a tribute to their unexpected durability and to the skill of the gentlemen amateurs who sailed them.

Another motor launch painted by Allfree, travelling at speed to engage a U-boat.
(Author's collection)

10

The Sea Skimmers

The story of the British 'Petrol Navy' does not end with the motor launches. For there were also the fast and sleek Coastal Motor Boats (CMBs), colloquially known as the 'sea skimmers'.

By mid 1915, the North Sea had become choked with mines. Extensive fields protected the German harbours around Wilhelmshaven and the Schillig Roads. British fields added to them in an attempt to prevent U-boat and minelayer egress. German and British minefields ran all the way down Britain's east coast with a narrow 'War Channel' allowing for access to ports and north to south sailings. Navigation was increasingly difficult and offensive thrusts against the German bases fraught with danger.

It was against this background that, in the summer of 1915, three officers of the Harwich Force, Lieutenants Geoffrey Hampden, William Bremner and John Anson,[1] approached the commander of the Harwich Force, Commodore (T) Reginald Tyrwhitt, with an idea for a new kind of offensive vessel, specifically intended to attack the German fleet in its harbours. This was the genesis of the coastal motor boat.

The proposed boats operated on the hydroplane principle: the concept developed by the three officers was that a very fast, shallow-draught vessel would be ideal for attacking German ships in their harbours. It would be able to pass over the defensive minefields without triggering mines, and its high speed would allow rapid strike and escape. Tyrwhitt 'supported the scheme very strongly',[2] as he had long wanted to take

Lieutenant William Bremner, one of the three 'inventors' of the coastal motor boat.
(Photograph by permission of David Bremner)

the attack directly to the German fleet. But the Admiralty was unimpressed; it 'was sceptical as to the design, raising doubts as to stability, trim, etc'.[3]*

Nonetheless, the concept was strongly backed by the navy's torpedo and mining school, HMS *Vernon*. They endorsed the original request for thirty-two such craft to be ordered, 'sufficient to make a thorough job of the attack'.[4] But in January 1916 the Admiralty grudgingly gave its consent to the acquisition of just twelve.

The Thornycroft company was approached to build them as '[they] are the exponents of that particular type of hull, and so the CMBs were ordered from that firm and were constructed on their patent *Miranda* principle'.[5] *Miranda IV* (1910) was the culmination of a series of experimental boats built by Thornycroft to explore hydrofoil or stepped hull designs. She was a 29ft-long, single-step hydroplane, capable of 35.5 knots. By the fitment of an angle or chine piece on the bow, such that the bow wave could not rise up but was thrown down laterally, the hull was greatly improved over previous models. *Miranda IV*, which became a successful racing boat, had this angle in the bow with concave sections below it which became flatter and recurved as they got to the step. The after body was slightly pinched in and hollow on the keel line, so that the water, having left the step, ran clear of the boat until shortly before it reached the transom. Thornycroft also designed a unique spiral propeller, which enabled the CMBs 'to jump over booms and wires without wrecking the propellers ... despite the strange shape very little speed was lost'.[6]

For the planned attack on the Schillig Roads they were to be carried across the North Sea at the light cruisers' davits, which put a limit on their size and weight, and they were built accordingly. They were 40ft in length, and weighed about 4 tons fully loaded.

The CMBs were of monocoque construction utilising Oregon pine stringers and American elm frames, with a 'skin' of Honduran mahogany backed by oil-soaked calico, or cork, soaked in paraffin wax, which 'fed' oil to the wood over time to prevent it drying out. The hulls had to be very elastic, so that they could give and take the severe strain on them by bumping over the water at speed. For instance, 'in the bows where the water just meets the hull, the hull worked in and out some three or four inches'.[7]

---

* The irascible retired Admiral Sir Percy Scott claimed in his autobiography that he had put the idea of the hydroplane boat to the Admiralty in 1915. 'We were very short of fast surface boats, the submarine's greatest enemy. In connection with this shortage rather a peculiar thing happened. On the 30th June, 1914, ... one of the guests at a dinner party asked what was the antidote for submarine. ... I mentioned that very fast surface boats carrying a gun would be useful. Exactly one year after this, on the 30th June, 1915, this gentleman brought me a good design of a very fast (40 knots) hydroplane motor boat, 60 feet long. I took the design to the Admiralty, and they promptly turned it down.' (Scott, *50 Years in the Royal Navy*, p288).

Power came initially from 250 brake horsepower V12 aircraft engines made by Sunbeam and Napier and later used engines from Green's, Fiat and of Thornycroft's own manufacture. This made them very fast (they could hit 40 knots and average 33–35) and able to skim over the top of minefields by aquaplaning. They were beautiful to look at. One naval officer wrote: 'I do not know who invented the CMB but this little vessel was a masterpiece of ingenuity, so much so that I wept with envy when I saw the first one go over from Dover to Dunkirk'.[8] However, CMBs were not good sea boats and could only really cope with sea state two.

They were armed with a single 18in Mark VIII torpedo, chosen on account of its heavy warhead charge and also because of its good depth-taking qualities. These were fired over the stern of the craft, tail first. It was carried in a cradle in a centreline trough and was launched by a bell-head ram which was impelled by a cordite charge exploded in a steel bottle; 1,500 grains of cordite were used for this charge, giving a pressure in the explosion bottle of 4 tons, but this reduced to 1,000lbs on reaching the ram. The torpedo firing lever was mounted to the right hand of the commanding officer. After firing the weapon, the CMB skipper then had to make a sharp turn away to avoid his own torpedo. Lewis guns on portable swivel mountings were also installed in the cockpit. Later modifications meant that the torpedo could be replaced by a couple of depth charges, rolled off the stern down the torpedo trough, and even a Stokes mortar* for close inshore bombardment. To prevent the torpedo-launching rails icing up in winter, the exhaust could be directed to warm them.

The usual crew of the 40ft boats was three to four men, one of whom was a mechanic to tend to the engines. They were 'young officers who could be spared from the RN, plus a sprinkling of selected RNVR and RNR officers … [and] artificers specially trained in motor engines'.[9] In many respects, the CMB men regarded themselves as the naval equivalent of the aviators, fast moving, in fragile craft, young men risking life and limb with new technology. This resemblance even extended to their garb, for as protection against the icy and blinding spray that the CMBs threw up, leather helmets and goggles were often worn. They were knights of the seas, mounted on their motorised destriers.

It was initially decided to base the CMBs away from Harwich and so the South Eastern and Chatham Railway Company's Queenborough pier was commandeered as their headquarters, where the boats could be hoisted out of the water by electric cranes and placed on trucks. Subsequently, a large base with workshops was set up at Dover and some CMBs were stationed at Dunkirk.

---

* A 3in trench mortar with a smooth bore, muzzle-loading and designed for high angles of fire.

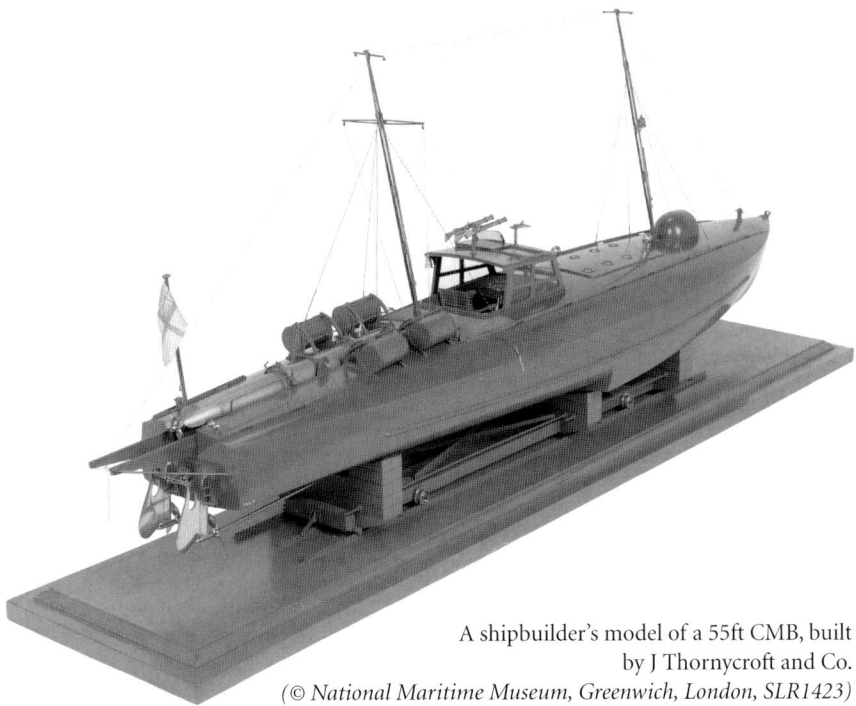

A shipbuilder's model of a 55ft CMB, built by J Thornycroft and Co.
(© *National Maritime Museum, Greenwich, London, SLR1423*)

Eventually, the Harwich Force, having 'invented' the coastal motor boats, lost them to the Dover Patrol command. But in March 1918 Harwich finally got the CMBs back and a base was established at Osea Island, on the River Blackwater, under the command of Captain Wilfred Frankland 'Froggie' French. French had 'both personality and enthusiasm in abundance, a first-class brain and a smile worth a guinea a minute'.[10] Here the boats were maintained and fitted out and some two thousand men, mechanics, sailors, officers and ratings were billeted in prefabricated huts. 'The idea was that this should eventually become the permanent peace base and so the most complete workshops of every description were erected'.[11]

As it became apparent that the concept of a fast sea-skimming vessel had utility, a larger version was designed, 55ft long and able to carry two torpedoes. Three to five men crewed the craft, which was also equipped with four machine guns. Hulls were constructed of double or even triple skins of mahogany, with mainly Thornycroft*, but sometimes Green's or Sunbeam engines. These vessels could attain 40 knots and were propelled by two

---

* The most widely used power unit was the Thornycroft V12 petrol motor of 375hp, two 6-cylinder cast-iron blocks made in one piece.

engines of 375 horsepower each, driving two propeller shafts. The power plants were installed lengthways; the forward starboard engine had a reversing gear, the port engine further aft had a hand-operated spring clutch. Displacement was 11–12.5 tons.

These craft were intended to operate as anti-submarine vessels as well as for attacks on surface targets. An American officer from the USN vessels at Portsmouth was given a ride in a 55ft boat on night patrol: '34 to 36 knots were claimed for them,' he wrote later, 'but when bucking a little chop they seemed to be making 60mph. They surely did get over the water'.[12]

And in early 1918 twelve 72ft-long CMBs were ordered. They were specifically designed to carry the new magnetic M-sinker mines, seven in number, or four depth charges or six torpedoes. And with regard to these larger craft, Jacky Fisher, as he often did, had got there first. Writing to Lord Esher in 1912, he imagined a revolutionary mother-ship with:

> ten motor boats carried on board in an armoured pit in the middle of her, where the funnels and the boilers used to be. Two of these motor boats are over sixty feet long and go 45 knots! And carry 21in torpedoes that go five miles! Imagine these let loose in a sea fight.[13]

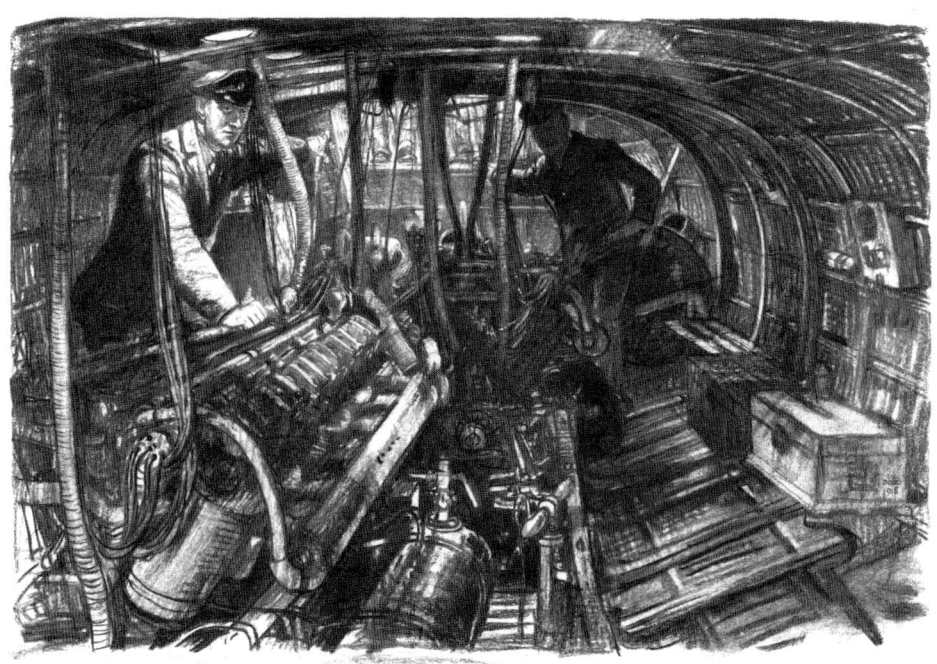

The confined engine space of *CMB-68B* in a drawing by Francis Dodd.
(Author's collection)

Thirty-nine 40ft boats were constructed and used in action. Two were built but not added to the Royal Navy, and sixteen were ordered and then cancelled. Seventy-two 55ft vessels were completed. And five 72-footers were delivered, with a further seven cancelled. Of those built, one was sold to Arthur Ernest Guinness, another Guinness scion with an interest in fast motor boats and faster cars, and three of the five even saw action in, and survived, the Second World War.[14]

CMBs in action
At Dover
In April 1917 CMBs provided a welcome success for the Dover Patrol. In a planned operation, Vice Admiral Reginald Bacon, commanding at Dover, ordered Zeebrugge to be heavily bombed by the Royal Naval Air Service (RNAS) late on the 7th. His intention was to drive German warships in the harbour out to sea where they could be more easily attacked. As he had expected, the Kaiserliche Marine vessels in harbour stood out to sea to avoid the bombing and anchored up for the night. Now came the CMBs.

At 0115 on the 8th Lieutenant Walter Napier Thomason Beckett* in *CMB-4* led a group of five coastal motor boats of the 3rd CMB division from Dunkirk into the harbour roads and the Wielingen channel and attacked the resting ships, launching their single torpedoes as they turned away. The German destroyer SMS *G-88* (1915) – armed with three 10.4cm (4.1in) guns, six torpedo tubes and carrying twenty-four mines – was hit amidships and sank, killing eighteen sailors, and another vessel was seriously damaged. Beckett and his force then retired over the German minefield. His own boat filled up with smoke and gas due to an exhaust problem and another boat was heavily shelled by a German destroyer. But all made it back to Dunkirk safely and there were no British losses. Beckett received the DSC for his planning and execution of the mission.[15]

But the limitations of the craft when pitted against a more alert enemy were exposed two months later. On 19 June a Dunkirk-based Short 184 seaplane, with two escorting Sopwith Baby seaplanes, took off to carry out a reconnaissance of the Belgian coast. Ten miles northeast of Nieuwpoort they were attacked by three German seaplanes. One German and two British planes were shot down, and a French destroyer, together with *CMB-1* and *CMB-9*, sailed to rescue the pilots. But the Germans got there first. Four German torpedo boats of the Flanders Flotilla arrived on the scene. *CMB-1*, under the command of an RNR lieutenant, took a direct hit and blew up

---

* A large, strong man, Beckett was another of the navy's 'characters', and was known to most people as 'Joe' Beckett, after a famous British boxer of the same period. Walter Beckett was also himself a capable amateur boxer, holding the title of Royal Navy heavyweight boxing champion for some time.

Two views of a restored CMB on the River Thames, with a close-up view of the torpedo launching trough. This boat was originally *CMB-9*. *(Photographs: Dr V A Michell)*

off Ostend. All the crew survived to become POWs, but two aircrew died. As a consequence of this particular action, air–sea rescue missions were abandoned when Allied aircraft crashed too close to the enemy coast, a decision perhaps not designed to increase the desire of pilots to fly such missions.

However, the navy did not desert the aviators altogether. Another such air–sea rescue was during a minelaying operation in the southern North Sea over the night of 25/26 September. A number of ships were out to support the minelayers, including the seaplane carrier *Vindex*. Two of her planes failed to return and on the afternoon of the 27th CMBs *8* and *13* were despatched to look for them. *CMB-8*'s steering gear broke down at 1800 and

CMB-13 took her in tow, but now came under fire from the shore. To add to their problems, they spotted ships' smoke, which proved to be from German torpedo boats. Then at 1640 *CMB-13* had engine problems and came to a halt causing number *8* to overrun the tow, which consequently became tangled in her propellers and killed off her engines. The crew were taken off, a demolition charge exploded, and she sank off the Belgian coast. *CMB-13* returned safely with both crews and with no lives lost. Meanwhile, the search had been abandoned.

Operation ZO

The CMBs, like the MLs, played a pivotal and dangerous role at Zeebrugge and Ostend. Primarily used for smoke-laying, they also filled a number of other key functions. At Zeebrugge, the Dover-based boats were under the command of twenty-five-year-old Lieutenant Arthur Eric Pole Welman RN.

He led his craft first in the laying of smokescreens, and then in undertaking attacks against enemy vessels, the seaplane shed and the Mole itself. During these assaults, Sub Lieutenant Cedric R L Outhwaite RNVR in *CMB-5* fired a torpedo at an enemy destroyer, which he observed to hit below her forward searchlight, putting out the light and stilling her gunfire. Only nineteen years of age, Outhwaite was the son of the radical Liberal Party politician, leading advocate of land reform and MP for Hanley, Robert Leonard Outhwaite.

In *CMB-7*, Sub Lieutenant Leslie Robert Blake RNR claimed a torpedo hit on a destroyer alongside the Mole, striking it below the forebridge. His boat was badly damaged in the attack, but he was able to nurse it back to harbour. And *CMB-32A* fired at the steamship *Brussels*; an explosion followed but the result was hidden by smoke.

Lieutenant Edward Eliot Hill in *CMB-35A* had set off from Dover with the others, but fouled his propeller when eighteen miles into the outward voyage. Undeterred, Hill picked up a tow from a drifter and arrived back at Dover at 2000. His boat was immediately hoisted out of the water and the propeller cleared, but as there was other damage he was not afloat again until 2140. Hill then hared away for the Belgian coast and was off Zeebrugge – about seventy miles – by 2350, taking up his smoke patrol at once, and continuing it for an hour, in the course of which he came under rather heavy fire from a battery at Blankenberge. A tactic of the CMBs was to drop a smoke float, approach the shore to draw fire, and then escape at speed into the smoke again, thus deflecting enemy attention from the main raiders.

At the first raid on Ostend, *CMB-10* under Sub Lieutenant Peter Booth Clarke RNR circled the abandoned blockship *Sirius*, searching for the ship's engineer who was thought to be still on board, in the course of which she came under heavy fire. And Sub Lieutenant Frank A W Ramsey in *CMB-19* dashed inshore to lay calcium flare buoys under a deluge of machine-gun fire.

At the second attack on Ostend, the smokescreen was so thick that *Vindictive* could not see the harbour and passed the entrance twice trying to locate it. It was not until *CMB-23* laid a million-candlepower flare that she could make out her goal. The CMB's commander was twenty-four-year-old Lieutenant the Honourable Cecil Edward Robert Spencer RN, son of Charles Robert Spencer, 6th Earl Spencer.*

Lieutenant William Bremner, one of the originators of the CMB, was at Second Ostend. When carrying out his smokescreening to put off the enemy shore batteries, he stumbled on a German torpedo boat, which switched on her searchlight and opened fire. Bremner had only Lewis guns, but returned

---

* And hence great-uncle to Diana, Princess of Wales, although the Hon Cecil died in a riding accident in 1928.

fire anyway and peppered the torpedo boat to such good effect that he drove her away from the harbour entrance and prevented her interfering with the blocking operation.

And Lieutenant Cuthbert F B Bowlby in *CMB-26* had escorted *Vindictive* close up to the entrance, then ran ahead and fired a torpedo at one of the piers. This proved counterproductive, for the shallow water and short range meant that the explosion shook the boat so severely as to damage the engines and open the seams. The CMB began to sink, but Bowlby got the leak stopped, restarted the engines, and brought his craft out of the fire zone, where he was taken in tow by the destroyer HMS *Broke*.

Roger Keyes was impressed by the courage and determination of the young CMB commanders, regular and reservist alike. 'The zest of most of the young officers in the coastal motor boats, like that of those in the motor launches, compels one's admiration,' he wrote in his subsequent despatch.[16] Keyes also ensured that they received some recognition for their efforts. Welman was awarded the DSO for Zeebrugge and then a bar to it at Second Ostend.[17] 'During the action the units of the coastal motor-boat flotilla under his command were handled in a masterly manner,' his medal citation read, 'rendering the greatest service in screening and rescue work. He, himself, was in a coastal motor boat, and was always in the most exposed positions across the harbour entrance'.[18] The French also gave him the Croix de Guerre. Outhwaite was awarded the DSC: 'Sub Lieutenant Cedric Robert Leonard Outhwaite RNVR in command of a coastal motor boat. Under considerable gunfire from shore defences, torpedoed an enemy destroyer proceeding eastward from Zeebrugge harbour.'[19]

Spencer had already earned the DSC[20] and was granted a bar to it for Ostend. Clarke also received a DSC ('he handled his boat with marked ability').[21] Blake too won the DSC. Hill was mentioned in despatches, as were many others. The Sea Skimmers had earned their corn.

At Harwich

Tactical doctrine for CMBs at the time, according to Lieutenant William Bremner, stated that:

> their proper function is to attack a definite known objective or to perform a set piece of work. They are, as well, quite suited to an offensive patrol by night in enemy waters, and in close vicinity to enemy ports. They should not be used for this work in daylight, as they are very vulnerable to machine gun attack from the air.[22]

But owing to the heavy mining in the Bight, and the prohibition by the

Admiralty of Tyrwhitt's Harwich-based forces going to within a hundred miles of it, for fear of mines, using CMBs against the German ships near their harbours was impossible.

Commodore Tyrwhitt, famously offensively minded, decided that instead they could be used against German minesweepers while they attempted to cut a passage through the British minefields off Heligoland. These fields had been laid originally to prevent U-boat egress and were now maintained, mainly by Harwich Force minelaying submarines, to delay the exit of the High Seas Fleet into the North Sea. By now the obstruction had worked back a long way from Wilhelmshaven as a result of repeated minelaying by British vessels. They had laid 15,686 mines in the North Sea in 1917, as opposed to 1,679 the year before,[23] which combined with mines laid by German forces to block the approach of Royal Navy's minelayers and other light craft. German minesweepers had to come some 150 miles out into the North Sea before they could start sweeping.

The plan called for the 40ft skimmers to be transported out to the minefield border on the davits of the light cruisers with the intention of finding the sweepers at the break of dawn and be back with the cruisers soon after daylight. They carried one torpedo and one or two Lewis guns apiece. Seaplanes were to operate in concert with the motor boats to provide air cover and to help them find their way back to the waiting 'mother-ships'.

The first such operation was conducted on 29 June 1918. The Harwich Force cruisers, each carrying two CMBs, dropped them just outside the British minefields around the Heligoland Bight. The problem was the weather conditions. Three flying boats had been towed out on lighters by the Harwich destroyers but only one, a Felixstowe F2A, succeeded in getting airborne. One of the others was so badly damaged while attempting to take off that it sank, and the third had to abandon its attempt to fly, as in the process it had come to grief. However, the single F2A did complete a reconnaissance flight before it suffered engine failure and had to ditch. The crew was rescued by a Dutch trawler and later transferred to a Harwich destroyer. No minesweepers were found.

Several more such operations were essayed, all bedevilled by seaplane problems and no minesweepers were encountered. Consequently, it was suggested, by the CMB crews themselves, that a daylight attempt might bear more fruit. On 10 August the operation began. The light cruisers *Curacoa*, *Coventry*, *Concord* and *Danae* set sail from Harwich at 2100, together with thirteen destroyers. Of these, *Retriever*, *Thisbe* and *Teazer* each towed a lighter with a seaplane on it, while *Redoubt* and *Starfish* jointly took out lighter H-5, fitted with a wooden take-off platform carrying a Sopwith Camel.

At 0600 on the 11th the flotilla had reached a point about twenty five miles northwest of Vlieland (one of the West Frisian Islands) and the skimmers were dropped to start a run which was to take them past Ameland (another West Frisian Island). Once again, the seaplanes could not get off, this time because it was too calm – there was not a breath of wind. The CMBs therefore headed eastward with no aerial escort. Tyrwhitt did not recall the boats, as he had arranged for a flight of aircraft from Yarmouth to rendezvous with him. These arrived at 0700, but the admiral's frantic signals to them did not get through and they acted independently all morning.

Meanwhile, the six coastal motor boats had reached Terschelling and were moving at high speed close to the shore. They were cruising in pairs arranged in a rough echelon, for the water through which the boats moved was so churned by the enormous bow wave that no boat could follow in another's wake. As they swept past the low sand dunes of Terschelling in bright, clear sunlight, six aeroplanes were sighted: three were ahead and three astern.

The CMB flotilla was under Lieutenant Commander Anthony Lancelot Henry Dean Coke RN. He at first thought the aircraft were his lost escort, but then he spotted the large black crosses under their wings. Coke ordered the flotilla to close up so as to concentrate the fire of their Lewis guns; the aeroplanes, by now eight in number, opened fire with their machine guns. Undismayed, Coke decided to continue with his reconnaissance.

'I was bound to be attacked by other machines whatever I did,'[24] he wrote later, and so a running fight developed, which continued for some thirty minutes. The aeroplanes swept up towards the motor boats from astern, firing through their propellers; when they reached the motor boats they rose sharply, and flew back to a position well in the wake of the flotilla. Given that the CMBs were travelling at well over 30 knots and the German seaplanes at around 70, it was surely the fastest action of the war to date. From time to time the German aeroplanes also dropped bombs, but none scored a hit.

Around 0800 Coke turned westward with Ameland lighthouse abeam. 'Up to now the flotilla had held its own,' states the navy's *Official History*. 'It had suffered no serious damage and one of the enemy's planes had been seen to come down sharply'.[25] But now the Germans had the sun behind them and four land-based fighter planes, each armed with two guns, had joined the fray. These machines, according to Lieutenant Commander Coke, 'caused more trouble and did more damage than the eight that had appeared previously'.[26] During the next quarter of an hour the coastal motor boats suffered badly, and by 0815 they had practically ceased to fire. In some the guns had jammed; in others the ammunition had been exhausted. The

Germans now flew over the boats almost at point blank range. But there was still some devil in the skimmers; with virtually their last rounds *CMB-40* and *CMB-44* peppered one of the German planes so heavily it crashed into the sea.

However, the flotilla was finished. Bullet-ridden, out of ammunition, *CMB-47* on fire, several with engines failing and holed hulls sinking under them, they were out of the fight. The Dutch coast was three or four miles away and *CMB-41* reached the shore, where the Dutch authorities impounded her. Royal Netherlands Navy torpedo boats came out and took the disabled *CMB-44* and *48* in tow and interned them, along with their crews. The other three (*CMB-40, 42* and *47*) were set on fire and abandoned by their crews; not one craft made it back to the supporting force. Nor did they ever sight a British aeroplane.

One of those interned by the Dutch was Cedric Outhwaite, awarded the DSC and mentioned in despatches by Vice Admiral Keyes for his actions in *CMB-5* during the Zeebrugge Raid. The *Abergavenny Chronicle and Monmouth Advertiser* noted that 'Cedric Outhwaite, DSC, RNVR, son of Mr R L Outhwaite MP, is reported safe and unwounded in Holland'. With perhaps a little exaggeration, it went on to state that 'aged only nineteen, he was in command of a coastal motor boat which took part in the action in the Heligoland Bight with a Zeppelin and a squadron of twenty German planes. He was picked up by a Dutch lifeboat'.[27]

Coke was awarded the DSO. The citation noted that:

> Lieutenant Commander Coke, who was Senior Officer of the flotilla, showed great determination, gallantry and courage in continuing his reconnaissance in spite of the presence of the enemy. The Coastal Motor Boats led by Lieutenant Commander Coke fought a very gallant action against superior odds, and continued to do so until all their ammunition was expended or their Lewis guns rendered useless by jambing [sic].[28]

But it was clear that the CMBs were very vulnerable without air cover when so close to the enemy coast, just as Bremner had noted. They were also a hard-lying duty, a fact attested to by Bremner and Thornycroft in a post-war paper to the Institution of Naval Architects. 'They were uncomfortable boats to be in, and only vigorous young men could stand for any length of time the exposure and general hardship'.[29]

Distant control boats
Archibald Montgomery Low was an engineer and inventor who, pre-war,

had invented a device for the transmission of visual images, 'Televista', a precursor to television. When war broke out, the twenty-six-year-old genius joined the RFC and was attached to the Royal Aircraft Factory with a brief to examine the potential for remotely controlled aircraft, a project code named Aerial Target or AT.

After he had created a prototype, General Sir David Henderson, the Director General of the Directorate of Military Aeronautics, ordered that an experimental works be established at Feltham to build an AT with an explosive warhead. Low was appointed head of the operation with the rank of army captain and given thirty hand-picked men, including jewellers, carpenters and aircraftsmen, in order to get a pilotless plane built as quickly as possible.

By 21 March 1917, Low had built one, based on a de Havilland Airco, which was launched from the back of a lorry using compressed air. Low and his team successfully demonstrated their ability to control the craft before engine failure led to its crash landing.

The Admiralty had followed these developments closely. With the imperative of countering Germany's unrestricted U-boat campaign, which was at its most successful around the time of Low's triumphant AT demonstration, it was mooted that Low develop a remote-control system for a small boat. Low was temporarily transferred to the Royal Navy and began a project to determine whether unmanned fast patrol boats armed with torpedoes could be controlled from the air and directed towards enemy targets. They were to be known as Distant Control Boats or DCBs and by mid 1918, Low was ready to begin a full trial.

The boats selected for the DCB trial were 40ft coastal motor boats; they were fast and they were available, had seen considerable service and cost £4,000 less than the newer 55ft craft. Additionally, a single engine was easier to remotely control than two, as in a 55-footer or a motor launch. The CMBs selected were *CMB-3, -9* and *-13*, which became *DCB-3, -1* and *-2* respectively. All were handed over in July 1918 and a process of experimentation began to assess the feasibility of whether boats armed with torpedoes, or packed with explosives, could be controlled remotely from the air and directed towards enemy targets.

Lieutenant Sidney Wright Rayner RNVR had joined the reserve in December 1915 and had been assigned to anti-aircraft duties at Eastchurch. Six months later he was transferred to CMBs and in June 1918 he was placed on HMS *Victory*'s books for special duty.[30] Rayner was to be part of the trials. His task was to take out one of the boats into the Solent where an aircraft overhead would try to link up to the in-boat system and gain control of the vessel. Rayner and his crew were there to take over if anything went wrong.

On at least one occasion, things did go amiss. Rayner was out in *DCB-1* when she suddenly started to take in water. The weight of extra equipment in the craft had caused the timber frames to open up. He went to maximum power to bring the bow out of the water and ran for Portsmouth harbour and a hoist.

Eventually, it was proven that a CMB could be remotely controlled from 16,000ft up and five miles distant. The transmitting and receiving gear could be made to operate for some four hours and moonlight operation had been successfully undertaken. But the war ended before the DCBs could be used in anger. Desultory experimentation continued for a short time but *CMB-13* was deleted from the navy's books in 1920 and *CMB-3* in 1921. *DCB-1/CMB-9* continued until 1935.

* * * * *

The motor boat had come a long way in just fifteen years: from Selwyn Edge and Dorothy Levitt winning the 1903 *Daily Mail* race to a high-speed, 72ft aquaplaning power boat and a self-propelled, remote-controlled bomb. War had proved once again to be the locomotive of change.

11

The American Submarine Chasers

When the European war broke out in 1914, President Woodrow Wilson committed to keep America out of the conflict. He, and many Americans such as his Secretary of State William Jennings Bryan, felt that America should adopt a studied neutrality. Others saw Germany as a considerable danger. Walter Hines Page, US Ambassador to the Court of St James, wrote to Wilson, 'again and again I thank Heaven for the Atlantic Ocean'.[1] And to Wilson's friend and acolyte Colonel Edward House he opined that Germany 'would try to conquer the United States and we should all go back ... to the domination of kings by divine right'.[2]

Wilson won re-election in 1916 on the platform of 'the man who kept us out of the war'. But the rape of Belgium, the savagery of the Western Front, the depredations wrought on neutral shipping, loss of American lives, and shifting public opinion gradually made neutrality untenable. The United States of America finally declared war on Germany on 6 April 1917.* Like Britain, the US Navy was unprepared in terms of numbers of small craft. Immediately, 'the Navy Department ... solicited the co-operation of the yachtsmen of the country'[3] and started to take up motor boats and yachts for naval duty.

As in Britain, there was a thriving yacht and motor boat community in America from which to recruit vessels, many of which were taken into the Naval Coast Defence Reserve. There was also an embryo motor patrol reserve for, as with Britain, there were some motor boat pioneers in the USA who had driven forwards the idea that yachtsmen and motor-powered craft could play a key role at sea should war come. First amongst them was Admiral Austin Melvin Knight, quondam commander of the USN Second District, headquartered at Newport, Rhode Island.

According to the March 1919 edition of *Motor Boating*, to Knight was brought in 1916 'the plan of a nationwide patrol squadron formed of patriotic yachtsmen willing to equip and train themselves to be of

---
* On 2 April 1917 President Woodrow Wilson appeared before a joint session of Congress to request a declaration of war against Germany. On the 4th the US Senate voted in support of war on Germany. The House concurred two days later. The United States later declared war on Germany's ally Austria–Hungary on 7 December.

Laneta, of the Detroit Motor Boat Club and pictured around 1910. She is typical of the leisure boats taken up by several navies for war purposes.
(Library of Congress, LC-D4-40365)

The US Navy took up small pleasure boats for patrol use on her entry to war. Depicted is *Wendy*, acquired by the USN on 1 July 1917 as *SP-448*. She was decommissioned and returned to her owner on 9 December 1918. A sailor is manning her bow gun, a 1pdr. The stern weapon is a Colt machine gun.
(US Naval History and Heritage Command, NH 102519)

The motor cruiser *Lynx II* became *SP-730* and patrolled along the Massachusetts seaboard. In this picture from *The Illustrated War News* of 11 April 1917, her 1pdr gun can be seen mounted immediately ahead of the steering position. *(Author's collection)*

immediate auxiliary use in time of emergency'. This became known as the 'Power Squadron' and Knight eventually enrolled its members into the Second Squadron's patrol resources. They and their motor craft were the US equivalent of the RNMBR. And so was their role, in this case the patrol of America's long eastern littoral.

And so, inter alia, the Detroit Motor Boat Club provided a Bayless-built boat, *Laneta*. *Hippocampus* of New York became a patrol craft, *Wendy* became *SP-448**. *Abalone* was a wooden-hull motor boat constructed in 1913 at Morris Heights, NY, by the New York Launch and Engine Building Co. She was acquired by the Navy on 27 April 1917 under a free lease from Arnold Schlaet of New York City, who had co-founded the Texas Fuel Company, predecessor to Texaco Inc. Commissioned on 10 May 1917, *Abalone* became *SP-208*, attached to the 3rd Naval District local patrol forces and based at New Haven, Connecticut. In her naval guise, *Abalone* could

---

* SP = Section Patrol.

The motor boat *Panama*, seen here in peacetime at a Florida port, was built at Key West, where she also served as *SP-101*, by Luther Finder.
(US Naval History and Heritage Command, NH 42996)

Some larger US Navy motor boats, pleasure cruisers converted to patrol craft shown in Lockwood's Basin, Boston, Massachusetts, c1918. They are (from left to right): motor boat USS *Paloma* (*SP-533*); motor yacht USS *Edithena* (*SP-624*); and twin Speedway-engined motor boat USS *Elsie III* (*SP-708*). *(US Navy History and Heritage Command, NH 45270)*

manage 10 knots, had a complement of eight men and was armed with a 1pdr gun and a single .30-calibre machine gun. She was eventually returned to her owner on Christmas Eve 1918.

Industrialist Nathaniel F Ayer, who had made his fortune in textiles, provided the large motor cruiser *Lynx II*. Built by the Herreshoff Manufacturing Company of Bristol, Rhode Island, she was of 22 tons, 58ft long and could achieve 21 knots. The USN purchased *Lynx II* and she was fitted with a single 1pdr gun and under reservist Chief Boatswain's Mate S O Joyce and his crew of eight, she commissioned on 9 July 1917 and spent the war patrolling the Massachusetts coast from Boston to Provincetown, and escorting arriving and departing merchant ships through the defensive sea area of the Port of Boston. She was sold out of the navy for $6,000 in 1919.

USS *Panama* (*SP-101*) had started life as a civilian motor boat with the Miami and Nassau Passenger Line in 1914. But on 29 April 1917 she joined the US Navy, was fitted with a 3pdr and a machine gun, and was sent to patrol around Key West and occasionally the Caribbean. Just about capable of 9.5 knots and 78ft long, she would have been outclassed by any enemy she could conceivably have stumbled upon.

Even vessels with no cabin were utilised. *Betty Jane 1* was a 36ft-long, open motor boat constructed in 1913 at Bayonne, New Jersey, by Elco. She was acquired by the USN on free lease from a wealthy brewer, Percy Ballantyne of South Montrose, Pennsylvania, on 4 September 1917 and commissioned later that day. USS *Betty Jane 1* joined the 6th Naval District and spent the remainder of the war patrolling the southeastern coast of the United States. She was not returned to her owner until 17 January 1919.

Or consider *Caprice* (1914), a 45ft Elco pleasure launch with a forward steering position, a canvas sunscreen overhead, and described by Elco in an advertisement as 'an ideal home all summer'. She was commissioned as USS *Caprice* (*SP-703*) on 24 August 1917 and returned to her owner on 24 January 1919.

The leisure sailors' clubhouses were also taken up by the navy, such as the Corinthian Yacht Club of New Jersey, which became a USN training centre.

Not everyone put forward their boats with entirely altruistic feelings; one boat owner told a friend: 'the thing to do is lease your yacht to the navy at a dollar a year and ship on it with a bunch of good fellows as crew. Then you sail around New York harbour all day and go ashore every night'.[4]

Using civilian craft in this way was all fine and dandy. But the depredations off the US east coast by *U-53* in October 1916, when she paid a surprise visit to Newport, rang alarm bells in some naval quarters. The

The Corinthian Yacht Club of Cape May, New Jersey, which was requisitioned by the USN as a naval training camp. *(US Naval History and Heritage Command, NH 116394)*

U-boat's captain was able to post a letter to the German embassy, chatted up inquisitive locals, waved goodbye, went to sea, and quickly sank six commercial vessels flying belligerent flags. So too did the ability of the large 'cargo' submarine *Deutschland* (1916) to sail easily from Heligoland to Baltimore, arriving on 10 July 1916. As a nation with two long and exposed coastlines, the US was extremely vulnerable to attack and/or blockade by U-boats and had nowhere near enough sea-capable small vessels to defend the littoral. What was to be done?

The submarine chasers

One of those who was alarmed by the situation was Assistant Secretary of the Navy, Franklin Delano Roosevelt, who had held the post in the Wilson Administration since 1913. Unlike his boss, Secretary of the Navy Josephus Daniels, Roosevelt was a supporter of the Preparedness Movement* and helped establish the United States Navy Reserve Force† before the US joined the fighting.

---

* The Preparedness Movement was a campaign led by former Chief of Staff of the US Army Leonard Wood and ex-President Theodore Roosevelt to strengthen the US armed forces after the outbreak of war in 1914.
† Legislation was finally passed on 3 March 1915 to bring the Navy Reserve Force into being.

Assistant Secretary of the Navy Franklin D Roosevelt, who played a key part in bringing the Naval Reserve Force and the Submarine Chasers into existence.
(Library of Congress, LC-USZ62-93456)

Roosevelt and others recognised that U-boats presented a clear and present danger to the US, and that the means to defend against them was lacking. Moreover, the evidence of sinkings around the coast of Britain and in the Mediterranean demonstrated that the whole Allied supply chain could be severely interrupted by submarine activity. This latter point was emphasised by Rear Admiral William Sims*, who had been despatched to Britain in secret, before the USA had joined the conflict, to liaise with the Admiralty and report on the naval situation obtaining.

---
* Vice admiral from 25 May 1917.

Admiral William Sowden Sims, officer commanding US Navy forces in Europe. *(Author's collection)*

Arriving after war had been declared, on 27 April 1917 Sims sent a message to President Wilson via Ambassador Walter Hines Page which bleakly addressed the problem:

> There is reason for the greatest alarm about the issue of the war caused by the increasing success of the German submarines. I have it from official sources that during the week ending 22nd April, eighty-eight ships of 237,000 tons Allied and neutral were lost. The number of vessels unsuccessfully attacked indicated a great increase in the number of submarines in action.

This means practically a million tons lost every month till the shorter days of autumn come. By that time the sea will be about clear of shipping. Most of the ships are sunk to the westward and southward of Ireland. The British have in that area every available anti-submarine craft, but their force is so insufficient that they hardly discourage the submarines.

The British transport of troops and supplies is already strained to the utmost, and the maintenance of the armies in the field is threatened …

Whatever help the United States may render at any time in the future, or in any theatre of the war, our help is now more seriously needed in this submarine area for the sake of all the Allies than it can ever be needed again, or anywhere else … There is no time to be lost.[5]

What was required, according to a contemporary writer, was 'an immense fleet of small, quickly built, easily manoeuvrable vessels, with power plants that could be shut down instantly in order to use the newly developed listening devices'.[6] Against the passive resistance of Daniels, Roosevelt was driving such a programme forward. And the result was the submarine chaser, generally known as sub chasers or SCs.

Building the sub chasers

At first, the USN considered adopting the Elco design which had already been produced in quantity for the Royal Navy. But the General Board held to the view that the MLs were too small to be effective sea boats and decided to go it alone. The Boston-based yacht and motor boat naval architect Albert Loring Swasey* was contracted to produce a new proposal, for which purpose he was enrolled as a lieutenant commander in the US Naval Reserve Force. The prevailing view was that a sub chaser should be very fast but Swasey disagreed, maintaining that extreme speed was not worth the price in the sacrifice of seaworthiness, cruising range and comfort. His plan was a 110ft-long, 15ft-beam boat, built for a top speed of 17 knots and a cruising range of 1,000 miles at 12 knots. Swasey adopted a bow flare similar to that of a big whaler with its hull cut off at the waterline aft, a type familiar to American east-coast shipbuilders and successful for sea work since ancient times. They were to draw less than 6ft.

---

* Swasey, amongst his many accomplishments, had been Commodore of the Massachusetts Institute of Technology (MIT) Yacht Club in 1897.

A sub chaser under construction at an unknown US shipyard in 1918. Their all-wooden build is clearly seen in this photograph. *(US Naval History and Heritage Command, 165-WW-506A-111)*

Steel was in short supply, for as America geared up for war it was needed for the regular navy and army, so the sub chasers were to be built of wood, primarily yellow pine, Oregon pine and white oak. Steel was only used for the bulkheads and one fore and aft beam. Displacement was 75 tons. The boats were originally intended to be driven by twin 300 horsepower (hp) engines, but a shortage of these engines resulted in the design being changed to use three 220hp petrol engines driving triple screws. The centre power plant could be uncoupled from the propeller to cruise economically on the two outer ones. The engines were manufactured by the Standard Motor Construction Company of Jersey City*, and were the same air-start, reversing units as used in the Royal Navy's motor launches; compressed air was generated by a 20hp auxiliary and stored in three metal tanks under pressure of 250lbs. The auxiliary also generated the electricity for the batteries which drove extractor fans, bilge pumps, radio equipment, a rudimentary heater, etc.

---

* Standard contracted out manufacture for some of the work to Lyons-Atlas Company of Indianapolis.

Building Submarine Chasers, a lithograph by the American print maker and illustrator Joseph Pennell. *(Library of Congress, LC-USZ62-36005)*

Marine engine technology was still in its infancy. The engines were open crankcase with a lubricating oil reservoir, which was filled by hand using a funnel. It took a chief petty officer and three artificers per shift to run the motors, working in a fume-filled environment full of smoke and petrol vapour. Accidental fires were not uncommon.

Working from the forepeak, the layout ran: paint locker and storage, crew head, forecastle which provided sleeping accommodation for twelve men and a mess table, coal stove for generating hot water, then the magazine. Next, amidships, were the listening tubes followed by the wireless room, and officers' sleeping and washing arrangements. These were less than perfect: 'When under way the gas [petrol] fumes come through the bulkhead as readily as they do through the deck ventilators, and it is often a question in the officers' minds whether they should not change their service records from deck to engineering duties'.[7] The engine room was aft of these quarters, then the depth-charge store and finally the engineers' mess and bunks. Under the officers' quarters sat 2,400-gallon capacity tanks of petrol. Up top, the chart house accomodated three engine annunciators, a wireless telephone receiver, dial plotting instrument, a bell to the engine room, general quarters' alarm, and speaking tubes fore and aft as well as to the bridge and crow's nest. It was all very compact.

The navy's Bureau of Construction and Repair was put in charge of the building programme, specifically supervised by Commander Julius A Furer USN. An initial order of 345 boats was placed in 1917 for delivery that same year (eventually 448 vessels would be ordered, of which 441 were constructed); they were built in thirty-seven different yards, including Elco, who produced twenty of the type. The USN did not name the little ships, but each boat was known by a number with an 'SC' prefix.

Rear Admiral Sims thought that the design was a success: 'The small sub chasers exhibited such remarkable sea-keeping qualities; this fact was a pleasant surprise to all sea-going men, particularly to naval officers who had had little experience with that type of craft'.[8] And Commander Francis Tower RNVR (last met in Chapter 4), who encountered the SCs when some joined the Coast of Ireland Command, thought well of them:

> I liked them as able to keep the seas in bad weather and capable of much … good beam, strongly built and with a real good rubbing strake were points which appealed to me. A good gun, and a number of depth charges well-arranged gave an armament not to be despised.[9]

Sailing the sub chasers

The designed complement of the sub chasers was two officers and twenty-two enlisted men*. And, just as with the motor launches in the Royal Navy, the crews were, almost to a man, volunteers; not regular navy men, but college boys and leisure sailors. Rear Admiral Sims recalled that:

> I do not think that the whole lot contained one per cent of graduates of Annapolis or five per cent of experienced sailors … Ignorant of salt water as these men at that time were, they really represented about the finest raw material in the nation for this service. Practically all, officers and men, were civilians; a minority were amateur yachtsmen, but the great mass were American college undergraduates. Boys of Yale, Harvard, Princeton – indeed, of practically every college and university in the land – had dropped their books, left the comforts of

---

* The personnel of a chaser's complement consist of: two commissioned officers, one chief petty officer in charge of the engine room, five engine room artificers, three radio operators, one boatswain's mate, one quartermaster, one coxswain, the listeners (for the hydrophones), one cook, one mess attendant, five seamen (Chambers, *United States Submarine Chasers*, pvi).

SC-2, unknown location or date. *(US Navy History and Heritage Command, NH 43601)*

their fraternity houses, and abandoned their athletic fields, eager for the great adventure against the Hun.[10]

They were inducted into the USNRF (United States Navy Reserve Force) and the commanding officers given the rank of ensign. The American Corinthians had answered their country's call.

One typical example was Ensign George S Dole, who took command of *SC-93*. He was an Olympic gold-medal-winning wrestler at the 1908 London Games, Yale graduate and amateur yachtsman. Or take twenty-six-year-old Alexander Moffat, Harvard graduate class of 1913, who was vice president of the Transport Tractor Company of Long Island City when the USA entered the war. He immediately volunteered into the USNRF and was given command of the 80ft motor yacht *Tamarack*, despite having 'experience only in small sailing yachts in coastwise cruising'.[11] Within weeks he would be appointed CO of *SC-77* and then *SC-143*. Then there was Ensign Ashley D Adams, skipper of *SC-137*, who had rowed for the Yale freshman eight.

Another volunteer was Harold Stirling 'Mike' Vanderbilt, a scion of the famous and fabulously rich Vanderbilt family. The great-grandson of the shipping and railroad tycoon Cornelius Vanderbilt, he was born to great wealth and privilege; as a child he was raised in Vanderbilt mansions, travelled frequently to Europe and sailed the world on yachts owned by his father. He was thirty-three years old when America entered the war, but immediately donated his power boat to the navy and volunteered for service.

Initially assigned to patrol boat number 8 at Rhode Island, he was reassigned to sub chasers on 17 July 1918 and joined Submarine Chaser Detachment Number 3 at Queenstown, serving there until the unit was disbanded on 25 November 1918.

The SCs were not comfortable ships. They were:

> a little sweat box or ice box (according to weather) which rolled 140 degrees in seven seconds (70 degrees each way), whose decks leaked so that everyone's clothes were soaking wet, and so small and overloaded with engines and anti-submarine gear ... that there were not enough bunks to go round.[12]

One new commanding officer wrote of his first ocean voyage in a sub chaser:

> in this area a big sea was running and the waves seemed to be as high as our mast. The directions as taught in school ashore, when the ocean is merely a conception of the imagination to most of the students, are to run down the side of the wave and with a sort of scenic railway effect shoot up the next. We found the chasers were just like corks in the sea, and corks can't be steered down one side; they just drop, and so did we. The fact that they were small and light with a flaring buoyant bow kept them from sticking their noses too far under. Plenty of green water was taken over decks for us beginners.[13]

They were wet boats for another reason too: their rapid construction had used unseasoned wood in places and this led to frequent leaks. Many had to

A line up of six sub chasers, (L–R) *SC-207, 37, 46, 181, 110, 329*, depicted in an Abrahams' postcard. *(Author's collection)*

dry-dock several times during the war to be recaulked. And when fully loaded the chasers were inches deeper than the designed waterline. This reduced their speed, but acted as a stabilising ballast for their narrow hull in which the beam was only one-seventh of the overall length. This might have made them safer, but produced 'a most uncomfortable snap roll, conducive to seasickness'.[14]

Around the east coast of America, the winter of 1917/18 was one of the coldest anyone could remember. 'This meant operating in ice anywhere from six to twelve inches thick,' wrote Ensign George Wallace USNRF. 'We had no heating systems but lived aboard just the same … [the] engines were only started after a thorough application of a blow torch on frozen cylinders'.[15] Sims admired the determination of these amateur sailors:

> Day after day the poor subchasers, coated with ice almost a foot thick, many with their engines wrecked, their planking torn and their propellers crumpled, were towed into the harbour and left at the first convenient mooring, where the ice immediately began to freeze them in. As was inevitable under such conditions, the crews, for the most part, suffered acutely in this terrible weather; they had had absolutely no training in ordinary seamanship, to say nothing of the detailed tactics demanded by the difficult work in which they were to engage.[16]

Despite the conditions, the sub chasers based at New London, Connecticut, trained and practised submarine hunting. Sometimes they had to force their way through miles of ice to reach the exercise grounds; and ice regularly formed inside the boats as a result of minimally functioning heaters.

And in warmer climes, the SCs were equally uncomfortable:

> the warmth of the summer latitudes struck us like the blast from an open furnace door, and we found that the chasers were difficult of ventilation. This lack of ventilating facilities was, I believe, the principal fault of the submarine chasers … Any sailor can accustom himself to the instability of his craft and will condone insufficient headroom or cramped quarters when he knows that these are necessary to the safety of his vessel, but there has yet to arise a race of men who can live without fresh air or sleep peacefully in the fumes of gasoline engines.[17]

But, like the MLs of the Royal Navy, they were a speedy solution to a pressing problem. Named by their crews 'splinter ships' for their all-wooden

3in gun drill on board a USN sub chaser.
(US Naval History and Heritage Command, NH 124131)

construction, by and large SCs were accepted for what they were and their USNRF officers and men simply got on with the job.

Arming the splinter ships

It had been initially intended that the sub chasers should be armed with two deck guns, fore and aft. However, the coming into service of the SCs coincided with the development of the Y-gun depth-charge thrower (see below) and the stern gun was replaced by this system. The single forward weapon was a 3in, 23-calibre, short-barrelled gun, used on USN destroyers as an anti-aircraft weapon, and manufactured by the Poole Engineering and Machine Company* of Baltimore. It had a long recoil with a vertical sliding breech block and weighed about 531lbs. The gun had open sights, was elevated by wheel and worm gear, and trained by shoulder movement. It fired fixed ammunition (ie, shell case and projectile handled as a single assembled unit) with a 13lb projectile and a range of 10,100yds at 45 degrees of elevation.

As the boats came into service, sufficient numbers of the Poole guns were not available and some of the chasers were fitted with other weapons, mainly the Davis non-recoil weapon. This was an American design which connected two guns back-to-back, with the backwards-facing gun loaded with lead balls and grease of the same weight as the shell in the other gun, thus acting as a counter to the recoil. Chasers with a Davis gun had a pipe frame erected

---

* The same design was also produced by Bethlehem Steel and Driggs Schroeder.

around them, to prevent accidentally firing the counter charge into the wheelhouse.

Firing the gun was fraught with danger to those in the chart house, for if the windows were closed they frequently blew out. On one occasion, *SC-128* fired thirteen rounds from her 3in gun

> The firing broke two windows in the chart house, smashed a chest and sand locker lashed to the deck breakwater, and below in the forecastle broke two metal bolts in the fore and aft midships beam, tore out the electric alarm bell and light fixture from the overhead and made our puppy, the ship's mascot, sick for the rest of the voyage.[18]

Two Colt or Browning machine guns were also fitted either side of the bridge and an assortment of pistols and rifles could be carried.

But the primary offensive weapon of a sub chaser was the depth charge. Early depth charges were simply rolled off the back of the attacking ship. In 1917 the British Thornycroft company created a single depth bomb thrower, developed from a trench mortar design, which could project to a range of 40yds. Subsequently, the USN Bureau of Ordnance produced an improved version which propelled two charges simultaneously. 'Y'-shaped and mounted on the centre line of the ship with the arms of the 'Y' pointing outboard, two depth charges slotted into the firing arms, where they rested on a cradle and expendable 'arbour'. A blank 3in shell was detonated in the

The Y-gun depth charge thrower on board *SC-267*.
(US Navy History and Heritage Command, NH 41995)

vertical column of the Y-gun by pulling a lanyard, which fired two depth charges about 45yds over each side of the ship. The first production quantities of this design were delivered in November 1917 and were manufactured by the New London Ship and Engine Company of Connecticut. As well as the Y-thrower, three parallel bomb racks were mounted aft, built on an angle so that the bombs resting on them could be dropped over the stern by either pulling a toggle or cutting a lashing.

Sub chasers were equipped with the US-designed Mark II depth charge, developed from the Royal Navy's D-type weapon. It contained 300lbs of TNT and could be set to explode at depths from 50ft to 200ft by adjusting a dial mounted on the casing. The usual war fit-out on board was twenty-four.

But the Y-thrower and the depth bombs were useless if the U-boat could not be located. As with the British MLs, various types of underwater locator devices were tried. At first, the chasers were equipped with a mechanism called a trailing wire. This was a reel of phosphor-bronze wire connected to an indicator in the pilot house. To detect a submerged submarine, the wire was reeled out with a weight attached to the end. If the wire made contact with a metal object, a small electrical current would sound an alarm in the indicator. The chasers would then run back and forth over the area of the attack searching for the submarine hull. As might be imagined, this system proved less than useful and was removed fairly early in the sub chasers' commission.

Similarly to the Royal Navy, American companies and scientists had been working on detector systems which could find a U-boat underwater by the sounds it emitted. By the beginning of 1918, the chasers were fitted with one or more of three different detectors.

The SC tube was installed on the port side of the keel forward and when not in use was hauled up to a protective housing built along the strake. It comprised a tube with two opposed rubber 'ears' and was lowered over the side to a depth of around 3ft. It was of limited utility for two reasons: when the chaser rolled at 20 degrees or more, the water washing against the ears made detection impossible. And the design meant that all the sounds in the search area were heard, which made it difficult to identify one from the other.

Next came the MB tube. It was fitted on the other side to the SC tube and had an elaborate array of sixteen ears; this made it possible to more accurately distinguish differing sound sources. However, it was a heavy and intricate device and, according to one authority, 'it was seldom used because of its complicated construction and susceptibility to leaks'.[19] Both of these pieces of equipment had an operating range of four to five miles. Hilary

Chambers, CO of *SC-128*, described the functioning of the SC and MB tubes thus:

> sound is transmitted to these ears from the water and follow tubing to the listener, who wears a stethoscope head apparatus. When this lower part is turned perpendicularly to the bearing of the sound, the noise is transmitted binaurally, of the same intensity in each ear, or centred.[20]

Finally, there was the K-hydrophone. This was a great improvement on the first two, with a listening range of up to thirty miles. It was a triangular-shaped brass pipe with rubber ears at the corners, suspended by an electrical cable to a depth of about 40ft. Twelve small floats carried the cable to the boat and the ears were filled with carbon particles which vibrated in response to a noise, creating an electrical signal, audible to the operator. By the adjustment of moveable dials, the reading of two ears could be obtained and, as the dials were graduated, the bearing of the sound source relative to the tube could be read from them. The tube itself was suspended 65ft below the surface. The K-system was particularly useful as the little buoys were fluorescent and thus readily identifiable at night, giving the SC crew an indication of the direction the sound was coming from.

The chasers worked in units of three. To detect a submarine, all three turned off their engines and drifted with the listening devices lowered. With the power off, the chasers would roll heavily, at times dipping the beam ends

SC-405 starboard side, at Brest, France, on 13 December 1918. *(Author's collection)*

under; crewmen had to operate the equipment and hold on for dear life at the same time. When sound readings were obtained, they were triangulated to determine the location of the submarine. The chasers would then start motors and head for the estimated enemy location. The Y-throwers were fired off to create a pattern of explosive; from line abreast, one ship forged straight ahead and released its bombs, one turned to port and one to starboard before firing off theirs. In this way a roughly triangular area of ocean could be plastered with explosives. The depth setting was down to the CO; there was as yet no way of tracking the enemy.

Co-ordinating an attack was aided by the fact that the sub chasers were equipped with wireless telephony. All chasers were fitted with radiotelephones, but the range was limited, five to twenty miles only, depending on atmospheric conditions. On detecting a sound:

> the commanding officer at once began talking with the other two boats, asking if they had picked up the noise. Unless all three vessels had heard the disturbance, nothing was done; but if all identified it nearly simultaneously, this unanimity was taken as evidence that something was really moving in the water … The middle chaser of the three was the flagship and her most interesting feature was the so-called plotting-room. Here one officer received constant telephone reports from all three boats, giving the nature of the sounds, and, more important still, their directions. He transferred these records to a chart as soon as they came in, rapidly made calculations, and in a few seconds, he was able to give the location of the submarine. This process was known as obtaining a 'fix.'[21]

And so, with the convergence of the new technologies of guns, depth charges, listening devices and telephony, coupled with the recently developed internal combustion engine, did the SCs hunt for U-boats.

12

The Splinter Ships Go to War

The sub chasers operated around the American coast, 303 being utilised in this way during the war. About half of them were deployed to US coastal bases in the northeast of the USA, where they exercised anti-submarine warfare and prepared for general A/S duties. And twelve chasers served along the southern Atlantic coast of America, again undertaking A/S patrols and convoy duties.

Despite the increasing activity of the splinter ships, the German government decided to widen its unrestricted U-boat campaign to American waters in the spring of 1918. The first boat, *U-151*, sailed in April, arriving off the US eastern coast a month later; it was followed by other submarines from June onwards – *U-155*, *U-140*, *U-139*, *U-156* and *U-117*. But the overall impact was not large. Six U-boats sank fewer than a hundred ships, two-thirds of which were small fishing vessels. German mines laid by *U-156* sank USS *San Diego* (1904) with the loss of six lives on 19 July, and another mine from *U-117* damaged USS *Minnesota* on 29 September. One U-boat shelled the Cape Cod Canal with the aim of shutting it down so coal barges and other commercial vessels were forced to go around the Cape, where they were less well protected from torpedo attacks.

USN submarine chaser *SC-201* in the Hampton Roads, June 1918. *(Author's collection)*

The armoured cruiser USS *San Diego*, four 8in and fourteen 6in guns, 13,680 tons, sunk by a mine from *U-156*. She was the only major USN warship lost in the war.
(Author's collection)

As a result of the U-boat presence, the chasers had several close encounters of a submarine kind off the Atlantic coast. Three such actions may speak for the whole. *SC-234* was escorting the battleship USS *South Carolina* (1908) to Delaware Bay on 9 June 1918 when a periscope was sighted about 500yds distant. While the battleship opened fire, *234* went full speed ahead and fired off the Y-gun. No impact was observed. A fortnight later, on 17 June two groups of chasers detected a submarine and gave chase; the U-boat zigzagged away and the chasers ran low on fuel, forcing them to give up the pursuit. And then on 1 July *SC-241*, on passage to Nova Scotia in heavy fog, spotted a torpedo headed towards a freighter at 1540. She altered to avoid its path and then five minutes later a U-boat emerged from the murk, on a parallel course. *SC-241* fired her Y-gun, and landed a bomb within 10yds of the conning tower; the German submerged and a large oil slick was seen.

In all these instances there is no record of a U-boat being sunk in the area; and indeed, the chasers did not destroy any submarine off the US coastline. But it was not for want of trying.

Additionally, thirteen sub chasers went to the West Coast and served with the Pacific Fleet, with tasks such as survey work and patrols along the Mexican and Central American littoral.* And twelve chasers were assigned to the entrances of the strategically vital Panama Canal; four watched the

---

* Four of these boats, *274*, *302*, *311* and *312*, were transferred to the Cuban government in November 1918.

Pacific side and the remainder the Atlantic one. *SC-309* and *SC-310*, built on the West Coast at Bremerton, were assigned to police and coastguard duties in Alaska.

To Europe

On 29 November 1917 the Allied Naval War Council agreed that sub chasers should be deployed to Plymouth and, later, Queenstown. Subsequently, Italy, Greece and France also gained chaser bases. Overall, a total of 133[*] of the chasers were sent to European waters to help hunt U-boats and protect trade and supply. Unlike the MLs, which transited the ocean on freighters, the splinter ships sailed across. Crossing the Atlantic was a difficult exercise, as they were not well suited to the rough oceanic waters. Constant leaks from decks and windows, choking petrol fumes in the officers' quarters, and ever-present seasickness from the rolling motion made them uncomfortable ocean boats, and in heavy weather they were almost awash, with only the pilot house showing above the waves. The Y-thrower and depth charges were felt to be too heavy by some skippers, making the little ships liable to take seas over the stern and they were 'tossed about like pieces of cork'.[1] The sub chasers sailed in convoy with a mother-ship, which was there primarily to refuel them on the crossing.

They were manned and commanded by 'young American reservists',[2] 'very few of whom,' according to Admiral Sims, 'had ever made an ocean voyage'. Sims went on to note 'who would ever have thought that a little wooden vessel … could have crossed more than three thousand miles of wintry sea'.[3]

Among the initial group of sub chasers to arrive at Portsmouth was *SC-177*. She and her sisters departed New London on 22 February 1918 and headed for Bermuda as first port of call. But on the 26th they ran into a strong gale, with high wind from the northeast. The naval tugs *Cherokee* and *Mariner* which were accompanying the chasers both foundered and for one of *SC-177*'s officers 'this storm was the worst ever … an eighty-to-ninety-mile gale blowing against the set of the Gulf Stream can better be imagined than described'.[4] For some of the college-boy sailors, the experience was almost overwhelming. Ensign Alexander Moffat, CO of *SC-143*, had sailed on 24 February and had 'no more idea how to use a sextant than a saxophone'. The raging seas made 'fear for my ship and for my own life lay like a quivering lump in my belly'.[5]

But somehow the chasers survived the experience and fought on to arrive in Hamilton on 1 March. Only two made it under their own power; the

---

[*] Nutting quotes 135, others sources 133.

The tanker USS *Chestnut Hill* (1917, 10,000 tons displacement) seen in port on 16 March 1918, two days after she was commissioned into the US Navy. She had been launched as SS *Desdemona* seven months earlier. *Chestnut Hill* refuelled two separate groups of sub chasers on their voyages from the USA to the Azores. For these trips, she was armed with one 5in and one 6pdr guns and was partially painted with dazzle camouflage. *SC-219* caught fire and was destroyed whilst refuelling from her.
(US History and Heritage Command, NH 70471-A)

remainder were variously disabled by the storm and had to be towed in. On 8 April they were on their way to the Azores, now accompanied by the depot ship USS *Leonidas* and refuelling from the tanker *Chestnut Hill* (1917). To take on petrol, the tanker held her course and speed while four chasers were fuelled at the same time, two aft and one on either side, delivered through a 3in hose. The voyage took fourteen days. On the 27th they were off again, this time for Brest and then on to England, to arrive in Portsmouth on 9 May. It had been a long and trying voyage, but the little wooden ships had acquitted themselves well.

Thirty-six vessels arrived at Plymouth in June, where they came under the command of Captain Lyman A Cotton USN, who was responsible for the American naval forces based there (known as Base 27). There were observers who were disbelieving that the chasers had made the voyage. Referring to their amateur crews, someone remarked to Cotton, 'Those boys can't bring a ship across the ocean.' Pointing to the little vessels now lying in Plymouth harbour, the captain replied, 'Perhaps they can't; but they have.'[6]

Cotton noted, in a letter to Captain A J Hepburn USN back at the chaser base in New London, that:

> Divisions E and F arrived in very good condition so far as sea-going qualities are concerned, but as you no doubt know, almost all of the

A view from the Cattewater of chaser Base No 27 at Plymouth. It shows the boats moored in the slip and *SC-47* and *258* underway, apparently going alongside to secure.
(US History and Heritage Command, NH 121467)

> MB tubes were out of condition, generally due to leaks. Also a number of guards had been lost en route due to the manner in which they were secured.[7]

The captain was disappointed with the early results of his new command's activities:

> the hunting down there [Corfu] seems to be much better than up here at present. Leigh* thinks that he has gotten one submarine to date, whereas since I arrived here, not one submarine has appeared in the entire Start Point – Lizard area, which is the part of the Channel assigned to me. However, since heretofore this has been such a favourite spot with the Hun submarine, I feel sure they will come back here eventually.[8]

And when he went out in one of the splinter ships, the experience was chastening.

---

* Captain Richard Leigh USN, at that time commanding at Corfu. He had been sent out to establish a base for the chasers.

> Have been able to get out for one hunt only on a sub chaser. It was most interesting but, I am compelled to say, most uncomfortable. What with seaplanes and dirigibles overhead, various types of patrol craft on the surface, and enumerable 'suspicious sounds' beneath the water, interspersed with an occasional 'SOS' or 'ALLO', there were very few dull moments, but the looked for submarines did not materialize. However, I do not feel badly so long as there has been no vessel even attacked in this area since we arrived. Incidentally, it is giving our people a good opportunity to shake down before the real thing happens.[9]

Here he makes a key point, which applied equally to the MLs: it was not necessary to sink a U-boat to be counted as successful – it was enough to keep them underwater and exhaust their batteries and air. The number of ships saved from doom by such activities is, of course, *ignoramus et ignorabimus*.

Ensign John Langdon Leighton was an intelligence officer working for Admiral Sims. He too makes this point:

> Plymouth and its vicinity were favourite area for submarines … before the chasers began to operate, there were sixty-five sightings of, sinkings by, and attacks by, submarines within 100 miles of Plymouth. In July, after they had been operating for two months, there were only forty-five … within the same distance of Plymouth … as months went by, submarine activity in the Channel became less.[10]

The units of three chasers operated with four days out at sea and four days in harbour for rest, repair and resupply. When on patrol, they worked from 0800 to dark: 'we would run from ten minutes to half an hour at a pretty good pace, [then] all the boats stopped simultaneously, dropped their listening tubes and listened for a pre-determined period'.[11] Sometimes a destroyer stood off at a distance in case a U-boat surfaced to engage the chasers with gunfire.

SC-177 claimed a U-boat sunk on the night of 29 May, off St Catherine's Point.* It 'popped up alongside … about 60 yards away … the Hun decided to ram us', but then 'began submerging'. The Y-gun fired off, and 'an explosion took place which knocked everyone in the engine room flat'.[12] Joined by *SC-143*, they chased off and almost ran over the half-submerged

---
* The southernmost point on the Isle of Wight.

Submarine chasers *SC-224, SC-97* and *SC-351* and three others in dry dock at Devonport in 1918. *(Naval History and Heritage Command, NH 1864)*

enemy. 'We rained machine gun bullets on the conning tower and deck so that it wouldn't be healthy for her crew to bring her gun into action'[13] and *177* fired one shell from her 3in as the U-boat dived once more. They laid up and listened, hearing the sounds of hammering and at first light dropped a dozen depth charges between them over the spot where they assumed the German was laying. 'Two weeks later, British trawlers found the wreck of her … this was the first sub which the chasers received credit for destroying from the British Admiralty'.[14]* It is a good story, told to a motor-boating magazine a year later, but no U-boat was sunk on the 29th or 30th, off the Isle of Wight or elsewhere, according to modern analysis.

SC-177 had another interesting U-boat encounter when a lookout in the crow's nest spotted that a barrel, floating on the surface like a piece of jetsam, suddenly seemed to start moving and generating a wake. General Quarters was sounded and the chasers set off in pursuit of a now rapidly accelerating barrel. They fired on it and the barrel lost headway; a U-boat had been using

---

* And sub chaser Unit One, the three-ship group which included *SC-177*, received a 'a star' for the action.

it to disguise its periscope as it spied on an approaching convoy and now submerged completely. The chasers laid down a pattern of depth charges, but all this achieved was to 'bring up thousands of dead or stunned fish, whose white bellies soon dotted the sea in all directions'.[15]

Unit One relocated to Weymouth where, when in harbour, they were locked in for the night by anti-submarine nets. On one occasion a U-boat took advantage of this to fire a few shells at them. 'As soon as the searchlights and guns of the fort began to search her out, she calmly submerged and as the gates were never opened at night we had to wait until morning to look for her'.[16]

Finally, they were sent to Plymouth and encountered an entirely different type of sea:

> The life on the chasers was so strenuous in those turbulent waters, that we were given an eight-day rest period after four days out ... after four days of being continually tossed about I have come in with every muscle in my body as sore as a boil ... it was impossible to stay in our bunks without lashing ourselves in.[17]

In these conditions of choppy cross seas and tide rips, the splinter ships usually drifted between dusk and dawn, which encouraged their natural tendency to roll and produced endemic seasickness amongst most of the crew.

Another thirty-six sub chasers arrived at Queenstown, Ireland, to be under the command of Captain Arthur Jepy Hepburn USN*, on 21 August 1918; they sailed up the River Lee, past Haulbowline Island and moored up at Passage West. Queenstown, near Cork, was the headquarters of the Coast of Ireland Command. It was also a major American base; the first USN destroyers to arrive in British waters docked there on 4 May 1917. They were initially greeted by the sub chasers' sister petrol navy craft, as *ML-181* and *ML-325*, the former flying a pilot's flag, came out to meet them and lead the American vessels into harbour. From that point, Queenstown grew to be a major US base, with destroyers, aircraft and all the other paraphernalia of war working alongside Royal Navy ships and men. And it was an integrated command; despite the numerical preponderance of American ships and crew, the CinC was Royal Navy Vice Admiral Lewis Bayly.

Arriving when they did, the chasers just missed a visit from their proponent and advocate, Franklin Delano Roosevelt. He had departed New

---

* Hepburn, Cotton's correspondent, had subsequently been posted to Queenstown to command the sub chasers there, known as Base 6.

York on 9 July on board the brand-new destroyer USS *Dyer* and arrived at Plymouth on the 21st. From there he travelled to Queenstown on the 24th, in the company of British First Lord of the Admiralty Sir Eric Geddes, and both stayed with Bayly at Admiralty House for two nights.

The splinter ships in Ireland spent until the end of September under training in Bantry Bay and were then assigned to Queenstown, Berehaven and Holyhead, each port hosting a division of six vessels, while two divisions were held in reserve. They finally went out on operational hunting patrols on 20 October. Less than a month later the war would be over and so their true potential was never revealed. Admiral Bayly thought that 'they would soon have become a great asset in working with the seaplanes off the coast'.[18]

And apart from the British Isles, the submarine chasers were stationed all over the Europe: inter alia, in France, the Mediterranean and the Azores (see also Appendix 6 for a full breakdown).

The Otranto Barrage

The activity of the MLs at Otranto was noted in Chapter 6. But the constant patrolling by MLs, drifters and other naval units was not sufficiently impeding the ability of Austro-Hungarian and German submarines to escape the Adriatic Sea and wreak havoc in the Mediterranean. With resources stretched and unwilling to risk larger ships in the confined seas around Otranto, the Royal Navy was fighting a losing battle. In May 1917, 150,000 tons of Allied shipping was lost in the Mediterranean and in January

USS *Leonidas* pictured in 1914 as a survey ship. In 1918 she served as tender to the USN sub chasers based at Corfu. *(US Naval History and Heritage Command, NH 51305)*

Captain Charles 'Juggy' Nelson (white uniform, shaking hands), commanding officer of the sub chasers operating at the Otranto Barrage.
(US Naval History and Heritage Command, NH 52757)

1918 alone, Austrian submarines based at Cattaro sank 26,020 tons. In addition to commerce losses, *U-27* sank the destroyer HMS *Phoenix* on 14 May 1918.

However, by early 1918, the Americans were keen to deny the enemy the use of bases in the Adriatic. Vice Admiral Sims' planning staff put forward a series of proposals which came to nothing – except the despatch of thirty-six sub chasers to the region.

On 5 May Captain Charles Preston 'Juggy' Nelson USN, commanding the tender/depot ship USS *Leonidas*, quondam collier, survey ship and now mother to a flock of sub chasers, was at Ponta Delgada in the Azores when he and the splinter ships under his command were ordered to Corfu. It was 2,800 miles away, the same distance again as they had already travelled. First Gibraltar, then Malta – where some essential maintenance delayed them, ten chasers fitted into the dry dock at one time – and finally to Corfu, where the first nine vessels arrived on 4 June, followed by *Leonidas* and the remaining chasers a few days later.

Whilst the climate was pleasant, if hot, the living conditions left something to be desired. Disease was rampant among the Serbians, Greeks

The USN sub chasers at Corfu, US Naval Base 25. *Leonidas* is centre top, with some twenty-one chasers and a tanker present.
(US Naval History and Heritage Command, NH 42570)

and Albanians who made up the civil population, but the base* was in an isolated bay below Comeni Head and there were few opportunities for mixing, entertainment or relaxation. Arranged into two squadrons of six units, three boats to a unit, the chasers were soon at work, and the patrolling of the barrage was remodelled to accommodate them. To the north, the first defence was a line of British destroyers; it was their main task to prevent the barrage from being raided by German and Austrian surface ships. Moving south, next came a line of trawlers, then drifters, next the Royal Navy motor launches, and finally the sub chasers – and above them a line of kite balloons flown from RN sloops kept watch. In July 1918, apart from the thirty-six chasers, there were twenty-seven British destroyers, twelve British and French submarines, four kite balloon sloops, three torpedo boats, fifty-two trawlers, 107 drifters and forty motor launches working on the barrage.

Repair work was an issue. All maintenance performed on the subchasers was the crews' responsibility and they often received little help from the rest of the USN. Much of the mens' free time was spent repairing the wooden vessels and their power plants, which broke down regularly. One officer

---
* It was formally known as Base 25 and informally as 'American Bay'.

noted that 'the boats are slowly going to pieces'.[19] *Leonidas* provided spare parts and tools, but it was up to the crews of the sub chasers to make the repairs, and the US Navy had nearly no supplies set aside for these little ships.

The splinter ships served in rotation, typically four days on and four days off. When not on patrol they would spend time resupplying from *Leonidas* or in training. The Italian navy provided the submarine *Nautilus* (1913) to act as a tracking target for instruction in hydrophone use and stalking the underwater prey.

The sub chasers reported thirty-seven separate U-boat hunts[20] and the listening devices made frequent contact with the enemy – and many times the chasers went to General Quarters. But sinkings were there none. For although it was now not practical for any submarine to pass through the Otranto Barrage in calm weather without being heard, it was always possible for the enemy to wait for the frequent stormy weather (which scrambled sound reception for the listening devices) to slip through this dangerous area without detection.

This did not stop wild claims of success; 'submarine chaser Detachment 2 is officially credited with fourteen submarines,' stated Lieutenant Walter P Groszman USNRF after the war.[21] In fact, later analysis demonstrated that no U-boat was sunk by the splinter ships, which in no way negates the hard and difficult work that was put in. And as the war came to its end, the U-boats operating in the Adriatic region were scuttled by their crews at the end of October rather than try to exit the region en masse.

The sub chasers and the raid on Durazzo

If Zeebrugge was the acme of the motor launches' war, Durazzo was the zenith of the chasers' contribution. Durazzo (Durrës) is a port on the Albanian coast. In 1915 it had been occupied by Italy, which held imperial ambitions in the territory, but they were evicted by the Austro-Hungarians in 1916, under which regime the port remained until late in the war. The waters off Durazzo were also the scene of the last naval action of any size in the Adriatic during the conflict.

On 14 September 1918 French General Louis Felix Marie François Franchet d'Espèrey, commanding the French and British forces in the Allied Army of the Orient (and known to the British troops as 'Desperate Frankie'), began an offensive on the Macedonian Front. The Bulgarian lines were broken and on 29 September the Bulgarian government sought an armistice, the first of the powers aligned with Germany to do so. D'Espèrey was concerned that the remaining German and Austrian forces ranged against him would be able to resupply via Durazzo and he asked the Allied navies to take action to neutralise the base. The Italians were initially reluctant to do so;* but when the French suggested that they would take unilateral action, all of the Allied navies in the Adriatic were pressed into service. And this included the US sub chasers.

On 28 September Captain Nelson was asked by Commodore Howard Kelly RN, commanding Allied naval forces at Brindisi, if he would detail twelve sub chasers to leave Corfu the following day to join up with the attacking group he was assembling. They left as requested, spent two days at the port being briefed and equipped, and finally sailed in company with the other Allied naval elements at 0230 on Wednesday 2 October. *SC-244* wrapped a wire around its propellers and had to be left behind.

A considerable bombardment force had been put together. Apart from the USN vessels, Allied forces included the Italian battleship *Dante Alighieri*, which was to provide distant cover, three Italian armoured cruisers, three Italian light cruisers, five British light cruisers, fourteen British destroyers, two Australian destroyers and eight Italian torpedo boats. Allied aircraft were also involved, along with several Italian MAS motor boats. The role of the sub chasers was to act as a screen for the heavy ships during the planned bombardment.

This all proved to be something of a hammer to crack a nut, for the Austro-Hungarian government had decided to withdraw most of their warships from Durazzo. Only two destroyers, one torpedo boat and two U-boats opposed the approaching fleet, together with a hospital ship. Three shore artillery batteries also offered opposition.

The gunnery ships formed in two lines and opened fire after a preliminary aircraft attack. Patrolling to the north and to the south of the battle area, the American chasers were on anti-submarine picket. Admiral Sims later set the scene:

> two subchaser units, six boats, were assigned as a screen to the Italian cruisers while the bombardment was under way. One unit, three boats, was stationed at Cape Pali, to the north, to prevent any submarines leaving Durazzo from attacking the British cruisers, which were to approach the scene of activities from that quarter, and another unit … was stationed off Cape Laghi. Thus the two critical capes were covered against submarine surprises, and the attacking vessels themselves were effectively screened.[22]

The Italian cruisers sailed back and forth for about an hour, blazing away at

---

* In the Treaty of London, Italy had been promised a protectorate over central Albania and she did not want the other Allies establishing any footholds there.

Durazzo, destroying such shipping as was in the harbour and knocking about military (and civilian) buildings.

Meanwhile, the three chasers of Unit B, commanded by Lieutenant Commander Paul Henry Bastedo, had started for their station at Cape Pali. The Austrian shore batteries at once opened upon the splinter ships, the 'water in their neighbourhood being generously churned up by the falling shells'.[23] The British cruisers, after steaming for a while east, turned south in order to take up the bombarding station which, according to the orders, the Italian warships were about to leave.

SC-129 was with the British cruisers, one of three USN craft of Unit B so detailed, steaming in line ahead. Suddenly, her CO, Ensign Maclear Jacoby USNRF, veered out of line to starboard and hared off at full speed. Observing this manoeuvre, *215* under Lieutenant Commander Bastedo, decided to follow, and saw a moving periscope. Commander Bastedo forgot all about *129*, and steered his own boat in the direction of a little column of spray. As the periscope itself became visible, *215* opened fire at it with the 3in gun and with the second shot a pillar of water and air plumed about 6ft into the air. By now the third chaser, *SC-128*, had joined him; as the U-boat turned away for safety to the south, *215* and *128*, followed, dropping depth charges and firing off the Y-gun. This occasioned a circle of roiled sea, debris and oil; Bastedo thought it a sinking.

But what of *SC-129*? She had signalled that she too had sighted a U-boat, attacked with depth charges and then found that the blast from them had disabled her engines. *SC-215* headed towards the stationary chaser and inquired as to where the U-boat was; in reply, Jacoby stated that he had sunk it. Later, Nelson and the US forces claimed two submarines killed. In fact, *SC-129* had engaged the Austrian boat *U-29*; *U-31* was

Maclear Jacoby USNRF, CO of *SC-129* at Durazzo. He was awarded the navy's Distinguished Service Medal for his actions in the raid.
(*US Naval History and Heritage Command, NH 48856*)

attacked by *215* and *128*. Neither were destroyed and both survived the war. Shells fired from on shore landed within 50yds of *129*, but no American sailor was injured on any of the USN vessels.

As for the hospital ship, *Baron Call*, it was intercepted by *SC-215*, *SC-128* and *SC-129* under heavy gunfire, boarded by a party from a destroyer, and escorted back to Brindisi, where it was released.

During the bombardment, *U-31* had torpedoed the light cruiser HMS *Weymouth* (1910), blowing off a large portion of her stern and killing four men. The final duty of the sub chasers in the action was to escort her back to port.

As some British ships made to enter the port, Ensign Henry R Dann, commanding officer on board *SC-130*, spotted a mine floating in the path of the advancing British screening destroyers. To his crew, it looked like a German Mark IV weapon. Dann pulled his boat out of formation and set course towards the mine, leaving *SC-324* and *337* to guard the starboard side of the British vessels. Dann fired once with the 3in gun and struck the mine, causing it to sink. Shortly afterwards, the crew noticed another floating mine 500yds away. Again, *130* steered towards the mine and idled alongside it in order to warn the British vessels of the danger. The Maxwell brothers later wrote that the chasers sank 'two mines at the entrance to the harbour, just as a flotilla of destroyers was coming in at high speed [and] probably saved many casualties'.[24]

The Durazzo action was the largest in which the USN participated during the war. Charles Nelson and Paul Bastedo were awarded the navy's Distinguished Service Medal and the Italians presented Lieutenant Commander Bastedo with the Silver Military Medal for Valour; Nelson received one too, and several other chaser COs gained the Bronze Military Medal. And the myth of the sunken U-boats was written into history in the DSM award script:

> The President of the United States of America takes pleasure in presenting the Navy Distinguished Service Medal to Lieutenant Commander Paul Henry Bastedo, United States Navy, for extraordinary heroism in the line of his profession as Commander of the Sub-Chaser Squadron One, Hunt Commander Otranto Barrage, and as Commander of a detachment of three Sub-Chasers in the engagement of Durazzo, when two enemy submarines were destroyed.[25]

As Professor Paul Halpern has written, 'the Americans for many years cherished the erroneous belief that their sub chasers had sunk two submarines that day. They had not'.[26]

Once again, the chasers had done good work without clocking up a kill, despite the belief at the time. But they had prevented two U-boats from inflicting more damage than they did.

Chasers and the Canadian Navy

The Royal Canadian Navy entered the war with two obsolete cruisers, HMCS *Niobe* (1897) and *Rainbow* (1891) and fewer than than 350 sailors. Neither ship was in working condition, having no ammunition and only partially crewed. Valiant efforts were made to prepare them and they soon put to sea. Moreover, British Columbia premier Sir Richard McBride secretly purchased two submarines from a shipyard in the United States. After significant work on submarines to get them seaworthy, they patrolled the west and east coasts during the war, but never saw action.

It had been intended that the protection of Canada's coasts should be undertaken by the Royal Navy. But the exigencies of war meant that the RN was committed in the North Sea and elsewhere, leaving Canada largely defenceless.

Like Britain, Canada turned to civilian craft. Motor pleasure boats were taken up from their more or less willing owners and pressed into service to patrol in the Gulf of St Lawrence and the Cabot Straits, working close to the littoral, under the overall command of a 'dug-out' officer, fifty-two-year-old Australian-born Captain Frederick Claude Coote Pasco RN. Pasco had been serving on the staff of the Governor of New South Wales before being placed on the retired list by the Admiralty in April 1915.[27] Having tried to join the Australian Expeditionary Force and being rejected by reason of his age, Pasco accepted Canada's offer to command the Gulf patrol flotilla and arrived at Sydney (Nova Scotia) on 5 September 1915.

By the war's end, Canada had assembled a force of 100 small vessels for these duties, which included twenty-six motor boats. They were manned by a mixture of RN and RNR officers and senior rates, together with Canadian volunteers.

In the spring of 1918 U-boats attacked Canada's east coasts as well, sinking ships off the eastern seaboard of America. The sub chasers came to the rescue. The USN loaned six splinter ships to the RCN, which arrived at Halifax on 16 May and would serve with RCN for the rest of the war.

The sub chasers were organised into two divisions of three units each and designated as convoy escorts. The slow convoys to Europe, designated 'HS', departed from Sydney, but when the St Lawrence froze in winter, moved to Halifax. Halifax was also the year-round assembly point for smaller 'HC' convoys of more valuable 'medium-speed' ships, which often included troop transports. For example, in early July, when convoy HS 47 assembled at

Sydney, it was escorted by *SC-51*, *SC-183* and *SC-241*, which based themselves there. One division of chasers looked after the slow convoy and one the faster one. They would remain with the convoys for the first twenty-four hours of passage, a distance of some 150 to 200 miles out into the Atlantic.

The merchant ships were most vulnerable near the coastline, and here slower RCN patrol vessels – the motor boats and a collection of Canadian-built trawlers and drifters – kept a watch at the harbour mouth before and during the departure of the merchantmen, and then did their best to keep up a screen around them as they picked up speed.

So sub chasers did their bit in Canadian waters too, and by the end of the conflict, the RCN had expanded to over five thousand men from its original 350, with another three thousand Canadians serving with various branches of the Royal Navy.

A Mediterranean predella

The end of the war did not see all the sub chasers leave the Mediterranean. Some of those that remained were assigned to the American Red Cross humanitarian mission to Salonika (Thessaloniki).

On 18 August 1917 a massive fire had completely destroyed the port of Salonika. The fire swept through the centre of the city, leaving 72,000 people homeless, at least 50,000 of whom were Jewish. Many businesses were destroyed, and as a result, some 70 per cent of the population were unemployed. Two churches and many synagogues and mosques were lost. In all, more than one quarter of the total population of approximately 271,157 became homeless.

The Greek government prohibited a speedy rebuilding of the city on the grounds that it wanted to implement a complete redesign in a European style urban plan prepared by French architects. Another consideration may have been that of population re-engineering, for following the Greco-Turkish war of 1919–1922, over 160,000 ethnic Greeks deported from the former Ottoman territories were resettled in Salonika, and many of the city's Muslims were deported to Turkey, perhaps 20,000 people in all. The Greeks thus became predominant in the region.

Whatever the reason, a major care crisis was precipitated and in 1919 a US Red Cross mission was sent to the area. They found the city and all its hospitals still packed with thousands of refugees and sufferers from the great fire. The Americans distributed medicines and re-equipped the largest hospital, and the USN placed six sub chasers at the Red Cross's disposal. These were used to ship in potential patients from outlying areas. The ships of war became vessels of peace.

Post-war, six American sub chasers in the Greek Islands were placed at the disposal of American Red Cross workers in Salonika. On the wharf, beside *SC-128* are some Greek boys and men who have been brought into Salonika to the Red Cross hospital. An RN battleship can be seen in the background. *(US Library of Congress, LC-USZ62-139293)*

Sub chaser losses

Six submarine chasers were lost between 1917 and November 1918. Three were sunk as a result of collisions: *SC-132* on 5 June 1918 with USS *Tacoma*; *SC-187* on 4 August 1918 with the Norwegian *Capeto* near the Cape Charles Light Vessel; and *SC-60* when she collided off New York with the tanker *Fred M Weller* on 1 October 1918. Two crew were killed.

SC-117 caught fire and burnt out at Fortress Munroe, Virginia, on 22 December 1917. *SC-209* was lost to friendly fire when fired on by the armed freighter USS *Felix Taussig* on 27 August 1918, when eighteen men were killed. In these two latter cases, it may be that her passing resemblance to a U-boat, a problem shared with the British motor launches, did not help her cause. Finally, an explosion did for *219*, on passage from Bermuda to the Azores, on 9 October; she was refuelling from USS *Chestnut Hill* when there was a petrol explosion in her radio room. Set afire by the blast, *SC-219* sank in less than two hours. Four men died, eight were injured and Chief Gunner's Mate Oscar Schmidt Jnr received the Medal of Honor for rescuing the survivors. No chaser was lost to enemy action.

Additionally, two chasers were badly damaged but salvaged. *SC-126* grounded and partially sank near Two Hocks Passage, Bermuda, and finally sank south of Agar's Island on 10 April 1918. And *SC-226* suffered when a depth charge exploded on board wrecking the engines. She was towed to Plymouth with no casualties.

ss *Felix Taussig* was constructed by the Newport News Shipbuilding and Dry Dock Company at Newport News, Virginia, in 1917. She was requisitioned by the Emergency Fleet Corporation for service and chartered by the US Army. She sank *SC-219* on 27 August 1918; two days later she was acquired by the USN and placed in commission as USS *Felix Taussig*. (US Navy History and Heritage Command, NH 65093-A)

13

Motor Boats in the Italian, French and German Navies

It was not just in the USA and Britain that the concept of internal combustion engine-powered warships took hold. Other Allied and Central Power navies were attracted to the petrol navy concept. This chapter considers some of the initiatives taken.

Italy

Italy, like Germany, was a modern creation, having existed in its fullest form only since 1871* after a series of wars and treaties known as the *Risorgimento*. In 1882 she joined the Triple Alliance with Germany and Austro-Hungary, largely because she shared borders with the latter, considered the Austrians as a potential enemy, and was worried about France's intentions. But when war came, Italy declared her neutrality. Her primary war aim in so doing was irredentism. Italy hoped to finally claim her ideal border at Austro-Hungary's expense by selling herself to the highest bidder; less publicly, 'she wanted to control the eastern Adriatic … and become a power in the Balkans'.[1] In the Treaty of London, signed on 26 April 1915, Italy agreed to declare war against the Central Powers in exchange for the territories of Friuli, Trentino and Dalmatia.†

Italian ports such as Genoa and Venice had for centuries past been known for their shipbuilding skills. And the Adriatic, home to irredentist ambition, was a limited closed sea, ideal as a proving ground for small, fast motor craft. Moreover, psychologically and culturally Italy was undergoing a revolution, driven by the likes of the poet and writer Gabriele D'Annunzio and Filippo Marinetti and the Futurists. This latter movement 'celebrated dynamism, energy, speed, novelty, mechanisation and violence'.[2] The concatenation of these conditions meant that Italy was ready and willing to adopt motorised sport, vehicles – and boats. As but one example, by 1906 Fiat had built a multipurpose motor boat armed with a 47mm gun (1.9in), two machine guns and two 14in torpedoes. Twin 80hp petrol engines delivered 16 knots.

---

* The Kingdom of Italy was formed in 1861 and gained further territories in 1871.
† In fact, Italy did not declare war until 23 May, and then only against Austro-Hungary. She did not declare war on Germany until late August 1916.

MOTOR BOATS IN THE ITALIAN, FRENCH AND GERMAN NAVIES   195

Italian MAS boat *MAS-15* on display in Rome in the Vittoriano (aka 'Altar of the Fatherland'). It was this craft that sank *Szent István* in June 1918. *(Creative Commons)*

As with the Royal Navy, on entering the war, Italy established a motor boat volunteer reserve, the CNVM (*Corpo Nazionale Volontari Motornauti*), which relied on pleasure boat amateur sailors bringing their craft for martial usage. This was not a success, 'because most of the vessels available were small, slow and insufficiently seaworthy civilian motor boats'.[3] Instead, the Italian naval command moved on to the concept of purpose-built, fast, torpedo-carrying craft, known as MAS boats.

Italian MAS boats

By the end of the war, the Italian navy had taken delivery of 359 motor boats[4] (known as MAS boats and numbered with an MAS prefix) of essentially two classes. There were various marks of fast torpedo armed craft, not unlike

CMBs and known as *Motoscafo Armato Silurante*;* and motor launches, largely acquired from Elco and essentially much the same as the Royal Navy's MLs of the first batch, *ML-1–151*.

The latter were 80ft long, powered by twin Standard engines. The Regia Marina Italiana took delivery of 137 of these little ships,[5] with another thirty-five being on order at the end of the war, all built by Elco. They were received between 1916 and 1919. The Italians denoted them Type C boats and armed them with a machine gun, an anti-aircraft weapon and a fore deck main gun, noted by *Jane's Fighting Ships* to be a 14pdr.[6] They were also known as MAS boats, in this instance from *Motoscafi AntiSommergibili*, or anti-submarine vessel. Elco built *MAS-63–90, 103–114, 253–302, 377–396*. In addition, *MAS-303–317* and *377–396* were Italian-built 'knock-offs' of the Elco design.

Not all deliveries from Elco went to plan. The USN had its own need for extra sub chaser-like vessels and in at least two instances, *MAS-77* and *MAS-78*, they snaffled the ships for themselves. They were taken up by the Americans in April 1917 and not released to the Regia Marina until the December, entering active service only in June 1918.

In the case of the *Motoscafo Armato Silurante*, the boats ranged over several types. In March 1915 the Regia Marina placed an order with the Societa Veneziana Automobili Navali (SVAN) for two 52ft-long boats powered by petrol engines with a speed of 30 knots, and a displacement of 12 tons. Armament consisted of two 18in torpedoes launched over the stern. They were named *Motorbarca Armata SVAN* and numbered as *MAS-1* and *MAS-2*. But they were clearly not considered a success, for in November 1915 they were rearmed with guns and restricted to submarine chasing.

Nonetheless, twenty more boats were ordered from SVAN, *MAS-3* to *MAS-22*. Built in cedar wood, these were given stronger hulls, but their speed suffered correspondingly and dropped to 21 knots; torpedoes were now stowed amidships and carried in launching 'slings'. They had a crew of eight: an officer, two engineers, a leading seaman, a gunner, a machine-gunner, a bowman, and between one and three seamen.

Some considered them too noisy for sneak attacks, and *MAS-20* and *21* were refitted with electric motors as an experiment. When this proved successful in an otherwise abortive raid of 1 November 1916, more were fitted with battery powered electric motors as auxiliaries, additional to their petrol engines. These were 44V, 5hp motors, one to each of two shafts, with power coming from a twenty-five-cell storage battery. On electric power only they could manage around 6 knots.

---

* Torpedo armed speedboat.

MAS-99 seen in 1917. *(US Navy History and Heritage Command, NH 47661)*

The next design iteration came from the Orlando Company of Livorno. They produced a dual-purpose torpedo or gunboat. These were designated *MAS-91* to *MAS-102* and *MAS-218* to *232*. Known as Type A, they carried either two 18in torpedoes or a 47mm QF gun, and their engines drove them at up to 26 knots; the power plants came from FIAT, Isotta-Fraschini, or the Sterling Gas Engine Company of Buffalo, NY. The next development of this idea was *MAS-204–217*, which were uprated to a 57mm (2.3in) gun; and finally, Type D – three vessels *MAS-397–400*, capable of 28 knots.

A key point in Italy's naval strategy was the concept of 'battle in harbour'. As the KuK Kriegsmarine generally remained tied to its base at Pola, the Regia Marina would have to bring the war into the port itself. Thus Italian ingenuity even produced a motor boat which could travel out of the water. In order to penetrate the defences protecting the Austrian fleet, safe behind several defensive booms, in 1918 the *Grillo* class of tracked torpedo motor boats or *Barchino Saltatore* (jumping boats), was designed, also officially known as *Tank Marino* (sea tank) or *MAS Speciale*.

These sported a pair of spiked continuous tracks, meant to assist them to clamber over the booms, which were made of large timber baulks. The boats were again powered by two 5hp electric motors for a silent approach, and carried two torpedoes mounted on drop collars either side. Four were built; the first two, *Cavalletta* and *Pulce*, were scuttled on 13 April 1918 when their slow speed failed to get them to the harbour barrier at Pola before daybreak; and in a second operation, *Grillo* made such a loud clattering noise climbing the obstructions that it was spotted and destroyed by gunfire, although she had by then crossed four of five booms. This seems to have

Motoscafo Armato Silurante (MAS) boats in the harbour of Durazzo, after the capture of the port by Allied forces. The right-hand boat's empty torpedo slings and the sole gun of the left-hand boat can be seen. *(US Naval History and Heritage Command, NH 111501)*

convinced the authorities that the concept was a dead end and the fourth, *Locusta*, was scrapped in 1920.*

MAS in action

The torpedo-carrying MAS boats were seen as new, innovative and representative of a modern, technologically savvy Italy. D'Annunzio wrote them into some of the wartime puffs he produced for the motivation of the nation and used the acronym MAS as his personal Latin motto, *Memento Audere Semper* (Remember always to dare).

And there were some daring actions. The fast MAS craft made a number of pinprick raids against Austrian shipping, such as that of 6 September 1916, when *MAS-5* and *MAS-7* sank the steamer *Lokrum* during an attack on shipping moored near Durazzo. On this occasion, they were escorted by French destroyers and this became the modus operandi; two or three boats would be towed into their starting position by larger craft (to save fuel and premature engine problems). Their escort was then available to shepherd them home, post the conclusion of the operation.

But the true lethal nature of these little craft was demonstrated late the

---

* The Italians also fitted tracks to a midget submarine, the B-class *B-3*, a small 40-ton verssel.

following year, and the leader of the attack was naval reservist Lieutenant Luigi Rizzo. Rizzo had already distinguished himself in the May when he captured the two pilots of an Austrian seaplane downed by engine failure. Now he was after a bigger prize.

SMS *Wien* (1895) and SMS *Budapest* (1896) were *Monarch*-class coastal defence battleships, with a main armament of two 240mm (9.4in) Krupp and six 150mm (5.9in) Skoda guns. The two sister-ships were sent to Trieste in August 1917 to bombard Italian fortifications in the Gulf of Trieste. They were still there during the night of 9/10 December, at anchor in Trieste's harbour, and protected by heavy hawsers positioned as a boom across the mooring's entrance.

Towed to his starting line by the torpedo boats *9-PN* and *11-PN*, and under cover of darkness, Rizzo took two boats, *MAS-9* (his own craft) and

SMS *Wien* (1895), one of three Austrian *Monarch*-class coastal defence ships and equipped with two 9.4in and six 5.9in guns. She was sunk by *MAS-9* on 9 December 1917. *(Author's collection)*

MAS-13, up to the barrier and used hydraulic shears to cut the protective cables. He was able to creep to within 220yds of the Austrian battleships. Suddenly going to full power, Rizzo fired two torpedoes at *Wien*, hitting her amidships. *MAS-13* launched at *Budapest* but missed; nonetheless, both little craft were able to escape without harm.

Rizzo's attack had blown a hole some 34ft wide abreast the boiler rooms. All of the watertight doors had been left open in *Wien* and the ship capsized in five minutes, despite an attempt to counter her list by flooding the trim tanks on the opposite side. Forty-six crewmen died. As for the bold Italian, he was awarded the Gold Medal of Military Valour. A motor-driven boat had just sunk a nearly 6,000-ton battleship. The Petrol Navy had scored a major success. And for the Italian government and people, it was a welcome riposte to the reverses at Caporetto in October and November.

Two months later, on 10/11 February 1918 Rizzo was in action again, this time commanding *MAS-96* and with Gabriele D'Annunzio on board as an observer. The plan was to sink Austrian shipping in the harbour at Buccari (now Bakar), a port in an enclosed bay (the Bay of Bakar) near Rijeka, at the head of the Kvarner Gulf. It lay some fifty miles along a sheltered waterway and, because of its distance from the open sea, was thought to be

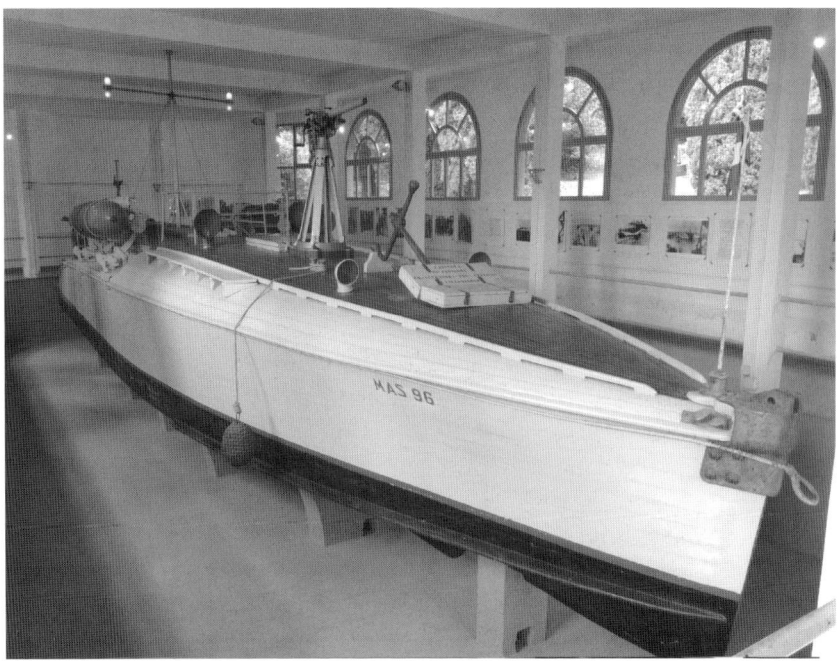

MAS-96, at the Vittoriale degli Italiani, in Gardone Riviera, on Lake Garda. With D'Annunzio on board, she took part in the Bakar raid. *(Creative Commons)*

beyond attack. Italian success would thus have a moral, as well as a physical, impact.

Three MAS boats, under the overall command of Capitano di Fregata Costanzo Ciano, were towed by torpedo boats under escort from two destroyers and a light cruiser for fourteen hours in order to reach the Farascina channel, between Istria and the island of Cherso (now Cres). From here, the flotilla spent several hours evading Austrian patrols and the shore batteries at Porto Re (now Kraljevica) to arrive outside the bay. The MAS boats slipped their tows, and the escort withdrew. At about a mile from the objective, the motor craft switched from petrol engines to their nearly silent electric motors for the final approach and as their targets came into range, all three boats fired their two torpedoes.

But the great adventure was to go unrewarded. On this occasion, they had not dealt with the port defences; five torpedoes became entangled in nets, or otherwise failed to explode, while the sixth slightly damaged a freighter and at last alerted the Austrians to the attack. The MAS boats withdrew to open water and all returned safely to base; and the nation was indeed uplifted by a remarkable journey by their little *motoscafi* and no doubt by D'Annunzio's reportage of it. The raid became known as the Bakar Mockery and is still remembered as such.

Then came June; and Luigi Rizzo, now elevated to the rank of *capitano di corvette*, was about to burnish his already shining reputation. The Austrian naval chief, Admiral Miklós Horthy, tiring of the presence of the Otranto Barrage, now being reinforced by USN sub chasers, decided upon a major raid to rid himself of this nuisance once and for all. His intent was also that his forces would be able to wreak havoc amongst the Allied vessels stationed there as the striking force was supported by capital ships of his latest and most modern type as well as their escorts and other smaller craft.

The best battleships in the Austro-Hungarian navy were the four *Tegetthof*-class dreadnoughts of the 1st Battle Squadron. They mounted twelve 30.5cm (12in) guns in four triple turrets, displaced nearly 21,700 tons and could achieve a speed of 20 knots. In the evening of 9 June 1918 two of them, *Szent István* (1914) and *Tegetthoff* (1912), left harbour later than the others, escorted by one destroyer and six torpedo boats and went to maximum speed to catch up. This caused the former's turbines to overheat and speed was reduced to a stately 12 knots. When *Szent István* again tried to increase speed, early on the 10th, she produced a voluminous cloud of dark smoke; even in the pre-dawn light, this was visible. And it was seen by two MAS boats.

Luigi Rizzo was in *MAS-15*, in company with *MAS-21*. Number *15* was an early model, launched in 1916, but she carried two 45cm (18in) torpedoes and a deck gun. The two boats were on the scene by accident; they had been towed into the northern Adriatic for a minesweeping mission. Off the coast of Premuda, both boats now went to full power and, evading the battleships' escorts, penetrated the screen. At 0325 they launched their torpedoes, Rizzo at *Szent István* and number *21* at *Tegetthoff*. *Szent István* was hit by at least two torpedoes* abreast her boiler rooms. The aft boiler room quickly flooded and gave the ship a ten-degree list to starboard. At 0612 she sank, eighty-nine officers and men perishing with her. Horthy immediately called the operation off.

In the Italian capital, the citizens celebrated as if the entire Austrian fleet had been sunk. Lieutenant Commander Charles R Train USN, the American naval attaché in Italy, reported to Vice Admiral Sims that:

> last evening a crowd of Romans, frenzied with delight by the victory over the Austrians, broke into the old German embassy, which is German property, and had a great time chucking out the valuables. They particularly enjoyed smashing up the emperor's picture and also that of the empress. The contents of the library, throne, etc, were burned, much to the delight of the crowd.[7]

Rizzo and his little wooden motor boat had sunk another major capital ship. It was a record that would not be equalled during the war. He was awarded the Knight's Cross of the Military Order of Savoy by King Victor Emmanuel III for his deed and gained the popular nickname 'The Sinker'.

Luigi Rizzo was an Italian Corinthian. Born in Sicily to a seafaring family, he became a student captain in the Italian merchant marine and joined the naval reserve on 17 March 1912. Twenty-eight years old when Italy joined the war, he soon volunteered for service in the MAS units. By the time he was thirty-one, he was a household name. And he had amply demonstrated the worth of the Petrol Navy to the world.

Austro-Hungary

One of the more creative ideas for a petrol-driven craft came from the Austro-Hungarian navy in their search for a very fast torpedo-carrying boat to solve the problem of fighting in the Adriatic.

Lieutenant Commander Dagobert Müller von Thomamühl was an inventive naval officer who had fought against the Boxers in China and commanded several Austrian naval vessels. In 1915 he developed the idea of the *Versuchsgleitboot* or 'glider boat'. This was a proto-hovercraft which

---

* Two hits were claimed at the time. Later scholarship suggests that one of *21*'s torpedoes may have hit her too, in addition to Rizzo's.

The Austro-Hungarian *Versuchsgleitboot*, or 'glider boat', of 1915. *(Author's collection)*

took advantage of the 'wing in ground effect'*. Unlike later hovercrafts, the *Versuchsgleitboot* had rigid 'skirts' on the sides to trap air but not on the entry or exit of the hull. Four aero engines drove two conventional shafts, but there was also a fifth, smaller, engine which powered an air compressor. This created an air cushion which was capable of lifting the boat up to 10in from the surface. Once 20 knots had been attained, the vessel was completely out of the water and rode on its air cushion.

Built by the Seearsenal yard at Pola, the prototype was launched in September 1915. Displacing 6.5 tons, it had a crew of five, was 43ft long, and was armed with two 450mm (18in) torpedoes, a handful of anti-submarine grenades and a Schwarzlose machine gun. The boat underwent extensive trials, experimenting with differing propeller set-ups, but it was found to be dangerously unstable in high seas and too unsteady a platform for launching torpedoes or depth charges. Development was not pursued. The vessel was scrapped and cannibalised for spares. But one wonders what might have happened if it had been perfected, for the craft could attain 35 knots and was thought to be capable of 40. Of course, so could a CMB, and the stepped

---

* The aerodynamic interaction between the moving wing and the surface below which enables a vessel to glide over a level surface (usually the sea) by making use of the ground effect.

hull design which made the coastal motor boat so effective a weapon was perhaps a technology more likely to succeed within the limits of engineering knowledge at the time.

The French

The French navy also made use of motor boats throughout the war but on a rather piecemeal basis. The use of the RNMBR and its craft on the Franco-Belgian waterways in 1914/15 has already been noted in Chapter 3. The French also operated native motor boats extensively for transportation on the canals and riverine systems of Belgium and France. They carried provisions, ammunition, mail and even troops, as well as towing strings of laden barges. In 1916 there were around 170 such vessels under naval control. They were operated by members of the French motor boat reserve, who wore a greyish-brown uniform with an armband of white and red.

Pre-war, there had been a secret agreement that, in the event of German attack on France, Britain would take the main responsibility for protecting her Atlantic coasts, while the French navy took the major part in the Mediterranean. Even so, the outbreak of war in August 1914 had come at the wrong time for the French navy. After decades of confusion and controversy, it was in the process of transforming itself from a 'fleet of samples' to an up-to-date battle fleet, a process that began with the naval programme of 1912. Construction work was in its early stages when the German occupation of the industrial areas of northeastern France, combined with the manpower and industrial demands of the French army, effectively suspended this programme. As a result, for the vitally needed smaller patrol craft, the navy had to make do as best it could. And this meant begging or borrowing from its Allies. Because of the disjointed nature of this process, records are difficult to identify and there is *désordre* between the usually accurate published sources such as Jane's, Conway's or French language sources. What follows is therefore a synthesis and reconciliation.

Motor launches

Forty Elco-built Royal Navy motor launches were transferred to France in 1916 and 1917, all from the first and second Admiralty orders. The first two arrived at Cherbourg in May and the French named them *Vedettes* (speedboats). The batch were allocated identifying numbers from *V-1* to *V-40,* and were armed with a single 75mm (3in) field gun on a naval mounting and carried two depth charges. The depth charges were later augmented by a Y-gun thrower. Of these vessels, *V-3* and *V-33* and two others saw action in Operation ZO, escorting 'M'-class monitors at Zeebrugge and at least three of these were lost during the war, *V-21, V-23* and *V-27*.

The French also built their own version of the Elco boats, roughly similar but around 10cm less in the beam. *V-41* to *V-53* were designed and constructed by Despujols at a yard at Neuilly and fitted with two Panhard engines, which proved to be highly unreliable. Four joined the Biscay Patrol Division and six the Dunkirk flotilla. Three were cancelled. And *V-54* to *V-61* were built by Cornilleau shipyard near Marseilles, delivered between January and June 1917. They were slightly larger, and were equipped with two American-built Wolverine petrol engines*. They served mainly in the Mediterranean. Finally, *V-62* to *V-72* were ordered directly by the French from Vickers Canada, for delivery in May 1918. They were slightly smaller than the standard Elcho boat, could attain 19 knots and, due to protracted trials, only entered service two days after the Armistice.

A French sub chaser (*chasseur*) wearing the French *tricolore* and with *matelots* on deck, but still bearing its USN designation as *SC-348*.
(US Naval History and Heritage Command, NH 110769)

Submarine chasers

The Ministry of Marine purchased a hundred 110ft sub chasers from the USA, of which 98 were delivered and became part of French naval forces. When built, the chasers were assigned an 'SC' number which was changed to a 'C' designation on joining the French fleet, becoming *C-1* to *C-98*.

Most were sailed across, not without incident. *SC-405* was damaged in transit and replaced by *SC-177*, already in European waters; *405* was

---

* Wolverine Motor Works, Grand Rapids, Michigan, USA, 'manufacturers of marine and stationary gas and gasoline engines and launches, single, twin screw and stern wheel launches, stationary gas and gasoline engines' (quoted from an 1898 brochure).

redesignated *177* when repaired. *SC-319* was lost with all hands in a storm at sea in January 1918. *SC-28* was disabled in the same storm and presumed lost on 15 January. Thirty-nine days later she arrived at Horta, Azores. The *New York Times* told her story

> An American submarine chaser, which became separated from her convoy in a gale at sea in January, and which had been given up for lost, has turned up safely at an unnamed port, according to information received officially by the Navy Department today. The chaser was thirty-nine days at sea on short rations and had to navigate by compass.[8]

Quoting Navy Secretary Josephus Daniels, the article went on to state that:

> the engines were disabled and the boat left adrift far out at sea. The crew managed to rig up a sail made from bed coverings, and were able to make two or three knots an hour before the wind. There were no navigating instruments, except a compass, aboard, and the crew had to estimate their positions.

Others were towed across. For example, *SC-67* was towed by the armed yacht *Venetia* in January 1918, via Bermuda, and the Azores, as was *SC-173*, by the yacht *Lydonia*. Having dropped her tow in Leixões, Portugal, *Venetia* then took *SC-172* to France.

SC-141, intended for France, was struck and sunk by *SC-174* off Philadelphia; all the rest were safely delivered, although there were occasional 'hiccoughs'. For example, the French suffered at the hands of *SC-143*; she had stripped the teeth on the rack and pinion of her steering gear. It was non-standard, but the same as *142*, moored nearby, crewed by French sailors as it had just been sold to the French navy. The skipper of *143* and his engineer dashed aboard and started to demolish the officers' quarters of *142* to get at the equipment they needed. Anticipating the discomfiture of their officers, the *matelots* joined in. *SC-143* was on the move within two hours. It took rather longer to get *142* to sail to France.*

And amazingly, eight of these hastily built and hard worked craft were still in French service at the start of the Second World War.

---

* On 15 April 1918 *SC-142* left Bermuda in a convoy with twenty-nine other submarine chasers, four USN tugs, two French tugs and destroyer tender *Bridgeport*. Cruiser *Salem* and armed yacht *Wadena* acted as escorts for the convoy. On 25 April *142* had to be taken under tow for a time by *Bridgeport*, and two days later, reached Ponta Delgada, Azores.

A wrecked French *chasseur*, sunk in a German bombing raid on Dunkirk and as depicted in a contemporary newspaper. Apparently, she was successfully repaired.
(Author's collection)

Russia

In 1906 the Tsarist navy purchased ten 'torpedo pinnaces' fitted with internal combustion engines from the USA, but 'they were technically unsatisfactory and, with one exception, served as harbour launches'.[9]

It seems that some Elco MLs were acquired by the Russian navy, and that they were developing their own types as well. As an example, the *Saska* class of armoured motor boats was originally intended for the Amur River flotilla; in fact, four went to the Baltic in 1915 as submarine chasers and four to the Black Sea.

Jane's Fighting Ships 1919 notes an unknown number of motor patrol boats of varying types stationed in the Baltic, White and Black seas, constructed chiefly by American companies between 1915 and 1916. There were Elco boats in the Black Sea squadron and a number of US-built motor boats were used for anti-submarine purposes.

And *Yachting Monthly* stated in August 1917 that 'it comes as a surprise that the Russian Government are building 72ft boats with a speed of 28 knots'. In fact, the yacht and fishing boatbuilders Greenport Basin and Construction Company of Long Island constructed eighteen 60ft wooden, petrol-driven boats for the Russian navy in 1916/17. They were powered by twin eight-cylinder Duesenberg engines with a reported speed of 30 knots. Their constructor designated them as 'gunboats', and the Russians intended them for use in the Black Sea for anti-submarine purposes. Post-delivery, some were converted to minelayers and taken by cruisers to mine the Bosphorus. One was fitted with a 38cm torpedo tube mounted obliquely to the deck, which fired at a sixty-five degree angle to starboard and was used in a commando attack in the Black Sea.

By the end of 1917, Russia had succumbed to widespread disorder and the October Revolution, with its resultant anarchy, eventually resulted in civil war. This effectively put paid to any further structured wartime developments.

Germany

Germany was a late adopter of the motor boat and only really took up the cause in 1916, driven by the need for a weapon with which to eliminate anti-U-boat and anti-torpedo boat nets laid by the Royal Navy off Ostend and Zeebrugge.

Some civilian craft, on hand at the time, were first tried: the racing boat *Boncourt* and the motor boats *Ursus*, *Max*, *Annette IV* and *Brase*, but they proved too lightly built for the open seas and too small to work on the heavy nets.

According to *Jane's Fighting Ships* of 1919, the Kaiserliche Marine built some forty-nine 'F'-class motor boats during 1916/17. These were about 55ft long and weighed 23 tons.

They joined a number of 'UZ'-class boats, possibly twenty-two in total. 'UZ' was an abbreviation of *Unterzeeboote Zerstörer* (submarine destroyer), designed to hunt submarines and for mine clearance. They could not

'German motor boats armed with anti-aircraft guns engaging a Russian biplane', taken from *The History of the Great War* (Waverley, 1920) The etching depicts vessels engaged in river patrol on the Eastern Front. The position of the exhaust manifold relative to the helmsman seems to indicate some artistic licence. *(Author's collection)*

operate outside of coastal waters and were seaworthy up to force 6 winds. The class was 85ft to 100ft long, about 60 tons, and power came from a Deutz or Daimler twelve-cylinder, four-stroke petrol engine, which could take them up to 15 knots; they were armed with a 5.2cm (2.0in) fast-loading cannon.

These vessels made sporadic attacks against Allied forces. Even in late August 1918 it was reported to the War Cabinet that on the 23rd enemy motor boats had made a raid in the Dunkirk Roads. The French claimed to have sunk one of the German boats. 'The German claim, which they have published, to the effect that two of our motor boats were sunk, is false',[10] reported First Sea Lord Wemyss.

But the most noteworthy of the German petrol-powered developments were the *Fernlenkboot* and *Luftschiffmotorboote* types.

Fernlenkboot (remote control boat)

As with the Royal Navy, the Kaiserliche Marine experimented with remotely controlled vessels. The *Fernlenkboot* or FL-boat was the end product. Its genesis was the need for a weapon to attack British bombardment ships, monitors and other ships, which from 1916 onwards were regularly off Flanders coast attempting to destroy German U-boat facilities and harbours. They were small boats powered by a powerful six-cylinder, 400hp engine of an advanced design, credited to the French speedboat racer Victor Despujols.

The story is that at a race in Monaco, the French Despujols-designed boat did not show up. After investigation it was found that the racer had been sold to some Germans, facilitated by the Bosch representatives at the port. They were acting on behalf of Siemens, and very shortly the boat was at the Siemens-Shuckert works and reverse engineered.

Come the war and the Siemens-Shuckert company used this industrial espionage to produce the power plant for the FL craft. The mode of operation was technically complex for the time. Once in the water, the boat

A German remote control *Fernlenkboot* being manhandled into its concrete shed, probably at Zeebrugge. *(Author's collection)*

was started up by its crew, who then abandoned her. Each boat had a spool of single-core, insulated electric cable between 30 to 50 miles long, which controlled speed and steering. An aircraft flew overhead and passed back to the operators on land the necessary corrections of course and speed. The system allowed the following commands to be transmitted: system test; engine start and stop; set rudder position; turn on a light (to enable the boat to be tracked at night); and later, self-detonate the warhead, to prevent capture if the target was missed. The 55ft-long craft could make 30 knots and carried 300–500lbs of explosive in the bows.*

The weapon saw limited action. In late December 1916 an FL-boat was sent after a British monitor sailing along the coast. After about ten miles the steering locked and the boat travelled around in circles. Apparently, a German destroyer had crossed the path of the boat and severed the wire. A warship was despatched to destroy the FL, to prevent it falling into enemy hands. As a result, an extra fuse was added to self-destruct the craft should the cable be cut. In February 1917 there was another effort against an RN vessel but the fuse failed and blew up the craft before it reached its intended target.

In March 1917 an attempt was made to use an FL to attack a land target from the sea; the control gear and wiring was loaded onto a trawler and launched against the harbour mole at Nieuwpoort. All functioned well, but little damage was caused, and the Royal Navy was able to recover some of the wreckage and gain a greater understanding of what the FL was and how it worked.

This helped on 6 September 1917 when the monitor *M-24* (1915) observed a motor boat bearing down on it. Taking no chances, she opened up with almost every gun on board until, with 300yds to run, the German boat was destroyed.

More success was achieved the following month. On 28 October the twin 15in-gunned monitor HMS *Erebus* (1916) was hit by an FL nine miles off Ostend. It blew a 50ft hole in her anti-torpedo bulge, but did little damage to the hull. Two seamen were killed and fifteen wounded by the blast, mainly members of the crew who had been standing on deck, watching the approaching boat and wondering what it was. Her anti-torpedo bulge suffered most of the impact, but it still took two days to nurse her back to harbour at Dover, from whence she was sent to Portsmouth for repairs. *Erebus* returned to service on 21 November.

Another monitor to be bothered by an FL (which the Royal Navy referred to as an electrically controlled motor boat or ECB) was HMS *Prince Eugene*

---

* Some sources suggest more, *Jane's* gives this value.

(1915, two 12in guns). In the morning of 3 November she was attacked by an 'electrically controlled motor boat accompanied by nineteen aeroplanes'.[11] The FL was sunk by gunfire and the monitor undamaged. But the War Cabinet was concerned that, post the damage to *Erebus*, the press was getting the wind up. They agreed that 'in the view of statements made in the press about the boat it would be desirable to communicate some more detailed information to the press'.[12] Admiral Jellicoe undertook to look into it.

There was another incident later in the month when an ECB had been observed making for the Belgian coast patrol vessels. 'Our ships had jammed their wireless and she had not been seen again'.[13] The final FL-boat attack seems to have been at the end of November, when the destroyer *North Star* observed a fast craft approaching and destroyed it with gunfire.

Technically innovative, the weapon proved of limited utility. The Germans switched their attention to another type of motor vessel.

Luftschiffmotorboote (airship-engined boats)

The Kaiserliche Marine turned to the development of crewed craft, initially with the idea of using them to clear the anti-submarine nets laid by the RN in the approaches to their U-boat bases at Zeebrugge and Ostend.

The Lürssen boatyard at Bremen was commissioned to design and build the prototype, and eventually twenty-one were produced from 1917 onwards, by Lürssen, Naglo, Rolandwerft and Oertz*. They were designated *LM-1*, etc, their naming being derived from the fact that they were powered by three lightweight Maybach Zeppelin engines. The first four were armed only with a 3.7cm gun and carried bow-mounted net cutters. Subsequent construction included an additional 45cm bow torpedo and a single machine gun. A top speed of 30 knots was claimed, but had to be reduced to 20 knots in order to fire the torpedo, and a crew of four manned the boat. They operated on a similar hydrofoil principle to the British CMBs and as a result were also known as *Gleitboote* (hydrogliders).

The LM-craft were deployed mainly at Flanders, but seven were sent to the Baltic, where the only sinking attributed to them occurred. The old British steamer ss *Penelope* (1871, 1202grt) on passage outward from Petrograd (while serving as commissioned transport in the Russian Baltic Fleet) was torpedoed and sunk in the Gulf of Riga by Oberleutnant zur See Georg Peytsch on 24 August 1917. Peytsch did not live long to celebrate his singular success, for at 1727 on 10 October his LM boat was observed from the shore to blow up, with all aboard killed. It had probably hit a drifting mine.

---

* *LM-19* was not delivered until after the hostilities had ended.

* * * * *

In all major combatants' navies, the internal combustion engine adapted for marine use had led to a number of innovative designs. If America and Britain had the advantage in terms of quantity, and probably quality, in Italy and in Germany some local success had been achieved too. The locomotive of war had driven the petrol navies of the world to become an established marine weapon.

14

Armistice, Occupation and a Revolution

At the eleventh hour of the eleventh day in the eleventh month of 1918 the war came to an end. Except that for many MLs, CMBs and sub chasers it didn't, as will be seen. But first they had to weather the Armistice.

On 8/9 November *SC-148* and her unit contacted a U-boat and unsuccessfully chased it during the night, the last such contact for a chaser in the war. Two days later:

> on 11 November, while we were plunging along on patrol about ten miles south of Eddystone Light, we picked up a radio message from Admiral Sims; 'Armistice signed; enemy submarines on the surface not to be attacked unless hostile intentions are obvious'. No words could express our elation over this news.

Number *148* requested and was granted permission to return to Plymouth where 'the long-standing enmity between our "gobs" and "limies" was for the time forgotten and former contenders in bloody street encounters could

USN sub chasers docked in Holyhead, Wales, decked with flags to celebrate Armistice Day.
(US Navy History and Heritage Command, UA 43.05.01)

be seen everywhere arm in arm, or drinking out of the same bottle'.[1]

News of the Armistice reached *SC-143* when they were on patrol off the Isle of Wight. On the way back to Plymouth, 'vessels dipped their colours, everyone waved and yelled like madmen'. RN ships hoisted signals for officers to repair on board for drinks and 'one sailing vessel had an effigy of the kaiser hung at the yardarm'.[2]

At Corfu, *Leonidas* sent a signal that an armistice had been signed at 0958. The depot ship and the chasers 'fired celebratory salutes'. The celebrations lasted until the following day, when 'representatives of the Allied fleets fired twenty-one guns at morning colours'.[3] According to Hilary Chambers, CO of *SC-128*, 'twenty-one chasers in column formation wound its way among the anchored ships, and on passing the flagship each fired the propulsion charge of its Y-gun'.[4]

And in Wales, sub chasers based in Holyhead decked themselves with flags to celebrate the great day. Lieutenant Gerald Aldridge, CO of *ML-382*, was on fourteen days' leave when the peace was announced. His diary entry for the day was rather quotidian: 'Armistice signed at 0500! Morning – gardening; Afternoon – downtown with J*, shops closed, streets crowded'.[5] Whereas in the Aegean, Sub Lieutenant Fred Cooper of *ML-228* reported that 'all ships dressed at 1100 for the rest of the day … there were great doings in Salonika, rockets fired at night by everybody in harbour'.[6]

But even before the 11th, MLs had been involved in 'peaceable' activities; after the Turkish surrender and Armistice of 30 October, motor launches were part of a minesweeping contingent sent to clear the minefields of the Dardanelles to allow the passage of a fleet into Constantinople, work which commenced two days later.

And MLs had a role to play after the guns stopped firing on the Western Front too. The terms of the Armistice required that the German fleet be interned; eventually it was decided that this would be at Scapa Flow for the surface ships and Harwich for the U-boats. On 19 November the submarines started to arrive at the latter port. The SNO Harwich had been asked to lend all available motor launches to assist in the process and Lieutenant Gordon Maxwell was in charge of a flotilla of MLs sent in response.

When the U-boats had anchored, they were boarded by a Royal Navy officer. He required the German CO to sign a paper which stated that the submarine was fit to be navigated, disarmed and not booby-trapped. The White Ensign was then hoisted above the German flag and when all the submarines were ready, they were sailed into harbour by Royal Navy submariners, with the Germans fallen in on the forecastle, and were made

---

* His wife, Mary Joanna.

A view from the Ehrenbreitstein Fortress, where the Rhine and Moselle meet at Coblenz, the US occupation HQ, 1919. *(US Naval History and Heritage Command, UA 570.16.03)*

fast in a submarine trot off Parkeston Quay. The MLs were responsible for carrying British sailors from their depot ships to the U-boats and the Germans to their accompanying transports for return to their bases. Lieutenant Maxwell:

> never thought at one time to have the deck of my ML crowded with German sailors but it was this day, when we took them off the U-boats back to their own ship. It was interesting to study them. They seemed to vary a good deal both in appearance and manner. One crew we took off looked the most bloodthirsty gang of unshaven ruffians I ever hope to meet, but other lots did not seem such bad fellows – that is, for Huns.[7]

The war was over; but in reality, fighting dragged on in Russia, the seas had to be cleared of mines and the German Armistice terms had to be enforced. And a part of this work fell to the Petrol Navy.

*Die Wacht am Rhein**

Among the conditions imposed on Germany in the 11 November Armistice was that of occupation, both to provide France with security against renewed attack and to serve as a guarantee for the payment of reparations. (For the appropriate terms of the Armistice, see Appendix 7.)

Occupying armies from Britain, France, Belgium and the USA marched

---

* 'The Watch on the Rhine', a German patriotic anthem written and composed in 1840.

ARMISTICE, OCCUPATION AND A REVOLUTION   217

The Watch on the Rhine by William Rothenstein was originally exhibited in Canada as part of the Canadian War Memorials exhibition of 1920. The painting's many symbolic elements represent Germany's defeat and the triumph of the Allied forces. In the foreground, a British howitzer faces out across the Rhine and a British sentry stands guard to one side. *(Author's collection)*

into Germany west of the Rhine, all of which was to be under Allied/US governance. Furthermore, the Allies and the USA took control of four right-bank bridgeheads and territory east of the Rhine which projected in a 30-kilometre (19 miles) radius around each of Cologne, Coblenz (Koblenz from 1926), Mayence (Mainz) and a 10-kilometre (6 miles) semi-circle around Kehl (directly opposite Strasbourg). Additionally, the left bank of the Rhine

MLs on the Rhine, led by *ML-542*, passing under the Hohenzollern Bridge at Cologne. *542* was still in service in 1924 and not disposed of until 1927. *(Author's collection)*

and a 50-kilometre (31 miles) wide strip east of the river was declared a demilitarised zone. Cologne came under British administration, Coblenz fell to the Americans, and Mayence to the French.*

Essential to the management of communications and commerce in the occupied territories was control of traffic on rivers and canals. Immediately after the signing of the Armistice, a Field Navigation Commission was established to regulate all navigable waterways within the occupied territories. This included rivers and canals in Belgium, 'the Rhine between Alsace-Lorraine and the Dutch frontier, the Moselle from Alsace-Lorraine to its junction with the Rhine, and the Saar from Alsace-Lorraine to its junction with the Moselle'.[8] To administer the Rhine itself 'an Inter-Allied Commission was formed with headquarters in Cologne and a sub-commission in Rotterdam'.[9]

And if you have water to control, you need the navy. The Americans

---

* The provisions were repeated in the Treaty of Versailles which limited the presence of the foreign troops to fifteen years after the signing of the treaty (ie until 1934). Following acceptance of the Young Plan, the occupation of the Rhineland was prematurely ended on 30 June 1930 and the area became a demilitarised zone. The administration of occupied Rhineland was until then under the jurisdiction of the Inter-Allied Rhineland High Commission with its seat at the Upper Presidium of the Rhine Province in Coblenz.

MLs patrolling on the Rhine, *ML-291* foreground. Drawn by Charles de Grineau for the *Illustrated London News* of 5 April 1919. *(Author's collection)*

provided a random collection of water craft at Coblenz; the French despatched their *vedettes* (MLs in French dress) and *chasseurs* (the French sub chasers obtained from the USA); and Britain sent Royal Navy motor launches and their mainly volunteer crews.

The Admiralty cut the first orders on 9 December 1918: 'MLs *8, 50, 121,*

287, 288, 291, 333, 345, 473, 541, 558, 566 should be commissioned forthwith as tenders to *Hermione* with two officers in each and a full crew for patrolling in the British section of the Rhine. Three MLs will have a lieutenant RN in command'.[10] The orders went on to specify that MLs *291* and *558* were to be fitted with W/T, silencers were to be replaced where they had been removed, depth charges were not to be carried, but the 3pdr gun would be retained on all the vessels detailed. In addition, one sub lieutenant RNVR and six chief motor mechanics were to be shipped aboard as a repair party. *ML-291* was designated as the commanding officer's boat and a paymaster lieutenant and a victualling chief petty officer were to be assigned to them and meet the flotilla at its destination.

On 14 December Commander the Honourable Patrick George Edward Cavendish Acheson MVO DSO RN received his sailing orders. He was to take the twelve MLs* to the Rhine and thence Cologne, routing through the rivers and canals of France; Acheson was not permitted to directly access the Rhine at Rotterdam in order to respect Dutch neutrality. His instructions also specified that 'French naval authorities have been requested to lend an officer for the passage through the canals to the Rhine and he will join at Havre. They have also been asked to supply petrol and a small quantity of drinking water at Paris and Toul'.[11] Once in place he was to act as Senior Naval Officer, Rhine Patrol.[12]

Thirty-six years old, Patrick Acheson was the son of Archibald Brabazon Sparrow Acheson, 4th Earl of Gosford†. He was, unusually for MLs, a career naval officer, having joined the Royal Navy in 1897 as a cadet. Acheson had been appointed a Member of the Royal Victorian Order in 1904, and in 1915 was awarded the DSO for bravery at Gallipoli when in HMS *Inflexible*. He had only served in big ships and had never exercised independent command. But he was 'a most excellent and hardworking executive officer', possessing 'very good command of both officers and men and most tactful in his dealings', according to Captain Edward Henry Fitzhardinge Heaton-Ellis, quondam captain of *Inflexible*, who felt moved to add 'plays most games'.[13] Now Acheson was to lead a flotilla of motor launches into the heart of Germany. Perhaps it was thought that tact would be important in the role.

Acheson's orders required him to leave Portsmouth on 17 December, but the weather delayed his departure. Eventually, the flotilla set sail on the 21st, although it would appear that the conditions had not much improved. On

---

* Of the MLs originally specified, *541* and *558* did not actually depart and were replaced in sailing orders dated 14 December by *358* and *542* (docs 1617, IWM).
† Lord Lieutenant of Armagh from 1883 to 1920, Vice Chamberlain of the Household of Queen Alexandra from 1901. He was also Honorary Colonel of the 3rd Battalion of the Royal Irish Fusiliers from 1899 and Vice Admiral of Ulster.

their way to Le Havre, the glass steadily fell and around 1900 a terrific gale sprang up, accompanied by a very uncomfortable sea. Seasickness became endemic through the little ships and the conditions caused the loss of two of them. *ML-121* sank about fifteen miles down the coast from Le Havre on the Seine Bank; her commander was Lieutenant John William Robinson RNVR, who had held the position for just eleven days, having joined from *ML-424*, the boat in which he had won the DSC at Zeebrugge. And *ML-566* foundered off Cape Barfleur. Both crews were rescued without loss. Two other MLs were badly damaged.

At Le Havre they collected two more MLs before entering the Seine. The flotilla made its way in stages across France by river and canal, passing through Rouen, Paris, Épernay, Verdun, Toul, Strasbourg, Coblenz and Bonn before finally reaching Cologne on 6 February 1919. Because of the often heavy rain, they frequently had to pause the journey to allow the waters to subside, such that they could pass under the stone canal bridges, and their route took them through '219 locks and [they] crossed the R Moselle by aqueduct'.[14]

Before the MLs had arrived at their destination, a second group was preparing to sail. On 3 January 1919 Lieutenant Reginald George Fife RNVR received orders to ship from Portsmouth with an additional four MLs* (one of them, *ML-229*, was under the command of the ill-starred John Robinson). Fife had served in motor boat *35*, *Minou*, commanded a number of MLs and finally took charge of *ML-569* for this assignment. He was yet another pre-war amateur sailor and a member of the Sussex Motor Yacht Club.

The MLs were to sail on 11 January 1919, following the same route as the main body of the original flotilla.[15] But once again, weather intervened and they eventually prepared to sail on 31 January, but then even this was delayed for twenty-four hours. Finally, they left at 1540 on 1 February and 'rolled all night', according to Lieutenant Aldridge in *ML-260*. Conditions were so bad that at 1220 the following day they returned to Portsmouth. Finally, on the 4th the MLs set off at 0100 and 'had a good crossing', despite having to 'wait a long time for locks to be opened before proceeding to berth' at Le Havre.[16]

There didn't seem to be a great sense of haste. The day after their arrival, a group of officers took a trip to Trouville in *ML-366* and when they did finally sail on the 7th there were frequent stops for excursions and visits to places of interest. At Rouen, Aldridge explored the cathedral, and found it 'a fine building'[17] on the 8th, and the following day returned for another look and took in the Abbey of St Ouen as well.

And as they proceeded up the Seine, 'there were some exquisite views

---

* These were *229*, *260*, *569* and *576* (docs 1617, IWM).

MLs in line astern beginning to manoeuvre to abreast, entering Cologne on 19 March 1919 accompanied by an aeroplane. Drawn by Charles de Grineau for the *Illustrated London News* of 5 April 1919. *(Author's collection)*

ARMISTICE, OCCUPATION AND A REVOLUTION 223

which were enhanced by the snow which had fallen in the night'.[18] The wheelhouse windows and fore deck were frozen over. Paris was reached on the fifth day of sailing. Here Lieutenant Aldridge visited the Place de la Concorde. But administrative provision for the journey had clearly failed, for he had to go to the British embassy on the morning of the 15th to draw 1,000 francs against his own pay in order to provision the ship and pay his crew. The following day a group of officers spent the entire morning and afternoon touring the sights of Paris. The boats left the city the next day and took to the River Marne.

Châlons was gained on 24 February, Nancy took until 4 March. Three days later, the little flotilla 'passed through front line trenches, saw very large shell holes, wire entanglements, temporary bridges … smashed up villages'[19] – the detritus of war.

On the 9th there was a near disaster. As *ML-229* was in a lock, a small boy, spectating from the lock side, toppled into the water. Lieutenant Robinson immediately dived in after him and effected a rescue, but was sucked into the sluice gates. Somehow, his fellow sailors pulled him out and

Field Marshal Douglas Haig making a tour of the motor launches at Cologne in March 1919 and going aboard *ML-576*. The naval officer ahead of him is Commander Acheson. General Herbert Plumer, the C-in-C of the British Army of the Rhine is on the left, obscured by another officer. In the background is the Hohenzollern Bridge.
(© *Imperial War Museum, Q3734*)

ARMISTICE, OCCUPATION AND A REVOLUTION   225

Aldridge gave his fellow commanding officer artificial respiration. Robinson survived and his courage was recognised with the presentation by the Royal Humane Society of a 'Testimonial on Vellum'.[20]

Finally, on 19 March the MLs arrived at Cologne. Their mammoth inland journey was finally over and they joined the other motor launches, which were now based at the requisitioned home of the Cologne Watersports Club. This was on a barge, just south of the Hohenzollern Bridge along the Frankenwerft.* Some officers had sent home for their families to come out and join them in rented accommodation.

That same month, the flotilla was honoured by a visit from Field Marshal Douglas Haig, as part of a tour of inspection of the British Army of Occupation. Commander Acheson took him on a tour of the MLs at Cologne and as he departed, he was given a rousing send-off by the crews, parading on the quayside. But the boats' duties were largely of a humdrum nature; on 2 April *ML-260* took a lieutenant colonel to Bonn. A day later they welcomed the deputy assistant provost marshal and transported him to the end of the British riverine sector. And on the 8th, they were off to Dusseldorf.

Putting on a show

On 15 April Acheson was sent detailed orders for a Rhine Flotilla review, in honour of General Charles 'The Butcher' Mangin, commanding the French 10th Army forces occupying the French sector. Acheson's instructions left him little room for personal initiative, detailing how the little vessels were to 'man the sides', speeds and revolutions, salutes to be fired, etc.[21]

The flotilla† sailed from Cologne on the 21st, arriving in Coblenz at 0925 the following day; from there they reached Mayence at 1620. The trip was not without its problems, for one ML hit some hidden rocks. That evening, the officers of the flotilla motored to Wiesbaden for dinner.

The grand review began on St George's Day, 23 April. After the flotilla had breakfasted, they watched the French guard of honour fall in at the quayside and then march to a square, a new silk ensign carried ahead of them and flanked by Mangin's personal bodyguard of North African *Tirailleurs*. In the square, the North African cavalry were lined up to receive the marching phalanx. 'All of the National Anthems were played [and] the British, French and Algerian horsemen marched off through the city and back to where the MLs were lying'.[22]

Now it was the two navies' turn to show off. 'At 1320 we all left our berths

---

* A promenade next to the river in the old part of the town. The club lay between the Hohenzollern Bridge and the Deutz Bridge.
† The boats involved were *291, 8, 576, 50, 473, 287, 288, 260, 358, 542, 569, 229*, organised in three groups of four with Acheson in *ML-291* (docs 1617, IWM).

MLs *576, 358, 542, 287*, moored at the Cologne Watersports club, the Deutz Bridge in the background. They are dressed for the 28 June 1919 Peace Day celebrations.
(Author's collection)

and moved up stream,' wrote Gerald Aldridge. 'A little later the French MLs came up but on the other side of the river'.[23] On board a Royal Navy ML, Mangin and Commander Acheson sailed up stream between the two lines and a seventeen-gun salute was fired by both nations' vessels.

The general disembarked and returned to his horsemen, whereupon 'we all passed him in turn and saluted the French flag'.[24] The formalities over, the MLs moored up at 1430, and at 1915 all the officers repaired to Mangin's 'palace'. Here they were wined and dined and there were 'coloured flags and fireworks on the river; there was also a torchlight procession'.[25] After years of wartime shortages, the food offered for the dinner must have seemed richly delicious. It included veal, pigeon, chicken and asparagus and was finished off with – in tribute to the raid which had taken place twelve months to the day a year earlier – 'Bombe Zeebrugge' (for details see Appendix 8).

Quite what the indigenous population thought of this display of foreign pageantry is a moot point. But this demonstration of German subjugation and French dominance may also have been to do with Mangin's political

Another view of MLs at the Cologne Watersports Club, this time MLs *287*, *473* and *50*. (*Author's collection*)

stance, for he had become a controversial figure due to his attempts to promote the creation of a pro-French Rhenish Republic, separate from Germany and thus denying Germany the west bank of the Rhine.

There were more celebrations three weeks later when, on 16 May, the flotilla sailed to Königswinter for an event in honour of Maréchal Ferdinand Foch. Eight MLs participated, joined by two French *chasseurs* and nine *vedettes*. Foch was greeted by gunnery salutes from all naval vessels present. Returning to Cologne, the MLs dressed ship and the French again fired off their weapons in salute. According to Lieutenant Aldridge, 'we had dinner in the ballroom and had as our own guests the French naval officers and representative [*sic*] ladies in Cologne. After dinner there was dancing until 0200'.[26] *

It would seem that it is with some justification that Violet Markham, wife

---

* Such parades were regular events. There were more celebrations in Cologne of Peace Day, 28 June 1919, and again in August when Winston Churchill was among the visitors.

A panoramic photograph of the review, in Cathedral Square, Cologne, of British troops by General Gouroud (Commanding Fourth French Army), August 1919. *(US Library of Congress, 2007663192)*

to James Carruthers, later the chief demobilisation officer for the British forces in the Rhineland, noted that 'life in Cologne is very pleasant for the occupying army'[27] and 'surely no army of occupation was ever so well housed or so comfortable as we are'.[28]

Certainly, the commanding officers of the occupying forces lived in some style. The British Rhine army chief, General Sir William Robertson:

> lives in a magnificent mansion out of the town on the banks of the Rhine in beautiful grounds. The owner of this house is a self-made man, who began life as a boy in the steelworks in Sheffield and then returned to Germany when he had made his fortune. The family had been turned out of this house, but the German servants were still there.[29]

Meanwhile, in between these jolly days, the luckless Lieutenant Robinson had yet more misfortune. On 12 May, about noon, his *ML-229* blew up after taking on fuel. Motor Mechanic Locke was killed and three men injured; the English language *Cologne Post* of 13 May 1919 reported that Lieutenant Robinson was dead, which must have come as a surprise to him for he had in fact 'sustained light burns'.[30] Chief Motor Mechanic Kennedy and Deckhand Patterson were also injured.

For Lieutenant Aldridge, his time in Germany was at an end. The navy

sent him back to England by train and on 28 May he was again at the depot ship HMS *Hermione*, still giving the ML officers a base, where he completed his demobilisation papers. The following day he was at his home, where he played tennis. His war was finally over.

And so was John William Robinson's, four months later. He became CO of *ML-576* in August and took her back to Le Havre; Robinson was demobilised on 17 September and returned to his native Newcastle-upon-Tyne.

Winding down

The end of the war had brought with it a need to rebuild the British economy and reduce military spending in all its forms, a process started in the same month as the Armistice. In a letter to First Lord of the Admiralty Eric Geddes on 23 November 1919, Chancellor of the Exchequer Andrew Bonar Law wrote to state that he was 'most anxious that the cutting down of unnecessary war expenditure should take place at once'.[31]

Thus in mid 1919 the Admiralty asked if the remaining eleven-strong flotilla in Cologne could be reduced, for reasons of cost saving. It was agreed that five boats could be withdrawn, leaving six on station. On 5 August Acheson drew up orders for Lieutenant Stanley Floyd Wood Laidlaw RN to take *ML-473* under his command and sail it and four others* to Le Havre for Southampton along the same canal and river route by which they had all arrived. Laidlaw, who had previously been serving on *473* as a supernumerary, had been badly injured in the first week of the war when

---

* In the end, *473* did not depart but *569*, *576*, *299*, *50* and *260* did (docs 1617, IWM).

HMS *Amphion* was mined off Harwich. Now aged thirty-six, he was 'v tactful, well-mannered and v fond of shooting' according to Commander Acheson.³² Quite how this latter accomplishment would help in the task at hand was not vouchsafed.

The Admiralty's decision to sail the MLs back to Britain was not universally praised at a time of stringent economies in military spending. In the House of Commons, Major W P Colfox, Conservative MP for North Dorset, asked the Parliamentary and Financial Secretary to the Admiralty, Dr Thomas Macnamara:

> what was the cost in fuel and otherwise of bringing motor launches home from the Rhine; what these motor launches were worth when they arrived in England; how much the country has lost by bringing them home rather than selling them or destroying them where they were when no longer needed.

Macnamara patiently explained the reasoning:

> the cost in fuel in bringing a motor launch home from the Rhine was about £30, but this is counterbalanced by the saving of the fares of the crew. Wherever possible the motor launches are sold where they lie, and this has been done in the Mediterranean and elsewhere, but there is apparently no market for them on the Rhine. The saleable value of the launches was in no way diminished by their being brought home. No loss has therefore been incurred by this action, and some money will eventually be realised by their sale. Five motor launches have already been brought home.³³

In fact, 100 MLs had already been sold off by October; the five returnees were presumably intended to join them.

For Acheson and his men, the round of dinners continued. These included one given by Colonel David H Biddle, Liaison Officer in the US Army, at the Hotel Excelsior, Cologne, in honour of General Robertson on 25 February 1920. And four motor launches were sent to Mayence for the *Semaine Hippique* between 26 and 30 August. They moored in front of the Feldbergplatz, next to the French flotilla, but only Acheson was offered accommodation ashore, at the Hotel Rose.

The sailors of the Rhine patrol designed and produced their own Christmas cards for 1919 and 1920, and by the beginning of 1921, Acheson's officers comprised a paymaster and an engineering lieutenant, ten other lieutenants and two sub lieutenants.³⁴ But the Admiralty continued to press

A US Army bugler plays the Last Post as the Americans leave the Rhineland, February 1923. The American handed over 'their' sector to the French. *(Author's collection)*

for the Rhine Patrol to be ended. However, General Sir William Robertson still resisted. Acheson, however, did depart, having contracted tuberculosis*, and on 7 March 1921 Queensland-born Commander Alan Robert Armitage MacDonald RN took over the flotilla from Acheson; and at the end of the year, possibly as a gesture from Robertson, it was reduced to five. The main reason for the patrol's retention appeared to be military pride: 'the suppression of the flotilla was again suggested from time to time but it was decided to retain it for the sake of prestige, as it would have to be replaced by the French'.[35] It was to remain in place until the British finally left both Cologne and the Rhineland, the last MLs leaving for home on 27 January 1926.†

MLs and a revolution

In Salonika, Sub Lieutenant Fred Cooper returned to *ML-228* on 15 November and sailed to Mudros, where from the 21st to the 26th they were trapped in harbour as it was 'blowing a gale'.[36] But by 4 December, *ML-228* and her sisters proudly sailed into the harbour of Constantinople, the

---
* He was invalided out of the navy in the 1920s and led a very restricted life, mainly in France, dying in 1957.
† Some British troops remained at Wiesbaden until 30 June 1930.

furthest east that any motor launch had voyaged. The following day, *228, 210, 236* and *509*, in company with the scout cruiser HMS *Sentinel* (1904), entered the Black Sea, sightseeing the ex-German battlecruiser *Goeben* en route. By the 9th, they had reached Sulina (the most eastern point of Romania) at the mouth of the Danube, where the MLs joined up with some Insect-class river monitors to cruise up the river. Christmas Day 1918 was spent in Bucharest.

On the second day of 1919, the little flotilla passed through the Iron Gates and on 6 January arrived in Belgrade. By the 27th they were in Budapest and availing himself of its attractions, Cooper saw a production of Wagner's *Lohengrin* at the Budapest Opera on 2 February and on 15 March attended a 'Grand Ball Masque'.

In between times, the MLs were inspected by Rear Admiral Troubridge on 12 February. Rear Admiral Ernest Troubridge (known as the Silver King on account of his mane of white hair) had incurred the displeasure of the Admiralty, and a court martial, for failing to engage, and allowing to escape to Turkey, the German battlecruiser SMS *Goeben*. Relived of his command, he was not offered another appointment until he begged First Lord Winston Churchill to give him a post. Churchill sent him to Serbia to organise the Serbian naval forces against Austrian Danube attack, and whilst there he became very close to the Serbian crown prince and armed forces commander, Prince Aleksander Karageorge. He also shared the horrendous retreat of the shattered Serbian forces over the mountains into Albania and eventual rescue by Italian naval forces.

After the war, the Allies urgently needed a Balkan specialist to head a commission to administrate the Danube waterway, one who would represent the victor's interests and be acceptable to the Serbs, Romanians and other interested non-European parties. The choice fell on Troubridge and he swiftly accepted; for him, it was another chance to rebuild his reputation. On 20 February 1919 Troubridge returned to the Balkans and set up his office in the ex-Austrian Embassy in Belgrade.

But further up the Danube, Budapest was in a state of uproar. Hunger stalked the land, a shattered and defeated nation faced a hostile Romania on its borders and Allied occupation of its trade routes; and insurrection was brewing. At the end of the war there was much territorial jostling at the borders of Hungary and Romania, and the Paris Peace Conference recommended the establishment of a neutral zone between the two countries, a proposal which favoured Romanian territorial ambitions. Hungary was not officially informed of this decision until one Lieutenant Colonel Vix, a French officer, informed the president of Hungary on 20 March, describing the line as a 'temporary political frontier'. He turned it into an ultimatum by demanding a response within thirty-two hours.

This démarche provoked widespread anger, and on 21 March 1919 the Hungarian Soviet Republic, the second Communist regime in Europe after Russia itself, was proclaimed. The pre-existing Hungarian government was deposed and a Bolshevik dictatorship, under an ex-muckraking journalist and quondam aide to Lenin, Bela Kun, was established.

On 22 March, at 0130, Fred Cooper recorded that 'the watch on deck' of *ML-228* 'was rushed and surrounded whilst the CO, self and crew were taken prisoner. The boat was ransacked'.[37] The prisoners were transported by guard boat to the Ritz [hotel] and the Bolshevik Red Flag was hoisted over the motor launch. The following day, the crew of *ML-210* were similarly interned and forced to the Ritz, from where both boats' men later broke out and returned to their craft.

Troubridge hurriedly put together a small scratch force consisting of an ML under the command of his number two Captain Haggard, and the former KuK (Austro-Hungarian) monitors *Bosna* and *Enns* flying the British and French flags respectively, which left Baja on 22 March for Budapest.

The crews of the MLs were told by the Communists that they must not leave Budapest; and by Captain Haggard that they must stay until the Allied missions had managed to depart safely. In fact, the MLs managed to sail for Baja on the 27th, and were back at Belgrade by 3 April. Here Cooper and his commanding officer met with Troubridge, who told them 'that as soon as the other MLs arrive from Mudros, they would be sent home'.[38] *

But this was not the end of the motor launches' involvement in the Hungarian revolution. As Bela Kun's short-lived regime began to fail, a ML took part in the so-called 'Battle of Baja' of June 1919, when two monitors and four armed gunboats of the former Austrian Navy, now under the control of revolutionary Hungarian forces, were seen to approach the British Danube base of Baja. Thirty-two-year-old Lieutenant Basil Gold Watney RNVR, an architect in peacetime and now commanding *ML-236*, sallied out to attack them and defend the base, only to discover that they were coming to surrender. For his courage and subsequent tact in negotiating their submission he was awarded the Distinguished Service Cross on 14 October[39], only to die a fortnight later of the 'Spanish Influenza'. He was buried in the Rákoskeresztúr cemetery of Budapest.

---

* As indeed they were, and Cooper was demobilised on 22 May.

15

In Russia and the North Sea

As was noted in the preceding chapter, the Armistice did not in fact see the end of the fighting for the petrol navies. For in Russia and some of its former territories, now struggling to be independent entities, the forces set loose by the Great War continued to be in conflict; a war – or more properly a set of wars – which would not end until 1921.

In the Baltic States – Estonia and Latvia in particular – the German army carried on fighting the Bolsheviks of Russia (at the demand of the Allies). German proxies battled to fulfil Teutonic dreams of a Reich-dominated eastern quasi-empire, as articulated in the German statement of war aims made in 1914 and reiterated in 1917*. In Russia, Finland and again in the Baltic States, White Russian forces, loyal to the monarchist cause and seeking a Tsarist restoration and the return of the Russian empire's lost territories, warred against the newly formed Red Army of the Bolsheviks, Trotsky and Lenin. The Bolshevik regime itself fought against its internal enemies, parties of the left and centre which were still attempting to bring about some democratic version of Russian government, with brutal repression and murder. Meanwhile, the Red Army attacked to the west to recover the rich lands which it had lost when Lenin took Russia out of the world war. And British, French, American and Japanese military missions were all committed to action within Russia, supporting the White Russian armies and their disparate leaders. They fought with the White Russians against the Reds, or vied with German revanchist armies, in the Baltic, the White Sea, the Black Sea, Siberia, the Caspian Sea and numerous other places. And coastal motor boats, motor launches and submarine chasers were there too.

Battle in the Baltic Sea

The war had barely ended when Britain sent a Royal Navy flotilla of light cruisers and destroyers into the Baltic Sea. On 26 November 1918 they sailed under Rear Admiral Edwyn Alexander-Sinclair; their mission was to help the fledgling states of Estonia and Latvia in their struggle to maintain their

---

* These included 'Poland and the Baltic group, annexed from Russia, would be under German sovereignty for "all time"' (Tuchman, *The Guns of August*, p315). These aims were reaffirmed on 17/18 May 1917 by Germany and Austro-Hungary.

independence in the face of attack by Lenin's Red Army and internal German-sponsored insurrection.* These aims were reaffirmed on 17/18 May 1917 by Germany and Austro-Hungary.

After some adventure, this force withdrew when the Baltic iced up in winter and was replaced in February 1919 by a similar force under Rear Admiral Walter Cowan. Neither of these groups of ships had a member of the Petrol Navy in their numbers. But soon two would be introduced into the region by stealth.

CMBs in the Baltic
Lieutenant Augustus Agar RN was kicking his heels at Osea Island when the call came for him to go to London for a mysterious meeting. Agar had been working with the CMBs at Osea; he knew them and their crews well. In London he found that he was to meet 'C', the legendary Mansfield George Smith-Cumming, head of Britain's Secret Intelligence Service. Cumming was running agents in Russia; but the flow of information had ceased, and his normal couriers had been either killed or imprisoned. He needed to be able to get agents and messages in and out of Russia, especially Petrograd, and a CMB, which could pass over the defensive minefields and travel quickly and stealthily, seemed the ideal vehicle.

Agar was given £1,000, told to pick his own crews and furnished with two CMBs. His orders instructed him to make his own way to Finland in secret and set up base there. The boats were painted white and shipped as deck cargo on a civilian ship. Once there and united with his CMBs and their crews, Agar planned to establish his operations in an old and derelict yacht club at Terrioki, thirty miles north of Biorko and just three miles from the Finnish-Russian border. He had selected five men he knew from Osea Island: two sub lieutenants, Edgar Robert 'Sinbad' Sindall and John White Hampsheir, together with Midshipman Richard Nigel Onslow Marshall, all reservists RNR, and two Chief Motor Mechanics, Hugh Beeley (an RNVR member, Rolls Royce trained) and Albert Victor Piper RNVR. All the men had volunteered for this special service.

Cowan was informed, but Agar was not under his command and he and his team were officially 'deniable'. Nonetheless, Agar managed to persuade Cowan to let him have two torpedoes for his boats, just in case he needed them. His instructions from Cumming forbade him to use his force for offensive purposes – but then any fool can obey orders. Bored with the

---

* The full account of the little-known story of the Royal Navy in the Baltic in 1919/20 is told in Steve R Dunn, *Battle in the Baltic*, Seaforth Publishing (Barnsley, 2020).

The Russian protected cruiser *Oleg* (1902), twelve 6in guns, sunk by *CMB-4* in June 1919. *(Author's collection)*

waiting in the gaps between running as courier, Agar resolved to take action against the Red fleet.

The garrison of the fortress of Krasnaya Gorka, which guarded the southern entrance to the Russian fleet base at Kronstadt, had revolted, arrested their commissars and hoisted a white flag as a signal to White Russian and Allied forces to come and rescue them. When Agar observed two battleships firing at the fort, he decided to act.

On Monday, 16 June Lieutenant Agar left his base at 2215 hours (Finnish time) and set course for the main Russian fleet base at Kronstadt with both CMBs, *CMB-7* now commanded by Sindall, and Agar himself in *CMB-4*. Out of courtesy, Agar had sent a message to Cowan giving his intentions. He and his men had their naval uniforms with them and both boats were flying small white ensigns.

The plan was to pass through the Russian defences and attack the bombarding ships with torpedoes at around midnight. But disaster struck. While rounding Tolbuhin Light, *CMB-7* struck a submerged obstacle, probably a 'dud' mine, which broke her propeller shaft. Marshall, although a non-swimmer, went over the side to see if he could fix the problem, to no avail. Agar took her in tow and they returned to Terrioki. Sindall's mechanic, Piper, immediately dived overboard to examine the shaft, but it was beyond repair; and they had no spares.

From a lookout point in a nearby church steeple, Agar observed that the two battleships seen earlier now had steam up and were under way, back to

The crew of *CMB-4* who sank *Oleg*. Midshipman Hampsheir (left), Lieutenant Agar (centre), who gained the VC for his actions, and Petty Officer Beeley (right). *(Author's collection)*

harbour. In their place had arrived a large cruiser, *Oleg*, with attendant destroyers. That afternoon, the cruiser restarted the bombardment of the fortress. It was now or never. The fortress needed help; there was a target of opportunity in the offering and he still had one CMB. Augustus Agar determined to attack that night, the 17th.

Hampsheir, Beeley and Agar once more put on their uniforms and mounted their charger. At 2230 local time, *CMB-4* slipped out of harbour. They were off to challenge the Russians to single combat.

The weather was worsening with a heavy swell, not ideal conditions for a small 40ft-long motor boat, but they reached the position of the cruiser around midnight. She was protected by a destroyer screen and the first task was to slip through it unobserved.

To ready the torpedo for launch, Agar ordered Hampsheir to remove the safety pin from the cartridge in the firing chamber. There was a sudden noise, the boat shook and Hampsheir reappeared with an agonised look. While trying to remove the safety pin from the firing pistol lanyard, it broke, leaving the pin still in. As Hampsheir fought with the device, the pin suddenly came out and the pistol fired. Fortunately, the linkage to the explosive firing charge was also faulty and the torpedo launching mechanism itself did not fire.

They now had to stop the boat and reload the cartridge, difficult on land, more so when the vessel was rolling in a sea. Beeley took over and removed the starting pistol and replaced the cartridge. At 2350 it was ready to use. The whole process had taken fifteen minutes, all the while with Russian destroyers 200–300yds to either side of them and the big cruiser in silhouette ahead. As Agar wrote later, 'I, of course, dared not leave the wheel and controls. I could see the black hulls of the destroyers and waited for gun flashes. We were a "dead sitter" but, luckily for us, remained unseen'.[1]

When Hampsheir finally called that all was well, Agar slipped the clutch and went to full speed. The little craft tore down on the cruiser. Holding on until the range was 500yds, he fired the torpedo and turned almost a complete circle, now heading back the way they had come, followed by the wind and, more worryingly, the first gunfire.

The torpedo hit abreast the foremost funnel and a huge column of black smoke rose up from the stricken beast. Russian forts and destroyers opened fire on them, fortunately going high, and they gave three cheers for themselves, unheard above the engine's roar, as they fled away. Shells exploded in the sea around them, soaking the men and their craft, but none

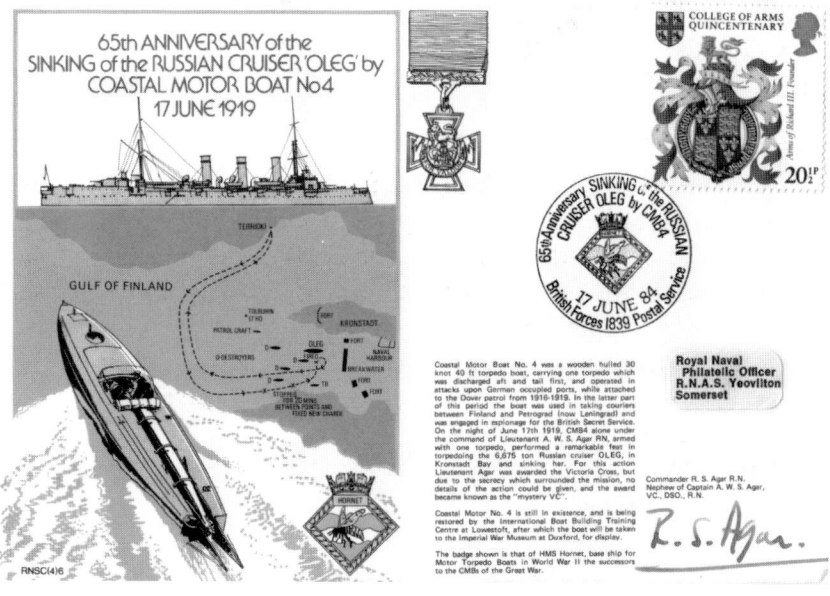

A British first day postal cover from 1984, commemorating Agar's sinking of *Oleg*. It is signed by Augustus Agar's nephew, Captain R S Agar. *(Author's collection)*

hit home. At 0300 they re-entered Terrioki; Agar and his crew had just sunk a large Russian armoured cruiser of twelve 6in guns, 576 men and 6,975 tons. St George had killed the dragon.

Cowan was delighted with this success and put Agar forward for the Victoria Cross. For his bravery in action, and on Cowan's recommendation, on 26 August 1919 Lieutenant Augustus Agar was awarded the VC. Because of the secret role he had been engaged on, and his 'unofficial' presence in the Baltic, the citation for the award merely stated that it was 'in recognition of his conspicuous gallantry, coolness and skill under extremely difficult conditions in action', for which reason it became known as 'the mystery VC'.[2]

Admiral Cowan now recognised that in CMBs he had a weapon which he could use to attack and neutralise the Bolshevik fleet at Kronstadt which, although seemingly unwilling to sally forth, presented a clear and present danger to his ships and to the littoral of the Estonian and Latvian states. He formally requested the Admiralty to send him a flotilla of the little craft which would be able to skim over the mines and barrage protecting the harbour.

But how to get them from the River Blackwater to the Baltic Sea? Part of Cowan's 20th Destroyer Flotilla was ordered to return to Britain to collect the motor boats. This time they were 55-footers, carrying two torpedoes rather than one, and up to four Lewis guns. The towing destroyers were to transport the motor boat spares, engines, torpedoes and the like, and one officer and one rating was to be on board the little craft while they were being towed. This latter instruction seemed to offer an uncomfortable passage to the unfortunates chosen. Eight CMBs were to be brought out to Cowan's base at Biorko.

It was no easy task and the 20th Flotilla suffered a total of sixteen breaks of tow on the voyage and made a very difficult passage. But Cowan's petrol-driven strike force eventually made it to Biorko on 8 August; and so did the man detailed to lead them, thirty-four-year-old Commander Claude Congreve Dobson DSO, until now a submarine specialist. He and the other crews had been asked by the Admiralty to volunteer for 'Special Service'. Some, such as nineteen-year-old Chief Motor Mechanic Baden Marples Masters RNVR*, had already been demobilised. He had returned to his apprenticeship at Rolls Royce when he received a telegram from the Admiralty requesting his services. He told his father that 'he would make his light shine if he got the chance'.[3]

---

* Initially assigned to MLs with *Hermione*, Masters transferred to CMBs on 1 October 1918 (ADM 337/98/994, TNA).

Map showing location and defences of Kronstadt Russian naval base. *(Peter Wilkinson)*

The plan called for a raid by the CMBs at night. The striking force of six boats were to attack the ships in the harbour whilst two guarded the entrance and, if necessary, neutralised the harbour barrier. The vessels would have to pass through the forts and the harbour mouth, which was only 50yds wide, without being detected. Aircraft would bomb the garrison to confuse and divert it. Cowan dubbed the raid Operation RK in homage to his great hero Roger Keyes.

At 2130 on 17 August the flotilla started their engines and shoved off from the aircraft carrier HMS *Vindictive*, where they had berthed during the day. Leaving Biorko at 2200, they proceeded in two groups, one led by Agar, one by Dobson, to the rendezvous at Inonemi Point. Dobson arrived at the meeting point and his flotilla joined him at midnight, while Agar, having piloted two other boats to the rendezvous, proceeded independently to patrol the harbour mouth. The flotilla then set out at 19 knots towards the North Channel. They were now slightly behind time and the air offensive had already started, but difficulties in navigation made Dobson chary of increasing speed. He could also see just two boats, *79* and *88* (Lieutenants William Bremner, last met in Chapter 10, and Archibald Dayrell-Reed respectively), following him, but decided that he should capitalise on the air diversion and attack immediately.

With Bremner, whose boat was full of cable-cutting equipment in case of a harbour boom, in the van, they proceeded up the Petrograd canal and found the destroyer *Gavriil* on guard duty but with no one on deck. Bremner, finding no barrier at the entrance, roared into the basin and launched his torpedoes at the cruiser/depot ship *Pamiat Azova*. Dobson, in *CMB-31BD*, followed him in and his number two, Lieutenant Russell McBean, fired two torpedoes at the battleship *Andrei Pervozvanny*. Behind him, Dobson saw *CMB-88* running in and thought she put one torpedo into *Andrei Pervozvanny* and another into the battleship *Petropavlovsk*.

But all was not well in *88*. Dayrell-Reed and his number two, Lieutenant Gordon Steele, heard the explosion as the depot ship was torpedoed and suddenly came under fire from both sides of their boat. Steele ducked down involuntarily and when he looked up again the whole surface of the water was pockmarked with shell splashes. The motor boat was headed straight towards a hospital ship, and Steele had just remarked, 'Where are you heading?' to his skipper when he realised that 'although still standing up and holding the wheel, his head was resting on the wooden conning tower top in front of him'.[4] He had been shot through the head. 'Mossy' Dayrell-Reed was a big man and it was with some difficulty that Steele lowered him to the cockpit floor so that he could take command. He was right on top of the *Andrei Pervozvanny* and must fire now or never. He fired and then stopped one engine to make an emergency turn away, firing at *Petropavlovsk* as he did so. As the boat turned, Steele saw and heard Dobson's torpedoes hit *Andrei Pervozvanny*, an explosion which drenched *88*'s crew with water and yellow picric acid powder before, seconds later, he observed his own weapons make their mark. The Soviets were now fully alert and there was a considerable volume of rifle and machine-gun fire being directed at the motor boats as all three CMBs began to retire.

Meanwhile, *CMB-72A*, under Lieutenant Edward Bodley, assigned to shoot at *Rurik*, finally arrived on station, having had trouble with her steering gear. The problem had not been rectified, which made it impossible for Bodley to manoeuvre into the basin, but he tried to launch his weapons anyway at a destroyer he saw as he approached the harbour entrance, only for the mechanism to misfire (it had in fact been shot away).

Now Lieutenant Lawrence Napier and Sub Lieutenant Osman Cyril Horton Giddy in *24A* entered the fray. Napier thought he had succeeded in torpedoing a destroyer, but in trying to make good his escape his boat was disabled by nets or the breakwaters and sunk by gunfire.

Behind them came Acting Lieutenant Commander Frank Brade in *62*. As Bremner was racing out, both boats collided and *79* was almost cut in half. The two boats were locked together, obstructing the entrance to the basin. Brade went to full speed, dragging both boats clear and then took *79*'s crew into his own vessel, while Bremner blew up his craft with guncotton. Brade then attacked a destroyer with his torpedoes but missed. *CMB-62* was now under fire from the destroyer's aft gun and a machine gun. The first shell fired hit the rear part of the cockpit and wounded all on board, fatally injuring Brade himself. Bremner took command and ordered the discharge of green Very lights, the signal for a disabled boat. Their Lewis guns had jammed and would not clear, giving the Russians uninterrupted target practice; their second shell hit the boat amidships and passed clear through whilst a third exploded on the cockpit, as did a fourth. Bremner, who had been wounded in three places whilst on his own boat, was now suffering from no less than eleven wounds. At this point a fifth shell hit forward and all the crew were thrown into the water as the motor boat blew up.

Agar, with Marshall and Sindall alongside him in the repaired *CMB-7*, had remained outside the harbour intending to attack any shipping that came out. At about 0200 he retired to Petrograd Bay and waited to assist any boats in trouble. When he decided that no more CMBs were likely to emerge, he went back in himself and fired his single torpedo into the harbour; it exploded, but Agar could not distinguish what he had hit.

Dobson withdrew in company with *88*, but then waited to see if any stragglers emerged. Coming under fire at first light, he again moved away and proceeded back to the flagship. For the remaining crew of Dayrell-Reed's boat, it was a tricky return journey. CMM Masters, himself wounded in the thigh, followed Dayrell-Reed's last command to him: 'For God's sake, Masters, keep the engines running'.[5] He 'had to keep filling my tin hat with oil and pouring it into the oil tank as it was shot through'. However, he believed that 'we gave the Bolshies h***'.[6]

Sub Lieutenant Francis Howard in *86BD*, who had been intended to attack the armoured cruiser *Rurik*, had experienced overwhelming problems with his steering and engine and had been left behind, unable to manage more than 7 knots. Nonetheless, although clearly not in a fighting condition, he proceeded through the defensive forts under heavy fire and patrolled Petrograd Bay, ready to engage any hostile craft and cover the retirement. But with his engines failing due to a seized big end, and hardly able to move at all, the guns zeroed in on his vessel. Fortunately, Sub Lieutenant Roland Hunter-Blair arrived in *72A* in the nick of time. On *86BD* Howard's number two, Sub Lieutenant Robert Leslie Wight, hastily prepared the crippled vessel for towing and *CMB-72A* took her under tow.

Onboard *88*, they administered morphine to Dayrell-Reed, who recovered consciousness once and tried to speak. Near Biorko they saw a destroyer and asked for a doctor. As they passed Cowan's flagship HMS *Delhi*, the admiral left the bridge to speak to them and when they reached their berth alongside *Vindictive* the ship's crew gave them a cheer. Dayrell-Reed died shortly afterwards.

Two Russian ships had been sunk, the 12in-gunned *Andrei Pervozvanny* and *Pamiat Azova*, and the battleship *Petropavlovsk* damaged. But there had been a cost. Three CMBs had been lost and two badly shot up and brave men had died. Four ratings, Leading Seaman Sidney Holmes, Able Seaman William G Smith, and two Chief Motor Mechanics RNVR, Francis Stephens and Francis Thatcher, perished in the fight. So did four officers, Sub Lieutenant Hector Forbes MacLean, Acting Lieutenant Commander Frank Tomkinson Brade RNR, Sub Lieutenant Thomas R G Usborne and Lieutenant Archibald Dayrell-Reed RNR, the latter a mariner who had served his apprenticeship in sailing ships. He had taken part in Operation ZO in 1918. Napier, Bremner, Giddy, two chief motor mechanics and an able seaman were taken from the water by the Bolsheviks and made prisoners of war, where they endured harsh conditions which nearly killed them too.

Part of the Red fleet had been disabled; indeed, never again would the big ships threaten the Baltic coast and Cowan had achieved command of the sea. Dobson and Steele joined Agar as holders of the Victoria Cross (see Appendix 9). The Petrol Navy had proved its worth again.

MLs in the Baltic

And there were motor launches in the Baltic War too. The whole area was riddled with mines, German, Russian, Danish and Swedish, and these offered considerable danger to Cowan's ships. Moreover, the Baltic is in parts heavily shoaled and the littoral areas are unpredictably varied in depth. What was needed were vessels able to sweep mines in very shallow waters.

In response to the admiral's pleas for vessels able to work in such waters, the Admiralty sent him four motor launches, MLs *98*, *124*, *125* and *156*, all of them towed out by destroyers, and Cowan put them to work sweeping and, occasionally, laying mines.

Only one of them made it back to the UK. When the time came for the Royal Navy's forces to leave the area, *ML-156* was out of action, having been mined. Whilst she was being hoisted out of the water at Reval for inspection and repair prior to being taken home, she was dropped from the crane and badly damaged. Her condition was judged to be beyond the dockyard's ability and she was left where she was to be sold off locally.

And on 29 December 1919 the minesweepers *Cattistock*, *Holderness* and *Heythorp* set out from Reval (now Tallinn), each towing a motor launch. They also headed into a great storm. On *Holderness*'s second night at sea, sailing for Copenhagen, the weather turned very nasty. She was towing *ML-124* which, in the freezing cold, 'looked like a miniature iceberg'.[7] *Holderness* was shipping water on deck and then the tow rope parted. A party was sent to board the motor launch, now adrift, and eventually a seaman on a lifeline managed to attach another towing hawser. The following night the tow snapped again and this time the hawser wound itself around the starboard propeller. Short of coal, with only one propeller, and in the teeth of what was now a violent storm, there was nothing for it but to run for the tiny port of Rønne on Danish Bornholm Island. The locals, taking pity on their plight, invited the crew to their New Year's Eve party. The ML washed ashore on the southern side of the island of Öland and was abandoned there.

Heythorp was towing *ML-98* and experienced similar issues with the weather. In snow squalls and gale-force winds the tow parted several times, being reconnected only with the utmost difficulty. Eventually, the tow broke for the final time at 0630 and the launch disappeared behind snow- and gale-lashed waves in which she foundered. Following her sister, and similarly low on coal, *Heythorp* ran for the shelter of Bornholm Island. Only *Cattistock* made it safely to Copenhagen, with *ML-125* in tow.

Action in the Caspian Sea

Back at Osea Island, requirements for CMB support came thick and fast.

They had a 'request from Black Sea asking for a flotilla to support their operations to regain control of the oil fields at Baku', and another for CMBs to support an expedition under General 'Tiny' Ironside 'to re-occupy Archangel and retrieve stores we left behind in the winter of 1918'.[8]

For the Caspian, twelve 40ft and 55ft CMBs were despatched from Osea on board the third-class cruiser *Diamond* (1904), which had been converted to carry six 40ft boats, and the Admiralty transport *War Stag* (1918, 5,249grt). The flotilla was under the orders of Commander Eric Gascoigne Robinson VC, a genuine war hero who had won his Victoria Cross in the Gallipoli campaign of 1915 where:

> Lieutenant Commander Robinson on the 26th February advanced alone, under heavy fire, into an enemy's gun position, which might well have been occupied, and destroying a four-inch gun, returned to his party for another charge with which the second gun was destroyed. Lieutenant Commander Robinson would not allow members of his demolition party to accompany him as their white uniforms rendered them very conspicuous. Lieutenant Commander Robinson took part in four attacks on the minefields – always under heavy fire.[9]

The flotilla sailed via the Dardanelles to Batoum (now Batumi, Georgia), on the Black Sea, from whence the boats were transferred to a special train for transport to Baku. This proved rather adventurous, as they were under constant threat from both Red and White troops, who wanted to lay hands on their supplies and stores; eventually the CMB crews and engineers had to man and control the train themselves.

At Baku they joined forces with a ragtag collection of improvised warships, made up from captured Russian merchant craft and commanded by Commodore David Thomas Norris RN, who had recently been made a CB, gazetted on 19 March 1919, for 'valuable services as SNO Caspian Sea during the summer of 1918'. Two of the captured ships (*Edinburgh Castle* and *Sergei*) were fitted out to carry the CMBs into action on their fore decks and kept at sea-readiness in case the Bolshevik Caspian Fleet sallied out.

Norris had established his base at Petrovsk. Lying at Baku was the nominally White Russian Centro-Caspian flotilla of gunboats and merchant ships. Unpaid for months and now pro-Bolshevik, if not yet openly so, they were unreliable and a potential threat. In early spring Norris decided to deal with them. Their commander was sent away on a train and – fearful of what might be in store for them – two of the gunboats and three armed steamers put to sea and anchored outside the port.

Four CMBs were sent to take care of the situation. Robinson gave the Russian ships an ultimatum: surrender and return to harbour or be sunk. Ten minutes were allowed for a reply and when none was forthcoming, the CMBs fired two torpedoes; embarrassingly both ran deep, but still produced an effect. As the entry in the log of one of the Russian ships, *Ardagan*, tersely noted:

> 3.25; they fired a torpedo
> 3.28; decided to surrender.[11]

Towards the end of April 1919, when the ice broke up in the northern Caspian, the remainder of the Bolshevik fleet ventured out of the River Volga and established a base at Fort Alexandrovsk on the eastern shore of the Caspian Sea. All through the winter months the fleet had been bottled up in the river port of Astrakhan.

In May, Norris received intelligence that the Reds intended to mount an assault against the base from the fort. He sailed to get his retaliation in first, taking the CMB carriers with him. Air reconnaissance demonstrated that some destroyers, two submarines and several barges and small armed craft were at anchor in the harbour. On 21 May he opened the assault with gunfire. The CMBs were intended to be used in the raid too, but the radio sets on *Sergei* and *Edinburgh Castle* were old and failed to pick up Norris's summoning signal.

Then, seven days later, six CMBs were sent to attack the harbour, led by Commander Robinson. They torpedoed a large barge and a submarine depot ship, but their depredations were stopped by a delegation of civilian sailors who put out in a launch to intercept Robinson's boat and inform him that the Bolsheviks had departed; the first strike had cost them a destroyer, a gun barge, a minelayer and several smaller craft. They had withdrawn to save further punishment. The CMBs, known to the Reds as 'Devil Ships', had played their part again.

The White Sea chasers

The Allied intervention in Russia began with a British landing at Murmansk in March 1918. This was followed in the August by a landing at, and eventual occupation of, Archangel (Archangelsk). The latter port had been a major centre for Allied supply of the Tsarist Russian army and a considerable amount of ammunition and weaponry was still stored there. As the Bolshevik Red Army began to expand its hold over the region, the British and French governments set their military three objectives. First, to prevent the Allied war materiel stockpiled at Archangel falling into German or

Bolshevik hands; secondly, to mount an offensive to rescue the Czechoslovak Legion, which was stranded along the Trans-Siberian Railway and resurrect the Eastern Front; and thirdly, by defeating the Bolshevik army with the assistance of the Czechoslovak Legion, to provide support to the White Russian armies battling the Reds across Russia.

But troops and support could hardly be spared from existing commitments. The Allies asked the Americans to help and, in September 1918, 4,500 US troops arrived at Archangel to join the fray.

The official end of the war in November 1918 did not bring peace to Russia; Britain, France and to a lesser extent the USA, all wanted to strangle the doctrine of Communism at birth and gave support to the White Russian armies while continuing to place their own men in the field.

But political vacilation, lack of resources, incompetence in the White Russian army and continued Bolshevik success all rendered the situation in the White Sea region difficult. The Northern Dvina River was an important line of communication and soon calls were being made for naval craft of shallow draught which could operate on this and other riverine routes. But the situation worried the commanders on the spot.

In February 1919 commander of American naval forces in Russia, Rear Admiral Newton A McCully, sent an urgent message to Admiral Sims, which Sims relayed to Admiral William S Benson, Chief of Naval Operations, on 25 February 1919:

> Following received from Admiral McCully quote Arrived Mourmansk [sic] February 23rd. While at Archangel visited railroad front and consider situation of Archangel forces precarious. About beginning of April headwaters of Dvina open up, releasing enemy Naval Forces of considerable strength with six-inch guns mounted afloat, while Allied Naval Forces will remain frozen in for another month. Enemy's land forces outnumber ours three to one, he has lately showed himself bold and confident and if he makes a determined effort we will meet disaster. Only heavy reinforcements of reliable troops can make the situation secure. For subsequent operations on Dvina River recommend that twelve submarine chasers with tender be sent, as vessels drawing over seven feet cannot operate in this river. Vessels of submarine chaser type can operate in all interior waterways of Russia from the White Sea to the Caspian. Unquote. Strongly recommend approval. Will hold twelve submarine chasers for this duty unless otherwise directed. In case chasers are not to be held, request that I be promptly informed as these chasers must be selected from those now under orders to return to the United States and are practically ready to sail. Sims.[12]

And so the sub chasers went to Russia. Twelve were selected, volunteer commanders called for, and *SC-1, 90, 95, 98, 137, 256, 257, 258, 262, 271, 321* and *354* were sent to Inverness. The Y-gun was removed and an extra 3in installed in its stead, .30 calibre-Lewis guns were taken aboard, as were Browning automatic and Springfield rifles, Colt pistols, ammunition and a host of other supplies. The listening devices were removed and the hulls strengthened against the ice they would likely encounter by sheathing them with steel. But they couldn't attempt the voyage without a fuel tanker and the one assigned was damaged on passage. Eventually the problem was solved and the chasers departed in early June.

SC-354, 95 and *256* sailed with the British RFA tanker *Birchol* (1917, 1,097grt). Their route took them along the coast of Norway, and here in calm weather they conserved fuel by hoisting improvised sails. Crossing the Arctic Circle, on 12 June they reached Tromsø and on the 18th entered the White Sea and Archangel, mooring next to the protected cruiser USS *Des Moines* (1902), which would act as flagship for the flotilla. USN orders required the naval forces to restrict themselves to 'observation, communications and reporting', and this, in effect, manifested itself in 'ferrying passengers around the White Sea and sometimes visiting with local residents'.[13]

Coastal motor boats arrived too. Walter 'Joe' Beckett (last met in Chapter 10) was sent to Archangel in May 1919 as second in command of the 'CMB Flotilla, Dvina River Force' and skipper of *CMB-28A*, a 55-footer. His CMBs fought Bolshevik ships on the Dvina and Beckett also worked with the military (on land), as a Lewis gun officer, and on mine-clearance duties on the river.

On 14 September Beckett was stationed on the Dvina near to the front line and was tasked to take a badly wounded officer back to Archangel. He filled his boat's fuel tanks and took an additional 200 gallons in cans aboard, strapped his officer cargo and his stretcher into a torpedo trough and set off by moonlight. In the morning, in the absence of marker buoys, the CMB ran aground and started to take on water, filling quickly. With great presence of mind, Beckett went to full power and rammed it into the riverbank, ripping the bottom out of the craft, but ensuring that it would not sink and drown his passenger. As luck would have it, he was able to make contact with a passing launch and transfer his human freight, remove anything of value from his vessel and set it alight.

The British pulled out in September. They left behind five motor launches, *ML-575, 567, 570, 578* and *579*, which were abandoned as not being worth taking home. *CMB-77A* was also not to return to Britain, when the cargo ship due to take her sailed before a crane was ready to lift the boat aboard.

In the meantime, by July, most of the US troops had been evacuated and there seemed little further reason for an American naval presence. On 4 July the chasers took part in an Independence Day celebration and the following morning began their long journey back to Britain and their next assignment. It was to be hunting, but not of U-boats – instead they were to hunt mines.

The splinter ships and the northern mine barrier

When the United States entered the war, one of its government's immediate concerns was that the transport of troops and materiel from America to Britain and Europe should be as safe as possible. The introduction of transatlantic convoy was one means of achieving this aim; another was to deny U-boats access to the Atlantic by laying a 250-mile mine barrier between the Scottish and Norwegian coasts. In May 1917 the US Navy Office of Operations proposed the project to the British, who found the idea faintly risible, due to their experiences with the Dover Barrage. As Professor Norman Friedman noted, 'given the problems [of] maintaining the short Dover Barrage, the idea must have seemed ludicrous'.[14]

But the plan was supported by Assistant Secretary of the US Navy Franklin D Roosevelt and the Americans persisted. The USN pressed the concept on First Sea Lord Jellicoe, who in turn brought it before the London Allied Naval Conference of 4/5 September. Roosevelt ensured that some 100,000 mines were manufactured in America and eventually, the US Navy got its way; the first mines were laid in March 1918.

The plan was to leave two corridors at either end of the barrage to allow transit of friendly craft, one (area B, sixty miles width) flanking the Orkney coast and one (area C, seventy miles width) the Norwegian. Area B was to be deep-mined so that vessels supporting the Scandinavian convoys could pass over them and the U-boats would be driven down on to them by patrol craft which, as it transpired, could not be provided in any meaningful way. Area C was mined with deep and shallow mines as it was considered too far away for patrolling. The main section (area A) was an American naval responsibility and B and C fell to the Royal Navy.

Vice Admiral David Beatty, CinC Grand Fleet, was not a supporter of the mine barrier concept. Indeed, in August 1918 Foreign Secretary Arthur Balfour wrote to Lord Robert Cecil that Beatty held a 'dislike of the whole thing'.[15] But he followed his orders and Rear Admiral Lewis Clinton-Baker was appointed to command the Royal Navy part of the minelaying force. The Americans sent Rear Admiral Strauss aboard the Atlantic Fleet Mine Force flagship USS *Black Hawk* (1913). Strauss's command included twelve minelaying vessels. They were stationed at Invergordon and Inverness.

But then the war ended. Now the mines had to be swept up again. 'The

Commander Mine Force, Rear Admiral Joseph Strauss, was informed that his organisation, which had just completed the construction of the barrage, would be required to remove it'.[16] Over 70,000 mines had been laid and these now had to be swept up.

The minelayers were deemed unsuitable because of their draught. There was another problem too:

> Built on an entirely new principle, these mines had made the construction of the North Sea barrage possible, for a long antenna stretching up above the mine enabled it to do the work for which three or four had previously been required. Now this same feature became our greatest problem. With the uppermost end of the antenna at an average of eight to ten feet below the surface of the water, it was impossible for a steel vessel to pass over and strike the mines without exploding them. A piece of iron or steel no larger than a nail was sufficient to operate the delicate firing mechanism.[17]

The mission was under US control, but the British chartered twenty minesweeping trawlers to the Americans. However, the trawlers' hulls had not been designed or built to withstand repeated underwater shocks from the exploding mines (often several detonated at a time as one set off another), and leaks and damage soon became apparent. Proving unsatisfactory for the task, most of them were returned to the Admiralty. Which made it all the more puzzling that the USN sent their sub chasers – but they did. The chasers began to arrive at Kirkwall in February 1919, including 'three which had previously been sent to Norway for exhibition and possible sale'.[18]

SC-354 arrived at Kirkwall from the White Sea on 28 July. In common with the other chasers the 3in gun was removed, as was any metal hull protection, fitted to guard against ice while on Russian duty; for the mines were 'fired by a magnetic field created when the metal hull of a vessel came into contact with the mine's antenna wire'.[19] As wooden boats, the chasers were unlikely to set off the mine; the steel-built sweepers, however, were equipped with a newly developed device which generated a neutralising electromagnetic field around the ship.*

And at the peak of what was a difficult and complicated operation, in which American lives were lost, thirty-two specially equipped USN minesweepers and twenty-four USN sub chasers were deployed. The role of

---

* The mines were the USN Mark VI, which had horns, but also a long copper antenna held upright by a float. When any part of a metal object came in contact with the horns or antenna, a magnetic field was produced which activated the trigger.

the chasers was to follow the sweepers and sink by rifle fire any unexploded mines cut free by the sweeps.

By October, it was considered that the job had been completed. But now there was the problem of returning the sub chasers to the USA. Efforts to sell the vessels in Europe had been unsuccessful and to lay them up in a British port until the following summer, when the weather conditions would have been more suitable for the long return voyage, was considered unduly expensive. It was decided that they should be taken home, escorted by the minesweepers, and the chasers departed Devonport for Brest on 12 October in a voyage which would be the reverse of the trip via the Azores and Bermuda they had made to get to Europe.

Not all of them made it back home; the third day out from the Azores, *SC-256*, which was under tow from USS *Falcon* (1918, a *Lapwing*-class minesweeper), was destroyed by a fire following a fuel explosion. The fire spread so rapidly that the boat was consumed by flames before any action could be taken to save her. The crew, of whom several had been badly burned, all succeeded in getting clear of the vessel and into the water.

The remaining little ships arrived safely, but now they had to report to the Commandant Third Naval District to be disarmed and placed on the sale list. The twenty-three survivors were decommissioned at the end of November. Each one had made two Atlantic crossings. Some had sailed to the Arctic Circle. But their usefulness was deemed to be at an end.

USS *Lapwing*, minesweeper no 1, and other ships of the squadron anchored in the Hudson River, off New York City, while being reviewed by Secretary of the Navy Josephus Daniels on 24 November 1919, following their return to the United States after taking part in clearing the North Sea mine barrage. Minesweeper no 21, *Lark*, can be seen in the background. Launched in 1918, the class mounted two 3in guns and could make 14 knots. *(US Navy History and Heritage Command, NH 44903)*

16
Last Rites

Britain and the USA disbanded their wartime petrol navies with almost unseemly haste.

At the time of the Armistice there were 507 MLs in Royal Navy service.[1] Some were fitted for minesweeping to take part in the great mine-clearance operation around the British coast. Others were kept as patrol vessels, or for directing traffic into mineswept channels. At Queenstown, for example, MLs *259*, *185*, *189*, *131*, *377* and *163* were engaged in the latter duty during November 1918. And by 2 December, the depth charges and single towed charges were removed from all Auxiliary Patrol vessels and returned to the Ordnance Depot at Haulbowline.

By early 1919, the MLs were progressively detached from their stations and assembled on the River Hamble for decommissioning. The Admiralty set up a committee under the chairmanship of Admiral of the Fleet Sir William Henry May to advise on the best method of sale.

For some in Parliament, the disposals could not come quickly enough. At the beginning of August 1919 Lieutenant Colonel A Murray, MP for Kincardine and Western Aberdeenshire, asked the First Lord of the Admiralty:

> whether there are, some 300 of His Majesty's motor launches moored in the River Hamble; if he will state the original cost, and the present expenditure per week for the maintenance, of a motor launch; whether any motor launches have been refitted with a view to sale; if so, at what cost; and can he state the policy of the Government with regard to the future retention or disposal of the motor launches in the River Hamble?

Replying for the Admiralty, Thomas Macnamara noted that:

> of the 300 craft referred to by my hon and gallant friend, 210 are motor launches, of which 187 are for disposal. The original cost of these motor launches was about £8,000 each. The present expenditure for the maintenance of one of these vessels is, roughly, £2 a week, including wages, stores, and the cost of three motor launches in commission for attendance on those paid off.[2]

Murray countered that 'would not the most economical thing to do be to scrap them'?

The cost of an ML, including armament, was around £8,609. Many were sold off in large lots at bargain prices: 200 at £275 each to Monsieur Eugene Bloch on 31 December 1919, ninety-five at £263 to W J O'Loghlen and thirty-two to A Cree at Malta for £50 each.[3] Many became the property of individuals who turned them into pleasure boats or houseboats, in both cases replacing the expensive-to-run engines, which consumed huge amounts of fuel, with something cheaper. Those on foreign stations were sold locally if possible. And some were lost at sea (see also Appendix 10).

By 30 October there were only seventy in commission, 'in which are serving 120 officers and 550 men'.[4] Of the seventy launches, some were employed on mine-clearance work, some 'on special and temporary patrol duties at home and abroad, and some on miscellaneous duties in connection with transport and other duties at home and in the Mediterranean'.[5] By May 1924, only *ML-8*, *287*, *291*, *307*, *339*, *473*, *519* and *542* remained in service, and all were gone by 1927.[6]

What of their depot ship? *Hermione* was sold out of the navy in October 1921 and then resold to the Marine Society a year later for use as a training ship, where she was renamed *Warspite*. She was finally scrapped in 1940.

Sixty-six coastal motor boats were in commission on 11 November 1918.[7] However, the large base created at Osea Island was closed in 1921. Captain Sir Leonard Pius Vavasour, 4th Baronet Hazlewood, was appointed to HMS *Vernon* to command the Haslar Coastal Motorboat Base and its flotilla, and the CMBs relocated there. Vavasour's appointment terminated on 1 September 1923, when he was succeeded by Commander Thomas Bernard Drew; Drew's appointment ended precisely two years later and he does not appear to have been replaced. Many of the boats were deleted from the Navy List c1921–23, with only a few lasting until the early 1930s. Forty-footers *CMB-121* and *122* lasted until 1929, *123* was sold to the Dutch navy in 1928, and number *12* was deleted in 1935. The remaining 55ft boats were deleted in 1932 and two 72ft craft, *103MT* and *104MT*, served in the Second World War, both having been laid up since 1928.

As for the USN sub chasers, as noted in the preceding chapter, they too were destined for the scrap heap. By spring 1920, hundreds of them were moored up at Port Newark Army Base in New Jersey awaiting disposal. The firm of C P Comerford and Co, ship breakers, was a purchaser of the chasers, and three of the vessels sold to them also illustrate the short life that most of them led. On 11 May 1921 Comerford's acquired *SC-241*, commissioned on 8 April 1918; *SC-216*, commissioned 14 February 1918; and *SC-225*, commissioned 10 December 1917.

Twenty-six sub chasers staged a race from Bermuda to New York as the final leg of their post-war return from Europe. It was won by *SC-131*, on 20 August 1919, seen here sailing up the Hudson. She had also had the distinction of being the first vessel to enter the Austrian base at Cattaro after the Armistice.
(US Navy History and Heritage Command, NH 42587)

Motor Boat magazine carried advertisements offering them for sale as private yachts at a price of $12,500 (they had cost around $80,000 each to build).[8] Thirteen sub chasers joined the US Army, four were transferred to Cuba, as noted in Chapter 12, and *SC-37* and *38* went to Mexico. Twenty-two boats were transferred to the United States Coast Guard during 1919/20, and at least three became trawlers; *SC-292* converted to *Chief Seattle*, *SC-293* turned into *George L Harvey* and *SC-300* was renamed *Joseph Kildall*.

But the splinter ships gained some sort of posterity when they starred in the John Ford-directed movie *Submarine Patrol* of 1938. The film was loosely based on a memoir *The Splinter Fleet of Otranto Barrage* (1936) written by an ex-chief mechanic in a sub chaser, Ray Millholland, and was adapted for the big screen by William Faulkner. As shot, the plot has an arrogant playboy, Perry Townsend III (played by Richard Greene), who signs up with the US Navy, but is demoted for negligence and put in command of a neglected sub chaser for anti-submarine duty. Greene has the conceit knocked out of him,

Waiting for the end. A trot of sub chasers tied up at the Port Newark Army Base, New Jersey, awaiting disposition, 13 May 1920.
(US Navy History and Heritage Command, NH 69166)

restores discipline to the crew, and wins the affections of an all-American girl, portrayed by Nancy Kelly.

Naval naissance
But at the same time as the unloved and unwanted launches and chasers were being removed from service, some took leading roles in the birth of new navies.

Ireland
At the end of 1921 Ireland gained dominion status under the Anglo-Irish Treaty of 6 December. The agreement provided for the establishment of the Irish Free State within a year as a self-governing dominion within the 'community of nations known as the British Empire'. Article 6 of the treaty stated that:

until an arrangement has been made between the British and Irish Governments whereby the Irish Free State undertakes her own coastal defence, the defence by sea of Great Britain and Ireland shall be undertaken by His Majesty's Imperial Forces. But this shall not prevent the construction or maintenance by the Government of the Irish Free State of such vessels as are necessary for the protection of the Revenue or the Fisheries.

It also afforded British naval forces the use of certain specified harbours.

The Free State came into existence on 15 January 1922. In May it was decided to initiate an Irish navy through the purchase of four ex-Royal Navy Elco motor launches. Irish naval historian Daire Brunicardi noted that 'this decision is interesting. It marks the first decision of a modern Irish government with regard to some form of maritime defence force'. The MLs were to be equipped with a 12pdr gun and a 'continuous wave wireless set with a range of fifty miles'.[9]

The four boats were obtained from a broker, Messrs Goad and Proctor of Southampton, and one Lieutenant Commander Blay RNR was contracted to deliver them to Kingstown. The Irish did not necessarily get a good deal; first, they paid about £1,100 each for the MLs, much more than the Admiralty had been selling them off for, and secondly, when they came to collect them, the launches were fitted with the standard 3pdr gun and had no wireless. Nevertheless, Blay set off with his little flotilla, now named *ML-1* to *ML-4* in Irish naval service.

Things did not go well. The flotilla left Southampton on 18 July 1922 in fair weather. But within twenty-four hours, a gale rose up and lashed the MLs. While rounding Land's End, *ML-2* struck something in the seaway and began taking on water, which contaminated her fuel supply, leading to engine failure. *ML-4* made repeated attempts to fix and maintain a tow to *ML-2*, but the latter flooded and was eventually abandoned. Number *4* meanwhile had suffered damage, but managed to get ashore at Bideford with both crews safely aboard. *ML-3* had to put in at Ilfracombe, and only *ML-1* made it to Ireland, arriving at Dublin and immediately going into the Port and Docks Board slip in the Alexandra Basin for urgent repairs.

The tale of woe was not over, for while still at Bideford *ML-4* suffered an engine-room fire at the quayside, in which the whole after end of the ship was heavily damaged. Fortunately, the integrity of the hull and engines were maintained, and she was repaired and eventually restored to service.

In June 1922 a vicious civil war broke out in Ireland. The MLs were incorporated into the Marine Investigation Department of the new Irish

Army and were stationed at Haulbowline, familiar territory for Queenstown-based MLs in the war. They operated around Fenit, Galway and Killybegs, often mooring up for the night in these ports, and patrolled the west and southern littoral. Additionally, the MLs were used to move small forces of government troops in flanking movements, and to support landings by larger vessels.

The civil war ended in May 1923, although pockets of violence dribbled on, and the Marine Investigation Department was disbanded. The MLs became part of the new Coastal and Marine Service, but in early 1924 were laid up and by the middle of the year had been disposed of. The 12pdrs were never fitted, neither the radio sets, but the MLs had contributed to the formation of the Irish Republic and its first true navy.

Poland

Out of the chaos of war in eastern Europe, a new Polish republic was formed in 1918 and guaranteed by agreements signed in the Treaty of Versailles in 1919, as laid out in Section VIII, article 87. This gave the Polish state access to the Baltic at and around the town of Puck (Putzig), a fact celebrated in 1920 by Poland's 'Wedding to the Sea', a ceremony meant to symbolise restored Polish access to the Baltic Sea, lost since 1793.

And if you have a bit of sea, you need a navy. By decree of 18 November 1918, one was legally proclaimed and Captain Bogumił Nowotny appointed its first commander. The new navy entered into conversations with the firm of Leszczynski, who offered two ex-German *Odin-* and *Siegfried*-class coastal defence vessels, an offer wisely rejected as being far too costly to maintain.

Instead, they purchased an old Royal Navy motor launch, for $12,000 – meaning that Leszczynski must have made a considerable profit. This vessel then underwent modifications, the most visible of which was to move the mast ahead of the pilot house. A 1908 model 7.92mm Maxim gun was installed (the boat had arrived unarmed), later replaced by a 3pdr Hotchkiss (47mm), and on 1 April 1921 she entered Polish service as *Mysliwy* (Hunter). She was deployed as an observation and security boat in the Naval Air Squadron. In 1922 she even briefly became the flagship of the nascent Polish fleet, in the aftermath of the Polish-Russian conflict.

Problems with her engines and lack of spare parts restricted *Mysliwy*'s utility, and in the autumn of 1925 she was laid up; on 15 January the following year the ML was sent for dismantling and crossed off the naval list. But briefly, an ML had flown a Fleet Command pennant, in the Baltic, where once the launches had served under Rear Admiral Cowan.

Two pictures of *CMB-4* at Duxford Museum. *(Author's collection)*

Survivors

There are three coastal motor boat survivors. *CMB-4*, Augustus Agar's boat in the sinking of *Oleg*, made it back to England and was exhibited at the Motor Boat Exhibition at Olympia in 1920*. Unfortunately, she then lay neglected at Hampton Wick for nearly thirty years. In 1967 she was placed on display at the Shipbuilding Industry Training Board's centre at Southampton, and between November 1982 and April 1984 *CMB-4* was painstakingly restored at the International Boat Building Training Centre at Lowestoft. From here she was removed to the Imperial War Museum, Duxford, where she was tucked away in a corner. In August 2019 *CMB-4* was moved again and became part of the collection at Boathouse 4, Portsmouth Historic Dockyard, where (at the time of writing) a replica of her is also being constructed.

CMB-9 was one of the boats converted to remote control and became *DCB-1* (see Chapter 10). Deleted from the navy in 1935, a botched attempt was made to convert her to a cabin cruiser and then she was abandoned before being acquired by present owner Robert Morley. He has painstakingly restored the craft, strapping up part of the hull that had sagged, repairing

---

* The Motor Boat and Marine and Stationary Engine Exhibition.

the hydroplane step, fitting new propeller shafts and rudders. Her engines are now twin Leyland 400 diesels, dating from the 1950s.

Finally, *CMB-103 MT* is one of the 72-footers. Built by Camper and Nicholson at Gosport in 1920, too late for the war, she was laid up in 1928, but recalled to service between 1942 and 1944, and took part in the D-Day landings. Restored in 2011, *CMB-103 MT* is now on public display at Chatham Historic Dockyard.

Of the 720 Elco motor launches built for the Allied nations[10] there is only one identified survivor, *ML-286*, and she is hanging on to life by the thinnest of threads.* *ML-286*, one of the 500 ordered in June 1915, seems to have spent much of her naval career at Scapa Flow, helping guard and service the Grand Fleet. One of her early skippers was Geoffrey Allfree (see Chapter 9). The Navy List for January 1920 shows her under the command of Lieutenant John Thompson, but she does not reappear in February, indicating that she may have been stricken at that point.

Sold off for private use, *286* was re-engined and became the pleasure cruiser *Cordon Rouge* and subsequently *Eothen*†. Under this latter name, she

---

* Dr Anthony Firth has informed the author that there is another ML, in very, very poor condition, in Norfolk but he has been unable to identify it.
† *Eothen* was a popular travelogue of journeys in the near east, written by Alexander William Kinglake and published in 1844.

Three views of the 72ft *CMB M-103*, now on display at Chatham Historic Dockyard. *(Author's collection)*

took part in the evacuation of the British Expeditionary Force from Dunkirk in May/June 1940 as one of the 'little ships', and was then briefly requisitioned to serve as a River Thames patrol vessel before being deemed unsuitable and returned to her owners in the August. She then led a peaceful life as a domestic cruiser on the Thames until the 1980s, when her owners took her to B J Wood's boatyard at Isleworth Ait for essential repairs. These proved unaffordable and *Eothen* was abandoned at the boatyard, where her rise and fall on the tide caused problems with an adjacent dry dock. Consequently, the boatyard decided to break open her hull to sink her and let her sit as a hulk, in which condition she still lies, in extremely poor repair. Despite her parlous state, fame of a kind came when, as *Eothen*, she was commemorated in 2015 by the issue of a 45-cent stamp which featured a picture of her in the 'little ships of Dunkirk' series, issued by the Republic of Palau.

The Thames Discovery Programme (TDP), a volunteer archaeology group, have made valiant attempts to preserve the remains of *286*, and in 2019 Dr Anthony Firth of Fjordr Ltd tried to put together a group including TDP, Museum of London Archaeology, the National Museum of the Royal Navy and the Coastal Forces Heritage Trust to professionally conserve, and possibly display, the remains. But at the time of writing, they have not yet been able to gain the necessary funding. It seems an ungrateful nation wants a last remaining piece of its naval heritage to disappear.

But MLs live on in at least one work of fiction. Percy F Westerman was a prolific writer of tales of derring-do, who was also a keen yachtsman and lived on a houseboat until aged seventy. He wrote about the motor launches in *The Thick of the Fray at Zeebrugge; April 1918* (Blackie and Son, 1919). The first edition has an illustration of a ML coming head on to the viewer, a bone between its teeth and sailors grouped around the gun. Chapter One introduces the hero:

> Guy Branscombe, Sub Lieutenant, RNVR, was one of those wartime productions whose existence, as members of the 'band of brothers' under the White Ensign, has been amply justified. He had been a candidate for Osborne, but had failed to satisfy the examiners. Now, taking advantage of his undoubted skill as an amateur yachtsman, he was doing good service both in deep sea and coastal navigation. These two branches are widely distinct. Generally speaking, officers of the 'pukka' navy are indifferent navigators in coastal waters. Inside the 'five fathom line' they often lack the confidence that the skilled amateur possesses. Thus the Admiralty soon found the need to accept the offers of British yachtsmen to take command of the shoal of MLs … the war record of which showed that official confidence had not been misplaced.

Stirring deeds follow. The cult of the Corinthian gifted amateur was very much Westerman's metier; in the RNVR officers of the MLs, he found his models.

Finally, two Italian MAS boats have survived and are preserved with honour. *MAS-15*, the craft with which Rizzo sank *Szent István* in June 1918, was restored and is on display in the Vittoriano, the Victor Emmanuel II

MAS-96 at the Vittoriale degli Italiani. (Photo: Julian Mannering)

monument, in the Shrine of the Flags, part of the Central Museum of the Risorgimento.

And *MAS-96*, in which Rizzo and D'Annunzio made the Bakar Mockery famous, is on public view at the Vittoriale degli Italiani (Shrine of Italian Victories) in Gardone Riviera, on Lake Garda. Now a museum, it is where Gabriele d'Annunzio lived, after his occupation of Fiume (now Rijeka) was ended in December 1920, until his death in 1938. The estate consists of his quondam residence, the *prioria* (priory), an amphitheatre, the protected cruiser *Puglia* set into a hillside, a boathouse holding *MAS-96*, and a circular mausoleum. Both craft seem today to be shown as quasi-religious memorials, honoured in a way that their British counterparts are not.

The volunteers

The Petrol Navy's volunteer officers and men of the RNVR were disposed of with even greater alacrity than their boats. But they probably felt little resentment, many of them having been in naval service since early in the war: careers interrupted needed to be resumed, families reunited, minds calmed, and sailing become once more a pleasure.

Group of five naval VCs, including three of those from the motor launches and CMBs, at a party given for holders of the Victoria Cross by King George V at Wellington Barracks. Left to right: Percy Thompson Dean (his 'wavy navy' rank stripes clearly visible), awarded the Victoria Cross for Zeebrugge and Ostend. Gordon Charles Steele, awarded the Victoria Cross for Kronstadt Harbour. Augustus William Shelton Agar, awarded the Victoria Cross for sinking *Oleg*. Admiral Sir Arthur Knyvet Wilson, awarded the Victoria Cross in Sudan 1884. Edward Unwin, awarded the Victoria Cross for Gallipoli.
(© *Imperial War Museum, Q66160*)

As but a few examples, Acting Captain Ion Hamilton Benn was demobbed at the end of December 1918, although not before he had received a CB at Buckingham Palace in the September.* Rowland Bourke VC was demobbed in January 1919, as was Percy Dean VC. Most of the others joined them as the year wore on. Gordon Maxwell paid off *ML-314* on the Hamble in May 1919 and left the navy:

> a little regretfully perhaps, with the storehouses of our minds filled with vivid recollections of the Little Grey Patrol and all that befell us in those days, when we went forth to a new life, and, learning wisdom by experience, carried on with our jobs to the best of our several

---
* He would be made a baronet in 1920, of Rollesby in the county of Norfolk.

abilities, gaining a sporting tolerance for our early failures, a generous appreciation of our desire to do our best, and, I venture to hope, some little credit for our subsequent successes.[11]

The Maxwell brothers were demobbed on 2 April 1919 (Donald) and 15 June 1919 (Gordon), and returned to their life of sailing, writing and painting; Gordon became a well-known author and Donald a sought-after artist and illustrator. Lieutenant Christopher Noel Luker RNVR emigrated to New Zealand after his demob, married a British émigré, became an army chaplain (4th class) with the rank of captain and was killed in action in 1942, aged sixty (and thus combined the chivalric trinity of courage, religion and self-sacrifice). Keith Hoare was demobilised in September, Reginald Fife left in October, having brought his launch back from Germany, and returned to sailing at the Sussex Motor Yacht Club; and Geoffrey Drummond VC was one of the last to go, in November 1919.

In America it was a similar story. Lieutenant Hilary Chambers left the navy in early 1919. George Dole brought his chaser back from service in Russia and on the North Sea mine barrier in December 1919, when both he and his craft were decommissioned.

By early 1920, the 'amateurs' had nearly all returned to civilian life. Like their vessels, the naval life of the volunteers had been ephemeral.

At least the RNVR officers gained some small financial reward from their service. In Parliament on 11 March 1919 Sir Clement Kinloch-Cooke, MP for Devonport (and thus with some sort of vested interest), demanded of Dr Macnamara whether 'the First Lord of the Admiralty … is now in a position to state the policy of the Government with regard to the war service gratuity of temporary naval officers?' The reply guaranteed that 'temporary naval officers will receive a war service gratuity on the same scale as that granted to temporary officers of the army, namely, 124 days' pay for the first year of service, and sixty-two days' pay for each succeeding year or part of a year of service'.[12]

This stood in stark contrast to the treatment of the crews of their sisters in the Auxiliary Patrol, the armed yachts. Responding to a question in July from William Tyson Wilson, MP for Westhoughton, Dr Macnamara stated that because of their different terms of service (a T-124Y agreement) 'they are … regarded as ineligible for the seamen's war gratuity, which is only paid to naval ratings who received naval rates of pay'.[13]

The petrol progenitors

To conclude this *Nunc Dimittis* for the Petrol Navy, what of the progenitors of the original motor boat reserve, the RNMBR, and the Americans who made the MLs and sub chasers possible?

Admiral Frederick Inglefield was placed on the retired list on 9 June 1916.[14] Inglefield lived out the war, was appointed deputy lieutenant of Derbyshire, and died in 1921 at his home in Windley, Derbyshire, 'from blood poisoning due, it is believed, to an accident sustained while rowing'.[15]

Having served as chief of staff to the admiral in command of gunboats on the Belgian canals, Morton Smart was attached to the 1st Army in France and later went with the gunboat flotilla to the Dardanelles, where he was wounded and received the DSO for saving the crew of a monitor under heavy shellfire. After commanding an ML flotilla which made the passage from England to Mudros (see Chapter 6), he served in the Aegean until near the end of the war, when he became senior naval officer at Trinidad in the West Indies, with command of the naval station. After this varied and adventurous naval career, he resumed his medical work in London in 1919.

Smart wrote on manipulative surgery in the *Medical Annual* and contributed to many professional journals. From 1943 to 1949 he was a member of the Physical Medicine Group Committee of the BMA and during the same period served on the Central Medical War Committee. For many years he attended members of the Royal Family. He was created CVO in 1932 and advanced to KCVO in the following year. In 1950, when he was a patient in the King Edward VII Hospital for Officers, George VI visited the hospital and invested him with the insignia of GCVO; all three of these honours were directly in the monarch's gift. Smart died in 1956.

Sir Francis Armstrong, who had been demobbed from the RNVR with the rank of commander, continued his interest in things that ran on petrol by becoming the secretary and general manager of the Royal Automobile Club (RAC) in 1923, a post he only relinquished in 1941. He died three years later.

And the part played by the Thornycroft company and chief designer John Isaac Thornycroft was formally recognised by the Admiralty. On 16 October 1919 the Secretary to the Admiralty Board wrote to the company that:

> your firm having taken a leading part, in association with the Admiralty, in producing the design of the Coastal Motor Boat … I am commanded by My Lords Commissioners of the Admiralty to inform you that They desire to express Their cordial thanks to members of your firm and the employees concerned for the efforts made and Their congratulations on the results achieved.[16]

What of the head of US naval forces in Europe, and proponent of convoy and the splinter ships, William Sims? In 1920 he published a book, *Victory at Sea*, which described his experiences during the war. A year later the book was awarded a Pulitzer Prize for history, making Sims the only career US naval officer to have gained such an accolade. Whilst still in the service, he became a vociferous critic of American naval policy and of Secretary Daniels in particular, which no doubt did his prospects of further advancement no good at all. Sims was placed on the retired list in October 1922, having reached the mandatory retirement age of sixty-four and died in Boston, Massachusetts, thirteen years later. His role in winning the war is not as well-known as it deserves to be, even in his own country. But Jellicoe certainly appreciated it, writing that 'it was fortunate indeed for the Allied cause that Admiral Sims should have been selected to command the United States forces in European waters, for … he [had] a habit of speaking his mind with absolute fearless disregard of the consequences'.[17]

Henry Sutphen continued his association with boatbuilding for peace and war. Under his direction, in the Second World War Elco built 400 PT (Patrol Torpedo) boats for the USN. He died 'in harness', aged seventy-five; the *New York Times* of 11 December 1950 reported that 'Henry Randolph Sutphen, since 1947 chairman of the executive committee of the Electric Boat Company, 445 Park Avenue, with which he had been associated since 1892, died unexpectedly yesterday morning of a stroke in his sleep at his residence, 876 Park Avenue.'

And Albert Loring Swasey, the man who designed the sub chasers, was decorated with the Silver Star and the Legion of Merit for his services in bringing them into existence. Post-war, he became a regional director of the Massachusetts branch of the Sea Scouts. He died in 1956, aged seventy-nine.

So, by 1956, all the pioneers of the Petrol Navy, and nearly all their original boats, had passed into posterity.

17

Conclusions

Apart from boats, this book has been about volunteerism. The RN's Auxiliary Patrol was very much initially a volunteer organisation, with RNVR, RNR and RNR(T) – fishermen – prominent. In this navy within a navy, by the end of the war 1,600 commissioned RNVR officers were employed and 1,000 RNVR midshipmen.[1]

Commencing in spring 1916, with the introduction of conscription, men joined the RNVR not necessarily from choice, but because of specialist skills or training, such as engineering, wireless and electrical knowledge. Many of the original pre-war members thought 'their' service was being made a 'waste basket of the navy and with their high ideals as volunteers and seamen, they resented their uniforms being worn by those they considered neither volunteers or seamen'.[2] It was a dilution of their chivalric ideals, of their Corinthian identity.

An unknown RNVR lieutenant (note the wavy line sleeve insignia) on board a motor launch, and with a telescope under his arm. *(Author's collection)*

A group of unidentified RNVR officers on an ML with a sub lieutenant in the foreground. *(Author's collection)*

Royal recognition of the volunteers came during the war when King George V appointed an RNVR officer to be one of his naval aides-de-camp; the Hon Rupert Edward Cecil Lee Guinness (later 2nd Lord Iveagh) was the first to be so honoured. Soon afterwards the Marquess of Graham (James Graham, later 6th Duke of Montrose) joined him. And Prince Arthur of Connaught (a grandson of Queen Victoria) was made an honorary captain RNVR.

The Royal Navy motor launches were almost entirely the preserve of the RNVR*, CMBs a little less so, and USN sub chasers largely officered by reservists. Many had been enthusiastic yachtsmen and leisure sailors pre-war; many RNMBR men brought their own pleasure boats with them.

And it is a measure of the prevalence of yachtsman and motor boat

---

* A total of 6,000 men served in motor launches during the war.

sailors in the volunteers that, of the three major national yachting magazines in Britain pre-war, one of them, *Yachting Monthly* founded in 1906, became a sort of house magazine for the RNVR during the conflict, carrying a plethora of features and articles about yachtsmen at war and/or their previous lives. It even changed its masthead to read 'Yachting Monthly and Magazine of the RNVR'.

The Edwardian sense of voluntary mission, of Arthurian self-sacrifice, had sent many men to the Western Front and death in the trenches, as well as to the RNMBR and the RNVR. It did not survive the war. The post-Armistice peace was dominated by different and new mores. As Stanley Baldwin observed to his friend John Maynard Keynes, Parliament's new intake of MPs in December 1918 were a 'lot of hard-faced men who look as if they had done well out of the war'.[3]

'Doing well out of the war' was much resented by the men who had gone to conflict voluntarily:

> The supporters of compulsory service replied by pointing with scorn to the inequalities of the voluntary system. The best men had already volunteered and a great number had been killed. The remainder were daily exposing their lives and suffering the most terrible hardships while their less patriotic colleagues – 'Cuthberts' they were called – had stepped into their places in civilian life and were earning high wages and living in comfort.[4]

Self-sacrifice and *noblesse oblige* was replaced by vested self-interest.

And the chivalric did not survive the war for another reason – the demise of the leisured and aristocratic classes. This was in part a deliberate policy, begun by Lloyd George and H H Asquith in pre-war budgets and continued by Lloyd George post-war. Using the vehicle of death duties and land taxation, the landed rich were denuded of their monied privilege. Death duties had first been applied to land in 1894 at a rate equivalent to two years' income. By 1897, the Duke of Bedford had already been moved to note that 'low prices, bad seasons and a crushing weight of taxation have entirely caused rent … to disappear from the Thorney Estate'.[5] The Liberal government's 'People's Budget' of 1909/10 attempted to apply the introduction of complete land valuation and a 20 per cent tax on increases in value when land changed hands. It was blocked by the Lords, but eventually received royal assent in 1910. Further taxes on land were introduced in 1914. The Finance Act of 1919/20 imposed a 30 per cent rate of income tax and a supertax which commenced at 7.5 per cent. It also raised death duties from 12 per cent to a maximum of 40 per cent, which encouraged many families to leave the land entirely. Between 1918 and 1927, some 6–8 million acres, including 25 per cent of Britain's farmland, changed hands, to the detriment of the rentiers.

But the amateur volunteering spirit did not entirely fade away and made a remarkable come-back in May and June 1940 when hundreds of yachtsmen, motor boat owners, fishermen and ferries, watermen and wherries, headed for Dunkirk to evacuate the British Expeditionary Force. And as late as 1957, the survivors of Operation ZO held a reunion dinner on St George's Day at the St Ermin's Hotel, Westminster. Collamer Calvin and Ion Benn were amongst the attendees.

And the concept of the Corinthian yachtsman survives. The organisers of the 2023 Ocean Globe race announced the advent of the competition in a press release which stated 'technology moves so fast, that sailors the world over, while marvelling at these advances, have been left behind and look back fondly at the Corinthian days of the 1973 Whitbread Race and dream'.[6]

The US Naval Reserve Force

The US Navy's reserve forces began with the formation of the Navy Reserve, which was officially established on 3 March 1915 with an eye on preparation for America's potential entry into the First World War. Initially, only previously enlisted navy veterans were eligible to join.

This was followed by the US Naval Reserve Force (USNRF), which was founded on 29 August 1916. This opened up recruitment to 'gifted amateurs', who were organised into six categories based on their experience or trade. By 1919, the USN had 245,789 USNRF sailors, who included those who sailed on the sub chasers, and which compared to only 210,365 regular navymen. There were also 12,000 female naval reservists.

If there were 441 chasers in service, then 882 officers were needed, the vast majority of whom were USNRF (see Chapter 11), together with 9,702 men, likewise largely from a non-naval background.

As in Britain, this reserve force was swiftly run down post-war but, in recognition of the benefit the reservists had brought, in 1926 a Naval Reserve Officer Training Corps (NROTC) was established at Harvard, Yale, Northwestern (Chicago), Georgia Institute of Technology, University of Washington, and University of California, Berkeley. University students would be trained up as a potential surge resource in war. As in in the Royal Navy, the reserves had made their mark.

The boats

The motor launches and sub chasers were entirely an American achievement. The vast resources of the USA, her surplus labour and

Two of Henry Ford's unfortunate *Eagle*-class patrol boats (*PE-46*, *PE-19*), seen here next to an *Omaha*-class cruiser in the 1920s at Boston Navy Yard. Their forward 4in gun (one of two) is clearly seen. (*US Naval History and Heritage Command, NH 54323*)

advanced manufacturing techniques *pace* Henry Ford*, the drive and energy of men like Sutphen and Swasey, meant that seemingly impossible numbers of craft were produced in a very short time: 550 motor launches for the Royal Navy in 488 days; over 440 sub chasers, plus 100 for France – a remarkable mobilisation of effort.

It should not be thought that this was an altruistic initiative, however. Significant profits were made, and the USA only entered the war when domestic emotions and German attacks on US ships and civilians made entry no longer resistible. And President Woodrow Wilson's war aims were clear. An avowed Anglophobe, he believed that 'destroying the empires of Britain and Germany would facilitate the advance of American trade',[7] and 'resolved to remove blockade from the international arsenal to advance American commercial interests'.[8] Wilson wanted to dictate the peace to

---

* Ford's genius for mass production did not, however, make him a successful boatbuilder. The USN *Eagle*-class patrol boats, intended as the successors to the sub chasers, were steam turbine-driven steel ships, smaller than contemporary destroyers, but having a greater operational radius than the chasers, and were built by Ford at President Wilson's instigation. Sixty were constructed, but did not see war service, and it was probably just as well. Reports on their performance at sea were at best mixed. Ford's insistence on using flanged plates instead of rolled plates, for ease of production, resulted in sea-keeping characteristics considerably less than ideal. They also suffered from never-ending leakage problems that plagued the ships. This combination meant that many of them were ordered to stay in harbour and were used as stationary aircraft tenders.

achieve those ends; and of course, the war transformed the USA from a debtor to a creditor nation, with Britain massively in her debt.

In contrast with the US-built vessels, coastal motor boats were a very British invention, the brainchild of a small number of naval officers faced with a problem, to the solving of which they brought creativity and knowledge. Build numbers were much lower than their petrol sisters, but the design and techniques were appreciated and copied, especially in Italy.

But can the Petrol Navy be considered a success? Keyes waxed lyrical about the MLs at Operation ZO:

> at the Zeebrugge–Ostend raid the duty of making smoke screens and laying smoke floats was imposed on a large fleet of motor launches. Without the service of these little vessels for this duty, and for inshore work generally, an attack of this nature could hardly have been considered. The rescue of the crews of the blockships by the motor launches, which had been standing by under heavy fire of every calibre, was carried out in the gallant manner which distinguished the work of the motor launches throughout the action.[9]

And three VCs were won in MLs and another three in the CMBs. That's quite a haul for small, swiftly built auxiliary vessels. Major awards went to the crews of the US sub chasers too.

However, how did they perform against the original objectives set for them? In the case of the MLs and chasers, they were designed as anti-submarine vessels. When rated versus the objective of killing U-boats, their achievements were scant, at least as now assessed by modern scholarship; at the time, greater glory was claimed. The motor boats have no defensible kills; the chasers none either. And the MLs sank one with one assist: *ML-413* destroyed *UB-71*, and HMS *Opossum* with *ML-135* finished off *UC-49*.

Perhaps it was this that led the self-appointed expert on all matters naval, Lieutenant Commander Joseph Kenworthy, MP for Central Hull, to claim, in a question to Admiralty Financial Secretary Macnamara in August 1919, that 'these motor launches were a complete failure in wartime, and, that being the case, will he consider the advisability of disposing of the whole lot?' Macnamara simply replied, 'I am not prepared to concur that they were a complete failure. In any case, it is not a wise thing to say when we are trying to sell them, and it is not correct'.[10]

And Dr Macnamara was right, for the real measure of the success of the chasers and MLs, as has been stated several times in this book, is that they kept the U-boats underwater, made them exhaust their batteries and oxygen, prevented them from surfacing to fire at passing merchant ships, and drove them away from trade routes. It is a negative proof, admittedly, but it remains a truth. As a U-boat captain working in the Adriatic commented with regard to the trawlers, MLs and chasers deployed there, 'we submerged to deep soundings, but when we put up to periscope depth again at 1930 our pursuers were still there and within three cables' length of us'.[11]

Moreover, the MLs proved successful as smokescreen boats, rescue craft, shallow-water minesweepers (and sometimes layers), despatch vessels, communication links, and just plain showing the flag in riverine waters. Likewise, sub chasers were found more than useful to assist with minesweeping, and a host of other duties, similar to the MLs and not really considered by their designers.

CMBs were conceived as a means of passing over obstacle or mine barriers, but they too morphed into minelayers and smoke vessels, and had their moment of fame in the post-Armistice Baltic campaign. And all these types of craft found usage in the other Allied naval forces, and in the navies of the Central Powers too. These faster motor boats proved on occasion to be a powerful weapon, but no navy developed cohesive or cogent fighting tactics for them and, in general, only undertook quick, surprise raids. These demonstrated that a good return could sometimes be generated for only a small investment in men and materiel. At night, in smooth coastal waters and off harbours, small, high-speed naval craft proved the potential to be a dangerous weapon of war.

As Frederick Dittmar and James Colledge have written: 'the CMBs with their high speed and torpedoes caused the enemy great concern and led to

Looking into Portsmouth Harbour, with two MLs crossing to Gosport, by W L Wyllie (c1916). A view looking north up Portsmouth Harbour with a spritsail barge coming out under sail. *Victory* is still afloat as port flagship in the background, with the Union flag at the main. Gosport and the Camper and Nicholson boat yard are on the left.
(© National Maritime Museum, Greenwich, London, PAE3299)

the worldwide development of the motor torpedo boat. In post war years many similar craft were built by Thornycroft for foreign governments obviously intended as test vehicles and prototypes'.[12] In 1925 two were sold by Thornycroft to Sweden: 'these boats follow very closely the lines of those already built by the same firm for the British Admiralty and the French, Japanese, Spanish and Siamese navies'.[13]

Thus an unproven technology, wooden boats and amateur crews combined to produce a set of vessels which filled a strategic gap. The Petrol Navy demonstrated that the small, internal combustion-engined craft could play a significant role in the war. And it was one which, as technological progress took place, saw them take an even bigger part in the next global conflict. But that is another book and another war.

A lasting memory?

Captain Thomas Henry Roberts-Wray CB OBE VD RNVR, sometime naval aide-de-camp to King George V, was a true Corinthian. An RNVR member since his youth, on 9 September 1914 he was appointed brigade major at the hastily requisitioned RNVR training depot of Crystal Palace, with a salary of £500 per annum*.[14] Subsequently he became executive officer of the camp, its second in command. Roberts-Wray stayed at his post all through the war, leaving only to visit his son in France after he had been badly wounded.† In June 1918 Roberts-Wray's service record was endorsed 'abil[ity] exceptional. Utmost value in organising and disciplining depot, work [has] been entirely exceptional'.[15] Throughout this period, Crystal Palace was used as a training establishment for the RNVR. It was officially known as HMS *Victory VI*, and informally as HMS *Crystal Palace*. During the war, 125,000 officers and men were trained there.‡

This was not an experience universally beloved. Not yet eighteen, trainee signalman Harry Chadwick-Smith RNVR, a volunteer from Leigh, remembered 'being received as if we were a bunch of criminals newly released from some hulk in Botany Bay ... it was a shattering experience and the beginning of a grand disillusionment'.[16] It was bitterly cold with no heating, frequently the subject of Zeppelin raids and involved six weeks of square-bashing. Fortunately, things improved for Harry when they moved to the Signal School on the same site.

Post-war, Roberts-Wray served on the Admiralty Volunteer Committee, alongside such luminaries as Captain the Marquess of Graham, Commander

---

* Perhaps £60,000 in 2022.
† The son, Kenneth, would later become a lawyer and civil servant. As an authority on Commonwealth and colonial law, he was legal adviser to the Commonwealth Relations Office (Dominions Office until 1947) and the Colonial Office between 1945 and 1960.
‡ For 'other ranks' the service number suffixes KP, KW, KX applied to Crystal Palace intakes up until conscription and thereafter PZ.

the Viscount Curzon and the Hon Commander the Marquess of Ailsa, all previously met in this book.[17] Special permission was gained from the Treasury to retain him for this role. It troubled the captain that, although many fine memorials were being raised to the navy's service and dead, there was no specific tribute to the men of the Volunteer Reserve, and he took it upon himself to right this wrong.* On 6 June 1931 the Prince of Wales (the future Edward VIII) unveiled the Royal Naval Volunteer Reserve Trophy, originally housed in a military building within the Crystal Palace complex, to commemorate the service of Royal Naval Volunteer Reserve officers and men in the Great War.

Wray conceived the design, which was elaborated by an architect, J A Hale. R H Hawkins was the sculptor, and builder Philip Roffey carried out the constructional work. All three had served in the RNVR during the war and had passed through HMS *Victory VI*. A dedicatory panel recorded that:

> This Trophy was unveiled on the 6th June 1931 by HRH the Prince of Wales KG to commemorate the service of RNVR officers and men in the Great War, including 125,000 officers and men who were trained for all branches of the Royal Navy at the Training Depot, HMS *Victory VI* at the Crystal Palace 1914–1918.

The structure was of two parts: a hipped-roofed, timber-framed, open-sided pavilion and within, a table and a memorial ship's bell. The ship's bell was supported by two large, upturned dolphins with swirling tails, standing on a table that had angled legs carved in the form of rope. A bronze medallion depicting a ship in full sail was mounted on the front face of the table and flanked by two anchors and with a banner mounted below.

Time has not been kind to the Trophy. It was damaged during the Second World War, vandalised in the 1950s and again in the 1970s, and restored and re-sited to its current position in Crystal Palace Park in 1992. The bronze medallion and scroll were lost at some point, as was the dedicatory plaque, and the Trophy now sits in a flowerbed behind iron bollards and railings.

Perhaps few of the people passing by today understand what it is, or means, or the past to which it stands in mute memorial. It symbolises, by its very neglect, the loss of that brave prelapsarian innocence with which men volunteered themselves and their boats for war service. The Corinthians are long gone. The golden age is forgotten. Today only money matters. But once upon a time men went down to the sea in ships; and we should remember them.

---
* In June 1924 a memorial to the RNVR London Division had been unveiled by Captain HRH Prince Arthur of Connaught.

Appendix 1
Motor Boats Lost 1914–1918

Date	Name	Reason
21 July 1915	*Dorothea*	Fire, Eastern Mediterranean
28 August 1915	*Dolores*	Fire, Douglas, Isle of Man
2 December 1915	*Nita Pita*	Fire, Poole
8 September 1916	*Allegro*, *Doreen*, *Griffin*	Lost when SS *Alexandria* (ex-*Achaia*) was mined off Oran harbour. Four motor boats were on board for transit to Cardiff. Only *Puffin II* (motor boat number 108) was saved
26 February 1917	*Seagull*	Mined off Folkestone

Source: author's research; Dittmar and Colledge, *British Warships*, p135.

Appendix 2

British and World Merchant Shipping Losses, 1917 and January – April 1918

Month	Tonnage (grt)	
1917	British	World
Jan	153,666	368,521
Feb	313,486	540,006
Mar	353,478	593,841
Apr	545,282	881,027
May	352,289	596,629
Jun	417,925	687,507
Jul	364,858	557,988
Aug	329,810	511,730
Sept	196,212	351,748
Oct	276,132	458,558
Nov	173,560	289,212
Dec	253,087	399,111
1918		
Jan	179,973	306,658
Feb	226,896	318,957
Mar	199,458	342,597
Apr	215,543	278,719

Source: Fayle, *Seaborne Trade*, vol III, p465.

Appendix 3

Tonnage of Allied and Neutral Merchant Shipping Lost, 1914–1918

Year	Britain grt '000	Total grt '000
1914	241.2	312.6
1915	855.7	1307.9
1916	1,237.6	2,327.3
1917	3,729.8	6,235.9
1918	1,694.7	2,666.9
Total	7,759.1	12,850.8

Source: Fayle, *Seaborne Trade*, vol III, p465.

Appendix 4
The Motor Launch VC Citations

Lieutenant Percy Thompson Dean RNVR **(Motor Launch 282)**
For most conspicuous gallantry. Lieutenant Dean handled his boat in a most magnificent and heroic manner when embarking the officers and men from the blockships at Zeebrugge. He followed the blockships in and closed *Intrepid* and *Iphigenia* under a constant and deadly fire from machine and heavy guns at point blank range, embarking over 100 officers and men. This completed, he was proceeding out of the canal, when he heard that an officer was in the water. He returned, rescued him, and then proceeded, handling his boat throughout as calmly as if engaged in a practice manoeuvre. Three men were shot down at his side whilst he conned his ship. On clearing the entrance to the canal the steering gear broke down. He manoeuvred his boat by the engines, and avoided complete destruction by steering so close in under the mole that the guns in the batteries could not depress sufficiently to fire on the boat. The whole of this operation was carried out under a constant machine-gun fire at a few yards range. It was solely due to this officer's courage and daring that *ML-282* succeeded in saving so many valuable lives.'

London Gazette, 19 July 1918

Lieutenant Geoffrey H Drummond RNVR
Volunteered for rescue work in command of *ML-254*. Following *Vindictive* to Ostend, when off the piers a shell burst on board, killing Lieutenant Gordon Ross and Deckhand J Thomas, wounding the coxswain, and also severely wounding Lieutenant Drummond in three places. Notwithstanding his wounds he remained on the bridge, navigated his vessel, which was already seriously damaged by shell fire, into Ostend harbour, placed her alongside *Vindictive* and took off two officers and thirty-eight men – some of whom were killed and many wounded while embarking. When informed that there was no one alive left on board he backed his vessel out clear of the piers before sinking exhausted from his wounds. When HMS *Warwick* fell in with *ML-254* off Ostend half an hour later the latter was in a sinking condition. It was due to the indomitable courage of this very gallant officer that the majority of the crew of the *Vindictive* were rescued.

London Gazette, 27 August 1918

Lieutenant Roland Bourke DSO RNVR

Volunteered for rescue work in command of *ML-276*, and followed *Vindictive* into Ostend, engaging the enemy's machine guns on both piers with Lewis guns. After *ML-254* had backed out Lieutenant Bourke laid his vessel alongside *Vindictive* to make further search. Finding no one he withdrew, but hearing cries in the water he again entered the harbour, and after a prolonged search eventually found Lieutenant Sir John Alleyne and two ratings, all badly wounded, in the water, clinging to an upended skiff, and rescued them. During all this time the motor launch was under a very heavy fire at close range, being hit in fifty-five places, once by a 6in shell – two of her small crew being killed and others wounded. The vessel was seriously damaged and speed greatly reduced. Lieutenant Bourke, however, managed to bring her out and carry on until he fell in with a Monitor, which took him in tow. This episode displayed daring and skill of a very high order, and Lieutenant Bourke's bravery and perseverance undoubtedly saved the lives of Lieutenant Alleyne and two of the *Vindictive*'s crew.

London Gazette, 27 August 1918

Appendix 5
Motor Launch Losses, 1914–1918

Date	ML number	Reason and location
31 Jan 1916	19	Fire, Harwich
18 May 1916	40	Fire, Suez
10 Sept 1916	149	Fire, Taranto
14 Sept 1916	230, 253, 255	Aboard ss *Inverbervie*, torpedoed off Cape Rizzuto
31 Jan 1917	197	Wrecked, Ballincourty Light House
13 April 1917	534	Fire, Taranto
22 April 1917	431	Fire, Poole
8 June 1917	540, 541	Aboard ss *Hunstrick*, torpedoed off Algiers
23 Jul 1917	474	Hit by shellfire, near Chios
29 Nov 1917	52	Fire, Sandown Bay
15 Jan 1918	278	Wrecked, Dunkirk Pier
28 Jan 1918	55	Fire, Sittingbourne
6 April 1918	421	Sunk after collision, off Whitby
12 April 1918	356	Sunk after collision and fire, off Dover
10 May 1918	254	Sunk to avoid capture, off Ostend
10 June 1918	64	Fire, Granton
23 April 1918	110, 424	In action, Zeebrugge Raid
22 Aug 1918	403	Blown up trying to salvage German torpedo, Runswick Bay
29 Sept 1918	247	Wrecked, Oar Rock, St Ives
21 Oct 1918	561	Mined, off Ostend
Total	24	

Source: Dittmar and Colledge, *British Warships*, p136.

Appendix 6

Number of USN Submarine Chasers Based in Europe by Port, 1918

Port	Number	Notes
Plymouth, England	53	Inc those at Queenstown
Corfu	34	Inc Otranto
Azores	14	
Gibraltar	14	
Brest, France	7	
Bordeaux, France	2	
Le Palleau, France	2	
Harwich, England	2	
Saint-Nazaire, France	1	
Total	129	

Derived from Nutting, *Cinderellas of the Fleet*, p178.

Appendix 7
Armistice Military Occupation Clauses

Conditions of the Armistice concluded with Germany

CLAUSES RELATING TO THE WESTERN FRONT

II – Immediate evacuation of invaded countries: Belgium, France, Alsace-Lorraine, Luxemburg, so ordered as to be completed within fourteen days from the signature of the armistice. German troops which have not left the above-mentioned territories within the period fixed will become prisoners of war. Occupation by the Allied and United States forces jointly will keep pace with evacuation in these areas. All movements of evacuation and occupation will be regulated in accordance with a note annexed to the stated terms.

V – Evacuation by the German armies of the countries on the left bank of the Rhine. The countries on the left bank of the Rhine shall be administered by the local troops of occupation. The occupation of these territories will be carried out by allied and United States garrisons holding the principal crossings of the Rhine (Mayence, Coblenz, Cologne), together with the bridgeheads at these points of a thirty-kilometre radius on the right bank and by garrisons similarly holding the strategic points of the regions. A neutral zone shall be reserved on the right bank of the Rhine between the stream and a line drawn parallel to the bridgeheads and to the stream and at a distance of ten kilometres, from the frontier of Holland up to the frontier of Switzerland. The evacuation by the enemy of the Rhinelands (left and right bank) shall be so ordered as to be completed within a further period of sixteen days, in all, thirty-one days after the signing of the armistice. All the movements of evacuation or occupation are regulated by the note (annexure No. 1) drawn up at the moment of the signing of the armistice.

Appendix 8
Menu, Dinner 23 April 1919

The full menu is given below, as it was presented on the day. The author's English translation is given, but there was no interpretation on the day.

Diner du 23 Avril 1919

Consommé au Profiteroles (clear soup with small choux pastry balls)

Rouelle de Veau Royale (leg of veal)

Timbale de Pigeon, Petit Pois (minced pigeon with peas)

Asperges Sauce Hollandaise (asparagus and hollandaise sauce)

Poulets de Grains Rotis Broche (rotisserie cooked corn-fed chicken)

Salad de Laitues (lettuce salad)

Fromage Mont-Blanc (French Alpine cheese)

✴ ✴ ✴

Bombe Zeebrugge (unknown but probably involved ice cream)

Source: original menu.

Appendix 9
Dobson and Steele VC Citations

The London Gazette, 11 November 1919 (from the Admiralty, S.W.)

The KING has been graciously pleased to approve of the award of the Victoria Cross to the undermentioned Officers:

Commander Claude Congreve Dobson DSO RN
For most conspicuous gallantry, skill and devotion to duty on the occasion of the attack on Kronstadt Harbour on the 18th August, 1919. Commander Dobson organised and was in command of the Coastal Motor Boat Flotilla. He led the flotilla through the chain of forts to the entrance of the harbour. Coastal Motor Boat No 31, from which he directed the general operations, then passed in, under a very heavy machine-gun fire, and torpedoed the Bolshevik Battleship *Andrei Pervozanni*, subsequently returning through the heavy fire of the forts and batteries to the open sea.

Lieutenant Gordon Charles Steele RN
For most conspicuous gallantry, skill and devotion to duty on the occasion of the attack on Kronstadt Harbour on the 18th August, 1919. Lieutenant Steele was second-in-command of H.M. Coastal Motor Boat No 88. After this boat had entered the harbour the Commanding Officer, Lieutenant Dayrell-Reed, was shot through the head and the boat thrown off her course. Lieutenant Steele took the wheel, steadied the boat, lifted Lieutenant Dayrell-Reed away from the steering and firing position and torpedoed the Bolshevik battleship *Andrei Pervozanni* at a hundred yards range. He had then a difficult manoeuvre to perform to get a clear view of the battleship *Petropavlovsk*, which was overlapped by the *Andrei Pervozanni* and obscured by smoke coming from that ship. The evolution, however, was skilfully carried out, and the *Petropavlovsk* torpedoed. This left Lieutenant. Steele with only just room to turn, in order to regain the entrance to the harbour, but he effected the movement with success and firing his machine guns along the wall on his way, passed under the line of forts through a heavy fire out of the harbour.

Appendix 10

Motor Launch Losses Post-war, 1918–1920

Date	ML number	Reason and location
22 Dec 1918	121	Collision off Seine Bank
22 Dec 1918	566	Swamped off Cape Barfleur
Unknown	196	Caught fire and sank or possibly entered Turkish harbour of Sivriji at night to search for possible damaged U-boat and was lost
Unknown	434	Caught fire on R Danube
12 May 1919	229	Caught fire whilst refuelling on the Rhine and blew up. One man killed, two injured
Unknown	97, 127	Sold in damaged condition
27 Sept 1919	575, 567, 570, 578, 579	Abandoned at Murmansk
29 Sept 1919	18, 62, 191	Lost on passage from Norway*
13 Dec 1919	521	Caught fire off Portsmouth after collision with a cargo lighter
30 Dec 1919	156	Mined, salved and written off in Baltic
30 Dec 1919	98, 124	Lost under tow returning from Baltic
2 Jan 1920	152	Grounded on South Oland Island, Sweden
Total	20	

Sources: Dittmar and Colledge, *British Warships*, p136, and author's research.

*Note: Dittmar and Colledge give this loss, but Hepper, *British Warship Losses*, p153, states that he can find no record of the event in the Admiralty files. They are included in this table for completeness.

The Plans

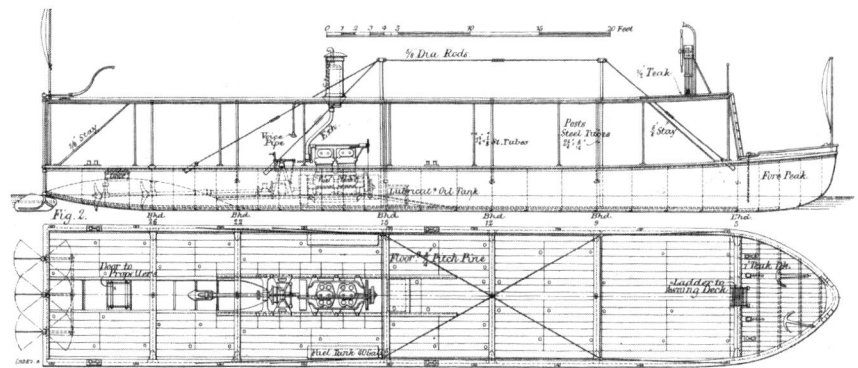

Plan of a Thornycroft river launch, built in 1906 for use on the West African rivers.
(Engineering, 6 March 1906)

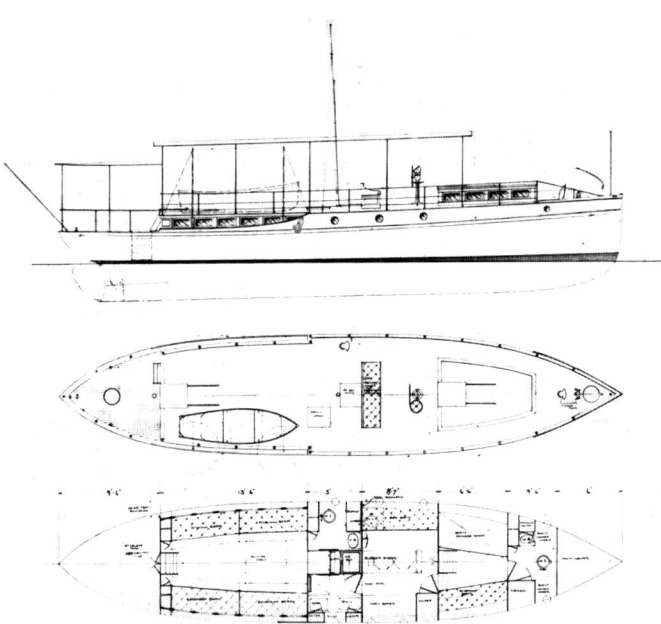

A plan by her builder (New York Yacht Launch and Engine Company, Morris Heights,
New York) of the 53ft motor boat *Hippocampus*, taken up by the US Navy in 1917.
This yard also built the sub chasers *SC-233–242* and *SC-393–402*.
(US Navy History and Heritage Command, NH101821)

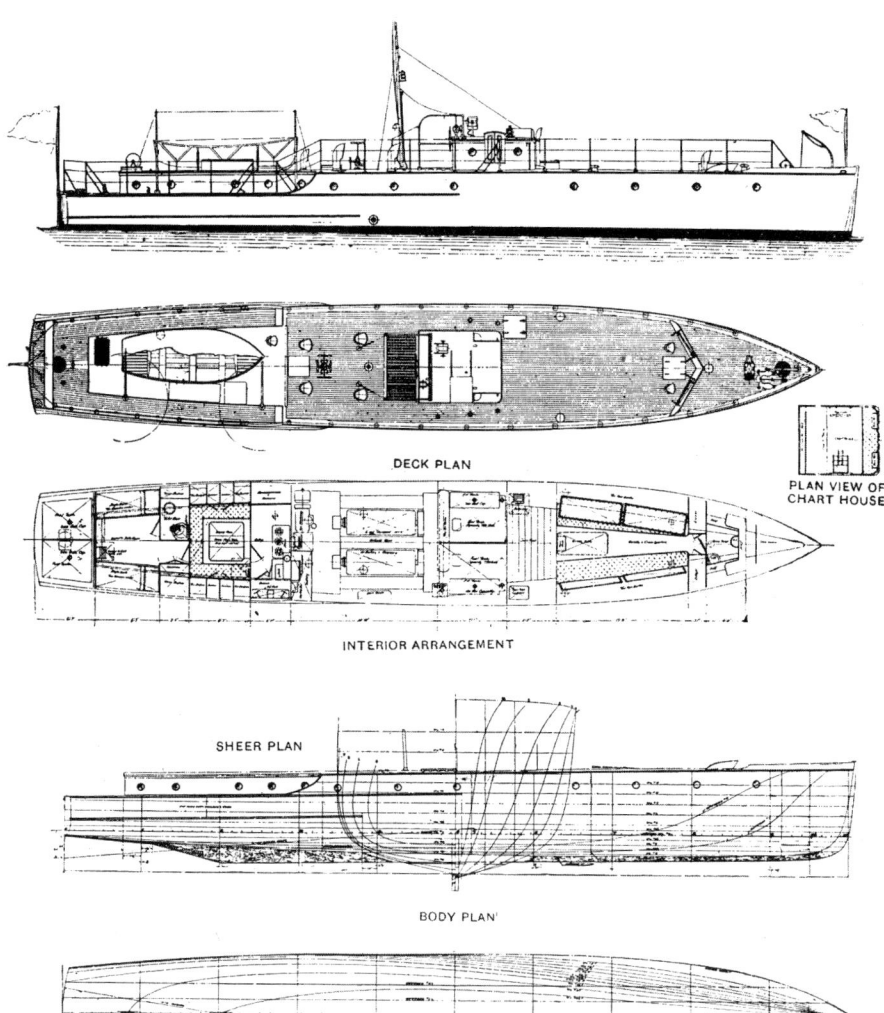

The design of the British M. L.'s.

The side, deck and sheer plan of a motor launch. *(From Cinderellas of the Fleet)*

THE PLANS 289

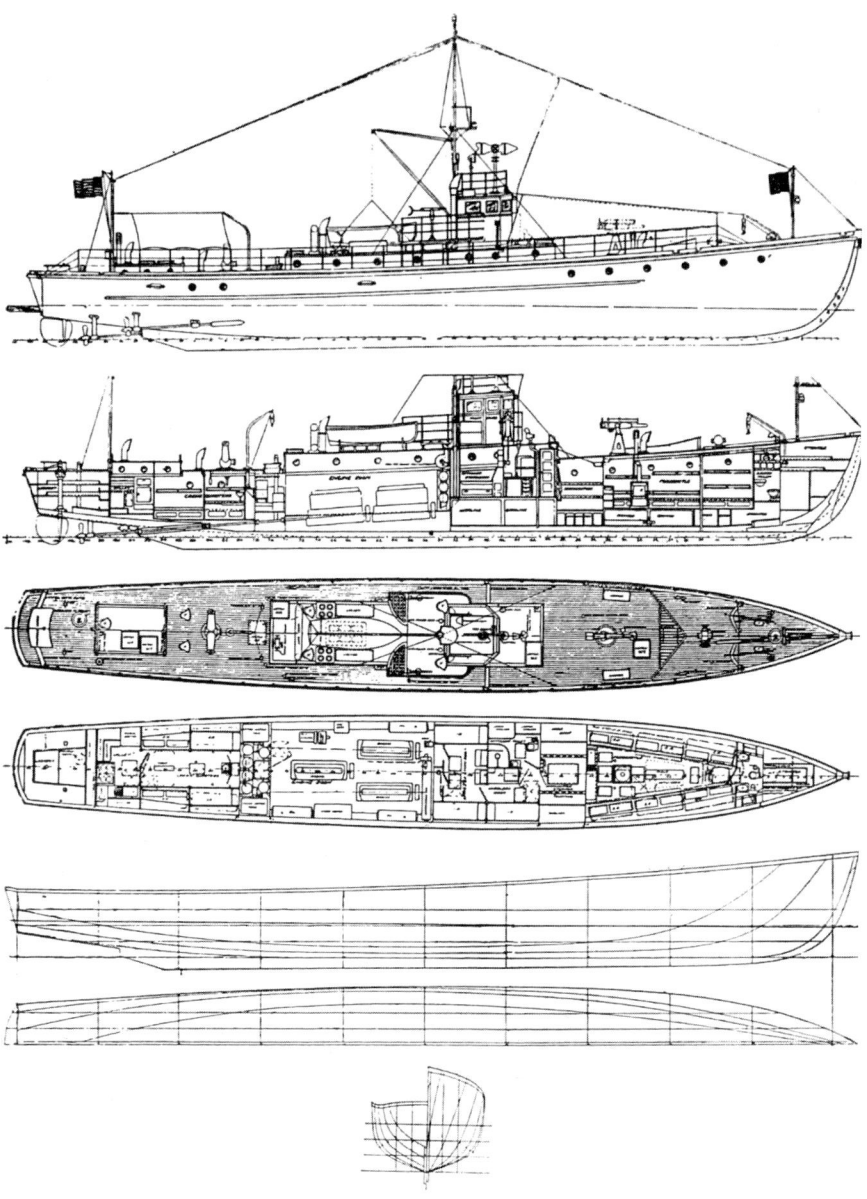

Profiles and plans of a USN sub chaser. *(From Cinderellas of the Fleet)*

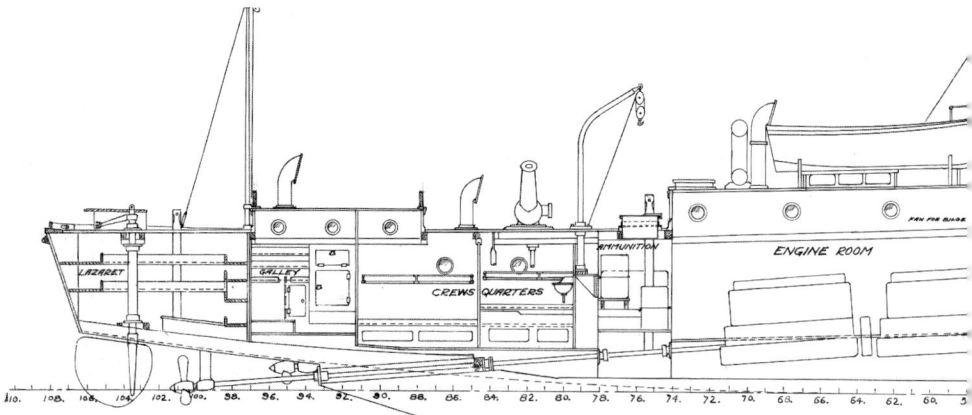

The inboard plans of a 110ft USN sub chaser.
(US National Archives at College Park, 30010079)

The outboard plans of a 110ft USN sub chaser.
(US National Archives at College Park 30010079)

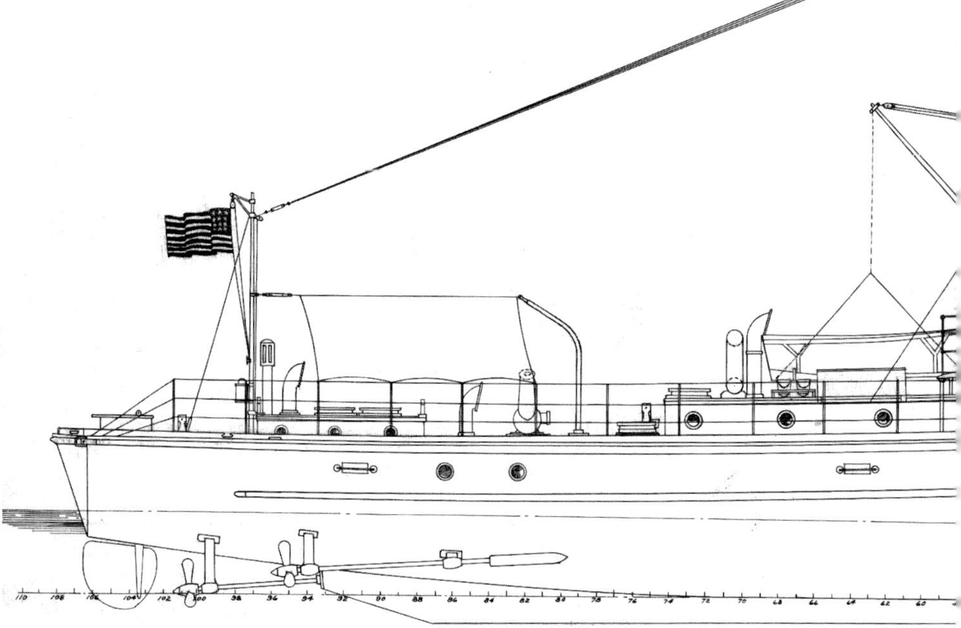

THE PLANS

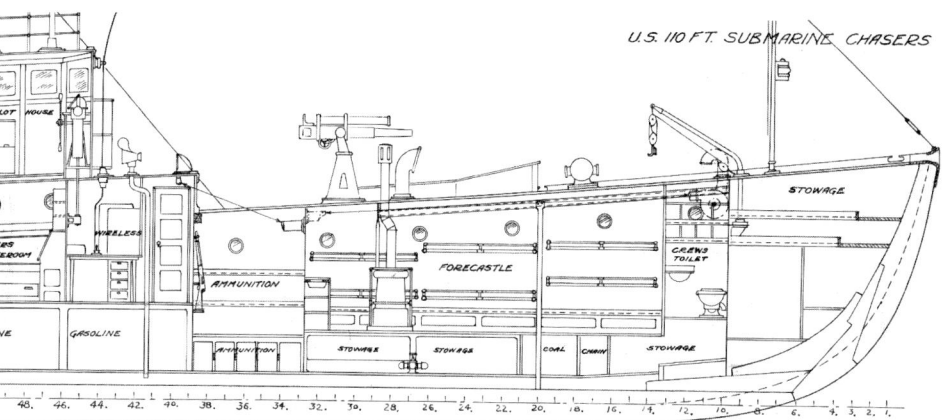

U.S. 110 FT. SUBMARINE CHASERS

U.S. 110 FT. SUBMARINE CHASERS

S.C. 448

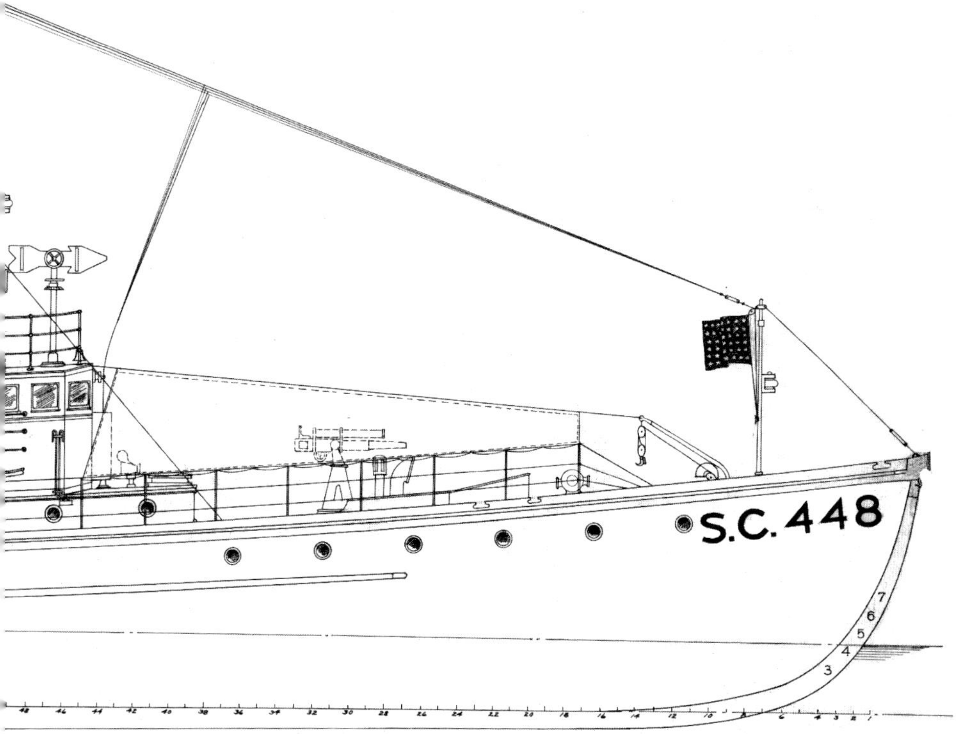

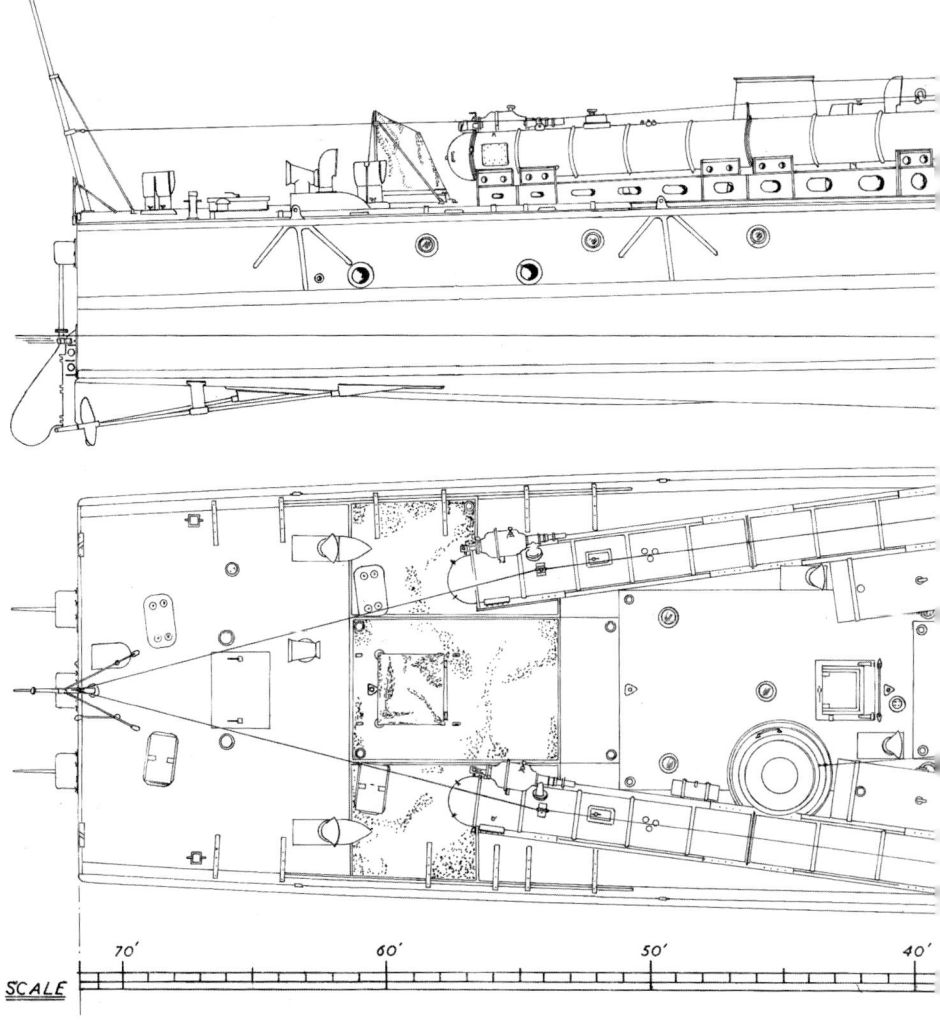

Technical drawing, profile and deck plans of a Thornycroft 40ft skimmer.
(© National Maritime Museum, Greenwich, London, THYB0171)

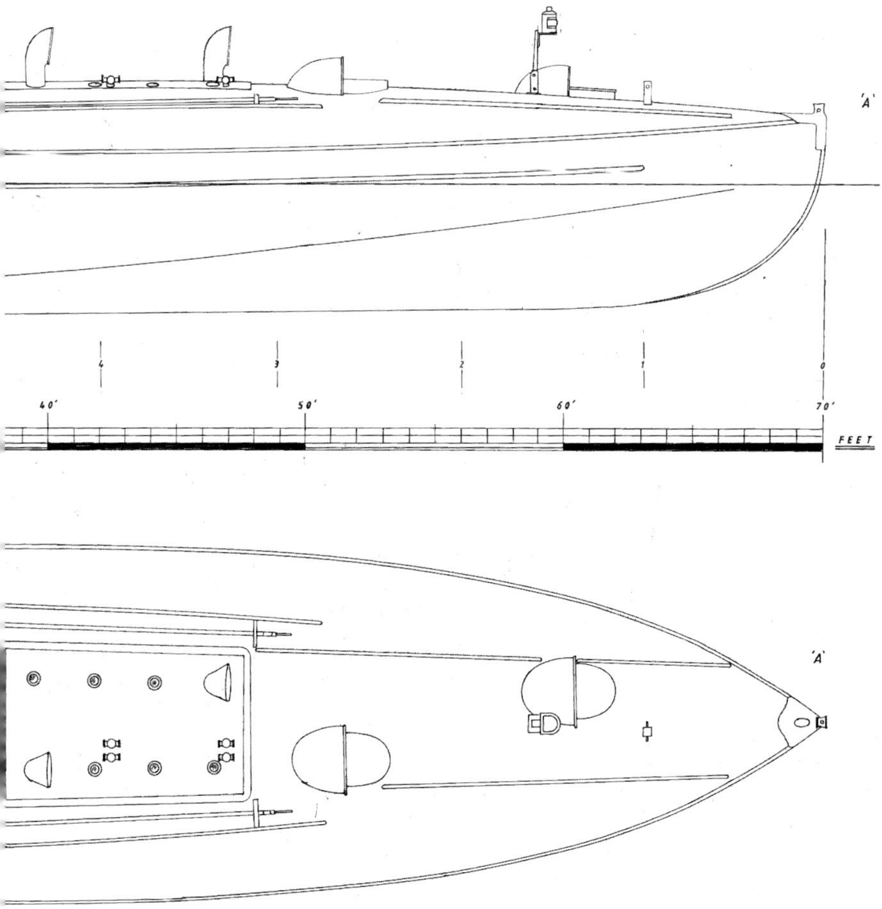

THE PLANS 297

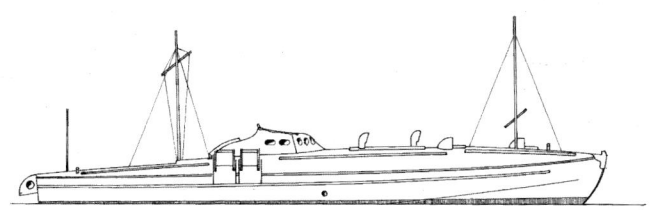

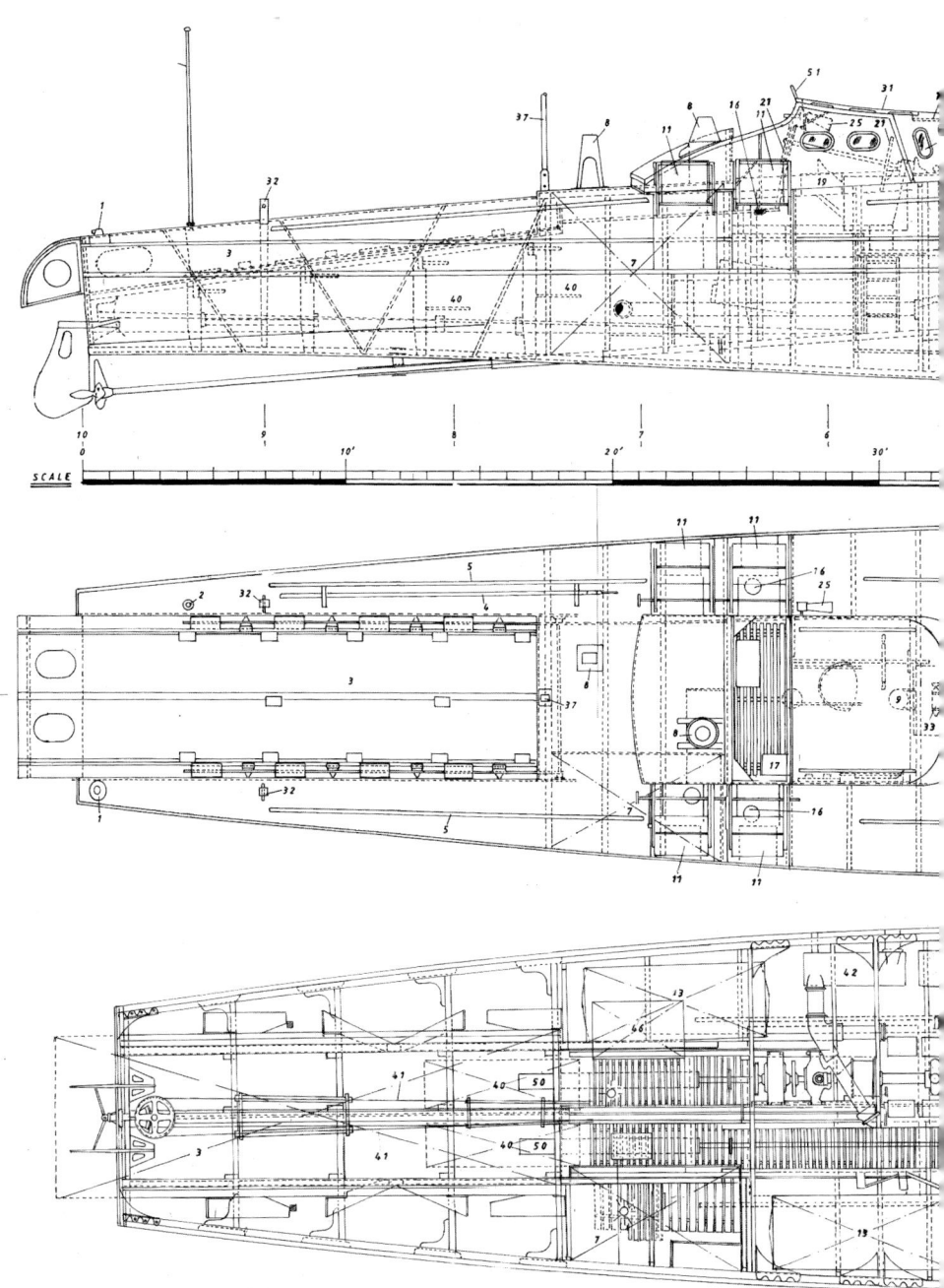

72ft Thornycroft coastal motor boat designed for minelaying.
(© John Lambert Collection/Seaforth Publishing, L-S-193B)

THE PLANS 299

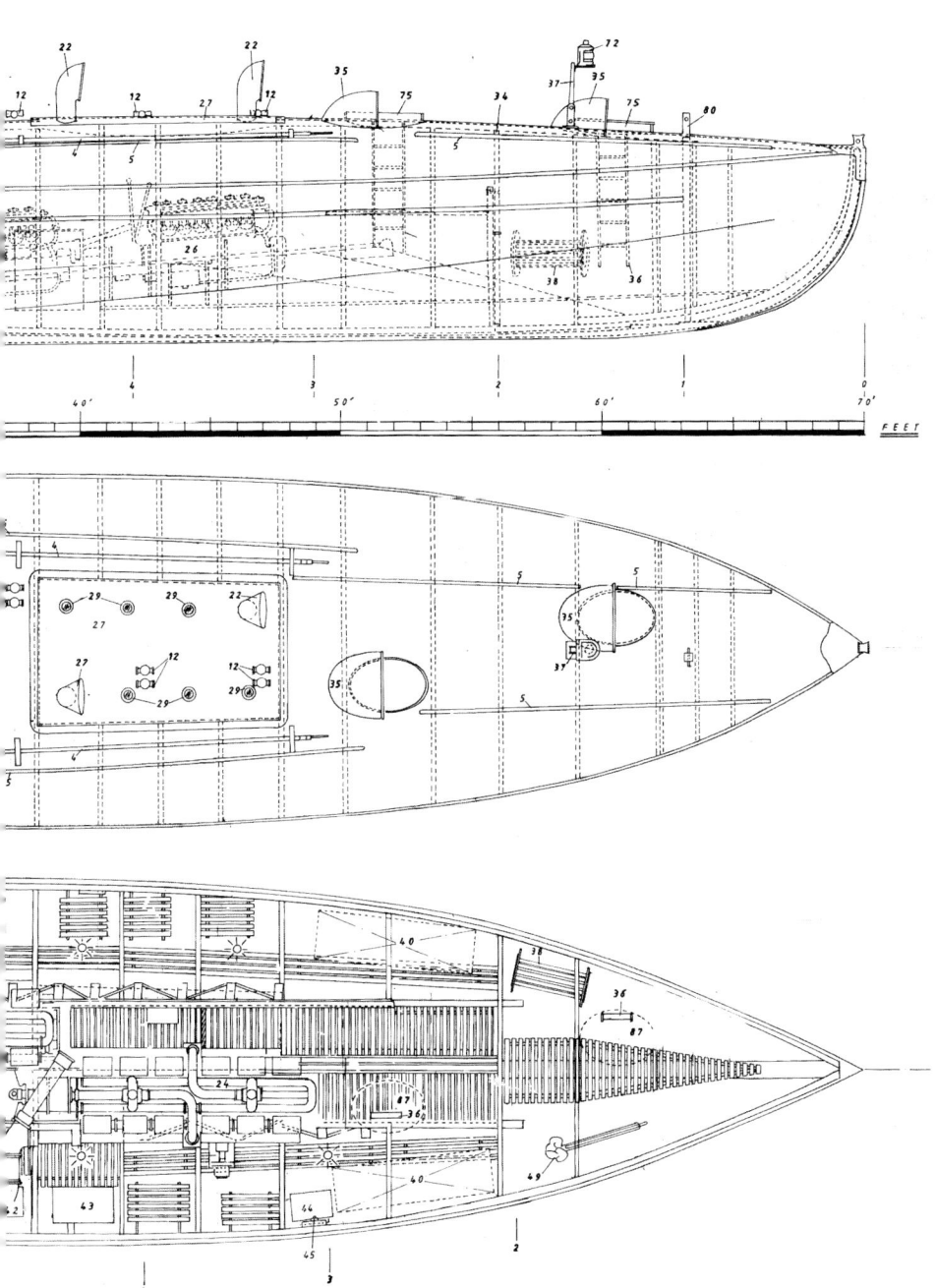

Author's Notes

I have previously written about the trawlers and drifters of the Auxiliary Patrol in the First World War, and it was this that stimulated my interest in examining other facets of that organisation. My publisher, Julian Mannering, ever-supportive, encouraged me to widen the scope to looking at the Petrol Navy as a whole and it seemed logical, given the strong American connections of the boats themselves, to consider the USN experience with petrol-driven craft, as well as similar craft in the French, Italian and German navies. The result is this book, which I hope has brought knowledge and enjoyment to the reader. More so, I trust that it has done justice to the men and vessels of the Petrol Navy and serves as a memorial to them.

My thanks are due to Dr Vaughn Michell, Chairman of the Britannia Naval Research Association for permission to use his two photographs of the restored *CMB-9*. David Bremner, Bristol Scout restorer extraordinaire, provided photographs and documents concerning his great-uncle. The Oxford Duplication Centre skilfully converted some old glass negatives into modern formats. Dr Anthony Firth kindly helped with information on *ML-286*. And Dr Christopher Phillips let me have an e-copy of his book *Civilian Specialists at War*.

Research was aided by the Special Collections Unit of the Library of Leeds University, who were most helpful, and as usual The National Archives at Kew and the Imperial War Museum in London proved fertile hunting grounds.

Three websites gave me an initial heads-up and helped me identify potential sources: Stephen Fisher's spitfiresofthesea.com; subchaser.org; and motorlaunchpatrol.net. I thank the owners of all three.

American picture archives are both extensive and more generous than British ones; many images are provided free of charge, a boon not granted by any British picture repository and more's the pity. As ever, I offer heartfelt thanks to the Library of Congress in Washington DC and the US Naval History and Heritage Command at the Washington Navy Yard for their generosity. Their imagery adds much to the comprehensive nature of this book.

My thanks are also due to Peter Wilkinson for the map of Kronstadt, Janet Andrew, who produced the index, and especially to Vivienne, without whose assistance and encouragement, none of my books would have been written.

I am not a 'yachtie', but in researching this book, it was clear that yachting/sailing was a very popular pre-First World War pastime, and that the yachtsmen of Britain (and the Empire) were ready and willing to answer their country's call. We owe a debt to them.

Notes and Sources

Abbreviations
The following abbreviations will be used for brevity.

Collections
IWM: Imperial War Museum, London
TNA: The National Archives, Kew
NMRN: National Museum of the Royal Navy, Portsmouth
CAC: Churchill Archive, Churchill College, Cambridge
BL: British Library, London
LC: Liddell Collection, Special Collections Unit, University of Leeds
NMM: National Maritime Museum, Greenwich
PC: Bremner MSS held in private collection

Books
FTDTSF: Marder, *From the Dreadnought to Scapa Flow*, vols I–V
NO: *Naval Operations, The History of the Great War based on Official Documents*, vols I–V

It is the convention that page numbers be given for citations. This is not always possible in the modern world. Some digitised documents lack page numbering and some archives hold unnumbered single or multiple sheets in bundles under one reference or none at all. Thus, page numbers will be given where possible but the reader will understand that they are not always available or, indeed, necessary.

1 Yachting and the Development of the Motor Boat
1. Scott, *50 Years in the Royal Navy*, p2.
2. Quoted in MacMillan, *War*, p120.
3. Ridley, *George V*, p88.
4. *OED*, vol 1, 1983 edn, definition B.
5. Brewer, *Dictionary*, p292.
6. *Engineering*, 9 March 1906.
7. *The Times*, 25 November 1904.
8. *Grace's Guide*, 1924.
9. *The Times*, 25 November 1904.
10. *Spectator*, July 1913.
11. Crawford, *Fallen Glory*, p84.
12. MacMillan, *War*, p62.
13. Pound, *Lost Generation*, p78.
14. Nicholson, *Gentry*, p195.
15. Docs 6726, IWM.
16. Williams, *Gentlemen and Players*, p20.

2 A Strategic Gap and a Motor Boat Solution
1. 26 Feb 1904 memo to Cabinet, quoted in Burk, *The Lion and the Eagle*, p363.
2. Lambert, *Admirals*, p312.
3. ADM 137/2864, TNA.
4. ADM 186/604, TNA.
5. DRAX 1/11, CAC.
6. Chatterton, *Auxiliary Patrol*, p25.
7. Ibid.
8. Kerr, *RNVR*, p24.
9. *The Times*, 16 April 1912.
10. Dawson, *Sound of the Guns*, p126.

3 To War in Boats
1. *The Times*, 4 August 1914.
2. Bailey, *Secret Rooms*, p232.
3. Marder, *FTDTSF*, vol 2, p357.
4. Chatterton, *Auxiliary Patrol*, p25.

5 Kerr, *RNVR*, p94.
6 Chatterton, *Auxiliary Patrol*, p26.
7 Ibid, p44.
8 Maxwell, *Motor Launch Patrol*, pp14–15.
9 Chatterton, *Auxiliary Patrol*, p26.
10 Navy List, 31 December 1914.
11 CHAR 13/49/24, CAC.
12 Navy List quarterly, July 1915.
13 Phillips, *Civilian Specialists at War*, p167.
14 *Yachting Monthly*, April 1919.
15 Ibid.
16 Palmer, *Gardeners of Salonika*, p52.
17 ADM 337/118/257, TNA.
18 Ibid.
19 ADM 337/117/176, TNA.
20 Ibid.
21 *NO*, vol I, p17.

4 The Birth of the Motor Launch
1 Chatterton, *Auxiliary Patrol*, p23.
2 ADM 337/121/144, TNA.
3 ADM 239/26, TNA.
4 ADM 238/2, 119, 142, TNA.
5 *London Gazette* 31248, 21 March 1919.
6 Fayle, *Seaborne Trade*, vol 3, p465.
7 Maxwell, *Motor Launch Patrol*, p1.
8 Ibid.
9 Woodrow Wilson, Message to 63rd Congress, 63rd Congress, 2nd Session, Senate Doc No 566, Washington, 1914, pp3–4.
10 M-P-S, *Hounding the Hun*, no page numbers (NP).
11 Ibid.
12 Ibid.
13 Kerr, *RNVR*, p98.
14 Ibid.
15 Ibid.
16 Ibid.
17 Bacon, *Dover Patrol*, vol 1, p72.
18 Maxwell, *Motor Launch Patrol*, p31.
19 Oliver, *Memoirs*, vol II, pp117–18.
20 Preston, *Wilful Murder*, p320.
21 Ibid, p409.
22 ADM 337/117/276, TNA.
23 ADM 337/117/797, TNA.
24 ADM 337/117/712, TNA.
25 ADM 337/117/780, TNA.
26 Ibid.
27 ADM 337/121/379, TNA.
28 Docs 25448, IWM.
29 Torpedo Bay Navy Museum online.
30 *The Motor Ship and Motor Boat Magazine*, 17 February 1916.
31 Chatterton, *Auxiliary Patrol*, p104.
32 Brown, Meehan, *Scapa Flow*, p84.
33 Maxwell, *Motor Launch Patrol*, pp16–17.
34 M-P-S, *Hounding the Hun*, NP.
35 Maxwell, *Motor Boat Patrol*, p53.
36 Ibid.
37 Ibid, p51.
38 Nutting, *Cinderellas of the Fleet*, p19.
39 Maxwell, *Motor Launch Patrol*, p51.
40 Bacon, *Dover Patrol*, vol 1, p72.
41 Brown, Meehan, *Scapa Flow*, pp82–3.
42 Ibid, p83.
43 Docs 11440 pt2, p21, IWM.
44 *Naval Monographs*, vol XVIII, part VIII, p33.
45 Bacon, *Dover Patrol*, vol 1, p71.

5 Motor Launches versus U-boats and Mines
1 Kerr, *RNVR*, p101.
2 DRAX 1/11, CAC.
3 Ibid.
4 Kerr, *RNVR*, p102.
5 Maxwell, *Motor Launch Patrol*, p55.
6 Jellicoe, *Crisis*, p65.
7 Details from ADM 53/51632, TNA.
8 Maxwell, *Motor Launch Patrol*, p54.
9 Dittmar, Colledge, *British Warships*, p147.
10 Ibid.
11 *London Gazette* 29877, 22 December 1916.
12 ADM 337/122/269, TNA.
13 Ibid.
14 *London Gazette* 30536, 19 February 1918.
15 ADM 337/120/25, TNA.
16 ADM 337/118/326, TNA.
17 *London Gazette* 30756, 18 June 1918.
18 Ibid, 31286, 8 April 1919.
19 Jellicoe, *Crisis*, pp64–5.
20 Chatterton, *Auxiliary Patrol*, p303.
21 Maxwell, *Motor Launch Patrol*, pp54–5.
22 Crossley, *Hidden Threat*, p111.
23 Lambert, *Planning Armageddon*, p53.
24 Taffrail, *Endless Story*, p105.
25 Ibid.
26 Carr, *Brass Hats and Bell Bottomed Trousers*, p128.

27 Nutting, *Cinderellas of the Fleet*, p30.
28 Carr, *Brass Hats and Bell Bottomed Trousers*, p162.
29 Chatterton, *Auxiliary Patrol*, p156.
30 Bacon, *Dover Patrol*, vol 1, p75.
31 Maxwell, *Motor Launch Patrol*, p55.

6 In Distant Waters
1 Winton, *The Victoria Cross at Sea*, p145.
2 Maxwell, *Motor Launch Patrol*, pp208–9.
3 *Yachting Monthly*, April 1919.
4 Ibid.
5 Bruce, *Last Crusade*, p82.
6 *Yachting Monthly*, April 1919.
7 Ibid.
8 Lloyd George, *War Memoirs*, vol 2, p1090.
9 *Yachting Monthly*, April 1919.
10 Ibid.
11 Maxwell, *Motor Launch Patrol*, p224.
12 Ibid.
13 *London Gazette* 31286, 8 April 1919.
14 *Yachting Monthly*, April 1919.
15 *London Gazette* 30694, 21 May 1918.

7 Operation ZO – The Raids on Zeebrugge and Ostend
1 *NO*, vol V, pp21–4.
2 Docs 25448, IWM.
3 2005.75, letter to family, NMRN.
4 *Yachting Monthly*, June 1918.
5 2008.7, p33, NMRN.
6 Diary 22 April 1918, LIDDLE/WW1/RNMN/005, LC.
7 Ibid.
8 Maxwell, *Motor Launch Patrol*, p119.
9 Chatterton, *Auxiliary Patrol*, p285.
10 Maxwell, *Motor Launch Patrol*, p114.
11 2008.7, 23 April 1918, NMRN.
12 Docs 25448, IWM.
13 Signal 23 April 1918, LIDDLE/WW1/RNMN/005, LC.
14 MSS 217, NMRN.
15 Winton, *The Victoria Cross at Sea*, p169.
16 Docs 3631, p3, IWM.
17 Ibid, p4.
18 Ibid, p6.
19 Ibid.
20 2008.7, p40, NMRN.
21 Maxwell, *Motor Launch Patrol*, p143.
22 *London Gazette* 30870, 27 August 1918.
23 MSS 217, NMRN.
24 *NO*, vol 5, p265.
25 Halpern, *Naval History of World War One*, p416.
26 Maxwell, *Motor Launch Patrol*, p149.

8 The Corinthians of ZO
1 *London Gazette* 30194, 20 July 1917, Honours for Miscellaneous Services.
2 Ibid, 30870, 27 August 1918 Ostend raid honours.
3 ADM 337/117/427, TNA.
4 *London Gazette*, 31483, 29 July 1919.
5 ADM 337/120/719, TNA.
6 Keyes' despatch, *London Gazette* 30870, 27 August 1918.
7 *London Gazette* 30807, 19 July 1918.
8 ADM 337/120/259, TNA.
9 Chatterton, *Auxiliary Patrol*, p284.
10 Snelling, *Naval VCs*, p279.
11 Ibid, p294.
12 Docs 12502, IWM.
13 *London Gazette*, 12 December 1918.
14 Snelling, *Naval VCs*, p298.
15 Kerr, *RNVR*, p106.

9 Motor Launch Losses
1 *London Gazette* 30267, 4 September 1917.
2 Jellicoe, *Crisis*, p191.
3 *London Gazette* 30852, 20 August 1918.
4 ADM 337/120/152, TNA.
5 Ibid.
6 *London Gazette* 30936, 4 October 1918.
7 ADM 337/121/532, TNA.
8 *London Gazette* 30870, 27 August 1918.
9 ADM 337/121/548, TNA.

10 The Sea Skimmers
1 FROB2/1, CAC.
2 Bremner, Lecture to RNSC, PC.
3 Ibid.
4 Ibid.
5 Ibid.
6 Barnaby, *100 Years*, p73.
7 Bremner, Lecture to RNSC, PC.
8 Evans, *Keeping the Seas*, p187.
9 Agar, *Footprints in the Sea*, p79.

10 Ibid, p78.
11 Bremner, RNSC lecture, PC.
12 *Pacific Motor Boat*, April 1920.
13 Letter 20 September 1912 in Fisher, *Memories*, p219.
14 Numerical data for CMB count from Dittmar and Colledge, *British Warships*, pp137–40.
15 *London Gazette* 30066, 11 May 1917.
16 Ibid, 31189, 18 February 1919.
17 Ibid, 30807, 19 July 1918 and 30870, 27 August 1918.
18 Ibid.
19 Ibid.
20 Ibid, 30909, 17 September 1918.
21 Ibid, 30807, 19 July 1918.
22 Bremner, RNSC lecture, PC.
23 Friedman, *Fighting the Great War at Sea*, p176.
24 *NO*, vol V, p345.
25 Ibid.
26 Ibid.
27 *Abergavenny Chronicle and Monmouth Advertiser*, 23 August 1918.
28 *London Gazette* 31038, 26 November 1918.
29 Fock, *Fast Fighting Boats*, p60.
30 ADM 337/120/564, TNA.

11 The American Submarine Chasers

1   Quoted in Neiberg, *Path to War*, p39.
2   Hendrick, *Life and Letters of Walter H Page*, pp327–8.
3   Nutting, *Cinderellas of the Fleet*, p57.
4   Moffat, *Maverick Navy*, p12.
5   Sims, *Victory at Sea*, pp38–9.
6   Nutting, *Cinderellas of the Fleet*, p58.
7   Chambers, *US Submarine Chasers*, p3.
8   Sims, *Victory at Sea*, p175.
9   Docs 11440, pt2, p24, IWM.
10 Sims, *Victory at Sea*, p176.
11 Moffat, *Maverick Navy*, p11.
12 Nutting, *Cinderellas of the Fleet*, p84.
13 Chambers, *US Submarine Chasers*, p13.
14 Moffat, *Maverick Navy*, p41.
15 Nutting, *Cinderellas of the Fleet*, p85.
16 Sims, *Victory at Sea*, p176.
17 *Motor Boating Magazine*, December 1919.
18 Chambers, *US Submarine Chasers*, pp27–8.
19 Nutting, *Cinderellas of the Fleet*, p73.
20 Chambers, *US Submarine Chasers*, pp2–3.
21 Sims, *Victory at Sea*, pp184–5.

12 The Splinter Ships Go to War

1   Sims, *Victory at Sea*, p173.
2   Nutting, *Cinderellas of the Fleet*, p81.
3   Sims, *Victory at Sea*, p168.
4   *Pacific Motor Boat*, April 1919.
5   Moffat, *Maverick Navy*, pp49, 51.
6   Sims, *Victory at Sea*, p178.
7   Cotton letter 9 July 1918, US Naval History and Heritage Command.
8   Ibid.
9   Ibid.
10 Quoted in Woofenden, *Hunters of the Steel Sharks*, p177.
11 *Pacific Motor Boat*, April 1919.
12 Ibid.
13 Ibid.
14 Ibid
15 *Pacific Motor Boat*, April 1920.
16 Ibid.
17 Ibid
18 Bayly, *Pull Together*, p252.
19 Still, *Crisis at Sea*, p500.
20 Woofenden, *Hunters of the Steel Sharks*, p93.
21 Nutting, *Cinderellas of the Fleet*, p101.
22 Sims, *Victory at Sea*, p201.
23 Ibid.
24 Maxwell, *Naval Front*, p187.
25 https://valor.militarytimes.com/hero/16379.
26 Halpern, *Naval History of World War One*, p176.
27 ADM 196/20/411, TNA.

13 Motor Boats in the Italian, French and German Navies

1   Thompson, *White War*, p4.
2   Ibid, p233.
3   Fock, *Fast Fighting Boats*, p32.
4   Ibid, p288.
5   Ibid.
6   *Jane's Fighting Ships*, p219.
7   Letter 25 June 1918, Naval History and Heritage Command.
8   *New York Times*, 26 February 1918.

9   Fock, *Fast Fighting Ships*, p59.
10 27 August 1918, CAB 23/7/27, TNA.
11 5 November 1917, CAB 23/4/39, TNA.
12 Ibid.
13 23 November 1917, CAB 23/4/55, TNA.

14 Armistice, Occupation and a Revolution

1   *Pacific Motor Boat*, May 1920.
2   Moffat, *Maverick Navy*, p127.
3   Woofenden, *Hunters of the Steel Sharks*, p106.
4   Chambers, *US Submarine Chasers*, p80.
5   Diary 11 November 1918, LIDDLE/WW1/RNMN/005, LC.
6   Docs 18309, IWM.
7   Maxwell, *Motor Launch Patrol*, p280.
8   Edmonds, *Occupation of the Rhineland*, p7.
9   Ibid, p98.
10 Admiralty telegram 9 December 1918, LIDDLE/WW1/RNMN/005, LC.
11 Docs 1617, IWM.
12 PGA/3/1, TNA.
13 ADM 196/125/42, TNA.
14 *Illustrated London News*, 5 April 1919.
15 PGA/3/1, TNA.
16 4 February 1919, LIDDLE/WW1/RNMN/005, LC.
17 Ibid, 8 February.
18 Ibid, 7 February.
19 Ibid.
20 ADM 337/122/284, TNA.
21 PGA/3/1, TNA.
22 23 April 1919, LIDDLE/WW1/RNMN/005, LC.
23 Ibid.
24 Ibid.
25 Ibid.
26 Ibid, 6 May 1919.
27 Markham, *Woman's Watch on the Rhine*, p39.
28 Ibid, p73.
29 WO 95/3991, TNA.
30 ADM 337/122/284, TNA.
31 Bonar Law to Geddes, 23 Nov 1918, ADM116/1809, TNA.
32 ADM 196/96/228, TNA.
33 Hansard HC Deb 27 October 1919, vol 120, cc290-1.
34 Docs 1617, IWM.
35 Edmonds, *Occupation of the Rhineland*, p102.
36 Docs 18309, IWM.
37 Ibid.
38 Ibid.
39 *London Gazette* 31604, 14 October 1919.

15 In Russia and the North Sea

1   Agar, *Baltic Episode*, p87.
2   Ibid.
3   Item 12, LIDDLE/WW1/RNMN/319, LC.
4   Agar, *Footprints in the Sea*, p324.
5   Item 12, LIDDLE/WW1/RNMN/319, LC.
6   *Derby Daily Telegraph*, 30 August 1919.
7   Docs 6898, IWM.
8   Agar, *Footprints in the Sea*, p82.
9   *London Gazette* 29264, 13 August 1915
10 ADM 196/89/199, TNA.
11 Wilson, *For Them the War Was Not Over*, p72.
12 US Naval History and Heritage Command.
13 Woofenden, *Hunters of the Steel Sharks*, p141.
14 Friedman, *Fighting the Great War at Sea*, p343.
15 Add Mss 49714, BL.
16 *The Northern Barrage*, p9.
17 Ibid, p8.
18 Ibid, p16.
19 Woofenden, *Hunters of the Steel Sharks*, p147.

16 Last Rites

1   *NO*, vol V, p430.
2   Hansard HC Deb 06 August 1919, vol 119, cc335-6335.
3   Dittmar and Colledge, *British Warships 1914–1919*, p136.
4   Hansard HC Deb 30 October 1919, vol 120, cc899-900.
5   Ibid.
6   Dittmar and Colledge, *British Warships 1914–1919*, p136.
7   *NO*, vol V, p430.
8   *Motor Boat Magazine*, 25 August 1920.

9 Brunicardi, *Sea Hound*, p57.
10 Nutting, *Cinderellas of the Fleet*, p170.
11 Maxwell, *Motor Launch Patrol*, p303.
12 Hansard HC Deb 11 March 1919, vol 113, c1109W.
13 Hansard HC Deb 30 July 1919, vol 118, c2122W.
14 *London Gazette* 29621, 13 June 1916.
15 *Dundee Evening Telegraph*, 9 August 1921.
16 Barnaby, *100 Years*, p75.
17 Jellicoe, *Crisis*, p116.

17 Conclusions
1 Kerr, *RNVR*, p114.
2 Ibid, p115.
3 Keynes, *Economic Consequences of the Peace*, p138.
4 Hankey, *Supreme Command*, vol 1, pp425–6.
5 Offer, *Agrarian Interpretation*, p114.
6 https://oceangloberace.com/, retrieved 14 September 2021.
7 Lambert, *British Way of War*, p342.
8 Ibid, p344.
9 Maxwell, *Motor Launch Patrol*, vii, viii.
10 Hansard HC Deb 06 August 1919, vol 119, cc335-6335.
11 Still, *Crisis at Sea*, p500.
12 Dittmar, Colledge, *British Warships 1914–1919*, p140.
13 *The Engineer*, 25 September 1925.
14 ADM 337/117/731, TNA.
15 ADM 337/117/11, TNA.
16 LIDDLE/WW1/RNMN/REC/015, LC.
17 Navy List June 1920, p1687.

Bibliography

The following resources have been cited in the text.

Primary sources
Various files in the ADM, WO and CAB series, individually cited, The National Archives, Kew
Rhine Patrol Flotilla Papers, PGA/3/1, The National Archives
Private papers of the Admiral the Hon Sir Reginald Aylmer Ranfurly Plunkett-Ernle-Erle-Drax, DRAX, Churchill Archive Centre, Cambridge
Various files in the CHAR 13 series, individually cited, Churchill Archive Centre
Private papers of Air Commodore Francis Banks, FROB 2/1, Churchill Archive Centre
Private papers of Captain Sir J M Alleyne RN, documents 3631, Imperial War Museum
Private papers of Commander F F Tower RNVR, documents 11440, Imperial War Museum
Private papers of A T Wilkinson, documents 6898, Imperial War Museum
Private papers of Captain P G E C Acheson RN, documents 1617, Imperial War Museum
Private papers of Commander C C Calvin RNVR, documents 25448, Imperial War Museum
Private papers of Commander J Petrie RNVR, documents 12502, Imperial War Museum
Private papers of F Cooper RNVR, documents 18309, Imperial War Museum
Private papers of Captain H U S Nisbet, documents 6726, Imperial War Museum
Private papers of Captain H Grant RN, MSS 217, National Museum of the Royal Navy, Portsmouth
Diary of William James Wood, 2008.7, National Museum of the Royal Navy, Portsmouth
Papers of Percy Pointer MSS, 2005.75, National Museum of the Royal Navy, Portsmouth
Add Mss 49714, British Library, London
Lieutenant (later Commander) William Bremner RN, Lecture Notes for the Royal Naval Staff College, 1922/23 term, held in private collection
Documents held by the US Naval History and Heritage Command, as referenced
Diary of Gerald Ashburner Mooring Aldridge, LIDDLE/WW1/RNMN/005, Liddle Collection, Special Collections Unit, University of Leeds
Oral history of Harry Chadwick-Smith, LIDDLE/WW1/RNMN/REC/015, Liddle Collection, Special Collections Unit, University of Leeds
Item 12, LIDDLE/WW1/RNMN/319, Liddle Collection, Special Collections Unit, University of Leeds

Secondary sources
Books
The place of publishing is London, unless otherwise stated.

Agar, A, *Footprints in the Sea*, Evans Brothers Ltd (1959)
——, *Baltic Episode*, Naval Institute Press (Annapolis, 1983, originally published Hodder & Stoughton, 1963)
Bacon, R, *The Dover Patrol*, 2 vols, George H Doran & Co (New York, 1919)
Bailey, C, *The Secret Rooms*, Penguin (2013)
Barnaby, K, *100 Years of Specialised Ship Building and Engineering*, Hutchinson (1964)

Bayly, L, *Pull Together* (George G Harrap & Co, 1939)
Brewer, E, *Dictionary of Phrase and Fable*, Blitz Editions (Leicester, 1990)
Brown, M, & P Meehan, *Scapa Flow*, Pan Books (2002)
Bruce, A, *The Last Crusade*, John Murray (1992)
Brunicardi D, *The Sea Hound*, Collins Press (Cork, 2001)
Burk, K, *The Lion and the Eagle*, Bloomsbury (2018)
Carr, W, *Brass Hats and Bell Bottomed Trousers: Unforgettable and Splendid Feats of the Harwich Patrol*, Hutchinson (1939)
Chambers, H, *United States Submarine Chasers in the Mediterranean, Adriatic and the Attack on Durazzo*, Knickerbocker Press (New York, 1920)
Chatterton, E, *The Auxiliary Patrol*, Sidgwick & Jackson (1923)
Corbett, J, & H Newbolt, *Naval Operations, The History of the Great War based on Official Documents*, vols I–V, republished Naval & Military Press and Imperial War Museum (2014)
Crawford, J, *Fallen Glory*, Old St Publishing (2016)
Crossley, J, *The Hidden Threat*, Pen & Sword Maritime (Barnsley, 2011)
Dawson, L, *Sound of the Guns*, Pen in Hand Publishing (Oxford, 1949)
Dittmar, F, & J Colledge, *British Warships 1914–1918*, Ian Allen (1972)
Edmonds, J, *The Occupation of the Rhineland*, HMSO (1987)
Evans, E, *Keeping the Seas*, Sampson, Low, Marston & Co (1920)
Fayle, C E, *Seaborne Trade*, vol III (Naval & Military Press, Sussex, facsimile edn; originally John Murray, 1924)
Fock, H, *Fast Fighting Boats*, Nautical Publishing Co (Lymington, 1978)
Friedman, N, *Fighting the Great War at Sea*, Seaforth Publishing (Barnsley, 2014)
Halpern, P, *A Naval History of World War 1*, UCL Press (1994)
Hankey, M, *Supreme Command*, vol 1, George, Allen & Unwin (1961)
Hendrick, B (ed), *The Life and Letters of Walter H Page*, vol 1, Doubleday, Page & Co (New York, 1922)
Hepper, D, *British Warship Losses in the Ironclad Era*, Chatham Publishing (2006)
Jane, F, *Jane's Fighting Ships of World War I*, Jane's Publishing Co (1919)
Jellicoe, J, *The Crisis of the Naval War*, George H Doran & Co (New York, 1920)
Keynes, J, *The Economic Consequences of the Peace* (reprint), Read Books (2013)
Kerr, J, & W Granville, *The RNVR*, George G Harrap & Co (1957)
Lambert, A, *Admirals*, Faber & Faber (2009)
——, *The British Way of War*, Yale University Press (2021)
Lambert, N, *Planning Armageddon*, Harvard University Press (Cambridge, Mass, 2012)
Lloyd George, D, *War Memoirs*, vol 2, Odhams Press (1938)
M-P-S, *Hounding the Hun from the Seas*, republished Naval & Military Press (Sussex, nd)
MacMillan, M, *War: How Conflict Shaped Us*, Profile Books (2020)
Marder, A, *From the Dreadnought to Scapa Flow*, vol 2, OUP (Oxford, 1965)
Markham, V, *A Woman's Watch on the Rhine*, George H Doran (New York, 1921)
Maxwell, G, *The Motor Launch Patrol*, J M Dent & Sons (1920)
Maxwell, G, & D Maxwell, *The Naval Front*, A & C Black (1920)
Moffat, A, *Maverick Navy*, Wesleyan University Press (Middletown, Conn, 1976)
Neiberg, M, *The Path to War*, OUP (Oxford, 2016)
Nicholson, A, *Gentry*, Harper Press (2012)
Nutting, W, *The Cinderellas of the Fleet*, Standard Motor Construction Co (Jersey City, 1920)
Offer, A, *The First World War: An Agrarian Interpretation*, Clarendon Press (Oxford, 1991)
Palmer, A, *The Gardeners of Salonika*, Faber & Faber (2009, originally published 1965)
Phillips, C, *Civilian Specialists at War*, University of London Press (2020)
Pound, R, *The Lost Generation*, Constable (1964)
Preston, D, *Wilful Murder*, Doubleday (2002)
Ridley, J, *George V*, Chatto & Windus (2021)

Sandford, C, *The Final Over*, Spellmount (Stroud, 2014)
Scott, P, *50 Years in the Royal Navy*, John Murray (1919)
Sims, W, *The Victory at Sea*, John Murray (1920)
Snelling, S, *The Naval VCs*, History Press (Stroud, 2013)
Still, W, *Crisis at Sea: the United States Navy in European Waters in World War I*, University of Florida Press (Gainesville, 2006)
'Taffrail', *Endless Story*, Hodder & Stoughton (1938)
Thompson, M, *The White War*, Faber & Faber (2008)
Tuchman, B, *The Guns of August*, Macmillan (New York, 1962)
Williams, C, *Gentlemen and Players*, Weidenfeld & Nicolson (2012)
Wilson, M, *For Them the War Was Not Over*, History Press (Stroud, 2010)
Winton, J, *The Victoria Cross at Sea*, Michael Joseph (1978)
Woofenden, T, *Hunters of the Steel Sharks*, Signal Light Books (Bowdoinham, ME, 2006)

Newspapers and magazines
Aberdeen Daily Journal
Abergavenny Chronicle and Monmouth Advertiser
Cologne Post
Derby Daily Telegraph
Dundee Evening Telegraph
Engineering
Fraserburgh Times
Illustrated London News
London Gazette
Motor Boat Magazine (USA)
Motor Boating
New York Times
Pacific Motor Boat
Spectator
The Engineer
The Motor Ship and Motor Boat Magazine
The Times
Yachting Monthly

Online resources
The Torpedo Bay Navy Museum, Auckland, New Zealand
Woodrow Wilson's Message to the 63rd Congress
Hall of Valor [*sic*] Project, online
www.oceangloberace.com

Other
British Vessels Lost at Sea 1914–1918 and 1939–1945, Patrick Stephens (1988)
Grace's Guide
Hansard
Naval Staff Monographs, vol XVIII, part VIII, Admiralty Training Department (1933)
The Navy List (various dates)
The Northern Barrage, US Navy Department, Office of Naval Records and Library (Historical Section), Publication Number 4
Shorter Oxford English Dictionary, vol 1 (1982)

Index

diag refers to a diagram; *ill* to an illustration; *n* to a note; *port* to a portrait

Abalone (US) 157–8
Acheson, Commander the Honourable Patrick George 220–1, 224*port*, 225–6, 229–30, 231
Adams, Ensign Ashley D 167
Admiral of Patrols 38, 40, 57
Admiralty Experimental Research Establishment 72
Admiralty Mining Committee 82
Admiralty Volunteer Committee 274
Adriatic Campaign 91–5
Aegean Campaign 104
Aerial Target (AT) 153
Agadir incident 33
Agamemnon (Br) 102*ill*, 103
Agar, Lieutenant Augustus 235–9, 237*port*, 241, 242, 243, 258, 263*port*
Agard (Br) 61
Aldridge, Lieutenant Gerald Ashburner Mooring 113, 117, 126, 215, 221, 224–5, 226, 227–9
Alexander, Grand Duke of Russia 51
Alexander, Chief Petty Officer Roy Leslie 122*n*
Alexander-Sinclair, Rear Admiral Edwyn 234
Allen, Chief Motor Mechanic Archibald 138
Allenby, General Edmund 97, 98*port*, 99
Alleyn, Lieutenant Sir John Meynell 119–20, 120*n*
Allfree, Geoffrey Stephen 59–60, 135–6, 259; artworks by 136*ill*, 137*ill*, 139*ill*
Allied Army of the Orient 104, 186
Allied Naval Conference 249
Allied Naval War Council 177
American Red Cross 191, 192*ill*
Amice (Br) 43
Amphion (Br) 230
Anacapa (Br) 101
Andrei Pervozvanny (Rus) 241–2, 243
Angier, Sir Theodore Vivian Samuel 28
Anglo-Irish Treaty (1921) 255–6

Anne (Br) 20
Annette IV (Ger) 208
Annie (Br) 90
Anson, John 140
Anzac (Br) 45
Archangel 246–7
Ardagan (Rus) 246
Armida (Br) 79
Armistice (1918) 214–16; celebrations for 225–9; celebratory menu 226, 284; conditions of 215, 283
Armstrong, Sir Francis 36, 37–8, 41, 265
Arnold-Forster, Hugh Oakeley 35
Arthur, Prince of Connaught 268
Asquith, Herbert 269
Astor, John Jacob 51
Austria–Hungary 34, 187, 202–4; KuK Kriegsmarine 197, 201, 233
Auxiliary Patrol 38, 40–1, 57, 252, 264, 267
Ayer, Nathaniel F 159

Bacon, Vice Admiral Reginald 55, 69, 83–4, 108, 111, 145
Bagot, Lieutenant Arthur 125, 133–4, 133*n*
Bakar Mockery 201, 262
Baldwin, Stanley 269
Balfour, Arthur 249
Balkan Wars (1912–13) 33–4
Ballard, Commander George 38
Baltic Campaign 15, 234–44, 240*map*, 273
Baltic War (1918–20) 244
Ballantyne, Percy 159
Baron Call (Aus) 189
Bastedo, Lieutenant Commander Paul Henry 188, 189
Bayly, Admiral Sir Lewis 76, 107, 182, 183
Beatty, Vice Admiral David 249
Beckett, Lieutenant Walter Napier Thomason 145, 145*n*, 248
Beeley, Chief Motor Mechanic Hugh 235, 237–8, 237*port*
Béla Kun 232
Belgium, canals in 44–5, 93, 204, 218
Bell, John Henry Atkinson 43, 43*n*, 59
Bell, Lieutenant Joseph Stephen 79

INDEX   311

Belleview (Br) 77, 132
Benn, Captain Ion Hamilton 116–17, 121, 124–5, 129, 131, 263, 270
Bennett, Paymaster Martin Gilbert 38, 38*n*
Benson, Admiral William S 247
Benz, Karl 23–4
Beresford, Admiral Sir Charles 70
Berlin (Ger) 33
Bernacchi, Louis Charles 43
Bethell, Admiral Sir Alexander 77
Bethlehem (Br) 90
Betty (Br) 124
Betty Jane I (US) 159
Biddle, Colonel David H 230
Bircham, Lieutenant Francis Richard Sam 46–7
Birchol (Br) 248
Bird, Lieutenant 'Dickie' 90
Black Hawk (US) 249
Blake, Sub Lieutenant Leslie Robert 148, 149
Blay, Lieutenant Commander 256
Bloch, Eugene 253
blockades 31–2
Blue Ensign 23, 23*n*
Boag, Thomas 126–7
Bodley, Lieutenant Edward 242
Boncourt (Ger) 208
Bonham-Carter, Lieutenant Stuart 112, 115
Bosna (Aus) 233
Bourke, Lieutenant Rowland Richard Louis 116–17, 119–20, 123, 130–1, 130*port*, 263, 280
Bowden-Smith, Lieutenant Commander Victor 137–8
Bowen, Lieutenant George 113
Bowlby, Lieutenant Cuthbert F B 149
Brade, Acting Lieutenant Commander Frank 242, 243
Brase (Ger) 208
Brayfield, Lieutenant 125
Bremner, Lieutenant William 140, 140*port*, 148–50, 241, 242, 243
Brett, Reginald, Viscount Esher 26, 144
Brilliant (Br) 109, 116–17
Briscoe, Arthur 60; *A Handbook on Sailing* 60
Britannia (Br) 22
British Expeditionary Force (BEF) 260, 270
British Motor Boat Club (BMBC) 26, 34
Brock, Wing Commander Frank Arthur 112, 112*n*
Broke (Br) 122, 149
Brooke, John Walter 26
Browning, Robert, *Epilogue to Asolando* 11

Bruce, Anthony 97
Bruges 106
Brunicardi, Daire 256
Brussels (Ger) 148
Bryan, William Jennings 155
Buccari 200–1
Budapest 232–3
Budapest (Aus) 199, 200
Bugg, Deckhand Rupert Walter 105, 105*n*
Bulgaria 33, 104, 186
Burrard (Can) 131
Burrastow (Br) 43, 59

California (Br) 44–5
Callaghan, Admiral George 32
Calvin, Collamer Chipman 63, 115, 116, 270
Campbell, Lieutenant Harold 111
Canada 53, 62, 190–1
canals 44–5, 93, 204, 218
Capeto (Nor) 192
Caprice (US) 159
Carpenter, Admiral Alfred F B 111, 115, 131
Carr, William Guy 83
Carruthers, James 228
Caspian Sea campaign 244–6
Cassidy, Lieutenant George Livingstone 80–1
Catania (Br) 91*ill*, 92
Catriona (Br) 43
Cattistock (Br) 244
Cavaletta (It) 197
Cecil, Lord Robert 249
Chadwick-Smith, Training Signalman Harry 274
Chadwyck-Healey, C E H 35
Chambers, Hilary 173–4, 215, 264
Chappell, Lieutenant Commander Lionel Sheard 114–15, 125
Charlton, Rear Admiral Edward Francis Benedict 'Ned' 40
Chase, Irwin 52
Chatterton, Edward Keble 34, 43, 59, 81, 83
Cherokee (US) 177
Chestnut Hill (US) 178, 178*ill*, 192
Chief Seattle (US) 254
Childers, Erskine, *The Riddle of the Sands* 61
Churchill, Captain James Ernest 77
Churchill, Winston, First Lord of the Admiralty 32, 52, 232
Ciano, Capitani di Fregata 201
Clarke, Sub Lieutenant Peter Booth 148, 149
Clinton-Baker, Rear Admiral Lewis 249
Coast of Ireland Command 76, 134, 166, 182

coastal motor boats (CMB) 15, 143*ill*, 144*ill*, 146–7*ill*, 149, 253, 272, 273–4, 294–5*diag*, 296–7*diag*, 298–9*diag*; armaments for 142; construction of 141–4; crews 142
CMB-1 145–6; *CMB-3* 153; *CMB-4* 145, 236–7, 258–9*ill*; *CMB-5* 148, 152; *CMB-7* 148, 236, 242; *CMB-8* 146–7; *CMB-9* 145–6, 153, 258; *CMB-10* 148; *CMB-12* 253; *CMB-13* 146–7, 153–4; *CMB-19* 148; *CMB-23* 149; *CMB-24A* 242; *CMB-26* 149; *CMB-28A* 248; *CMB-31BD* 241; *CMB-32A* 148; *CMB-33* 110; *CMB-35A* 148; *CMB-40* 152; *CMB-41* 152; *CMB-42* 152; *CMB-44* 152; *CMB-47* 152; *CMB-48* 152; *CMB-62* 242; *CMB-68B* 144*ill*; *CMB-72A* 242, 243; *CMB-77A* 248; *CMB-79* 242; *CMB-86BD* 243; *CMB-88* 241, 243; *CMB-103MT* 259, 260*ill*; *CMB-121* 253; *CMB-122* 253; *CMB-M-103* 260*ill*
Coblenz, US occupation HQ 216*ill*
Cochrane, Alexander Smith 49
Coke, Lieutenant Commander Anthony Lancelot Henry Dean 151, 152
Colfox, Major W P 230
Colledge, James 273–4
Colleen (Br) 76, 76*n*
Collins, Captain Ralph 114–5
Cologne 228; Cathedral Square 228*ill*
Cologne Watersports Club 225, 226*ill*, 227*ill*
Colonsay (Br) 58
Columbian Exposition (1893) 50–1, 51*ill*
Concord (Br) 150
convoys 88, 107, 249
Conway (Br) 61
Cooper, Frank 231–2, 233; *Sailing Tours* 20
Cooper, Sub Lieutenant Fred 104, 215, 231, 233
Corbett, Julian 48
Cordon Rouge (Br) 259
Corfu 184–5, 185*ill*, 215
Corinthian ethic 14, 19–20, 110, 267, 270, 274; definitions of 20
Corinthian Football Club 19
Corinthian Yacht Club, NJ 159, 160*ill*
Cotton, Captain Lyman A 178–80
Coventry (Br) 150
Cowan, Admiral Walter 38, 235–6, 239, 241, 243, 244
Cowes Week 18, 21, 22
Crabb, Chief Motor Mechanic George E 78
Cree, A 253

Crutchley, First Lieutenant Victor 118–19, 121
Cumberland (Br) 37
Cunard Steamship Company 37
Curacoa (Br) 150
Curzon, Francis, Viscount Scarsdale 27–8, 275

D'Annunzio, Gabriele 194, 198, 200, 201, 262
d'Espèrey, General Franchet 104, 186
Daffodil (Br) 109, 111, 116
Danae (Br) 150
Daniels, Josephus 160, 206, 266
Dann, Ensign Henry R 189
Dante Alighieri (It) 187
Dawson, Sir Trevor 52, 52*n*
Dayrell, Reed, Archibald 'Mossy' 241–3
de Grey, Frederick, Marquess of Ripon 19
de Robeck, Rear Admiral Sir John 36, 38
Dean, Lieutenant Percy 115, 123, 127–8, 127*n* 128*n*, 263, 263*port*, 279
Defensively Armed Merchant Ships 55–6
Delhi (Br) 243
Delmar-Morgan, John Godfrey Yule 43
Denison-Pender, Sir John 40
depth charges 72, 171–2, 177; G-type depth charges 68*ill*; guncotton charges 72; Y-gun depth charge thrower 170–2, 171*ill*, 174, 177
Des Moines (US) 248
Despajols, Victor 210
Deutschland (Ger) 160
Devonport Local Defence Flotilla 79
Diamond (Br) 245
distant control boats (DCB) 153–4
Dittmar, Frederick 273–4
Dobson, Commander Claude Congreve 239, 241–3, 285
Dole, Ensign George S 167, 264
Dorling, Commander Taprell 83
Dorothea (Br) 44
Douglas, Honourable Charles Watson Sholto 42
Douglas-Scott-Montagu, John Walter Edward, Baron Montagu of Beaulieu 43–4
Dover Barrage 47, 106, 249
Dover Flare 112*n*
Dover Patrol 70, 107, 143, 145
Dragonfly (Br) 42
Drake, 1st Air Mechanic 113
Drew, Commander Thomas Bernard 253
Drummond, Lieutenant Geoffrey Heneage 118–19, 121, 123, 128–9, 129*port*, 264, 279

Durazzo 186–90
Dyer (US) 183

Eagle class (US) 271*ill*, 271*n*
Eastern Mediterranean campaign 95–9
Edge, Selwyn Francis 24–5, 154
Edinburgh Castle (Br) 245–6
Edison, Thomas 51
Edithena (US) 158*ill*
Edward VII, King 17–18, 19, 22, 25, 30
Egyptian Expeditionary Force (EEF) 96
El Arish 95–7
Elco motor launches 14, 15, 54–5, 69, 70, 91, 196, 204–5, 266
Electric Launch Company (Elco) 50–4
electrically controlled motor boats (ECB) 211–12
Elsie III (US) 158*ill*
Enns (Aus) 233
Eothen (Br) 45, 259–61
Erebus (Br) 211
Esquimalt (Can) 131
Estonia 234–5, 239
Eun Mara (Br) 79
Europa (Br) 104
Euryalus (Br) 137
Evans, Captain Edward 'Teddy' 122
Eve, Thomas Lawrence Burls 46
Excellent (Br) 64, 126
Excellent Gunnery School 19
Eyres, Rear Admiral Cresswell John 38, 44

Falcon (US) 251
Felix Taussig (US) 192, 193*ill*
Felixstowe F2A (Br) 150
Fife, Lieutenant Reginald George 221, 264
Finland 234, 235
Firth, Anthony 261
Firth of Forth 32, 70
Fisgard (Br) 59, 64, 79
Fisher, Admiral Sir John 'Jacky' 30*port*, 31–2, 52, 144
flying boats F2A 150; Italian 197
Foch, Maréchal Ferdinand 227
Ford, Henry 14, 51, 271
Foster, Reginald Erskine 'Tip' 19
France 30–1, 33, 177, 204; canals in 44–5, 93, 204, 218
Frances (Br) 43
Franco-Prussian War (1870) 30
Fred M Weller (US) 192
French, Captain Wilfred Frankland 'Froggie' 143
Friedman, Norman 249

Fry, C B 19, 19*n*, 125
Furer, Commander Julius 166
Futurist movement 194

Gallipoli 94, 245
Gavril (Rus) 241
Gaza 97–8
Geddes, First Lord of the Admiralty, Sir Eric 183, 229
George V, King 19, 22, 268
George L Harvey (US) 254
Germany 30–1, 33, 208–13; Flanders Flotilla 145; High Seas Fleet 150; hydrogliders (*Gleitboote*) 212; Kaiserliche Marine 106, 145, 208, 212; Kriegsmarine 208, 212; surrender of 215; unrestricted submarine warfare by 88, 106, 153, 162–3, 175; war aims of 234, 234*n*
Gibson, Lieutenant Robert 41
Giddy, Sub Lieutenant Osman Cyril Horton 242, 243
Givenchy (Can) 131
glider boats (*Versuchsleitboot*) 202–4, 203*ill*
Godsal, Commander Alfred Edmund 116, 117, 118
Goeben (Ger) 232
Goodwin, Engineer Lieutenant Commander Frank Rheuben 38, 38*n*
Gough-Calthorpe, Admiral Somerset Arthur 103*port*
Grahame, Kenneth, *The Wind in the Willows* 11
Grant, Captain Herbert 109, 118
Greco-Turkish War (1919–22) 191
Greta (Br) 75
Grillo (It) 197
Griscom, William Woodnut 50
Groszman, Lieutenant Walter P 186
Guinness, Algernon Arthur St Lawrence Lee 43, 58–9, 268
Guinness, Arthur Ernest 145
Guinness, Honourable Rupert Edward Cecil Lee 268
Gyrinus II (Br) 25

Haggard, Captain 233
Haifa 99
Haig, Field Marshal Douglas 224*port*, 225
Halcyon (Br) 90
Hale, J A 275
Halifax, Nova Scotia 190–1
Halpern, Paul 189
Hampden, Lieutenant Geoffrey 140
Hampsheir, John White 235, 237*port*, 237–8

Hamshaw, Leading Deckhand Joseph 119
Harmsworth, Alfred, Viscount Northcliffe 24
Harwich, surrender of German submarines in 215
Harwich Force 15, 143, 150
Hawkins, R H 275
Heaton-Ellis, Captain Edward Henry Fitzhardinge 220
Helicon, later *Enchantress* (Br) 64*ill*, 65
Heligoland 150, 152
Henderson, General Sir David 153
Henry, Duke of Cumberland and Strathearn 34
Hepburn, Captain Arthur Japy 178–80, 182
Hermione (Br) 61, 64*ill*, 65–6, 65*ill*, 65*n*, 78, 104, 125, 220, 229, 253
Heythorp (Br) 244
Hill, Lieutenant Edward Eliot 148, 149
Hill, Lieutenant Samuel George 132
Hippocampus (US) 157, 287*diag*
Hoare, Lieutenant Keith Robin 116, 125, 133–4, 264
Holderness (Br) 244
Holmes, Leading Seaman Sidney 243
Holmes light 121*n*
Hong Kong Naval Volunteer Force 127
Hooley, Deckhand J H 78
Hornby, A H 39
Horthy, Admiral Miklós 201
Hounding the Hun (author M-P-S) 53–4, 66
House, Colonel Edward 155
Howard, Sub Lieutenant Francis 243
Hungary 232–3
Hunstrick (Br) 139
Hunt, Sub Lieutenant 99
Hunter, Lieutenant John D 62–3, 77, 78
Hunter-Blair, Sub Lieutenant Roland 243
hydrophones 72–4, 73*ill*, 74*ill*, 75; K-hydrophones 173; Portable Directional (PDS) 73, 75; Portable General Service (PGS) 72–3
hydroplanes 140, 141*n*

indicator nets 47; steel indicator nets 91
Indomitable (Br) 89–90
Inflexible (Br) 220
Inglefield, Vice Admiral Sir Frederick 34, 38, 41, 58, 265
Inter-Allied Commission 218
internal combustion engine 14, 26, 213
Intrepid (Br) 109, 112, 115
Inverbervie (Br) 139
Inverclyde, James Cleland, 3rd Lord Inverclyde 28, 36–7, 36*port*, 41

Inverclyde, John, 1st Baron Inverclyde 37
Iphigenia (Br) 109, 115
Ireland 76, 255–7; Marine Investigation Department 256–7
Irish Civil War (1922) 256–7
Iris (Br) 109, 111, 114, 115, 116
Ironside, General 'Tiny' 245
Isabella Alexandra (Br) 61
Isotta-Fraschini Company 197
Italy 15, 177, 194–203; 'battle in harbour' strategy 197; *Corpo Nazionale Volontari Moyonauti* (CNVM) 195; Motor Boat Volunteer Reserve (CNVM) 195; Regia Marina Italiano 196, 197; Risorgimento 194; Societa Veneziana Automobili Navali (SVAN) 196

Jackson, Admiral Sir Henry 32
Jacoby, Ensign Maclear 188*port*
James Graham, Marquess of Montrose 35, 268, 274
Jane's Fighting Ships 196, 208
Jean (Br) 43, 59
Jellicoe, Admiral John 72, 75, 80*port*, 81, 106, 108, 134, 212, 249, 265, 266
Johnstone, Sir George Charles Keppel 43
Joseph Kildall (US) 254
Joyce, Chief Boatswain's Mate 159

Karageorge, Prince Aleksandr 232
Katherine (Br) 20
Kelly, Commodore Howard 187
Kelpie (Br) 61
Kennedy, Admiral Sir William Robert 26, 27*port*
Kennedy, Archibald, Marquess of Ailsa 26, 275
Kennedy, Chief Motor Mechanic 228
Kenworthy, Lieutenant Commander Joseph 272
Keyes, Vice Admiral Roger 107–10, 107*port*, 125, 126, 129, 135, 149, 241, 272; and raid on Ostend 116, 118, 121, 122, 152
Keynes, John Maynard 269
Kia Ora (Br) 125
Killoh, Leading Seaman Noah 39
Kilrush, Ireland 76
King, Signalman Edwin F, 63, 67
Kinghorn, John 59
Kinglake, Alexander William 259*n*
Kinloch-Cooke, Sir Clement 264
Kitson, Lieutenant John Francis Buller 78
Knight, Admiral Austin Melvin 155–6, 157
Krasnaya Gorka Fortress 236–7
Kronstadt 236, 239, 240*map*

Laidlaw, Lieutenant Stanley Floyd Wood 229–30
Lambert, Andrew 31
Lambert, Nick 82
Laneta (US) 156*ill*, 157
Lang, Eugene 59
Lapwing (US) 251*ill*
Latvia 234–5, 239
Law, Andrew Bonar 229
Leigh, Captain Richard 179*n*
Leighton, Ensign John Langdon 180
Leonidas (US) 178, 183*ill*, 184, 185–6, 185*ill*, 215
Levitt, Dorothy 24*ill*, 25, 25*n*, 36, 154
Liberty (Br) 126
Lightning (Br) 12*ill*, 13–14
Littleton, Lieutenant Hugh Alexander 112, 125–6, 129
Lloyd George, David 33, 97, 99, 269
Locke, Motor Mechanic 228
Locomotives on Highways Act (1896) 26
Locusta (It) 198
Lokrum (Aus) 198
London Gazette 90, 132–3
Lord Clive (Br) 113, 117
Lough Ree Yacht Club 21
Louis, Prince of Battenburg 25–6
Low, Archibald Montgomery 152–3
Lowry, Sir Robert Swinburne 47
Lucia (Br) 137
Luker, Sub Lieutenant Christopher Noel 45–6, 95, 96, 97–9, 103, 264
Luppis, Capitano Giovanni 13
Lusitania (Br) 52, 58
Lydia (Br) 104
Lydonia (Fr) 206
Lynes, Commodore Hubert 109, 118
Lynx II (US) 157*ill*, 159

McBean, Lieutenant Russell 241
McBride, Sir Richard 190
McCully, Rear Admiral Newton A 247
MacDonald, Commander Alan Robert Armitage 231
Mackie, Lieutenant Anthony Charles 135
MacLean, Sub Lieutenant Hector Forbes 243
MacMillan, Margaret 29
Macnamara, Thomas 230, 252, 264, 272
Mairi (Br) 126
Mangin, General Charles 'The Butcher' 225–7
Mann, Chief Motor Mechanic Herbert 134
Mansura (Br) 43
Marguerite (Br) 94

Marine Motoring Association (MMA) 26–7
Marine Society 253
Mariner (US) 177
Marinetti, Filippo 194
Markham, Violet 227–8
Marland, Chief Motor Mechanic John 78
Marsh, Edward 44
Marshall, Midshipman Richard Nigel Onslow 235, 236, 242
Martin, Lieutenant Frederick 133, 133*n*
Mary (Br) 20
Mary Rose (Br) 44, 45
Mason, Frank Henry Algernon 60–1
Masters, Chief Motor Mechanic Baden Marples 239–40, 243
Max (Ger) 208
Maxwell, Donald 60, 264; artworks by 93*ill*, 94*ill*, 100–1*ill*
Maxwell, Sub Lieutenant Gordon 42, 55, 60, 65–7, 81, 73, 94, 102, 121, 123, 215–16, 263–4
May, Admiral of the Fleet Sir William Henry 252
Mayfair (Br) 46–7
Mediterranean Auxiliary Patrol Area VIII 104
Megiddo, Battle of 99
Memphis (Br) 45–6
merchant shipping, losses of 50, 70, 88, 277–8
Mercury (Br) 19, 125
Mersey, Lord 58
Meteor (Ger) 22, 61
Miéville, Lieutenant Commander Jean S 122
Milholland, Ray, *The Splinter Fleet of the Otranto Barrage* 254–5
mines and mining 82–7, 85*ill*, 138, 249–51; cruiser mines 72; EC mine nets 47; fixed-mine sweep 82
Minnehaha (Br) 45
Minou (Br) 42, 60, 221
Minnesota (US) 175
Miranda IV (Br) 141
Moffatt, Ensign Alexander 167, 177
Mole (Zeebrugge harbour) 108–11, 114–16, 148
Morandy (Br) 135
Morley, Robert 258–9
Motor Boat 63, 155, 254
motor boats
 British; armaments for 196; losses of 50, 276
 German (*Luftschiffmotorboote*) 212
 Italian (*Motobarca Armata* SVAN) 15, 198*ill*

MAS-1 196; MAS-2 196; MAS-3 196; MAS-5 198; MAS-7 198; MAS-9 199; MAS-13 200; MAS-15 195*ill*, 201–2, 261; MAS-20 196; MAS-21 196, 201–2; MAS-22 196; MAS-77 196; MAS-78 196; MAS-91 197; MAS-96 200, 200*ill*, 262*ill*; MAS-99 197*ill*; MAS-102 197; MAS-204–217 197; MAS-218 197; MAS-232 197

motor launches (ML) 56*ill*, 57, 93*ill*, 100*ill*, 136*ill*, 137*ill*, 139*ill*, 177, 288*diag* and air rescue 89; as anti-submarine boats 57, 70–1, 74–5, 272–3; armaments for 55–7; costs of 253; crews 58–66, 71*ill*; decommissioning of 252; impact of weather on 95, 99; living conditions on 66–9; losses of 132–9, 281, 286; and mining 70, 83–7, 85*ill*; production of 53–4; survivors of 258–62 ML-1 256;

  ML-1–151 196; ML-2 58, 256; ML-3 256; ML-4 79, 256; ML-5 61, 125; ML-7 59; ML-8 219, 253; ML-9 98; ML-12 12; ML-19 132; ML-21 125, 138; ML-22 58*ill*; ML-23 58, 90; ML-27 138; ML-31 58; ML-33 61; ML-34 101; ML-38 96; ML-40 132; ML-49 132; ML-50 219, 227*ill*; ML-51–260 53; ML-52 133; ML-53 126; ML-54 138; ML-55 124*ill*, 133; ML-59 58, 59*ill*, 60; ML-64 134; ML-98 244; ML-101 127; ML-102 61; ML-105/6 86–7*ill*, 121; ML-110 113, 139; ML-121 219, 221; ML-124 244; ML-125 244; ML-128 113, 114, 122, 125; ML-131 252; ML-132 75; ML-135 79–80, 272; ML-139 60; ML-154 60, 61; ML-155 81; ML-156 244; ML-163 252; ML-167 75; ML-168 79, 95; ML-181 59, 75, 182; ML-185 252; ML-187 75; ML-194 61, 134–5; ML-197 134–5; ML-206 77, 93, 99, 101–2, 101*ill*; ML-210 232, 233; ML-211 63, 77, 78; ML-215 89*ill*; ML-228 104, 215, 231–2, 233; ML-229 71, 221, 224, 228; ML-230 139; ML-234 77, 93, 102; ML-236 232, 233; ML-240 77, 93, 102; ML-247 60, 135–6; ML-248 77, 93, 98, 100*ill*, 101–2; ML-252 116; ML-253 139; ML-254 118–19, 121, 122, 139; ML-255 139; ML-259 252; ML-260 221, 225; ML 262– 550 53; ML-276 116, 119, 126, 131; ML-278 135; ML-279 135; ML-280 122; ML-282 114*ill*, 115; ML-283 116; ML-285 105, 105*ill*, 259–60; ML-286 259–61; ML-287 113, 220; ML-288 220; ML-289 105; ML-291 220; ML-299 90; ML-304 135; ML-307 60*ill*; ML-313 90*ill*; ML-314 60; ML-320 75; ML-324 134;

ML-325 75, 182; ML-333 220; ML-339 253; ML-341 130; ML-345 220; ML-350 61; ML-354 226*ill*; ML-356 133; ML-357 78, 88; ML-358 226*ill*; ML-366 221; ML-373 81; ML-374 76; ML-377 252; ML-382 113, 215; ML-399 66*ill*; ML-403 63, 136–7; ML-407 75; ML-410 75; ML-413 79; ML-420 116; ML-424 113, 114, 139, 221; ML-425 61; ML-428 94; ML-431 132; ML-432 93, 94; ML-438 93; ML-440 93; ML-448 112; ML-463 88*ill*; ML-473 220, 227*ill*, 229, 253; ML-474 139; ML-487 75; ML-505 93–4; ML-509 232; ML-512 110, 115; ML-516 92*ill*, 93; ML-519 253; ML-524 62*ill*; ML-526 112; ML-530 93; ML-532 117, 117*ill*; ML-534 132; ML-535 93–4; ML-538 112; ML-540 139; ML-541 139, 220; ML-542 218, 253; ML-551 61; ML-556 121; ML-557 117*ill*; ML-558 109–10, 114, 220; ML-559 119; ML-561 138; ML-562 13; ML-566 220, 221; ML-567 248; ML-569 221; ML-570 248; ML-575 248; ML-576 224*ill*, 226*ill*, 229; ML-578 248; ML-579 248

French (*Vedettes*) 15, 204–5, 205*ill* German 15, 208–13, 209*ill*

Murray, General Sir Archibald James 96, 97
Murray, Lieutenant Colonel A 252
My Lady Molly (Br) 45
Mysliwy (Pol) 257

Napier I (Br) 24, 24*ill*
Napier, Lieutenant Lawrence 242, 243
Nash, Sub Lieutenant Charles 132–3
Naval Discipline Act (1866) 35
Naval Forces Act (1903) 35
Naval Reserve Act (1859) 32
Nelson, Captain Charles 'Juggy' 184, 184*port*, 187, 188–9
New Zealand 62–3
Nicholas II, Tsar 51
Nina d'Asty (Br) 45
Niobe (Can) 190
Nisbet, Ulric 29
Norcock, Lieutenant Commander Charles Vernon Lowcay 75
Nord Est (Br) 42
Norris, Commodore David Thomas 245–6
North Sea 32; mining in 82, 140, 150
North Sea Barrage 249, 250–1, 250*n*
North Star (Br) 212
Northern Dvina River 247–8
Nowotny, Captain Bogumił 257

O'Brien, Edward Conor Marshall 61
O'Loghlen, W J 253
Official History (WWI) 48
Official History of the Navy 48, 151
Oleg (Rus) 237–9, 236*ill*, 238*ill*, 258
Oliver, Vice Admiral Sir Henry 57
Omaha class (US) 271*ill*
Oomala (Br) 45
Operation RK 241
Operation ZO *see* Zeebrugge/Ostend raid
Opossum (Br) 79–81, 272
Osea Island 143, 235, 244–5, 253
Osiris (Br) 104
Osprey (Br) 42
Ostend, raid on 116–23; *see also* Zeebrugge/Ostend raid
Otranto Barrage 91–5, 93*ill*, 183–6, 201
Ottoman Empire 99–100, 103
Outhwaite, Sub Lieutenant Cedric R L 148, 149, 152

Page, Walter Hines 155, 162
Paget, Lieutenant Ferrand 79
Paloma (US) 158*ill*
Pamiat Azova (Rus) 241, 243
Panama (US) 159
Panther (Ger) 33
paravanes 83, 84*ill*
Paris Peace Conference (1919–20) 232
Pasco, Captain Frederick Claude Coote 190
Paton, Sub Lieutenant Norman Giles 138
Patterson, Deckhand 228
Payne, Arthur 124
Penelope (Br) 44, 45, 212
'People's Budget' (1909–10) 269
Perlona (Br) 43
Petrie, Sub Lieutenant James 119–20, 126–7
Petropavlovsk (Rus) 241–2, 243
Peytsch, Oberleutnant zur See, Georg 212
Phillips, Christopher 44
Phoenix (Br) 184
Piper, Chief Motor Mechanic Albert Victor 235, 236
Platypus (Br) 58, 60
Plumer, General Herbert 224*port*
Plunkett, Commander Reginald 33, 70
Plymouth 177, 178, 180, 182; Base 27 (US) 178, 179*ill*
Pointer, Percy 110
Poland 257
Pooley, Chief Motor Mechanic Ernest 132–3, 133*n*
Port Said 95, 97–8
Portsmouth Harbour 273*ill*

Powley, Deckhand Herbert 132
Preparedness Movement 160, 160*n*
President (Br) 47, 64
Prince Eugene (Br) 211–12
Privet (Br) 81
Proctor, Deckhand C H 78
Proctor, Lieutenant Rawsthorne 121–2
Prynne, Douglas Gordon 58
Puffin II (Br) 45
Puglia (It) 262
Pulce (It) 197
Pursuit (Br) 43
Purvis, Lieutenant John Eiston 138–9

Queenstown, Ireland 24, 76, 177, 182–3, 252

Rainbow (Can) 190
Ramsey, Sub Lieutenant Frank A W 148
Ranjitsinhji, K S 20
Rauf Bey 103
Rayner, Lieutenant Sidney Wright 153–4
Redoubt (Br) 150
remote control boats (*Fernlenkboot*) 210–12, 210*ill*
Resource II (Br) 65
Retriever (Br) 150
Rhine River, MLs on 218*ill*, 219*ill*
Rhineland, occupation of 15, 216–25, 222–3*ill*; withdrawal from 229–31, 231*ill*
Rice, Isaac Leopold 50–1
Richardson, Lieutenant Commander Francis Joseph 41, 42
Richmond, Captain Herbert 107
Rizzo, Capitano di Corvette, Luigi 199–202, 261–2
Roberts-Wray, Captain Thomas Henry 274–5
Robertson, General Sir William 228, 230–1
Robinson, Commander Eric Gascoigne 245–6
Robinson, Frederick Oliver, 2nd Marquess of Ripon 19
Robinson, Lieutenant John William 113, 221, 225, 229, 228
Robinson, Lieutenant Oswald 113
Roffey, Philip 275
Romani, Battle of 96
Romania 33, 232
Roosevelt, Franklin Delano 160–1, 161*port*, 182–3, 249
Roots, James Dennis 24
Ross, Lieutenant Gordon 119
Rothschild, Nathaniel Mayer, Baron de 23
Royal Canadian Navy 190
Royal Clyde Yacht Club 37

Royal Flying Corps (RFC) 95–6
Royal Garrison Artillery 105
Royal Harwich Yacht Club 22
Royal Motor Yacht Club 65
Royal Naval Air Service (RNAS) 89, 145
Royal Naval Artillery Volunteers (RNAV) 35
Royal Naval Coast Volunteers (RNCV) 35
Royal Naval Motor Boat Reserve (RNMBR) 14, 36, 41–4, 46, 57, 110, 204, 269; commemorative brooch 41*ill*; Scottish motor boats 42
Royal Naval Reserve (RNR) 32–3, 35–6, 39, 267; Trawler Section (RNRT) 33, 82, 267
Royal Naval Reserve Act (1859) 35
Royal Naval Volunteer Reserve (RNVR) 14–15, 34, 35–6, 40, 41, 57, 110, 267–9, 267*ill*, 268*ill*; Crystal Palace training depot 274; Trophy (1931) 275
Royal Navy 18–19; 20th Destroyer Flotilla 239; class attitudes of 18–19; Home Fleet 31; Minesweeping Division 40; Motor Gunboat Flotilla 45; Nore Command 32; reorganisation of 31; Rhine Flotilla 225, 229–31
Royal Sussex Yacht Club 27
Royal Temple Yacht Club 23
Royal Thames Yacht Club 34
Royal Western Yacht Club 22–3
Royal Yacht Squadron 21–2
Rurik (Rus) 242, 243
Russell, Herbrand Arthur, Duke of Bedford 269
Russia 207–8, 234
Russian Revolution 208, 234; Allied intervention in 234–49
Russo-Japanese War 82
Rutland, 8th Duke of 40

Sackville, Gilbert, 8th Earl de la Warr 42
St George (Br) 38, 46
Salmon (Br) 49–50
Salonika campaign 46, 191, 192*ill*, 231
San Diego (US) 175, 176*ill*
Sandford, Lieutenant Richard Douglas 111
Saoirse (Br) 61
Sappho (Br) 118
Saska class (Russ) 208
Saudadoes (Br) 20
Saunders, Lieutenant Raphael 114, 122, 125
Sayonara (Br) 61
Scapa Flow 32, 215
Schlaet, Arnold 157
Schmidt, Chief Gunner's Mate Oscar 193
Scott, Admiral Sir Percy 18, 141*n*

Scott, Captain Robert Falcon 43
Sea Fencibles 34–5
seaplanes 87*ill*; Short 184 145; Sopwith Baby 145
Selborne, Admiral William Waldegrave 31, 35
Sentinel (Br) 232
Serbia 34, 232
Sergei (Br) 245–6
Sharon, Battle of 99
Shea, Lieutenant Maurice Patrick 88
Shillington, Lieutenant John Melville 96, 96*n*
Sidon 100*ill*, 101–2
Sidon (Br) 102
Siemens-Shuckert Company 210–11
Sim, Leading Seaman Alexander 39
Sims, Rear Admiral William Sowden 161–2, 162*port*, 166–7, 177, 184, 187, 202, 247; *Victory at Sea* 265–6
Sindall, Edgar Robert 'Sinbad' 235, 236, 242
Sirius (Br) 109, 116–17, 149
Skinner, Lieutenant Alan Leonard Dorney 135
Smart, Morton Warrack 36, 37, 41, 43, 44, 45, 93, 265
Smith, Able Seaman William G 243
Smith-Cumming, Commander Mansfield George 25, 235
Smith-Dorrien, General Horace 19
smoke-laying 112–13
Sneyd, Commander Ralph 111
Snowden, Viscount Philip 128
Song of the Sea Slugs, The 11
South Carolina (US) 176
Spectator 28
Spencer, Lieutenant George 116
Spencer, Lieutenant Honourable Cecil Edward Robert 148, 149
Spencer-Churchill, Charles, 9th Duke of Marlborough 17*n*
Spider (Br) 26
splinter ships *see* submarine chasers
Stanners, Deckhand John George 105, 105*n*
Starfish (Br) 150
Startin, Commodore 134
Stately (Br) 126
Steele, Lieutenant Gordon 241, 243, 263*port*, 285
Stephens, Chief Motor Mechanic Francis 243
Stewart, Ninian Ballantyne 43, 58
Strauss, Rear Admiral Joseph 249–50
Stubbs, J W Laurie 78
submarine chasers (SC) 15, 163–74, 164*ill*,

165*ill*, 168*ill*, 170*ill*, 128*ill*, 214*ill*, 255*ill*, 270–1, 282, 289*diag*, 290*diag*; armaments for 170–4; construction of 164–6, 168–70; crews 166–7, 166*n*; decommissioning of 253–4; living conditions on 168–70; losses of 192
  SC-1 248; *SC-2* 167*ill*; *SC-37* 168, 254; *SC-38* 254; *SC-46* 168; *SC-47* 179*ill*; *SC-51* 191; *SC-60* 192; *SC-67* 206; *SC-77* 167; *SC-90* 248; *SC-93* 167; *SC-95* 248; *SC-98* 248; *SC-110* 168; *SC-117* 192; *SC-126* 198; *SC-128* 171, 173, 188–9, 192*ill*, 215; *SC-129* 188–9; *SC-130* 189; *SC-131* 254*ill*; *SC-132* 192; *SC-137* 167, 248; *SC-141* 206; *SC-142* 206, 206*n*; *SC-143* 167, 177, 180, 206, 215; *SC-148* 214–15; *SC-172* 206; *SC-173* 206; *SC-174* 206; *SC-177* 180–2, 205–6; *SC-181* 168; *SC-183* 191; *SC-187* 192; *SC-201* 175*ill*; *SC-207* 168; *SC-209* 192; *SC-215* 188–9; *SC-217* 253; *SC-219* 192–3; *SC-224* 181*ill*; *SC-225* 253; *SC-226* 198; *SC-234* 176; *SC-241* 176, 191, 253; *SC-244* 187; *SC-256* 248, 251; *SC-257* 248; *SC-258* 179*ill*, 248; *SC-262* 248; *SC-271* 248; *SC-292* 254; *SC-293* 254; *SC-300* 254; *SC-309* 177; *SC-310* 177; *SC-319* 206; *SC-321* 248; *SC-324* 189; *SC-337* 189; *SC-351* 181*ill*; *SC-354* 248, 250; *SC-405* 173*ill*, 205–6
  French 205–6, 205*ill*, 207*ill*
Submarine Patrol (film) 254–5
submarines: detection of 72, 172–4
  Austrian 184; *U-4* 139; *U-6* 95; *U-29* 188
  British 70; *E-54* 50
  German 50, 209*ill*
    U-27 184; *U-27* class 57; *U-31* 188–9; *U-34* 81; *U-39* 139; *U-53* 159–60; *U-117* 175; *U-139* 175; *U-140* 175; *U-151* 175; *U-155* 175; *U-156* 175; *UB-II* class 57; *UB-71* 79, 27; *UC* class 82–3; *UC-7* 50; *UC-10* 50; *UC-II* class 57; *UC-49* 79–81, 272;
    UZ class 208–9
Suez Canal 45–6
Sunfish (Br) 77
Sunrise (Br) 94*ill*
Supreme War Council, Versailles 99
Sussex Motor Yacht Club 27–8
Sutherland-Leveson-Gower, George, 5th Duke of Sutherland 92–3
Sutphen, Henry Randolph 52, 53, 54, 266, 271
Swasey, Albert Loring 163, 266, 271
Sycamore, Edward Isaac 61, 89
Szent István (Aus) 201–2, 261

Tacoma (US) 192
Tagore, Arthur Hildebrand Ramsden 43, 58
Tamarack (US) 167
Tank Marino (It) 197
Tarlair (Br) 72
Teazer (Br) 150
Tegetthoff (Aus) 201–2
Televista 153
Temple-West, Lieutenant Francis Edward 49–50
Terror (Br) 138
Thatcher, Chief Motor Mechanic Francis 243
Thetis (Br) 109, 111, 126
Thisbe (Br) 150
Thistle (Ger) 21*ill*, 22
Thomamühl, Lieutenant Commander Dagobert Müller von 202
Thompson, Lieutenant John 259
Thornycroft, John Isaac 13, 265
Thornycroft Company 24, 25, 26, 141, 171, 274; motor launch 287*diag*; skimmer 292–3*diag*
Thring, Fleet Paymaster Ernest 88
Tirpitz, Alfred von 31
Tower, Commander Francis Fitzpatrick 69, 166
Tracey, Lieutenant Herbert 116, 126
Train, Lieutenant Commander Charles R 202
Treaty of London (1915) 187*n*, 194
Treaty of Paris (1856) 31*n*
Treaty of Versailles (1919) 218, 257
Tricase, Italy 94
Trident (Br) 125
Trieste 199
Trinidad 104–5
Triple Alliance 194
Troubridge, Rear Admiral Ernest 232, 233
Trumble, Lieutenant Frederick 121–2, 121*n*
Turner, Captain William 58
Turner, Edwin S 59
Tyre 100–2
Tyrwhitt, Commodore Reginald 108, 140–1, 150, 151

U-boats *see* submarines
United States 53, 155, 249; role in WWI 52, 249, 271–2
United States Navy 163, 196; Bureau of Construction and Repairs 166; Bureau of Ordnance 171; Coast Guard 254; Naval Coast Defence Reserve 155; Naval Reserve Officer Training Corps (NROTC) 270; Navy Reserve Force

(USNRF) 167, 270; Power Squadron 157
Unwin, Edward 263*port*
upper classes 14, 18–19, 42, 269–70; marriage to American millionaires 17–18
Ursus (Ger) 208
Usborne, Sub Lieutenant Thomas R G 243

Valhalla (Br) 22, 22*ill*
Vanderbilt, Alfred Gwynne 28, 28*n*
Vanderbilt, Harold Stirling 'Mike' 167–8
Vavasour, Captain Sir Leonard Pius, 4th Baronet Hazlewood 253
Velox (Br) 122
Venetia (Fr) 206
Vernon (Br) 64, 72, 82, 137, 141, 253
Victor Emmanuel II monument 261–2
Victoria, Queen 22, 23
Victory (Br) 64, 153, 273*ill*
Victory VI (Br) 274, 275
Vindex (Br) 146
Vindictive (Br) 109, 110–11, 114, 115, 118–19, 120, 122, 125, 148, 149, 241, 243
Vittoriale degli Italiani 262
Vix, Lieutenant Colonel 232–3
volunteer crews 16, 34–5, 39, 110, 262–4, 267–70; Admiralty opposition to 35; ranks of 42

Wace, *Roman de Brut* 11
'*Wacht am Rhein*' (Watch on the Rhine) 216, 217*ill*
Wallace, Ensign George 169
War Stag (Br) 245
Ward, Honourable John 26
Warspite, formerly *Hermione* (Br) 253
Warwick (Br) 109, 112, 115, 116, 119, 121, 122
Waterhouse, Lawrence Maxwell 43
Watney, Lieutenant Basil Gold 233
Watson, Commander William Wordie 121
Wells, Lieutenant Arthur 101, 102
Welman, Lieutenant Arthur Eric Pole 147–8, 149
Wemyss, First Sea Lord Rosslyn 110, 126, 210
Wendy (US) 156*ill*, 157
Westerman, Percy F, *The Thick of the Fray at Zeebrugge, April 1918* 261
Weymouth (Br) 189
What Next (Br) 43
White Sea campaign 246–9
Whitehead, Robert 13
Whiting, Lieutenant Arthur 137–8
Wien (Aus) 199, 199*ill*, 200
Wight, Sub Lieutenant Robert Leslie 243
Wilhelm II, Kaiser 31, 65*n*

Willacy, Leading Deckhand J H 78
Wilson, Admiral Sir Arthur Knyvet 263*port*
Wilson, William Tyson 264
Wilson, Woodrow 53, 155, 155*n*, 162, 271–2
Winton, John 91–2
Wood, Signalman William 112
Wright, Deckhand Norman 78
Wright, Lieutenant James Courtenay Keith 'Shiner' 115, 126
Wylie W L 35; artworks by 114*ill*, 273*ill*
Wynn, Honourable Thomas 42

yacht clubs 21–3; class and character of members of 28–9
Yacht Racing Association 23
yachting 20–3; yachting artists 59–61
Yachting Monthly 59, 60, 112, 208, 269
Young, Lieutenant Commander James Dawbarn 113–14, 126
Young, Seaman Patrick 136

Zarefah (Br) 40
Zeebrugge/Ostend raid (1918) 15, 106–23, 133, 145, 147–9, 270, 272; volunteers in 110–12
Zwaluw (Br) 90